The Success Secret

Published by CelebrityPress™, Orlando, FL
A division of The Celebrity Branding Agency®

Celebrity Branding® is a registered trademark
Printed in the United States of America.

ISBN: 978-0-9853643-7-3
LCCN: 2012939172

This publication is designed to provide accurate and authoritative
information with regard to the subject matter covered. It is sold with
the understanding that the publisher is not engaged in rendering legal,
accounting, or other professional advice. If legal advice or other expert
assistance is required, the services of a competent professional should
be sought. The opinions expressed by the authors in this book are not
endorsed by CelebrityPress™ and are the sole responsibility of the
author rendering the opinion.

Most CelebrityPress™ titles are available at special quantity discounts
for bulk purchases for sales promotions, premiums, fundraising, and
educational use. Special versions or book excerpts can also be created
to fit specific needs.

For more information, please write:

CelebrityPress™,
520 N. Orlando Ave, #2
Winter Park, FL 32789

or call 1.877.261.4930

Visit us online at www.CelebrityPressPublishing.com

The Success Secret

Contents

CHAPTER 1

Success Made Simple

By Jack Canfield

The big secret about success is that *there is no secret*. The fundamentals of success have been known for centuries. However, there is a fail-safe formula that always works. I have been studying and teaching about success for more than forty years, and there is a tried and true formula that has produced financial abundance, breakthrough results, and deep fulfillment in my life as well as the lives of hundreds of thousands of my students. This system always works, as long as you consistently work the system. So here it is—a success system that never fails, in eight simple steps.

STEP 1. DECIDE EXACTLY WHAT YOU WANT

Most people never take the time to sit down and design the life they want to live. They live by default instead of by choice. They live a life determined by past conditioning and habit rather than consciously creating the life of their dreams. So the first step is to sit down and spend several hours asking yourself where you would like to be one year from now, five years from now, and ten years from now. Clarify your vision of your ideal life in all the areas that matter to you. The ones I identified for myself are financial, job and career, relationships, health and fitness, fun and recreation, possessions, personal and spiritual growth, and contribution to the world. I want my life to be outrageous in all eight of those areas.

I want to encourage you to think big when you do this. General Wesley Clark, the former Commander of the Allied Forces under NATO, once said, "It doesn't take any more effort to dream a big dream than it does to dream a small dream." Think about that. Why not dream big? You might be telling yourself, *I can't dream that big of a dream, because I don't know how to make such a dream come true.* In step one you don't need to know "the how." You just need to decide what you really want. So many of my students get stuck here, so it is really important that you be honest with yourself about what you want. Don't let the HOW get in the way of your dreams. Trust me, the how will become clear in the process. Right now all you have to do is believe that anything is possible. It's true that in order to reach your goals you may need to learn new skills, make new friends, build new networks, let go of old habits and develop new disciplines, and replace your limiting beliefs with new more empowering ones, but all of that will become clear as you proceed.

What you may not know is you have a built-in GPS system (like the one in your car) that will figure out the route to your chosen destination. This internal GPS system is your subconscious creative mind which is connected to everything in the universe through your intuition. All you have to do is to properly put in the destination. (We'll discuss how to do that in Step 3.) The GPS system will then provide a set of directions from where you currently are to where you want to go. Of course, you will have to follow the directions by taking action.

STEP 2. TURN YOUR VISION INTO SPECIFIC AND MEASURABLE GOALS

The second step, and this is critical, is that you have to turn each part of the vision of your ideal life into specific and measurable goals. The key questions in this step are "how much?" and "by when?" Until you turn each part of your vision into a specific and measurable goal, you just have a wish or a dream. "I'd like to live in a big house on the ocean someday" is a very different statement than "I will live in a 5,000-square-foot house on the west coast of Maui, Hawaii, by December 31st, 2016 at 5 p.m."

You want to state each of your goals in such a measurable way that an outside observer could come in at any designated time to observe and *know* that you had achieved it. "I want to lose 30 pounds" would become "I will weigh 135 pounds or less by June 30th, 2013 at 5 p.m." That way someone could show up at 5 p.m. on June 30 and watch you stand on a scale and know whether or not you had achieved your goal.

This is a critical step in properly programming the GPS system in your brain for success.

STEP 3. SUPERCHARGE YOUR GOALS WITH AFFIRMATIONS AND VISUALIZATION

This next step is one often given lip service, but rarely implemented correctly. And it is one of the most important steps in this system. Skipping this step is like trying to open a combination lock when you are missing one of the numbers in the combination. You must create an affirmation for each of your goals and a visual picture of what it would look like if you had already achieved the goal. This is how you lock the destination (your goals) into your internal GPS system.

Here is a simple formula for creating affirmations that work. Just start each affirmation with the words "I am so happy and grateful that I now _____." Then fill in the blank with a description of what you would be experiencing if the goal was already achieved. For example, "I am so happy and grateful that I now am driving my new BMW 750i down the Pacific Coast Highway." Or "I am so happy and grateful that I now have built three new elementary schools for girls in Nigeria."

Once you have an affirmation for each of your goals, take the time to read the affirmation and then close your eyes and create an internal picture of what you would be seeing if you had already achieved the goal. It might be the image of a sunset from the patio of your 5,000-square-foot home in Maui, your hands on the steering wheel of your new BMW, or the image of your 135-pound body in the mirror.

The last step is to engage in the following daily practice. Read one of your affirmations, then close your eyes and visualize the picture you created in your mind for that affirmation. And here is the most important part—actually *feel* the feeling you would feel if you had already achieved that goal. Generate that feeling in your body and bathe in it for at least 30 seconds. Then open your eyes, read your next affirmation, close your eyes and visualize that goal as complete, and feel the feeling you would feel if that goal were complete. Repeat the process until you have gone through all of your affirmations. I usually am working on about 20 affirmations so the process takes me about 10 minutes in the morning.

If you want to accelerate your success, do it once again in the evening before going to bed—ideally right before you get into bed. This is a much better use of your time than watching TV right before you fall asleep. Recent research tells us two very important things. First, what you read about, listen to on the radio, watch on television and talk about during the last 45 minutes before you fall asleep gets processed more deeply during the sleep state than everything else that you experienced during the day.

Second, we now know that to get the greatest value from affirmations and visualization, you must first do them for thirty days in a row without interruption. If you skip them on Day 15, you're on Day One again on Day 16. This piece of research tells us one of the main reasons people do not get the results they want when engaging in personal development programs or practices. They fail to utilize this "30-day principle" when visualizing, creating a new habit, committing to an exercise program, implementing a new management program at work, or developing a new attitude or belief.

STEP 4. CREATE AN ACTION PLAN

The next step is to create an action plan (as best you can at this stage) for how you will get from where you are to where you want to be. Often the challenge is that you don't know what to do to make it happen. That is okay. One solution is to ask someone who has already done it. Almost anything you want to do—from becoming a millionaire or a bestselling author to filling your practice with high-paying clients or reaching the top level in your network marketing company—has been done by somebody else. Locate someone who has done what you want to do and ask them to spend a half-hour mentoring you on the necessary steps you'll need to take.

When Mark Victor Hansen and I wrote our first *Chicken Soup for the Soul* book, we asked 10 bestselling authors like Ken Blanchard (*The One Minute Manager*), John Gray (*Men Are from Mars, Women Are from Venus*) and Scott Peck (*The Road Less Traveled,* which was on the New York Times bestseller list for 12 years!) what we needed to do to get on the bestseller lists. We followed their advice, and it worked.

Another way to learn what to do is to take advantage of all the "how-to" resources that exist in the world. There are books written by experts who have already accomplished it in every field—from songwriting and relationship building to investing and business building. You can also learn from multimedia home study courses, coaching programs, seminars, trainings, webinars and boot camps. And of course, there is also a ton of information on the Internet.

Once you have the information you need, create a plan with action steps and timelines and then work your plan. Know that not everything you plan will work out exactly as you plan it, but it will get you into action, and then you can make corrections along the way. And remember, even if you can't see all of the steps when you start, as you take each step, the next steps will appear. And remember this: After 30 days of doing your affirmation and visualization process, you will start to get creative and inspired ideas for actions you can take from your subconscious GPS system. They may come in the shower, while you're meditating, as you're driving to work or when you are taking a walk. But whenever they come, write them down and then act on them. The main thing is to get in the game and start.

STEP 5. TAKE ACTION TO CREATE IT

In life, the thing that most separates winners from losers is that winners take action. Most people wait around for the perfect conditions before they act. They spend their whole life getting ready. Don't wait. Get started now. As the Nike ads say—Just Do It! I love the fact that the last six letters in the word *satisfaction* are *a-c-t-i-o-n*. Here are a couple of tips to get you started.

My friend Lee Brower taught me this simple technique that has got me off the dime numerous times with meditation, reading, exercise and writing. It's the "One-Minute Technique." A friend of Lee's asked him if he had ever read The Bible all the way through. Lee replied he hadn't because he didn't have the time. His friend asked him if he'd be willing to commit to reading it for just one minute a day. Lee agreed. What he found is that once he started reading for that minute, he would often get hooked and read for 15 minutes or longer. Eventually he got through the entire Bible.

Another valuable technique Mark and I developed is called "The Rule of Five." When the first *Chicken Soup for the Soul* book was published we decided to do five things *every day* to promote the sale of the book. We would send out five review copies to reviewers or celebrities who might promote our book, do five radio interviews by phone, make five sales calls to network sales organizations that might purchase our book to motivate their down lines, or call five churches to see if they would have us come speak to their congregations and let us sell our books afterwards—five specific action steps every single day *no matter what.* As a result of this commitment, which we maintained for more than two years, *Chicken Soup for the Soul* went on to sell more than 10 million copies in the United States and was eventually translated into more than 40 languages around the world.

One of the most important actions you can take is asking—asking people to buy, to enroll, to support, to invest, to lend, to endorse, to advise, to participate, to volunteer, or to contribute. Often, the only thing that separates the successful from the unsuccessful is their willingness to ask for what they need and want. Unfortunately, many people are uncomfortable asking. Some are even paralyzed. They are afraid of rejection. They are afraid of hearing the word NO. What got me over this fear of rejection was a formula that was taught to me by the girl who has the Guinness World Record for selling the most boxes of Girl Scout cookies in a single year—3526 boxes! Her formula was SWSWSWSW, which stands for Some Will, Some Won't, So What, Someone's Waiting. Don't let the fear of NO stop you. In fact, you can make a game out of it. Get excited about the NOs. See how many you can get in one day…because what you'll learn is that the more NOs you get, the more YES's you'll eventually get. Remember, someone is waiting to say YES!

And think about this: There really is no such thing as rejection. If I get a NO, I am no worse off than I was before I asked. If I ask someone to lend me one thousand dollars and they say no, I didn't have a thousand dollars before I asked, and I don't have a thousand dollars after I asked. My life didn't get worse. It stayed the same. When we were trying to find a publisher for *Chicken Soup for the Soul,* we were rejected by 144 publishers over the course of a year. If we had given up after 100 rejections, I wouldn't be writing this chapter right now. No one would care. A rejection is just a step along the way to success.

STEP 6. SOLICIT *AND RESPOND* TO FEEDBACK

It is a fact of life that not all the actions you take are going to work out exactly the way you want. However, every action you take will produce some sort of result, and that result is feedback. All feedback is valuable. Pay attention to the external feedback (lack of results, no sales, complaints, criticism, discord, loss) and the internal feedback (illness, physical pain, boredom, stress) that says you are off course. Just keep making the necessary corrections until you get the results that you want. Sometimes you have to keep experimenting until you get it right.

Here's one of the most important things I ever learned. It's a series of two questions for soliciting valuable feedback from others in both your professional and personal life.

1. On a scale of 1 to 10, how would you rate the quality of [our relationship, this product, our service, this meeting, me as a manager/employee/spouse/father/teacher] during this past [week, month, quarter]?

Anything less than a 10 as an answer gets this follow up question:

2. What would it take to make it a 10?

This is where the valuable information comes from. Have the courage to ask this question, listen to the answers without defensiveness, and act on the feedback.

STEP 7. PRACTICE PERSEVERANCE

In order to be successful you have to persevere in the face of resistance, disappointment, obstacles, setbacks and failures. There may be many times when you want to give in and quit, but the one quality more than any other that guarantees success is the willingness to stick with it, to see it through to the end, to refuse to settle for anything less than your dream. And remember, adversity and challenge is what gives you the opportunity to develop qualities such as courage, patience, tenacity, and compassion. And here's an encouraging statistic: the average millionaire in America has gone bankrupt or out of business 3.5 times on their way to becoming a millionaire.

STEP 8. PRACTICE GRATITUDE

The first *and* last step of achieving your goals is to have an attitude of gratitude—to be grateful for and appreciate all that you have. Most people starting out tend to focus on what they don't have rather than what they do have. What we have learned from movies and books like *The Secret*, which focus on the law of attraction, is that we get more of what we focus on. If we focus on our lack of money, friends, health or opportunities, we get more of that—lack. If we focus on all that we do have, and express gratitude for that, we get more to be grateful for.

Take a few moments every day to express appreciation for the many blessings in your life. Whether you write it down in your journal or simply make note of it in your mind, refocus your attention on those things you already have. Express that gratitude to God/Source/the Universe through prayer, meditation or the simple act of appreciation. Also express your appreciation to those people who contribute to your life and your happiness—from your family members, friends and coworkers to the waiters, mechanics and others who serve you. You'll be amazed at the miracles that will begin to occur when you come from an attitude of gratitude and express appreciation.

Well, that completes the eight fundamental steps of a success system that never fails. All you have to do is to dedicate yourself to putting it into action along with all of the other insights, principles and strategies you will learn in this book. I invite you to live your life as if everything I have written here is true for a minimum of ninety days and see what happens. I know you will be astounded at the results!

About Jack

Jack Canfield, known as America's #1 Success Coach, is the CEO of the Canfield Training Group in Santa Barbara, CA, which trains and coaches entrepreneurs, corporate leaders, managers, sales professionals and the general public in how to accelerate the achievement of their personal, professional and financial goals.

He is best known as the coauthor of the #1 New York Times best-selling *Chicken Soup for the Soul®* book series, which has sold more than 500 million books in 47 languages, including 11 New York Times #1 best sellers. As the CEO of Chicken Soup for the Soul Enterprises he helped grow the Chicken Soup for the Soul® brand into a virtual empire of books, children's books, audios, videos, CDs, classroom materials, a syndicated column and a television show, as well as a vigorous program of licensed products that includes everything from clothing and board games to nutraceuticals and a successful line of Chicken Soup for the Pet Lover's Soul® cat and dog foods.

His other books include *The Success Principles™: How to Get from Where You Are to Where You Want to Be, The Success Principles for Teens, The Aladdin Factor, Dare to Win, Heart at Work, The Power of Focus: How to Hit Your Personal, Financial and Business Goals with Absolute Certainty, You've Got to Read This Book, Tapping into Ultimate Success, Jack Canfield's Key to Living the Law Attraction,* and his recent novel—*The Golden Motorcycle Gang: A Story of Transformation.*

Jack is a dynamic speaker and was recently inducted into the National Speakers Association's Speakers Hall of Fame. He has appeared on more than 1000 radio and television shows including Oprah, Montel, Larry King Live, the Today Show, Fox and Friends, and two hour-long PBS Specials devoted exclusively to his work. Jack is also a featured teacher in 12 movies including The Secret, The Meta-Secret, The Truth, The Keeper of the Keys, Tapping into the Source, and The Tapping Solution.

Jack has personally helped hundreds of thousands of people on six different continents become multimillionaires, business leaders, best-selling authors, leading sales professionals, successful entrepreneurs, and world-class athletes while at the same time creating balanced, fulfilling and healthy lives.

His corporate clients have included Virgin Records, SONY Pictures, Daimler-Chrysler, Federal Express, GE, Johnson & Johnson, Merrill Lynch, Campbell's Soup, Re/Max, The Million Dollar Forum, The Million Dollar Roundtable, The Entrepreneur Organization, The Young Presidents Organization, the Executive Committee, and the World Business Council.

He is the founder of the Transformational Leadership Council and a member of Evolutionary Leaders, two groups devoted to helping create a world that works for everyone.

Jack is a graduate of Harvard, earned his M.Ed. from the University of Massachusetts and has received three honorary doctorates in psychology and public service. He is married, has three children and two stepchildren.

For more information visit: www.JackCanfield.com

CHAPTER 2

Success by Choice

By Alana McKinney

I am from Chicagoland. Colonel Robert R. McCormick's newspaper, *The Chicago Tribune,* is said to have coined the term in 1926. People in the suburbs liked the idea of being associated with Chicago without really living within the city limits, so it stuck. The term gives a general idea of where one lives in northern Illinois.

I attend a lot of business networking events throughout the US and Canada. A frequent question that I am asked after "…so where do you live?" is "Have you ever been to the Oprah Show?"

When I answer, "as a matter of fact I have", it takes most people by surprise. The questions change from trying to connect with me to, "Give me the inside scoop on Oprah." I have been asked: "Were you there when she was heavy or thin?" and "what perfume was she wearing?" A guy even told me his mother was dying and asked if I could score him four tickets to the "My Favorite Things" show.

One of the more exciting Oprah Shows I attended was by luck (some would say). I think it is more along the lines of the "Law of Attraction" kicking in. To build an audience, before the last segment of most shows, a topic and phone number would flash on the screen. If you would like to attend the show that featured a particular topic, you were instructed to call in and get as many as four general admission tickets. This was a true test of persistence. I spent an hour and a half 'speed dialing' and miracle of miracles someone picked up the phone. There were still four tickets available to the show that asked the question "Can you create a 'designer look' without the high price tag?" I could barely wait to tell three of my friends, "We're goin' to Oprah!"

Our general admission tickets got us in the doors, but after that it was every gal for herself to find a seat! Our little group did manage to snag seats together in the back section of the studio. As we settled down into our seats, I noticed a Director walk through the audience making introductions and small talk. She asked about the topic of the day as she made her way through the crowd. When she got to my section she asked me, "So... can you dress couture without spending a fortune?" I introduced myself and told her that I was a wardrobe consultant. I made it one of my top priorities to recommend garments that looked high end, yet did not have a high price tag. When she asked me how, I told her that I look for trendy style, high quality fabrics and impeccable construction. She thanked me and proceeded down to the stage. Within a few minutes, I was told that my new seat was waiting for me on the front row. Oprah came on stage and finalized the show preparation, and the Director introduced me to Ms. Winfrey as someone knowledgeable on the subject matter, who could speak on camera if needed. Wow, I was shocked at the testimonial I received!

That evening when reflecting on the events of the day, I was still in awe. I was seen on national television by friends, family, and clients as well as gave Oprah talking points on the fashions that were featured on her show. During the commercial she wanted my opinion and why I thought the way I did. She discussed what we spoke about during the commercial breaks to add to her commentary.

It wasn't until sometime after my experience when I realized what really happened that day at Harpo Studios. I had received a private lesson on success from one of the most recognized successful people on earth. However, I overestimated the importance of being on the show and undervalued the importance *of the processes* that brought me to that point in time. What should I learn from the experience to guide my future?

John C. Maxwell writes of the Law of Process in his book, *The 21 Irrefutable Laws of Leadership*. Successful people seem to know instinctively that success develops daily, not in one single day. If one is to attain their goals and dreams of success, one must nurture and grow characteristics that only the successful practice and master.

Life would truly be a bore if we did not have events on our calendar to give us inspiration and motivation to move on to the next level. Don't make the mistake as I did though, thinking that the event is as powerful as the process. Your daily routine and habits will determine your future more than anything else.

Have you defined success? When asking this question to an audience, I have found a variety of answers. Yet most of us visualize success as a destination, not a journey. It has taken me several years (due to bouts of A.A.D.) to realize I can choose to be a success in the present moment as well as in the future. I have found that being curious and asking questions makes me the learner of relevant knowledge that adds value not only to me, but also to others. I personally have defined success as: knowing who I am, building value in others and choosing to grow.

MINDSETS TO SUCCESS BY CHOICE

1. Choose to know who I am. You must know yourself to grow yourself. Imagine for a moment that you knew you were dying and had only one month to live. What would you want to share in your last interview? For Steve Jobs it was to know your 'passion' and be all over it like a dog with a bone. Does that surprise you? Would you have thought that he would have said something different?

Steve Jobs knew that when one works in their strength zone, they develop strategies that make them intentionally focused, supernaturally persistent and not only able to grow but also multiply their skill sets. He jokingly remarked that "any sane person would have quit long ago!

Recently, I participated in a workshop facilitated by my international renown speaking coach and mentor Roddy Galbraith. The workshop was two-fold. One we were to prepare a speech and two we were to give feedback to a select few in the workshop. The only caveat being, we were to recognize the positive points of the speech we critiqued. This was not as easy for some as you might think. Many have been conditioned to think that constructive criticism is negative feedback. The misconception is the one on the receiving end of the negative criticism has something to work on. In reality, most who work on their weaknesses have only marginal improvement. The issue is not that one has to have someone point out our weak areas. Studies conducted have shown participants that were asked to list their strengths and weaknesses listed

5x more weaknesses than strengths. The purpose of the exercise Roddy had us do was to intently focus on our strengths. By doing so, we could become more creative in developing strategies that would eventually expand our skill set.

2. Choose to build value in others by helping face reality. Before every flight, part of the safety instruction says, "In the unlikely event there is a loss of cabin pressure, oxygen masks will drop down. Securely place the mask over *your* mouth and nose before helping others." It has been my experience Southwest Airlines has more fun with the safety fundamentals than most airlines. I think that they have hit on something that gets the job done. Using humor encourages passengers to listen for the joke which seems to get the timely message across. The reality in an emergency (God forbid) there will be those who cannot physically comply with the safety measures, those that freeze, others that deny the reality of danger and the heroes who assist the crew in helping others. The flight attendants are reminding us in the remote possibility how to behave when helping others. Hopefully, you are those helping in the emergency and not one that needs help.

Uncertain economical times breed many who are insecure and have a lack of direction or purpose. They are in an emergency. Reminding them that their goals and dreams are built on reality can put them in a more positive place to recover. Assessing your reality and positively acting upon it is the foundational cornerstone to success.

Second, value all your relationships. In my Oprah story there were two relationships that had value added. Over 25 years Oprah learned her strengths. She evaluated what was most important for her to do personally in each show and she delegated the rest. Just think how much trust Oprah had in the Director whose job it was to find knowledgeable audience members. Think how capable the Director was in finding relevant, interesting material that was to support an hour long show. Would you trust your assistant with that degree of responsibility? Most entrepreneurs and small business owners would rather eat nails than delegate at that level. Successful people know they must give up to go up.

The next relationship that built value was between myself and the Director. I was chosen to add my expertise and be seen on camera multiple times. The Director was given the authority to canvass the audience and choose the best for the job. I guess you could say I was lucky (if you stop to think luck is when preparation and opportunity meet).

3. Choose to build your character. Character determines your personal and professional reputation and growth. Trade offs are inevitable if you are to mature and be successful. Life will make you pay. The higher you go, the bigger the tradeoffs. When growing up I heard my Mom say, "play now, pay later" or "pay now, play later." Though this may sound so last century the truth still rings true. Being disciplined enough to take care of business in the present will cost you less in the long run. If you decide to play first you will have to pay with higher interest.

We have known people who are climbing the ladder of success and think that all they need is to cultivate and grow their talent. Whitney Houston's tragic death should remind us that talent and right choices are needed to enjoy our success. Without good character as a foundation one is destine to be just a "candle in the wind."

Making a decision to build good basic core values is just the beginning. Aligning 4 traits of strong character will not only add but multiply your success.

- **Values**—What values would you say without a shadow of a doubt you would go to the mat for? You may have learned them from your parents, grandparents, teachers, the Bible or a religious figure like Mother Theresa. Evaluate and place your core values firmly in your heart and mind.

- **Thoughts**—Do you control your thoughts or do they control you? Being successful day to day means that you do not 'campout' on what you cannot change but focus on what you can change.

- **Feelings**—Do you let your feelings dictate your actions? Move toward your goals even when you do not feel like it. Feelings have a way of catching up with you.

- **Actions**—Decide your action steps when you are on the mountain top and not in the valley. The valley tends to cloud our view of what we are capable of doing. A body in motion has a tendency to stay in motion. A body at rest has a tendency to stay at rest.

Successful people have a more deliberate mindset different than most when it comes to achieving their highest goals. They have discovered their purpose in life. Their daily routine is full of action steps they passionately know will help them achieve their purpose. They grow in their potential and team up with others whose strengths will complement their weaknesses. They consciously build, give and serve in their relationships to add mutual value. By doing so, a successful person transforms into a successful leader.

And finally, by nurturing relationships to bring them to their full potential, the successful leader has the opportunity to leave a legacy that is admired, studied and copied for generations to come.

About Alana

Alana McKinney is the Entrepreneur's Networking Advocate by taking the mystery out of Social Capital.

She discovered the power of networking years ago when a gun shop opened across from her children's high school. Realizing she couldn't change the situation on her own, Alana reached out to others—including First Lady Hilary Clinton, the late Senator Henry Hyde, and Sarah and Jim Brady. Her crusade was picked up nationally, and the gun shop agreed to move. Alana then used networking to expand her women's clothing business. This brought her into contact with Business Network International (BNI). Its philosophy of "Giver's Gain" spoke to her. Alana became an Executive Director and Partner for the Chicagoland region, responsible for the operations, marketing/PR and nurturing of a franchise of more than 80+ BNI chapters.

Today, Alana advocates the benefits of networking and word-of-mouth referral marketing to BNI members, entrepreneurs, businesspeople and not-for-profits. She is a frequent presenter and coach on networking strategies and techniques. She has worked with business professionals in Action Coach International, The Brian Buffini Organization, Herbal Life, Mary Kay Cosmetics, SendOutCards, Shaklee Corporation, and Signs by Tomorrow, among many others.

Alana became a 2011 Quilly Award Winner given by the National Academy of Best-Selling Authors for her collaboration in the book, *Building the Ultimate Network*.

In early 2012 Alana became a Founding Partner on the Dr. John C. Maxwell Team as well as a certified trainer and speaker in the following programs: Becoming a Person of Influence; Everyone Communicates, Few Connect; How to be a REAL Success; Leadership Gold; Put Your Dreams to the Test.

Alana has been featured on The Oprah Winfrey Show, The Today Show, NBC Nightly News, CNN, ABC, NBC and CBS, as well as in USA Today, The Chicago Tribune, The Chicago Sun-Times, and radio interviews.

Her favorite saying is: *Intelligent people know facts; successful people know people.*

To learn more about Alana, to arrange a speaking engagement or coaching relationship, contact her at: Contact@AlanaMcKinney.com

or visit her blog at: www.AlanaMcKinney.com.

CHAPTER 3

The "It" Factor: Gaining Ownership of Your Life, Health & Goals

By Angel Boyce

What is "It"?

No matter where we are or what we're doing, there is an "It" that is the strongest motivating factor in our lives at that moment. "It" drives you forward to your most cherished goals—as well as to your own personal happiness and satisfaction.

In my various careers as a nurse, a corporate consultant, educator and a business owner, I always followed my own "It" to reach the next rung up the ladder of my personal and professional development. Sometimes that "It" has been about career. Mostly, in recent years, "It" has been about my family.

But sometimes, "It" wasn't about anything all that serious. For example, when I was younger, I worked at The Gap every morning for ten years... just because I liked trying on clothes!

There's nothing wrong with that—I made money doing something I loved to do and, when it was time to give it up, I did. And now, as I continue to pursue my own entrepreneurial goals, as I continue to raise my beautiful daughter Ally with my husband Chuck, as I continue to pursue a Doctorate. I continue to live each day according to whatever

"It" is pushing me forward.

So what's your "It?" And what's "It" all about?

BALANCING "IT"

First of all, "It" is about balance and nourishing your three main areas of living—Mind, Body and Spirit. Various personal gurus have their own labels for this kind of three-pronged approach, but we all know that if one of these "Big Three" gets out of whack, the other two suffer as well.

For instance, if you suffer from chronic pain (Body), you're going to have trouble concentrating on your work (Mind) and possibly get depressed about the future (Spirit). If a close relationship is in turmoil (Spirit), it could not only affect your attitude (Mind), but could even impact your actual physical health (Body).

Health is so important. It affects how we approach everything in life—if our health isn't good, it's as if someone dimmed our inner light. Health isn't just about going to the gym everyday, it's about your mindset and your lifestyle. Are you eating okay? Are you taking care of yourself? Are you getting enough sleep? Are your friends and family stressing you out or nourishing you? Do you need more time alone?

And what do you do to recharge yourself? When our schedules are packed with family and work, we often don't realize how run down we're getting and how low our energy has become. That's when it's important to say, "Hey, we just need to go play and have fun." That can be quite an important "It" if you need a break (which is why The Gap was my recharger for so many years!)

When something throws us off balance, then that becomes our most important "It," and we really can't get back on track until it's addressed. I was all set to write this chapter a few days ago; then, I received an urgent call that a close relative was heading to the emergency room. My "It" suddenly changed and I had to put this chapter (as well as everything else) on hold until I could make sure that person was okay. Fortunately, she was—and only when I knew that for sure could I shift back to my previous priorities.

There is a flow to life that we all have to respect. Going with the flow and trying not to fight it is a big part of how we keep our overall balance. We may get freaked out when our "It" is forced to shift with the current...but that current is what gets us to where we're supposed to go!

YOU CAN'T DO "IT" ALONE!

When we're growing and working towards our dreams, a little help from those around us can be the "make-or-break" difference between moving forward or staying in one place.

Too often, however, we look up instead of down when it comes to the people in our lives. What I mean is that, we ingratiate ourselves with those in charge and overlook the essential "supporting cast."

A few years ago, I became a school nurse for reasons I'll talk about shortly. I always made it a point at Christmas time to give little gifts to the school's custodial and kitchen staff. These were small gifts of chocolate cherries and a card, or even just Starbursts in a fancy jar, to show that I thought about them during the holidays and I appreciated their work.

This gesture didn't cost me a whole lot—a few dollars per person—but you would have thought I had given them each a brand new BMW convertible. They began to always greet me with a smile, ask if I needed help with something and, in general, treat me like a queen. And a few of them confided in me that no one had ever thought to "gift" them like that. They had grown accustomed to doing their jobs without anyone ever recognizing their contributions, since they weren't that high on the professional totem pole in most people's eyes.

Well, when it comes down to it, these people are actually the ones who know what's going on at the school more than anyone. They're the "boots on the ground" day after day. When I need help or I need to understand a situation, they give me valuable assistance and help me resolve the problem.

And that's because I did reach out and build those relationships. So say hello to all of those around you, no matter where they are perceived in the "pecking order." Build your network of contacts and you'll have the support you need when the time comes.

That way, you'll always have "It" covered!

MAKING "IT" WORK

As I mentioned, my "It" in recent years has been mostly about family. I wanted to be the best mom I could to my daughter, Ally, which meant some big changes in my life—changes I embraced because it took me to where I wanted to go, and enabled me to be the mother I aspired to be.

When Ally was born, I had a great job at Proctor and Gamble. I made an awesome salary, there was a lot of opportunity for growth and it was a great company to work for. I got to help provide direct care to over 350 employees and their families and design workplace educational sessions about vital health topics, such as stress, nutrition and ergonomics, as well as making sure our emergency response teams were up-to-date in their training and education.

Professionally, I couldn't be more satisfied. When Ally was a baby, it wasn't a problem to continue with my career. I was able to put her in daycare where I worked. I had a 45-minute commute to the office each way, and those 45 minutes provided us with some real quality time together.

Well, for the moment, I had an "It" that was a big win-win. I love all of P&G's systems, their philosophy, the people I worked with, and of course I loved having all that special "alone" time in the car with Ally. Note, however, that I said "for the moment." Because that current is always changing and we have to change with it.

When Ally was a couple of years old, that "It" suddenly changed. She wanted to be more social with friends around where she lived. Chuck and I both wanted to be in a neighborhood with a good school, where family and church were nearby. That wasn't going to happen where my job was located.

So, I left Proctor and Gamble and began consulting to work closer to home. We made that home where "It" would work for all of us.

The problem was, when Ally began kindergarten, I was still working long days. Even when I did get home at my normal time of 5:30, that didn't leave a lot of family time for us all. It was hectic and busy and not fun—I was losing my balance.

I firmly believe that if your current situation is not healthy, you should change your plan. You should instead go create and build a new situation that will work for you. Again, it's all about going with the flow.

In this case, my husband Chuck was already a busy entrepreneur. He had ended up missing Ally's first birthday party due to the work demands for his job. He had decided to change his personal "It". I just knew we couldn't have two entrepreneurs in one house. It can work well—and I could still support Chuck's efforts in my off-hours—but sometimes, your "It" takes you in a different direction.

And that's how I became a school nurse. It's an ideal schedule. I work roughly the same time as Ally is attending her school, and I'm off summers when she is out also. The best part is I can totally control my schedule. My hours at the school are very predictable, and I have enough time for other activities and work. For example, I not only work at the school, I also teach at the college, I work at an urgent care center and, as I said earlier, I'm pursuing my doctorate. At the same time, I can always be there when Ally needs me.

HAVING "IT" ALL

Now...if you read that last paragraph closely, you might be wondering, "How does she have time for all that?"

Well, it may seem like I'm overscheduled and over challenged, but, to me, it's how I find my balance—and it's how I fulfill my "It." The real secret is to have a lot of people nearby that you both give to and get from; when you're in need, they're there—and when they're in need, you're there.

By going full-out, going after and doing all these different things, I have not only kept my health training and education as current as possible, but I've also gained a great deal of business acumen and marketing savvy.

That means I'm far from being just a nurse. I'm someone who knows how to go into a company and tackle their health issues and challenges. I can help keep their workforce strong and educate everyone, and also help the company itself when it comes to business issues.

For example, in our company, we had an employee who slipped in the rain in the early morning hours on our premises. Someone overheard her say that she was going to sue and they came to me and said, "Angel, what should we do?" I told the person that we should quickly get a witness statement from her, then get on the phone with our worker's comp carrier to get a first report file, so someone could immediately start investigating the accident. When the employee came back to work, we should make sure she has a note from her doctor detailing if there are any restrictions on what she can do. In other words, there was a process we could follow that would enable us to possibly avoid a potentially complicated and expensive litigation and lost employee productivity.

Well, by the time the person was going to be interviewed by our worker comp person, she backed off, because she saw she couldn't get away with any exaggerations.

That's the value of what I can bring into a situation. Believe it or not, companies get nervous about answering questions as seemingly simple as, "Should we or should we not offer flu shots?" And rightfully so, in today's environment. It takes the right combination of information, experience and expertise to really be able to find your way through these thorny issues and safeguard your employees as well as your business.

So where is my "It" taking me next? Well, I'm really excited about pursuing the next phase of my life—combining my education and training with my business knowledge, and applying them to coaching and mentoring individuals, as well as speaking to groups and consulting with businesses. Health is my passion; it's wonderful knowing you can add a unique value to the world as well as help improve the health of those around you.

To sum up, I believe you can have everything you want out of life. Yes, you can have it all. You just can't have it all at any given moment. "It" is as simple as that.

And that's "It!"

About Angel

Angel is much more than a nurse–she's also a scientist, a corporate consultant, an educator and a business owner. Her lifelong commitment to education has given her the tools to provide expertise in a variety of situations; making her as comfortable helping a major corporation tackle its health issues and challenges as she is delivering individualized care to a student population as a school nurse.

A lifelong resident of the State of Delaware, Angel received her BA in Biology from the University of Delaware in Newark in 1992 and parlayed her degree into a career as a scientist. When she discovered her true passion was for helping people, she returned to the University to earn her BS in Nursing, with a minor in Psychology, in 1992. Later, she earned a Masters of Nursing Leadership and a Post Masters Certificate as a Family Nurse Practitioner from Wilmington University in 2008. Today, she continues to learn everything she can about the nursing profession by pursuing her doctorate.

Angel launched her nursing career as a consultant, and later became the Occupational Health Nurse at Proctor and Gamble. During her five years with the corporation, she helped to provide direct care to over 350 employees and their families, designed workplace educational sessions about vital health topics, such as stress, nutrition and ergonomics, and made sure the company's emergency response teams were up-to-date in their training and education.

The birth of her daughter, Ally, led Angel to refocus her energy on how to best grow her career as a working mother. She returned to consulting when her daughter was young, and when Ally started school, she became a school nurse in order to optimize her schedule. She has also spent over 10 years in occupational nursing, community nursing and hospital nursing, as well as a CPR and First Aid instructor, and teaches college nursing classes.

Angel is a Registered Nurse in the States of Delaware and holds a multitude of professional certifications in occupational health, school nursing and family practice. She has held leadership roles in nursing professional organizations by serving as Past President of the Delaware Association of Occupational Health Nurses and currently as Treasurer for the Delaware Association of School Nurses.

Angel has received numerous honors and awards including the 2005 NEAOHN Leadership Award, the 2011 FMC BioPolymer Grant and the Healthy Schools Program Bronze Award from the Alliance for A Healthier Generation for her school. She is a passionate advocate for health and strives to add value to the world by helping to improve the health—and lives—of the people around her.

CHAPTER 4

Success through Discovering Your Purpose and Designing Your Destiny

By L. Aynn Daniels, M.Ed., CPM

Your genetic code was created the moment you were conceived. You were designed for great things…and you have a unique purpose—an assignment.

Your purpose may remain dormant, unrealized, for your entire life, but it can never be destroyed. It may be delayed, even momentarily defeated, but never destroyed. The dictionary defines purpose as: An object or result aimed at – Intention; Resolution; Determination.

Unlike all other living creatures we humans are guided to ask, "What is my reason for being?" Your destiny is designed by discovering your purpose. Living purposefully allows you to channel fulfillment into your life and manifest the abundance you deserve.

Your purpose is often displayed as you go around in a constant whirl-pool of unfulfilled jobs, dates with different partners, obsession with buying cars, houses, and any other things you could possibly imagine that do not contribute to your true purpose. We all make ill-informed decisions as we seek our way.

Yet, we all possess a spirit, an inner wisdom – an essential silent partner. Whether of a spiritual persuasion or otherwise, most would agree that your purpose is already "within you." You don't "find" your purpose but rather you "discover" or turn within yourself and claim your purpose.

The current circumstances of your life may be more a representation of who you *were* than who you *are*. To move to a life of purpose, you must let go of the idea that past negative results represent who you are. You must plan for the future but live purposefully in the present. Focus on becoming a more human "being" in fulfilling your purpose and less of a human "doing."

When you are inspired by a sense of purpose, your thoughts break their boundaries, and your mind literally transcends all limitations. Your purpose is revealed at the intersection of your Divine Assignment, Intentions, Passions, Talents/Skills and Values.

ASK BETTER QUESTIONS

1. Am I going through life or is life going through me?

A life of purpose is the purpose of life. A life of purpose allows you to do those things that truly give you fulfillment, joy and peace. If you're having more "oh-no" days than "ah-ha days," it's time to flip the script. Your thoughts, self-image, beliefs, attitudes and emotional habits are central to a life of purpose.

Take a piece of paper. On one side, list the number of "oh-no" days you've had over the past three months. Beside each of those days list what you did or experienced that caused you to have this sense of dismay. List the people, places, and things in each experience. Describe what *you* might do over the next three months to not re-live those experiences.

On the opposite side of the paper, list the number of "ah-ha" days you've had over the past three months. Beside each of those days list what you did or experienced that caused you to have this sense of fulfillment. List the people, places, and things in each experience. To fill your emotional bank, describe what *you* might do over the next three months to re-live those experiences. Not only should you write these "ah-ha" experiences, but you should speak those experiences - speaking helps to solidify your commitment. Your destiny is designed by discovering your purpose through continuous connection with your inner wisdom… the basis of your success.

2. Am I living life from the dashboard or from the rearview mirror?

What would it be like to drive to your next destination looking only through the rearview mirror? What would be the chances of getting safely to your destination? A life of purpose allows you to experience a sense of empowerment and direction. Purpose is a dashboard experience.

Moving while looking forward often takes you out of your comfort zone. When you are not living life purposefully, you may end up in the backseat of an endless ride or gazing from the rearview mirror. The rearview mirror has its place; but those who don't learn from their past may be destined to repeat it. You can't move forward by constantly looking back. When you are on purpose, the people, resources and opportunities you need naturally seem to gravitate toward you. When you are looking back, you may miss what is right in front of you.

3. Am I sitting on my A.S.S.E.T.S. and dragging my butt?

A.S.S.E.T.S. are defined here as **A**uthentic **S**trengths and **S**kills that **E**ffectively **T**ransform **S**elf. We all have strengths and skills. These assets are often unrealized and untapped; we simply sit on them. You have divine and in-borne gifts. There's no one on earth like you. Your potential may be meaningless unless you do something with it and move to perform. As you move to your authentic self, ask:

- What does my inner wisdom, intuition or spirit say to me?
- What will fulfill me and move me to a sense of completeness?
- What strengths/skills (gifts/talents) do I currently have?
- What strengths/skills do I want to acquire, why, and by when?
- What steps will I take to acquire them?
- What is standing in the way of living my purpose; what are my fears?
- Am I asking the right questions, or simply giving the wrong answers?
- How will I feel when I move into living life on purpose?

You may say -

- BUT I don't have enough money or education.
- BUT coulda, woulda, shoulda…

Often these are merely excuses disguised as legitimate reasons for not becoming an action-driven person. Adversities can serve either as stumbling blocks or stepping stones. The person you become in life is dependent upon whether you focus on your strengths or focus on your weaknesses. You can be pitiful *or* powerful, but not both. Change your focus and you change your future.

You are your answer.

People may struggle in discovering their purpose due to lack of a strong sense of self so they often latch onto the actions and the self of others. They lack an authentic self which is the essence of purpose and destiny.

YOU ARE BORN TO SOAR

The story is told of a man who found an eagle's egg and put it into the nest of a barnyard hen. The eagle hatched with the flock of chicks and grew up with them. All his life, the eagle did what the barnyard chicks did, thinking he was a barnyard chicken. He scratched the earth for worms and insects. He would cackle as barnyard chickens do, thrash his wings and fly a few feet in the air.

Years passed and the eagle grew very old. One day, the ole eagle saw a magnificent bird above him in the cloudless sky. The eagle glided in graceful mastery among powerful wind currents, with its strong golden wings.

The ole eagle, that had grown up with chickens looked up in awe. "Who's that?" he asked. "That's an eagle, the king of the birds," said one of his chicken friends. "He belongs to the sky. We belong to the earth – we're chickens."

So the ole eagle, raised with chickens, lived and died a chicken, for that's what he thought he was. That's unrealized purpose. There is divine purpose inside each and every one of us. On our way to fulfilling our "purpose" – our journey to the "palace" – we sometimes find ourselves in the "pit" of life. The ole eagle in the story was out of his purpose.

He was born to soar. The sad part is that the eagle raised with chickens could not recognize the similarity, even when confronted with a replica of himself, the eagle. Sadly, that's true for many of us.

THE PIT, THE PROCESS AND YOUR PURPOSE

The pit, the state of adversity and challenge in your life, is not always a bad place. It can be a place of "positioning"; a ground zero. But that glorious process of momentous change is called transformation.

Your purpose has as much to do with your character as it does with your actions. Purpose is not simply what you do, but why and how you do it.

The palace, that place of purpose in your life, is a place of promise and tremendous provision. Between the pit and the palace is the process. Process is that place of potential. The process is as important, if not more so, than the palace. Your only way out may be the way through. You can't find *peace* until you find the *pieces*. You cannot go from the pit to the palace without going through a *process* of transformation:

Step 1: *Self-Actualization.* This requires a thorough examination of your A.S.S.E.T.S. There can be no actualization without examination. Self-examination allows you to know who you are, to discover your "are-ness." Self-actualization offers opportunities for prayer, self-reflection and meditation. It refers to a desire for fulfillment - the tendency to fulfill your potential - to become everything that you are capable of becoming. Purpose is defined as you move from self-consciousness to a strong God consciousness.

Step 2: *Make Quality Decisions.* Your purpose is displayed in your choices and decisions. Your choices and decisions, positive or negative, design your destiny. Follow the Five C's:

1. *Conviction* based on positive, healthy and sound values, and your discovered purpose.
2. *Challenge* yourself and seek new opportunities.
3. *Control* yourself by doing those things you can do and letting go of things you cannot do.
4. *Connection* to positive people, places and things for support
5. *Commitment* to acting on your convictions

A decision not to decide is still a decision.

Step 3: *Renew Your Mind.* ["As a man thinketh, so is he"]

   R - Rejoice and reflect on the positive things in your life.

   E - Envision and visualize what you want to accomplish in life, honoring your purpose

   N - Nullify and eliminate negative thoughts and fears

   E - Energize and ignite your life with positive people, places and things

   W- Watch your thoughts

Step 4: *Bloom Where you are Planted.* Trees are not swayed by "the grass is greener on the other side." Trees do their best and grow right where they are. Trees sink their roots deep. They don't waste time wishing they were someone or somewhere else. Trees thrive on more sunlight and water, but they will never just pull up and move somewhere "better" – they bloom where they're planted. Become like a tree.

Step 5: *Build Boundaries.* If you don't stand up for something, you'll fall for anything. Set allowable limits. Do not tolerate the intolerable. Learn to say No, or Yes with a condition. Your character is viewed by what you'll do when people are looking. Your integrity is determined by what you'll do when people are not looking.

Step 6: *Be Selective.* Be careful of what you expose yourself to. Guard your heart: be careful what you see, what you hear, and what you say. You may need to cut ties with certain people, places and things in order to fulfill your purpose. Hang a "No Rider" sign on your life and stop picking up everything and everybody.

Step 7: *Dissociate With the Past.* Forgiveness is an act of faith. It urges you to imagine a better future where your hurt will not be the final word on the matter and shows you can survive the pain and grow from it. Develop an attitude of perseverance and tenacity. The greatest defeat of your purpose is an attitude of "un-forgiveness" of yourself and others. He who angers you controls you. Forgiveness is an act that changes us from prisoners of our past to liberated people at peace with our memories. Let it go.

Step 8: *Develop an Attitude of Gratitude.* Thankfulness and appreciation for all life has to offer is rewarding. Gratitude is an act of unconditional love that allows you to redefine your purpose as a supportive extension of God, not as some fleeting detachment of the universe. Asking better questions and going through the process of transformation will position you to discover your purpose and design your destiny.

About L. Aynn

L. Aynn Daniels, M.Ed., CPM is a life coach, personal and organizational development trainer, consultant, writer, blogger and entrepreneur. Her writing can be viewed at www.AynnDaniels.com where she provides strategies and resources on discovering your purpose, defining your passion and designing your destiny. She conducts live workshops through her coaching company, *Increasing Your Awareness.* Her personal development model, *The Twelve Commitments for Success* is a practical and inspiring workshop that helps individuals to manage personal change, develop hardiness and resiliency, and learn the "power of arrival" in their personal and professional lives. Aynn's definition of success is best expressed in the biblical verse from Proverbs 3:5-6 – "Trust in the LORD with all your heart, and lean not unto your own understanding; in all your ways acknowledge Him, and He shall direct your paths."

Aynn is a member of the International Association of Risk and Compliance Professionals, and the National Association of Professional Women. She serves as consultant to several universities, secondary schools, community based, and health–human service agencies and has conducted over 500 seminars and workshops on personal and organizational development.

Aynn is a regular contributor to the online, international magazine *The Life Skills Magazine.* As a Certified Project Manager (CPM), Aynn is President and CEO of her own administrative consulting firm (LIANDA Consulting Group, Inc./DBA: LIANDA Resource Solutions) where she and her team provide project and operations management, grant writing/management, resource development, internal controls-compliance, and business development services. To learn more about her services go to www.AynnDaniels.com/lianda-resource-solutions. Aynn was an Assistant Professor of Family and Community Medicine at the prestigious Wake Forest University School of Medicine for 25 years. She has been an adjunct instructor with Pfeiffer University teaching in the dual degree Master of Business Administration/Master of Health Administration (MBA/MHA) program, and the Master of Science in Organizational Management (MSOM) program.

Aynn is completing a book entitled, *"Roger Fromwell and His Threefold Destiny."* This is an inspiring fable about a young man who leaves home looking for love, luxury, and leadership. Upon his return he learns powerful and practical lessons about discovering his purpose, defining his passion, and designing his destiny.

380-H Knollwood Street, Suite 181
Winston Salem North Carolina 27103
Office: (336) 577-3054
www.AynnDaniels.com
www.AynnDaniels.com/lianda-resource-solutions
info@ayndaniels.com

CHAPTER 5

7 Secret Money Breakthrough Strategies:
How to Overcome Obstacles & get a Money Breakthrough

By Charles Mixson

These are tough economic times. Every day you read of hardworking people being laid off their jobs, struggling with debt and losing their homes. You may be facing some of these dire situations yourself. Don't give up. There is life after economic set backs. You, and only you, can turn your financial situation around and get back on track.

A friend of mine went through a divorce at the age of 42. She also suffered with several health issues and finally, a bankruptcy. At a time when she thought her life would be settled and stable she was forced into starting completely over–from scratch. No home, no money, no income. Her worst fear was she'd end up a homeless bag lady. But she didn't. She used the seven steps I'm going to describe to you to turn her life around. She now has her own freelance writing business and lives in a house a block from the beach.

Though your situation may be different, it probably feels just as hopeless. You may think you've done everything you can and nothing gets better. You're still broke and the bills are still pouring in quickly while the money comes in slowly. You're not alone.

You can change your situation, though. The seven secrets I'm going to share with you can change your life. But before you read further you need to understand one thing: the first thing you'll have to change is YOU. Your circumstances will never change, your bank account will never change, your financial well-being will never change...unless you make a decision to change.

The secret of these steps are not in each individual step. The power of the steps is how they all work together. You can do one step and your life may improve some; but you won't see the results you need until you act on every step. Face your obstacles head on. Don't ignore them.

Let's get started.

STEP 1. CHANGE YOUR MIND

This is how it all begins. Until you've changed your thoughts and your beliefs, everything will stay the same. You have to lose the victim mentality that is so prevalent in today's society. "If only the economy was better," or " if only I had a better education," or" if only I had grown up in a family with money." On and on it goes. Stop. Right now. Today.

Stop focusing on the past and start thinking about the future. Your own mind is your biggest obstacle to financial freedom. Let me say that one more time: your own mind is your biggest obstacle to financial freedom.

Don't feel sorry for yourself anymore. Figure out what you want to change in your life and start thinking about how you feel when those changes are a reality.

How will you feel when you have enough money in the bank to pay all the bills and some left over?

How will you feel when you own a home?

How will it feel to run your own business?

You control your money. It should not control you.

When you start thinking of how you want things to be you'll notice a slight shift in your thinking. Build on this! At first it may be a simple, "I could probably do better if I tried a little harder," "I know I could manage my money better if I wasn't so depressed," and finally, "I could start a side-line business if I had more energy." Then switch it around.

Say, "I'm going to try harder."

"I'm going to manage my money better so I'll feel happier."

"I have the energy to build a business."

What you say will start to become your reality. This works in a positive or a negative way. You've been using the negative. As of today, stop the negative mind talk and start with the positive.

Will positive thinking alone change your life? No. But it's the first step. Overcome this obstacle and you're well on your way to success.

STEP 2. CHANGE YOUR GOALS

How do you want your life to change?

List in detail what you would like to achieve in your life. Be specific. Don't say, "I want a new career." Say, "I want to make a full-time living selling my paintings online." Or, "I want to start a travel blog and be able to write from anywhere in the world."

You'll never get to where you want to go without a clear vision.

This is the second biggest obstacle that keeps people from moving forward; they have no idea where they want to go! It's not enough to think you don't like your present job or your present financial situation. Start thinking clearly about what career you want and what you want your financial statement to look like.

Choose changes you can be passionate about. Passion works as fuel to push you towards your goals. Passion will help keep you motivated. Passion will add excitement and energy to your plans.

If it helps, put pictures of your goals on a bulletin board or tape them up someplace where you will see them daily.

Begin to let your vision crystallize in your mind so it's not a vague dream.

Draw yourself a map of where you are now to where you want to be in six months, a year, five years.

Then write down practical goals to achieve along your path.

Take classes.

Read books.

Send out resumes.

Start writing your novel.

Then, celebrate every success on your journey.

STEP 3. CHANGE YOUR HABITS

Move out of Denial. Get your head out of the sand and figure out exactly where you are financially. List all of your monthly bills as a start. Then, keep a notebook for one week where you write down every penny you spend. You'll discover a lot of leaks in your money bag.

This step is important for several reasons:

- You can't move forward without facing the present.

- You can't fix a problem that you don't admit you have.

- You must face the reality of your situation.

Money problems affect every area of your life. Your relationship with your spouse, your emotions, your feelings of self-worth, and the example you set for your children. Don't settle for letting your money control you.

Trying to spend less money is somewhat like trying to lose weight. The more depressed you feel about being overweight; the more you eat comfort food to make yourself feel better. Spenders tend to do the same thing. The more depressed they are about being in debt the more apt they are to spend money on "little" things to make themselves feel better. Lunch out with a friend, a new shirt at a department store sale, a new CD to cheer you up, a bigger television so you can zone out every night. You know how it works.

This step is necessary from a practical point of view and from an emotional one. By letting yourself feel the pain of your current situation you'll remember exactly why things *must* change.

Look over your expenses and see what you can cut. Do you really need cable or can you do without it for six months? Can you take your lunch to work at least three times a week instead of eating out every day?

Then change your habits. Stop spending money mindlessly. This is not an act of depriving yourself of things you want; it's the act of making choices.

Choose to spend your money on the things that are most important; not things that are merely habit.

Break the habit of spending money to make yourself "feel" better.

STEP 4. CHANGE YOUR HEALTH

Worrying about money is stress. Stress causes health problems. This is a vicious cycle, and the more you worry, the more tired you feel. The more tired you feel, the less energy you have to make changes.

You need to start taking better care of your physical body. This can be hard at first; but after you make a few needed changes you'll start feeling better, have more energy, and the cycle becomes an upward spiral instead of downward. Energy breeds energy. You already know what to do to take better care of yourself; but now you need to actually do it!

Get at least eight hours of sleep a night. Turn off all electronic devices at least an hour before you go to bed. Read a chapter of fiction before you go to bed to get your mind off work and business. Make sure you're sleeping in a room with some type of light on.

Drink plenty of water. Many people drink coffee, sodas and tea all day and wonder why they can't sleep at night. Cut down on everything that contains caffeine, especially after 7 p.m. When you're dehydrated you're going to feel tired and listless. And caffeinated beverages do *not* hydrate you. They have the opposite effect. Staying hydrated can go a long way in raising your energy level.

Eat more veggies, fruit, protein, and good fats. Eliminate sugar, fast foods, and highly processed foods as much as possible. There are a wealth of diet plans, but these are the essential components.

You may be dealing with more serious health problems. Though they may be an obstacle, they are not an insurmountable problem. Do everything you can to take care of your physical body. Don't dwell on your health issues or let them control all your thoughts.

STEP 5. CHANGE YOUR INFLUENCES

If you spend thirty minutes or more watching the news you'll probably feel depressed. Same thing with the newspaper. They don't stay in business by airing or publishing good news.

When you hear the unemployment rate has gone up yet again, of course you'll feel bad. What is the end result of feeling bad? If you're like most people it hinders taking action. Why try to find a job when there are so few available? Why try to start a business if many are failing?

Turn off negative news. This doesn't mean sticking your head in the sand. You can catch the most important headlines in five minutes on Yahoo or MSN. But stop pumping your mind with bad news and negative images.

This includes the people you spend time with and talk to on a regular basis. If all they do is whine and complain about how terrible their life is, then you need to find new people to spend time with. At least limit your exposure to them as much as possible. Don't agree with them or find their complaints. Try to change the subject back to something positive. If that doesn't work, then excuse yourself and move on.

Don't waste hours every night watching mindless television shows. If your life is going great and you have time to waste then that's one thing. But if you honestly want to change your life then don't throw away the spare time you have available.

Read books about successful people. Find out how they changed their life.

Study books in your career field to increase your value to your company.

Talk to successful people. Join groups like the Toastmaster or local Chamber of Commerce associations. Take someone you admire out to lunch and ask them how they achieved their success.

Fill your life with positive influences.

STEP 6. CHANGE YOUR ACTIONS

Do you want a better job? Then find out what jobs are available in your company and what you need to do to move into one.

Do you want to work at a different company? Research companies and pick the top 20 you would like to work for. Spend some time writing a great resume. Send them to your chosen companies with a cover letter tailored to each company. Show them specifically what you've done for your current company and how you can do the same for them. If you haven't done anything for the company you work for now, then start today. Start being an employee that produces results and document everything you do for inclusion on your resume.

Do you want to learn a new skill? Then sign up for a local class or try to get hired as an apprentice. It may take some time but you'll be steadily moving towards your goal.

Do research online about possible businesses you could start. With the power of the internet it's never been cheaper to start your own company. You can offer freelance services or sell a product. For less than $50 you can have your own webpage or blog. With four or five hours a week invested you can have your own moneymaking business. You can use this for extra cash or eventually build it to a full-time business.

But after you do the research you must keep moving. This is where people freeze. They don't take action.

Make a plan and work the plan. Get a website or blog set up. Start making posts two or three times a week. Write articles about your topic. Find out how to monetize the blog to bring in money. Write an eBook and sell it on your blog and on Amazon as a Kindle book.

There are countless ways to improve your economic situation once your mind is open to finding opportunities and taking action.

Many things can be used as excuses not to take action. Here are the top action killers:

Information Overload–Reading and researching are wonderful things to do. You should never stop learning and growing as a person. But at some point you have to stop studying and start DOING. Take what you already know to do and then do it. Don't wait until you think you know everything. That day will never come. There's always more to learn. But you must be willing to fail to move forward.

Fear–List the worst things that could possibly happen if you take action. Will you die if you start a new business and it doesn't take off right away? Fear is paralyzing. Look your worst fears in the face and move past them.

Procrastination–This can be a huge obstacle if you let it control you. Don't let yourself get caught up in the, "I'll do it tomorrow," cycle or the, "I'll change my life next year," or "I'll change my life after my children are grown." Take action NOW.

STEP 7. NOTICE HOW YOUR LIFE STARTS TO CHANGE

Your money breakthrough will happen because of the previous changes. Don't get so busy that you don't notice the gradual changes that are taking place in your life.

- You'll spend less money on "feel good" worthless items.
- Your career will start to move forward.
- You'll start bringing in extra income from your side-line business.
- Your family will notice you're happier and more relaxed.
- You'll have more energy because you're taking better care of yourself.
- You won't stress over money because you'll know you're taking action and making consistent progress.

One day you'll realize that while you were busy taking action; you achieved the money breakthrough you needed.

About Charles

Charles Mixson is a Georgia native who has traveled all over the World changing lives one breakthrough at a time. He is highly sought after Author, Life Coach and Speaker because of his innate ability to tap into the talents of others to help them achieve their dreams. Charles has spent a lifetime helping countless individuals & companies bridge the gap between where they are and where they want to go.

As owner of Augusta, Georgia based firm Phoenix & Dragon Lucky 8 Marketing, Charles has been able to see positive change happen in tangible ways with his clients. Through workshops, trainings, and one-on-one sessions, he has serviced over 7,000 clients in the areas of self-development, personal finance, career & life coaching and business development. His passion for making a difference in the lives of others has been proven to be key in the transformation that needs to happen for a true breakthrough to occur.

Charles is an energetic & dynamic speaker who prides himself on making a connection with everyone he encounters. He has been heralded as the Breakthrough Specialist because of his unique and uncanny ability to see the greatness of others & set it free. With over 40 years of experience, Charles' passion is to share the secrets to success to the masses.

Charles Mixson
"The Breakthrough Specialist"
Augusta, GA USA
www.womensecretmoneycures.com

CHAPTER 6

Beyond Life's High Hurdles Lies Success

By Diana Todd-Banks

The room was black.

Pitch black, no windows, no light seeped through cracks—just complete-ly pitch black. Totally surrounded by this blackness, my life was like solitary confinement in some dreaded faraway jail.

The fast-paced life of international business was challenging and stimu-lating, but I had allowed it to engulf my life to the point that my health screamed, "That's it, time out! No more! Like it or not, you're stop-ping!"

Which is why barely able to speak or walk, I felt completely imprisoned and confined in this dark black room, terrified of what was going to hap-pen to me, given how my life had changed, so suddenly. Or that's how it seemed.

As I crawled around my home on my hands and knees, only occasion-ally walking a few steps, I did not understand how and why my life had so quickly come to this. What happened? What caused this sudden change?

One thing was obvious regardless; I still had to manage and survive liv-ing on my own somehow.

Stress and exhaustion can do untold damage to the body, which at first may not be noticeable. But if unchecked the impact can have a severe affect on one's life, in different insidious ways, as I found out.

Constantly the health specialist's reports indicated there was nothing wrong except I was exceptionally tired and stressed. One said, 'Even if you could talk, don't, don't even try, not for three months and after that you will need the help of a speech therapist to learn to speak again.' It seemed, the muscles in my shoulders and neck were so tense they seriously strained my vocal chords. It was stress.

Not talking seemed one sensible but seemingly difficult solution. But other issues had to exist. Why would a person sleep 14 hours every day, still be tired, and still be perceived as healthy; and why without any bone breaks, would a person be unable to walk properly?

A little voice inside me, my intuition kept saying, "I was not down or depressed, as some specialists were trying to insist, but there was definitely something wrong, and since it had not been identified, don't use strong pills and potions as a panacea."

My life remained on that path for another fourteen difficult months — aimlessly sitting, lying and crawling around. During that time the pitch black room became even more intense and real to me at night, causing countless thoughts to run through my mind. Many negative, but some positive. From what was going to happen to me, to happy, positive thoughts.

One stood out!

If I ever recover, I will do something to help other people; something that helped others achieve and have a better life, just as I hoped would happen to me … some day.

But self-doubt came to the fore, "what a stupid thought. I can hardly walk, or talk or think clearly … let alone work."

Other realities also emerged and recovery seemed totally impossible. No government or health agencies could help me, as I didn't fit into any of their 'slots.' Nursing or aged care, or retirement homes, could not and would not accept me, as I was deemed too young.

Despite continuing to see different health specialists, no sound solution was suggested other than not talking. It was a traumatic, frightening, lonely time that could have lasted decades.

But for the foreseeable future, I had to survive without an income and without my business. I had to close that, say goodbye to staff; family ignored me, and friends too, deserted me, except for five.

Somehow I found some strength to keep writing for several newspapers even though I was paid a pittance. It didn't seem to matter that it would take days to write one page of text, but writing was my only anchor to life and anchor to remain mentally strong. I had no other, except the will to live and to regain my health.

The future then looked very bleak.

What is going to happen to me? What do I have to do to change my life? How can I change?

Every day those questions pounded my mind but my energy would run out trying to come up with solutions.

My life seemed so totally utterly hopeless.

In one of those moments of desperation I recalled a thought I had very early in my life.

"I am not going to live the rest of my life this way! I am in this world once and will have a great life again!"

In difficult times, that thought was the fuel that kept me going; somehow a solution would emerge—become evident. And, yes it did.

Something positive did happen.

The Universe, divine intervention or whatever name you choose to use, came to my aid.

Hearing about my predicament, one health specialist thought there may be a solution. Looking at my tests in horror they indicated my entire body was highly toxic. I was diagnosed with a severe case of Chronic Fatigue Syndrome (CFS), poisoned with heavy toxic metals. At the time CFS was not recognised by most health professionals. How fortunate one did.

Thankfully it is more recognised today.

Finally, I thought there might be a slim glimmer of hope to regain my health and life. Despite being told resolving that would take several years, it didn't seem to matter, and how those heavy metals came to be present did matter, but that is another story for another time.

Clinging on to any good snippet of news, that dark black room began to have cracks of light creep in. I was not going to let this health hurdle beat me. I would have a life again. I would find a way and do whatever I had to do to achieve that.

Intense thinking took a lot of energy, and still eluded me then. So, when affirmations and creative visualisation were first mentioned as being highly beneficial, I ignored the suggestion because they sounded a strange hard approach to adopt. It was clear I had not read about them then.

A good friend persisted saying they would be helpful, plus a little voice began gnawing at me, saying, 'give them a go' …'try them they might help.' Agreeing, this friend gave me a wonderful book, which I still hold sacred today–*Creative Visualization* by Shakti Gawain.

That book was my turning point.

I set some goals, and created visualisations and affirmations to regain my health and become stronger physically, mentally, and spiritually, in essence starting over and gaining a new life in the process.

I began to imagine 'what if.' What if I did regain my health what would I or could I do to help people, recalling the thought I had months earlier? It had to be something different to the way my life and work had been to that point.

Days and months went by dreaming, visualizing and thinking about that. Certainly becoming involved with charities was an option, but I saw myself doing something very different, but what?

Then I came across another of life's wonderful surprises. Learning how to meditate and reach the Alpha state. After continual use I came to find out, not only was it a wonderful form of relaxation, it also helped me cement the goals I began setting for myself.

Slowly strength came back and while I persisted with the new health regime it did take another two years to feel 'life' again.

There is a powerful adage, be careful what you wish for.

Or it could also be said, be careful how you craft your affirmations and visualisations because they do produce results negative or positive.

Then quite unexpectedly, my mother died but wasn't found for several days.

Despite still recovering from three years of being unwell, and being unable to work, I nevertheless was charged with handling all her personal affects. Personal effects spanning 80 years. A mammoth task to sort through!

A few years later, after packing up other relatives and friends possessions after they passed on, I decided to write a book to help others at this very difficult time. No book seemed to exist on the subject. After conducting further research, I began writing a practical guidebook about the process of how to pack up.

Throwing my heart and soul into the project, and still following a strict health regime, I began to feel joy again, joy at living and joy once again at having a purpose in life.

After what became a rather expensive self-publishing experience, I published the book, which as I found out later was a world first on the subject.

This became my major break into the world of helping others. I had achieved the goal I set when I could not walk or speak. I had come full circle of needing immense help myself to now helping others. That was, and still is, a great feeling.

In the past I had helped others in small ways, by teaching guitar to children with disabilities; teaching classic guitar to adults who in their childhood were told they hadn't a musical bone in their body; and teaching PR to small business owners.

Writing *Wrapping It Up - the Ultimate Guide*, was an exhausting, exciting accomplishment considering the subject matter and the health issues I had finally conquered.

A symbol of great achievement for me, it shows when a goal has passion, emotion and feeling associated with it, it is possible to achieve the goal no matter how high; and it is entirely possible to resolve life's tough hurdles and to have a positive new beginning.

With that accomplishment behind me, I felt there was still something more I wanted do to help others in some positive way.

The most common thread throughout my life has been the resounding thought it's never too late or too difficult to change your life, which I had done more than once after divorce, a major health setback after four deaths and after other of life's losses and setbacks. This is why I became accredited as a Life Coach specialising in Change, New Directions and above all Starting Over.

Despite life's hurdles you can turn your life and your business around just as I have done, because there are extraordinary opportunities that lie ahead for each of us, if, we take care of ourselves, listen to our intuition and apply our mind… positively.

Reflecting back on my experiences the most powerful tools I learned and have applied along the way are ones I still use today.

- For a goal to be real, it must have passion, emotion and feeling associated with it.
- If you believe something is so, be persistent.
- Do not ignore your intuitive impulses and gut feelings. Everyone is born with intuition, yet most of us ignore the signs and discount even the tiniest of signals and in doing so miss opportunities.
- Learn how to develop this innate sense, and become more aware of your intuitive skills. There are exercises to achieve that.
- Take time to learn how to correctly craft affirmations and creative visualisations; and practice them daily. These are very powerful tools.
- Learn and use meditation to reach the Alpha state.

Most people use a form of meditation, but not always to achieve the Alpha brainwave frequency, where you are not asleep, but deeply relaxed, focussed and aware. If you do, the results are remarkable and the process can even help you increase your ability to learn. And, once learned, it can be done anywhere, anytime.

- To care for others, first, take care yourself.

- You have more of life to live than you think. It is my hope this life experience proves why despite difficult hurdles, it is important to never give up.

- If your intuition says there is or must be a solution to an issue, be persistent if you have a yearning to do something more with your life; or if you want to change direction, do not ignore these signs. If any similar thoughts are present, do not give up, listen and have the courage to follow your intuition.

Here is another reason why it's never too late to begin again or too difficult to start over: Most of us are conditioned to look at our existing age and reflect on how many years we have lived as being the bench mark of how many years we have left.

There is a positive way to view your current age. By doing this simple exercise you will be surprised at just how many more years you have to begin a new career, or to engage in new activities you can look forward to and enjoy. In the western world, statistics show 83 as an average age when people pass away. Subtract your current age from 83 and that is how many years you may have to live life to the fullest. But why assume 83 is your limit, many people live vibrant lives way beyond that. If you are 45 then you have 38 years, nearly 4 decades. Or if you are 55 then you have 28 years, nearly 3 decades.

Don't waste those years thinking it's too late to start over. Ponder for a moment, what would happen if your life suddenly stopped? It can happen to anyone, at anytime and, unexpectedly. Don't procrastinate. There are many years remaining where you can make this next phase of your life the best chapter ever. Which is why this is worth remembering:

It is easy to neglect ourselves, because other parts of life seem important, but it is more important to cherish and treasure *our own* life because only then *can we* treasure others in our personal and professional lives. To achieve that, our body and mind needs to 'last', and to do that we must put them *first*! **Life *is* a constant work in progress.**

About Diana

Diana Todd-Banks is a woman who has had an incredibly varied life, has conquered very high hurdles to make things happen and overcome many deep lows.

Picking herself up, dusting herself off from these lows, she has moved forward with a positive outlook on life which ultimately has opened up many new doors and opportunities.

Combining her vast wealth of experiences and insight with practical coaching strategies, Diana works with clients to help them start over and create a new life following a loss or a setback. Also, she works with clients who have specific wellness and lifestyle goals they want to achieve.

As host of a weekly Internet TV & Radio program which focuses on Integrative Health & Lifestyle issues, Diana interviews guests from around the world, as a way of helping steer public awareness into a healthier more pro-active direction.

A very down to earth woman, Di has received extensive print media coverage and appeared on television and radio in both Australia and the United States. For twenty years she lived, worked and owned businesses in the US.

She was a U.S. wine and food importer, and an international marketing consultant for Australian businesses seeking new niche opportunities in the US. Prior to that, she gained a degree in Classic Guitar in Chicago.

In Australia her groundbreaking book, has drawn significant media attention, since it was a world first on the subject: *Wrapping It Up- Packing Up Possessions & Other End of Life Matters.'* This was followed by, *'Estate Organizer – The Ultimate Guide to Recording Your Life Matters.'*

This year, Di is a co-author alongside other top world inspirational, self-development speakers and best selling authors:

'In The Spirit of Success' with Deepak Chopra, Dr. Wayne Dyer, Esther & Jerry Hicks, Mark Victor Hansen, Neale Donald Walsch, and Sandy Forster is now available.

In the second book, Di is a co-author with the best selling self-development author Brian Tracy. Entitled *'Cracking The Success Code,'* this is expected to be released mid 2012.

To learn more about Diana and other benefits she offers visit: http://dianatoddbanks.com/

By registering you can receive a free eBook *"15 Steps To Embrace Change."* Also visit, www.wrappingitup.com.au to learn more about the book *'nobody wants but everyone needs. Read it before you need it.'*

You can email Di at diana@dianatoddbanks.com.

http://dianatoddbanks.com/

CHAPTER 7

The Seven Secret Steps to Success–UNLEASH YOUR POWER NOW

By Sugar Singleton, M.D.

I am a doctor. These days, everyone is (or wants to be) a doctor of some sort; so to be clear, I am a medical doctor. That means a lot of little things—I was a great student, graduated top of my class on the Deans list, Presidents list and the Honor roll, that I excelled in college and spent four years in medical school learning about illness, disease and how to treat the sick. I learned the parts of the body, how they malfunction, typical signs and symptoms of disease and things you must never miss. I learned really long names of medicines and complex biochemical equations. I learned a million really important things, and a million not so important things, as I was lovingly beaten over the head with the sledgehammer of knowledge.

When I was in medical school, I was hungry for this knowledge, and I devoured it all as I learned each and every organ system, every muscle, bone, ligament, tendon, cell, hormone and biochemical pathway—and I loved every minute of it. I loved it all so much that when I was studying the female anatomy, I felt sure I wanted to be a gynecologist; then when studying the brain, I was confident that, in fact, I wanted to be a neurologist, and then with the study of the heart, I moved forward ready to become a cardiologist.

I was in the middle of a heart bypass surgery during a cardio-thoracic surgery rotation and we were about to place the patient on ECMO (a machine that takes the place of the heart and pumps blood through the body during the open heart surgery). The beating heart was lying there in the patient's open chest and I remember feeling this deep desire to touch it, to caress it…the surgeon somehow sensed my desire and she said to me, "Go ahead, take a feel" as I placed my gloved hand on the smooth surface of the heart the surgeon said, "gently place your hand deep into the chest … under the heart." I still vividly recall that moment when time stood still and I held a beating heart in the palm of my hand…lub dub…lub dub….lub dub. I was in love with my profession and in love with the idea of being a doctor and making a difference. Over those years in medical school, I loved it all so much that in the end, I couldn't decide what to specialize in so I decided to pursue a residency in Family Medicine. I chose to specialize in treating not just the whole body but also treating the whole family.

Family Medicine Specialists do everything from gynecology and neurology to orthopedics and everything in between. We take care of moms, dads, grandparents, kids and yes, even deliver babies. After residency, I chose a career at a high volume Urgent Care Center in rural New Mexico. Our Urgent Care is owned by the local hospital and essentially functions as a satellite Emergency Room. Long hours, busy days, and critical dying patients mixed in with the usual sore throats, constipation and broken bones. I love being a doctor and over the years, I have discovered many interesting things about medicine and myself, which I choose to share as we delve into the secrets of success.

SUCCESS SECRET #1:
PREVENTION IS ALWAYS BETTER THAN TREATMENT.

The inspiration to choose things like eating healthy organic fruits and vegetables, drinking alkaline water, and daily practices of exercise, yoga and meditation as we take a vested interest in the future of our own health is somewhat of a new concept—the concept of being a *partner* in our healthy body, as opposed to turning all power over to a white coat with a prescription pad and expecting all the answers and a little white pill to fix the years of abuse and neglect. Generally speaking, most of us know what is good for us and what is not. It's not rocket science, just choices we make each day. It is one thing to treat disease. It is entirely more powerful to fall in love with your body and have a burning desire to do everything possible to honor that amazing body to vitality so it may thrive to a ripe old age.

SUCCESS SECRET #2:
WHEN YOU BELIEVE... ANYTHING IS POSSIBLE.

What the patient BELIEVES is a critical and often overlooked factor in successful treatment. When I was in medical school, something happened that changed the way I viewed everything about life. I was blessed to have a beautiful, successful, wise, and loving mother. She loved life and lived to inspire success in people. She was amazing at encouraging those around her to achieve more than they ever thought they could. When I was in medical school, my "perfectly healthy" mom was diagnosed with terminal cancer. We took her to the best hospitals and the best oncologists for the grim prognosis of "two to four months." I remember sitting at her bedside one day as she said to me, "Sugar, I am not ready to die." I took her hand in mine, looked her in the eye, and said, "Mom, I need you to do one thing for me. I need you to believe with all of your heart and soul that you will get better, and don't worry about anything else."

I am so grateful to say that we turned that two-month deadline on life into almost ten full and fabulous years. Sure we incorporated years of medical treatments but what struck me as a doctor was that even with her terminal condition, she was still able to live life positively, passionately, and with a full sense of purpose. After my mom passed away there was a question that haunted me and yet fascinated me all at the same time.

"How could this happen? How could the best doctors in the world say that someone would only live 2 months and she lives for almost 10 years?" I set about investing a great deal of time and resources over the next several years searching for the answer to that question. Today, I truly believe my mom loved the miracle of life to an extent that on some level, the passion and inspiration inside of her contributed to a much longer and happier journey than even most doctors believed was possible. That realization became my own yearning to not only live like her, but most importantly, it fueled a burning desire within me to inspire others to live a life of purpose, abundance, and total wellness.

Watching my mom's courageous battle with cancer allowed me to become a stronger woman and a more compassionate doctor. Now I under-

75

stand what an honor and a privilege it is to be able to talk to people and teach them about their total heath—not just their illness, to assist women in raising self esteem as it is the foundation of true health, to make others aware of the relationship between their Mind and their Body, and overall to inspire others to live in a place of abundance, peace and gratitude.

SUCCESS SECRET #3:
THERE ARE MANY ROADS TO HEALING

I absolutely love being a doctor and I honor my profession. Having said that, I have come to realize medicine is a fickle profession. In a profession like healing, where one might expect to find humility, the opposite is often found (in the form of ego). I'm sure you've noticed this if you've ever hung around many healers. It seems the medical doctors think they are superior to doctors of Chinese medicine; the acupuncturists look down their noses at Ayurvedic doctors; the herbologists have little tolerance for the osteopaths, the Reiki masters or the naturopaths; the Chiropractors think the chakra healers and the homeopaths are out in left field, while the energy light workers are just trying to hold the space for everyone to figure it all out. You get the idea.

SUCCESS SECRET #4:
HAVE AN OPEN MIND AND A DESIRE TO LEARN.

At this point I am definitely not giving medical advice on how to treat disease, however I have come to realize that there are many roads to healing and that there is usually no harm (and often times, incredible benefits) from allowing a patient the opportunity to explore many of these roads with an open mind, especially if they truly BELIEVE it will aid in their healing journey.

There are many roads to healing and I feel we could all benefit by reading a few more maps. As we continue, I'd like to share with you one of my favorite road maps and a powerful secret to my own success. Over the years, I came to realize that my purpose and my passion lay in something much deeper than just the routine practice of medicine. I realized I was passionate about working with women on a very deep level. I began to see that women everywhere have unconscious blocks that stop them from truly being happy, healthy, fulfilled, confident, and from really thriving.

SUCCESS SECRET #5:
TREAT THE CAUSE, NOT JUST THE SYMPTOM.

I had to learn how to release my unproductive cellular memories, which are those subconscious blocks that hold us back from living an abundant life. The process, once discovered, was incredible, fast, easy and powerful! I remember experiencing it for the first time and knowing that the woman I used to be was going to leave transformed. I recall looking into my own eyes in a mirror and seeing someone that had been waiting to blossom out of me! I had discovered how to shift on a Cellular level! I gave birth to a *woman* waiting inside of me that I didn't even know existed, and let me tell you, it wasn't even painful, I just had never known how to do that before!

That's when I fell in love with the concept of cellular memory and what it took to release my own personal blocks. The interesting thing is I was unaware of most of these blocks on a conscious level; I just had a feeling my greatest work was yet to be done.

So I began a very committed and meaningful journey into the world of cellular memory release. I learned what it meant to release my own unproductive cellular memory. That's when a whole new level of me emerged! It was the beginning of an abundant and thriving life for me, and my family. It was during this time that I had a profound realization. I recognized that I was called to be a healer, not just a medical doctor!

You see sometimes when we, doctors, just practice traditional medicine, it can almost become a bit superficial. It's like a band-aid. Fix what is wrong today when you never really get to work on the root of the problem. When I allowed myself to listen and follow my ultimate purpose, I began to see that I needed to pay attention to the cause of the malfunction. If you put a tight rubber band on your finger, the flow of blood will be blocked. As a result, the tip of your finger will start to turn blue because it's struggling to receive sufficient blood flow. Now, if we were to only pay attention to the symptom, we'd want to fix it. By doing what? Perhaps rubbing a cream on the tip of the finger? Or would we inject the finger or maybe swallow a pill? Nothing will allow the flow to return to its optimal capacity unless the rubber band itself is removed, because that's the cause, and that's the block. As a healer, I now go for the cause! Working with releasing cellular blocks, I teach women how to release their deepest blocks toward fulfillment, purpose, and the flow of prosperity.

SUCCESS SECRET #6:
DISCOVER THE TRUE FOUNDATION OF LASTING CHANGE.

I have seen it over and over again—women who carry subconscious issues in their cells for years (not even knowing so on a conscious level). These unproductive cellular memories serve as blocks that hold them back from being happy, having high self esteem, and from creating their desired personal & professional results.

The foundation of lasting change is releasing blocks on this level, at the core, going beyond an emotional and mental level, and getting right down to the cellular level. This is where there are no blocks and it just flows!

The inner conflicts are blocked energies, which are being unconsciously held in the form of cellular memory!

Some general examples of **Inner Conflict:**

On a **PERSONAL** level:

- Obsessive behaviors such as Perfection
- Self Sabotage
- Fear of Abandonment
- Being sensitive and having your buttons pushed by other people
- Fear of owning your voice (have you ever had a burning or choking feeling in your throat when you were about to speak your truth?)

On a **PROFESSIONAL** level:

- Fear of rejection
- Fear of money/success
- Fear of successful people
- Fear or even anger toward other successful/confident women
- Fear of selling or marketing
- Or have you ever felt resistance toward other people who sell something? The feeling of resistance is like feeling emotionally hot in the body combined with a hint of an-

ger! That's an example of inner conflict. It's unproductive cellular memory.

On a **GLOBAL** level (global because these blocks are within the collective psyche of the female gender) and therefore at some level, are a part of our individual cellular memory:

- Fear of not being good enough
- Lack of self worth
- Having guilt/worry
- Fear of other beautiful women
- Lack of trust, and so many more.

SUCCESS SECRET #7:
FORGET ABOUT SURVIVING, IT IS TIME TO THRIVE!

Now is the time to thrive personally & professionally. The secret is releasing the unproductive cellular blocks.

Every cell in our body has memory. Unfortunately, much of the cellular memory we hold onto is unproductive and manifesting as confusion, depression, unworthiness, worry, lack, struggle, procrastination, lack of fulfillment, relationship challenges, etc. Most women don't know they are holding onto these unproductive cellular memories, or how to release on this level.

Cellular memory release is the foundation of a shift toward:

- A thriving level of self-esteem
- True fulfillment
- And the flow of prosperity

Let's use a computer as an analogy. Our body is the hard drive of the computer. Our lifetime experiences become cellular memory. Cellular memory is the data stored on the hard drive. Over the years we have numerous files that we put on our hard drives called cellular memory. What happens when your computer has a lot of data on its hard drive? It operates slower, has technical difficulties, even crashes!

When we delete some files or clear the cookies/cache (in computer terms), and do it in the right way, that type of RELEASING unproductive memory, RESTORES the computer's ability to operate at a whole new level!

I love being a physician but looking back, that part of the journey is not what gave me inner peace or even abundance. It meant I could listen to someone's physical symptoms, put a name on their disease and match a medicine to it, write a prescription or even deliver a baby and bring life into this world. My real education didn't truly begin until I learned to feel joy and happiness on a CELLULAR level. When I learned to embody the feeling that comes when I say 'I LOVE MY LIFE' with all of its ups & downs, trials and triumphs. I have learned to be grounded, to be joyous, to be confident, to be prosperous, and all of it on a deep level! My cellular memories now work *with* me instead of unconsciously against me! Learning how to Release was the best investment I have ever made in *myself*. It's my purpose to bring this type of cellular shift to you. If you want to make this year the best year you've ever had on a personal and professional level, it may be time to consider releasing your cellular blocks, and stimulating the energy of fulfillment & prosperity in your cells!

About Dr. Singleton

Dr. Sugar Singleton, MD, Cellular Memory Expert, Best-Selling Author and International Speaker, is a practicing medical doctor, a loving wife and mother, and a powerful resource for women and their well being. Dr. Sugar has dedicated her life to helping women break through barriers and transform their lives. Her specialty is "working with women to take their lives to the next level, to achieve the breakthrough that they desire and absolutely deserve to receive."

An exhilarating speaker and presenter, Dr. Sugar takes women on a journey of discovery to their highest potential. As a cellular memory expert, she conducts regular *Release* experiences in the U.S. in order to assist women to release unproductive cellular memories that are blocking them from achieving true fulfillment, a thriving self-esteem and a flow of prosperity. Her presentations are transformational and can be applied to all aspects of everyday life.

What's unique about Dr. Sugar is that she has a love for true healing as opposed to the traditional ways of just treating disease. Being someone who always follows her heart, she has dedicated her life to being a healer. Today, in addition to saving people's lives in the urgent care, she spends most of her time in assisting women to release the blocks that are getting in the way of their true self-esteem, fulfillment, and prosperity. This passion has led her to become www.BraveHeartWomen.com an exclusive expert on cellular memory.

At regularly scheduled opportunities, women come together from different parts of the world to spend quality time with Dr. Sugar. She helps them gain clarity about the causes of their resistance and to learn the tools that give them permanent transformation on a deep cellular level. They soon find out that she's an authentic woman who loves to make a difference and also have fun. Want to find out what its like to have a slumber party in a mansion while having the most transformational experience of a lifetime then schedule yourself some "SugarTime".

Dr. Sugar is a lifetime member of the prestigious medical honor society Alpha Omega Alpha; she served as Chief Resident at UNM Hospital; she is board certified in Family Medicine and has served as Vice-President American Academy of Family Physicians, NM. She is married to her soul mate, Rick, and they have three healthy, beautiful children who reside with them in the Land of Enchantment.

Dr. Ellie Drake, the founder of the BraveHeart Women global community, describes her as "one of the most grounded and purposeful women I have had the privilege of connecting with. She is genuine, intelligent, focused, and--above all—inspiring."

In 2011, Dr. Sugar Singleton, received a Golden Quill Award from The National Academy of Best-Selling Authors™. She was honored for becoming a bestseller with her first book *Pushing To The Front: Front Line Strategies From The World's Leading Entrepreneurs.* The book features top advice from leading entrepreneurs and marketing experts from across the globe.

To learn more about Dr. Sugar and receive information on the next *Unleash Your Power Now Experience* visit Dr. Sugar's website at www.sugarsingleton.com, send an Email to: info@sugarsingleton.com or call Toll Free: 1-855-Dr-Sugar.

CHAPTER 8

The Law of Attraction

By John Jochem and Gloriana Ron Da

Napoleon Hill once said, "Whatever the mind can conceive and believe, the mind can achieve." We can attract into our lives the outcomes we desire or think about with faith, intention, focus, affirmations, vision and believing.

If your goal is to become a leader in some type of field, then you need to study. Learning and experience helps us stretch and grow as we work towards that goal. In the process, we acquire the intangibles of a leader in order to receive the tangible results. So essentially in the process, achieving the intangibles must come first. Desiring a multi-million dollar home or finding the right mate will require working on the intangibles within first to create the achieved outcome.

Fear and doubt are the ingredients which prevent success or guarantee not to get your desired results. Here is an example. Many years ago, Gloriana used the following affirmation every day as a mantra as she desired a new healing practice:

I am a young, powerful, successful, healthy and beautiful woman, producing $10,000 a month easily and effortlessly.

When the client base and income increased approximately two months later, she became paralyzed with fear of success; she became terrified of her power, feeling unworthy and not good enough. The affirmation was stopped abruptly, resulting in a decreasing client base, income and well-being. The lesson was learned. Much inner work was needed.

Affirmations are not enough by themselves, though. We must also heal the counter voices such as 'I can't have it,' 'I'm not good enough,' 'If I have money they will kill me,' 'I am afraid of my power,' or 'I am afraid of success.' Inner healing work needs to be consistently worked through to get beyond.

One aspect of our healing mission is to *feel* deeply inside that we are worthy. If we do not, then the law of attraction will create something we don't want. When one goes deep inside within oneself and takes personal accountability, stops blaming and utilizing negativity, then the channels for goodness to manifest are open.

GOALS STRETCH US AND SO DOES FLOW

Flow is life's unfoldment. Flow is an energy and does exist. Amazing things happen to us utilizing this energy. Synchronicities happen. Law of attraction works so much better when you think more positively and you take time, stop reacting impulsively or using force to get a desired outcome. We allow the flow to take over and lead us the way to accomplish our desired goal or outcome.

Sometimes the goal may not actually be what you think you want. Will the million dollar house make you happy? Remember, the joy lives inside you—not the house.

Gloriana had a goal to attend a specific seminar for five years. That was the right time for her. Five years later, and not a moment before. She would not have been ready if it happened any earlier.

Gloriana is a healer and has had many years of healing work, from body to mental growth work seminars; even therapy, in order to breakdown her own personal barriers and obstacles. John has attended many seminars for his growth work as well. We attended a past seminar by Jack Canfield. He taught students how important it is to take 100% responsibility for where we are in our life and stop blaming others—that helped Gloriana realize, she was her own obstacle, her worst enemy. Gloriana chose to face the truth and be accountable for where she was in her life and not blame anyone else. Every situation in her life *she* created. Now, it wasn't easy to accept that. She felt the voice inside her head say, "Go away!" as if Gloriana was holding out her hand to someone and saying stop, I don't want to look at that. But she did her inventory, ruthlessly and honestly. In reality, Gloriana got the lesson.

The immense fears from her past, the victimhood issue, anger, bitterness, resentment, consistent negativity in thinking—those things added up and they created blockages, negativity, and lowered her vibration. When you clear those out, you make room that creates a space for something good and new (like in a vacuum cleaner). The positive energy and other things need to occupy the empty space are positive affirmations, emotions, thoughts, and confidence. What comes out of that vessel? More joy, fun, laughter and lightness. Feeling good about oneself is the right combination. Flow works so much better because you can take charge with utilizing your inner power.

FLOW

The law of attraction states that the things you focus on can become your reality. Flow is either a good thing, or what appears to be challenging and not always pleasant. Good flow simply means everything is easy for your success and the patterns of disharmony go away. Road blocks disappear more quickly and the correct people show up and assist in a speedy fashion. Synchronicity happens. Good flow is like swimming downstream.

Paying attention to flow can exponentially increase your business intuition, offer more clarity and focus with groundedness, utilizing logic and creating better decision making with positive outcomes.

Characteristics of blocking good flow are drama, judgment, unforgiveness of self and others, complaining, bitterness, rage, resentment, festering negativity, guilt, shame, not feeling good enough, lack of self worth or self doubt, and even a huge ego. When you feel negative thoughts toward yourself or others, you are hurting yourself and stopping flow. So remember, you can create what you want with the law of attraction, even unconsciously. Good flow works with positivity, enthusiasm, passion, excitement, happiness, laughter and love. The more you become aware of what you are thinking and your conscious thoughts, the more you attract good flow for more goodness in your life.

Our huge subconscious hinders us and if we follow flow, even when it feels like it isn't working, we may find it opens a door for something good. You may be blessed with a wonderful outcome from an important lesson. Some people might think that is bad flow, but in reality it is not. There is always a purpose. Maybe flow is attempting to teach us an important lesson we couldn't learn otherwise, and what seems like a bad experience is actually assisting us to find our way to the good. That could be a blessing in disguise.

You can attract the flow—positive or negative. A negative flow might be a life lesson or teacher for you. What if it wakes you up from some faulty thinking? Would that not be a blessing in reality? Just because something happens that you don't like doesn't mean there is something wrong with the flow. Wait and see. Maybe a person needs to learn from that experience and then they grow. If one can distill the gift from this experience, one's life can be healed, emotionally, and more goodness can be the result in one's life. There is always something to learn.

PAY ATTENTION TO FLOW

Flow is life's unfoldment. So when flow isn't working, it's *you* that isn't working. Flow is always working and available. The question remains: Are you in alignment with flow? We wouldn't say God is not working. If you really want to manifest something, perhaps you are not congruent with whatever flow or goodness can be in your life. We have free will, we have choice. Every single one of us has blockages. So the lesson to life is to learn how to go along with flow and allow it to unfold with us in more positive ways.

When issues or complications arise, and it seems like you are pushing a ball up a hill, than flow is your teacher. Control freaks try to power their way to success. However, by paying attention to flow, your success can be easier. You can ask yourself "Why is this so challenging?" If a few things go wrong, then "Maybe I should pay attention to flow." When opportunities present themselves and things are easy, then you have good flow. When flow stops you need to change directions, do something else or ask yourself why is this situation happening?

We all have challenging flow at times. People who pay attention can avoid bad decisions. Success is easier when you work with flow instead of against flow. You become more aware of what you haven't been aware of yourself subconsciously. And then you can say, thank you flow. Albert Einstein said, "Problems cannot be solved at the same level of thinking, when we created them." By paying attention to flow, your level of awareness increases and you can solve your challenges or achieve success with more ease.

Here is an example of a challenging flow: Writers can experience writer's block which can be frightening or frustrating. Some students can write a paper in an hour, while others may take a month to write the same paper. Do not force flow. Walk away and don't take things seriously. Withdraw from the situation; when frustrated it isn't necessary to take on negativity as that in itself at the moment reduces flow. The emotion "frustration" now is blocking flow. Take a break as if you are clicking on the refresh button of a computer. Practice detached involvement from the situation, so that when you return, more than likely you will pick up where you left off and your creativity has returned.

When Flow Stops you could:

- Become aware of what you are thinking
- Take a break
- Walk away and come back at another time
- Take a different direction or course of action
- Get rid of fear
- Practice detached involvement and do a retake of the goal/process and ask yourself what to do next
- Find ways to accomplish other aspect of a goal/process and come back to the issue
- Delegate
- Don't try to control flow: it will not work

Formulas for Success with Flow:

- Inner confidence
- Inner trust
- Positive attitude
- Groundedness/realistic
- Forgiveness for self and others
- Creativity
- Faith
- Passion
- Enthusiasm

- Be joyful
- Visualize
- Gratefulness
- Love

In order to Thrive, Flourish and Prosper we need to let go of:
- Not **feeling** good enough
- Reactiveness
- Yelling
- Anger
- Drama
- Bitterness
- Resentment
- Unforgiving self and others
- Judgment
- Festering negativity
- Guilt
- Shame
- Feeling like a victim
- Self doubt
- Negative people
- Conflict

The reason it is so important to release these feelings is the feeling impedes the process of flow and hinders your ability to prosper. We need to go within our self and release the FEELING if we want to increase prosperity in our life. Prosperity is the law of abundance. It is a journey. Sooner or later you will know when you reach the tipping point and then the physical will begin reflecting back to you. Just remember, we have a huge subconscious and it takes a while before enough of you is healed and remaining in the positive energy to reach the tipping point.

The conscious mind is the tip of the iceberg, and the rest is hidden underneath. Unfortunately, it is difficult to know how much has been transformed when healing. One must keep working on self and at a certain point the tipping begins. There might be ups and downs; perhaps challenges, or triggers. One cannot always expect smooth sailing, having a bad day once in a while is okay.

When one heals and clears out more negativity, the heart opens and shifts, which can effect your whole life in so many positive and wonderful ways. An example is forgiveness. Forgiveness is a *huge* factor in prosperity. When we hold something against others we actually block the goodness that can flow into our very own life. If someone did something wrong, it is your responsibility to forgive them. You do not forget what happened, but it shifts your energy, your body, clears your own heart, and then flow will open more goodness in your life. That's just the way it works. So it is imperative to forgive yourself and others. That is a key ingredient to attracting more of what you want in your life.

Flow can bring about synchronicity. Being in the right place, right time, or with the right person can provide exactly what you need to learn, to grow and to manifest. That's a key you're on to something.

How do we get rid of the items we need to let go in order to thrive, flourish and prosper? How do we eliminate the blocks, which prevent positive flow and hinder the law of attraction? Through healing and there are numerous techniques out there. One process is called Emotional Freedom Technique or EFT, and it could be very helpful and instrumental in your process. EFT is a tapping technique, and when repeated, has very good and effective results.

EFT is an easy pattern interrupt, which is successful with the law of attraction and flow due to its powerful and gentle nature of creating a space for the positive to take root as you release the negative thoughts. That is why it is more effective than just only repeating affirmations. If one only does positive affirmations and still has all the negative content in the subconscious, you're just sugar coating the negativity—the negativity is still going to run your life. With EFT, you are naming specifically what you want to let go of, and then you create the space for the positive to fit right in. It is very important in healing work to do affirmations and also negations to be truly effective. EFT is one way to do just that.

SUCCESS

Some people want to be told what to do in order to achieve success. Take action in becoming who you really are. Get rid of those obstacles to find the real you. Then in the process, attract success and pay attention to flow. Always be honest and follow integrity. Focus on yourself growth. Remember, you will get knocked down, but you can get yourself back up! Find the people who will lift you up and keep you going. Live your life as an example to your Higher Power. Be grateful for everything good and be accountable.

If a magic wand would be waved for your success, you would be totally accountable for all of your actions. It is not about the money or the dream house: it is about becoming the right person within who can attract the money, the joy, the health, the happiness and the significant other into your life and keep them.

GLORIANA'S FINAL THOUGHTS

So many people read positive self help books from very successful people who have managed to create a wonderful life with the law of attraction. It appears those people have a perfect life and so many of us feel like failures because we compare ourselves to them. In reality, it's okay—there's always more work and healing to be done, whether you are a multi-millionaire or without savings in the bank. Life is a journey so keep growing, evolving and learning and becoming so you can thrive, flourish and prosper. It is your birth right. And every one of us deserves goodness in our lives.

I am a work in progress as anyone who wishes to improve one's inner self surely understands. I'm not really where I want to be yet, but I am getting there and working on it. I am enjoying so much of what I have manifested in my life on this journey. It's okay to say there is more inner work to be done. No one is ever finished if they truly choose to continue to want a better life, not even a multi-millionaire because it is what you FEEL inside that matters. Just having millions of dollars would feel empty and be very lonely without self love and joy. It is the core work inside yourself that is required to shift that makes you HAPPY. Over time you can begin to see the outer manifestations mirror what is going on within yourself. Self love leads to prosperity, and all good things.

Now I have remarkable intuition, clarity, discernment, so much joy, access to inner guidance, self love and more flow! What appears to be a wrong decision can still happen now and then, and I am learning from those experiences. Now I can create and now I can flow better. I now have insightfulness. It's okay, there's more inner work to be done. I am so much in joy now. Life is so good!

I want to lead by example with humbleness, honesty, truth and integrity. If I can do this journey of change and flow, so can you. May the flow be with you and bring you more joy, positivity, great health, courage, unlimited prosperity and love to each and every one of you.

About John

John Jochem is a best-selling author. He has co-authored books with Jack Canfield of *Chicken Soup for the Soul,* Tom Hopkins, who wrote *How to Master the Art of Selling* and Brian Tracy, who wrote *Goals.* John's books are *The Success Secret, In it to Win it* and *Counter Attack.* John is a certified Zig Ziglar speaker and trainer, a success coach and a consultant. John has spent months on the road with Tony Robbins and has been mentored by Jack Canfield and Brian Tracy.

In 2000, Tom Hopkins named John #1 out of a hundred thousand students, whom he trained. Corporately, John worked for 5 of the top 10 diabetic supply companies, and his best month in sales was 1,250 individual transactions. John did corporate acquisitions for three of the top four diabetic supply companies; the biggest was about $25,000,000. His largest advertising budget was $62,000,000. He has worked with the No. 2 power wheel chair company and helped to establish the No. 2 respiratory wholesale company in America.

Educationally, John's highest level is doctorate work —he has a MBA from the University of Phoenix and undergraduate BBA with dual majors in marketing and finance from the University of Miami. He has taught college students business concepts in management courses. To contact John for consulting or coaching, email him at johnfjochem@gmail.com.

About Gloriana

Gloriana Ron Da is a traveler on the journey of life, relishing each new day. Gloriana is an author, Reiki Master teacher and practitioner since 1996. She also utilizes other energy systems for the betterment of her clients for activating self awareness, growth, and healing. It gives her great joy and happiness to help others. One of Gloriana's areas of expertise is long distance energy healing work. She enjoys dancing, art, beading, music, nature, social activities, meeting people and discussing inspirational topics. To contact Gloriana, email her at rondatherapies@aol.com.

CHAPTER 9

The Art of Authentic Power

By Karl R. Wolfe

For years, I've had the opportunity to help individuals and organizations achieve massive success. Often they begin to double, triple or add zeros to their income within a few days or weeks of my program.

This isn't about learning a new strategy or technique. I simply lead them to the richness of the experience of *being themselves*, and help them to stop doing what doesn't work.

Everyone has something they do that their ego thinks if they do it repetitively they will eventually get a result. This is addictive behavior.

The magic happens when they discover that all they have to do is stop! They stop faking their lives. It's as if they take off the brakes and everything begins to move like magic. They stop the rational strategy, speak from their authentic voice and everything begins to change for the better. They stop running tape on who they think they should be and discover their own voice. There is nothing easier in the world than being yourself. People waste a lifetime practicing to be someone else, rather than being themselves. There is no one like you anywhere in the world, so why not just show up and be you?

I am going to share some simple truths about how to make a distinction between operating from your head, the rational mind (the ego) or from feeling, (the intuitive)–the *Authentic-Self*.

CHANGE

There are times in life when you realize everything is about to change. In earlier times, this change often took generations. Today with the interconnectedness of the world, through the internet, this change can happen in an instant. Strategies that worked for generations lose their power in moments.

As children, each of us is filled with impulses, aptitudes, uncertainties, ideas, memories, needs, fears and longings. We all depend on models from the outer world to help organize this highly active interior landscape; to give ourselves direction in life. Those who touch us emotionally influence this inner organization. We consciously and unconsciously mimic those to whom we were most strongly repulsed by or drawn to. For a time, this may work for us, or against us!

Today, culture trumps every strategy. If you do not know who you are, or if you have little sense of your unique inner culture, life will be a challenge. Within each of us, there is an innate culture—a cellular memory that is grounded, free of a need for approval, acknowledgment, and self-consciousness. It is free of the need for any external reference to act. This is the *Authentic-Self*. In all disciplines, this place of innate experience, true self-actualization, whether in art, business, music or sports, is often acknowledged as the *zone* or *the flow*. Accept the inevitability of constant change and you can abandon your need to control, to trust and go with the *flow*.

You must break the rules that paralyze your life, take risks, and be willing to make mistakes. If you are willing to do it wrong, you accelerate your learning curve and results. You can change everything overnight if you break even *one rule* that binds. Change a few basic assumptions about yourself and your whole world will move from stagnation to unbridled change. To succeed in the world today, you must adapt quickly and capitalize on instability.

Doing things the way they've always been done squelches adaptation. Culture always trumps strategy. Animals in the wild don't waste time sitting around contemplating strategies. They act on instinct. Strategies and techniques for gaining personal power are things of the past. You may have attended personal growth seminars where you found that the techniques worked for a few days or at most weeks. Most of those seminars are dinosaurs. Contemporary culture engenders constant change. The Internet was the end of marketing strategies and techniques as we know it. If you know who you are, you will weather all types of chaos and change. You can't learn strategies and techniques fast enough to catch up with today's connected world.

PERSONAL POWER

Power is more than the ability to exert your will upon another person or situation with a strategy. There is no real inner security in that kind of power. That kind of power is an effect of the moment; as time changes the sense of power also changes. You may have a strong body but that will change with time. If you have a physical beauty that you use to influence others, that will change. What will you do then? If you have an intellectual capacity with which you manipulate others, what happens if you miss an opportunity to use your strategy?

Authentic power is energy formed by the intentions of the *Authentic-Self*. You lose power whenever you identify with fear. Fear is just a thought and has no power (nor do any of the activities generated by fear). When you identify with fear, you allow yourself to become a victim and therefore less powerful. It is victimhood. It is never constructive to suppress emotions or disregard what you feel. If you are out of touch with your emotions, you cannot come to know the fractured nature of your personality, those energies that do not serve your development. More importantly, you cannot face and ultimately challenge those aspects. When energy leaks from you through fear or distrust, it cannot return anything but pain and discomfort. Authentic Power requires no strategy and comes from one who releases energy only through love and trust.

FOR WHAT DO YOU STAND?

You are only as powerful as that for which you stand. Do you stand for more money in the bank, a bigger house, an attractive partner or imposing your way of thinking upon others? These are indicators of a personality seeking to satisfy its ego's wants and desires and to amass personal power through strategy and technique. This is one approach to life and can be achieved at great cost to self and others. For a while, it may seem as if you are winning. However, in the end, you and everyone you interact with will lose.

There is another way of being. You can stand for perfection, for beauty and compassion, the power of love, the clarity of wisdom. You can stand for forgiveness and humbleness. Align with the later attributes and your personality is aligned with the *Authentic-Self*. This is the position of *true power*.

Those who know true humility are free to love and be who they are. They have no artificial standards to live up to. They are present to themselves in each moment. They are not drawn to the symbols of external power. There's no competition for external power. That does not mean that they are not spurred onward by fellow humans when that is appropriate to the situation.

If you can hear your inner voice, the *Authentic-self*, you are connected to the mystery and power of your inner culture. When connected, you know who you are, and what you want to do. You have vision. Once you know who you are, you'll find a vehicle to express that in the world. You have passion and stay focused on your vision. If instead you are self-conscious and focus on the inner or outer noise, then noise becomes your vision and that is what you create.

FEAR

Fear, doubt and worry are among the greatest obstacles. Stay true to your vision. Nothing will ever be the way it was. You feel the fear and do it anyway. That is one of the keys to success. The biggest mistake people make is waiting for the feelings of fear to subside or disappear before they are willing to act. These people usually wait forever.

There is no need to figure everything out. Successful people find comfort in the unknown and change. There is no need to get rid of the fear in order to succeed. Successful people have fear, doubts, and worries just like anyone, the difference is that they don't let any of those feelings stop them. Notice the part of you that is frightened is not the part that makes choices and takes action. Fear has no power to stop you. Successful people feel everything and then make choices and take informed action.

Action is the Bridge to Success

- Your vision determines your destiny.
- What are you or your organization trying to do?
- Be willing to risk and fail.
- Complacency is a seductress.
- Learn from the failure of others.
- Find solace in uncertainty.
- Living in your comfort zone equals death.
- Question the strategy of rational thought, and delete the need to understand.

I became a successful competitive ice skater at an early age, because I was willing to fall down thousands of times. Early on, I noticed that fear was just a story I created about the energy that wanted to move me at high speed across the ice. When I let go of the story of what I thought the feeling of fear was, I became the fastest skater in the rink. When you are in relationship with fear, rather than stopping forward progress, it becomes the creative force that propels you through life.

That is why I was able to run a company with 2,000 employees at the age of 28. It was just like skating. I had a relationship with the feeling of the unknown and this created great success for me and my company. As a child I had learned to feel fear and set it aside and take action anyway. This translated into great success in the real world. If you are terrified of the feeling of fear (the fear of fear), you avoid change and life. If you are afraid of fear, you are preoccupied and focused on death (avoiding death) therefore death becomes more real than life—there is no trust—you take no risks—you have no life.

To experience the fullness of life, in the moment, your ego must face its own death, to die to itself—the moment you die to your personal self-definition—is the moment you give birth to the *Authentic-Self*. The truth is, when you are out of control, you are actually *in* control, because then you connect with the love and support of universal consciousness and this accelerates everything in your life.

Who are you?

- You are not what other people say about you.
- Who are you inside?
- What do you feel certain about?
- Do you choose leading or following?
- Are you a person who makes a difference or are you a victim?
- Are you someone who is constantly looking for a way to grow, or are you someone who is constantly looking for an excuse to stay small and contracted?
- Are you merely a collection of habit patterns and behaviors, or are you something richer, something deeper?
- Are you merely your mythic past, or are you what you are defining for yourself now, in each moment?
- What makes you different and unique?
- You are more than what you do.
- Externals have no power to define you.

Notice how you may describe yourself, possibly from feedback you received in the past, or from self-definitions such as:

- I am worthless.
- I am powerless.
- I am unlovable.
- I am not alright the way I am.
- I am not good enough.
- I am evil.
- I am dangerous.
- I am stupid.
- I am beautiful.
- I am superior and on and on the stories go.

You may have defined yourself by what you think you are not, "I am not this or I am not that." Some people define themselves based upon past failures. Others define themselves based upon their future, who they think they will become. Until you become conscious and aware, your life is defined by your beliefs, the convictions of who you think you are from moment to moment.

Turn on your observer. Become aware of your unconscious myths—who you believe you are. Notice what you believe about yourself. What we believe usually isn't true. Take some time and write these down. Just because you once believed something about yourself in the past, does not mean that it is still or ever was true.

You can only continue a round of self-betraying behavior, if you think you're going to get something different from that next cycle. All addictions are self-betrayal. Defining yourself as an object is self-betrayal. You are not your beliefs, your personality or your job.

The greatest fear is not defining yourself at all. When you get close to not defining yourself in any manner, the greatest fear is that you will not exist. It is a strong, deep, fear in which conditioning is attached—if you stop the strategies and; the constant thinking, then you will not exist! And it is true. If you stop defining yourself, you do exist, and yet not as any definition. You exist as who you are, indefinable, undeniable; infinite consciousness—*Authentic-Self.*

There must be a willingness to give up the self-doubt and the aggression. There must be a willingness to stop resisting yourself; in whatever way that has taken form over you. Suffering must be practiced. Any strategy or thing you do to avoid suffering is a practice that will only bring on more of the same. Left unseen, we have this inner battle, a play between self-doubt and arrogance, ego and superego, and deeper than all of that is the truth. *The truth is closer than any strategy, suffering or self-definition.* The truth requires no defense. The truth requires no practice. The truth is closer than any thought. I invite you to live in the truth and stop suffering.

AUTHENTICITY - YOUR TRUE POWER

The invitation is to first recognize your *Authentic-Self* as truth. Then, recognize the lies your ego constructs—as they appear against this background of inner truth—the temptations, the elaborate explanations and justifications, now with the capacity to choose truth. When the binding to the story around resisting and seeking the truth is cut, then there is an opening. There is freedom, happiness and infinite open space.

In truth, nothing can make you happy. If you are not happy without money, you will not be happy with money. Happiness cannot be practiced; it is your innate condition. You must be willing to face the fear of your ego disappearing, in the stopping of the self-definition, in order to experience the freedom of your true nature and *Authentic-Self.*

There is nothing more annoying than being with someone filled with the self-loathing indicative of an inflated ego and nothing more refreshing than being with someone who knows who they are and isn't rehearsing to be someone else.

About Karl

Karl R. Wolfe mentors Executives and projects in every industry, including top studios: such as Warner Brothers, MGM, Paramount, Universal, the major Television Networks, also record companies and their recording artists such as: Dream Works, Sony, Michael Jackson Productions and major law firms and medical institutions.

Karl uncovers the one thing that prevents you from achieving everything you want in life. He developed a video technology that helps everyone see the invisible and unconscious narratives and myths that hold them back and, at the same time, what works. The diagnostic process is equivalent to 5 or 10 years of traditional therapy. It is illuminating, revealing, unusual, enjoyable and it works. In less than two hours, the client sees how their inner conflicts inhibit their ability to manifest their vision. A step beyond therapy, this process is known for getting immediate, practical and ongoing results. Often within in a few days everything changes for the better.

His process has been mentioned in *Vanity Fair, Newsweek* and *Time.* Barbara Walters, with ABC's 20/20 and the Oprah Winfrey Show, featured these seminars and how they transform his clients' lives from average to outstanding. Dr. Stanley Krippner documents Karl's work in the recent book, *Spiritual Dimensions of Healing,* first published in German and more recently in English. The book chronicles the practices of ten practitioners in North America—from native healers to contemporary health care providers.

Karl edited the recent bestsellers: *The Lazy Mans Way to Riches,* by Joe Karbo, revised and expanded by Richard G. Nixon, and the companion workbook *Roadmap to Riches,* by Richard G. Nixon. He is currently finishing two new books dealing with the topics of personal growth and organizational transformation: *Millionaire Body-Millionaire Mind-How to Get Everything in Your Life Moving and Fingers Pointing at the Moon—A Journey to the Authentic-Self.* His most recent book, *"The Only Business Book You'll Ever Need"* hit three separate Amazon.com bestseller lists.

As Creative Consultant to United Paramount Television Network News KCOP TV 13 in Los Angeles, and as Consulting Producer and Creative Consultant, he developed an award winning highly rated series of Feature News, Science and Technology Documentaries.

He was Manager of Engineering with a subsidiary of the Atlantic Richfield Company, in New York, administering an annual capital budget of more than $300 million. He then accepted the position of Director of Marketing and Design with a high technology company in San Francisco; specializing in Industrial Automation. Then with more than $500 Million in successful design projects completed; he established a Counseling and Consulting practice in San Francisco, where he also lectured and was research associate in the Graduate School for the Study of Human Consciousness, at John F. Kennedy University, in Orinda, California. With more than 30 patents, his accomplishments brought honorable mention in Who's Who in Technology and many other publications. Several other Who's Who publications document more recent achievements, as Creative Consultant and Mentor.

Visit the website www.truesilence.com to find out more about consultations and seminars, to read articles and receive his recent eBook or you may call: (888) 296-0084.

CHAPTER 10

Leave Your Baggage at The Curb And Move Forward After Divorce!

By Kathy Van Liere

Have you ever wondered to yourself, "Why can't I move forward?" Or, perhaps "Why do I keep attracting the same bad relationships or the same bad experiences over and over again?" I've certainly asked myself those questions.

When I divorced several years ago, I found myself alone, depressed, angry, filled with feelings of hopelessness and paralyzed with fear. I was also 25 pounds overweight. There were days when I struggled to even get out of bed. I was literally numb. It was as if I were living in a fog.

How did I get to a place of such despair?

Although I was married at the young age of 19, I still managed to bring lots of emotional baggage into my marriage. I was physically and emotionally abused as a child—I was always being punished, even when I did as I was told.

When I married, I felt like I was always trying to win my husband's love by being the best wife, homemaker, and lover I could be, and contributing my fair share financially by working. But no matter how hard I tried,

I still felt stupid and never good enough! I had this illusion if I give of myself freely, I'll get back what I've given. I thought I'd get back the love I was showing him. What I got back was usually something quite different.

My husband's nickname for me early in our marriage was "Bozo!" I'd tell him to stop calling me that because to me, it was the same as calling me "Stupid." However, he continued to call me "Bozo" for many years; he said it was a term of endearment, and I was just overacting when I'd tell him to stop.

One afternoon, in the first year of our marriage, my husband sat me down and told me that as part of his relationship with other women, sometimes sex would be involved. I looked at him in shock. I couldn't believe what I was hearing.

My immediate response to him was, "If I ever find out you've had sex with another woman, I will divorce you immediately!"

I didn't realize what I actually told him was, don't let me *find out* you've had sex with another woman, because then I'll have to divorce you.

He didn't tell me he'd already had an affair, but when we went to one of his company parties I saw him with the other woman. I got so good at blocking this woman (and the others) out of my head I managed to convince two of my best girlfriends many years later that my husband could never possibly have an affair like their husbands' had. That's how good I got at pretending to myself and to others!

Over the course of our marriage what I thought was punishment came in the form of taking away many of things I loved…like communication, sex, doing activities together, and so on. At first he'd stop talking to me for a day or two at a time, then he would go six months not talking to me.

To survive, I immersed myself into our two fabulous children and into my work. I was a good mom to our son and daughter, and I became a very successful CFO for a variety of companies over the years.

It was as though I'd become two very different personalities. By day, I was this strong professional woman and by night I was this weak submissive woman.

While there had been many good things about our marriage, we stopped communicating long before our marriage ended; the intimacy, romance and sex between us had become virtually nonexistent. We both gave up on our marriage. We just co-existed. We were in a loveless, sexless marriage.

When I've shared my story, people wonder why we stayed married for over 30 years. Unfortunately, when someone learns to carry his or her emotional baggage as well as I did, I honestly didn't know any better. And, I have to admit I ultimately believed when you get married, it was for better or for worse. And the worse in our marriage really wasn't just about my husband; I brought my emotional baggage into our marriage too.

When I think back, how could we possibly have had a healthy, loving relationship if we didn't talk to one another, we weren't each other's best friends, we didn't share activities we enjoyed together anymore, and the romance, intimacy and sex were virtually gone?

PRACTICING SACRED SELF-FULLNESS...SELF-LOVE

About a year before my marriage ended in divorce, I attended a real estate investing seminar in Atlanta. When the seminar ended, it was a Sunday evening but my flight back home didn't leave until the next morning. I went into the hotel bar to have dinner and read a book. I was sitting at a table reading when the ball on the arm of my chair fell off and rolled to the feet of the only other person sitting in the bar area. This set in motion a conversation and a dear friendship that continues today between Carla and me.

As Carla and I talked that evening, we found out we both had many similarities throughout our lives. And, even though she didn't tell me until after I filed for divorce, Carla knew that very first evening we met she was brought into my life to help me through my divorce. At that time, I wasn't even thinking about divorce!

About a month after I filed for divorce, Carla and I were talking on the phone. I don't remember what I said, but Carla told me she was going to send me some links to some self-help clips she'd found. She thought they might help me get out of my funk.

Once I got the self-help clips, I listened to them over and over again, what I heard made sense to me. I learned if I keep focusing on what's ugly, I will attract more ugliness in my thoughts, into my emotions and ultimately into my life. I wanted to stop the vicious cycle I was on and move forward! This was the beginning of my emotional healing!

I started to walk. I found walking to be great therapy for me and it also helped me lose my extra weight. As I walked, I listened to a playlist of upbeat music and played little games of appreciation. I'd say to myself what I appreciated in each yard as I walked by them. Rather than having all the negative, angry thoughts about my soon to be ex-husband go over and over in my mind, my thoughts became positive.

During that time, I lived in a golf community. One bright sunny day, I walked down a path between the 6th green and the 7th tee box. Ahead of me was a pond and in the distance were snowcapped mountains. As I walked down the path, I was thinking to myself how wonderful it would be to share this beautiful moment with someone who loved me. It was then that I realized I was sharing this moment with someone who loved me, and that someone was ME! Amazingly, this was the first time I realized I loved myself! How can I expect anyone to love me, if I didn't love myself?

I could tell I must have been changing, because neighbors and complete strangers were stopping to talk with me or just say "Hi!" as I walked by them. On one of my walks, a neighbor asked me how I was doing and wanted to know if I'd like to borrow her DVD of "The Secret." After watching this movie, my focus became even more intently on looking forward and not repeating the same stories in my head about the past, my past.

Instinctively, I knew I had to forgive my ex-husband if I was going to move forward. My forgiveness wasn't about him; it was about me. I didn't tell him directly that I forgave him because I knew at the time he wouldn't take my forgiveness in the spirit it was being given. I also knew I had to forgive my parents, especially my father, if I was going to move forward. More importantly, I had to forgive myself to move forward!

As my journey to emotional healing continued, I started to learn the importance of taking care of myself first. If I didn't take care of myself first, I didn't have the best of myself to give to me, a relationship partner, my family, friends, co-workers or my community. I learned to practice what I would call 'Sacred Self-Fullness or Self-Love,' which was totally foreign to me at the time. In fact, I thought how selfish it was of me to take care of myself first. Like most of us, I was taught it's better to give than to receive. What I realized it was actually selfish for me not to take care of myself first. If I didn't take care of myself first, I was giving myself and everyone else an exhausted, rundown, cranky, overextended, and unable-to-fully-concentrate version of me. Not a pretty sight!

Over time, I found myself attracting many people into my life who helped me along my emotional healing journey. I learned about the neuroplasticity of our brains. Amazingly, we can actually change our brains! I used meditation, mantras, walking, and many other ways to move myself forward. When I felt panicky, I had a short emergency mantra I used to take back control of my feelings. Some of the longer mantras were just too hard for me to remember when I needed help *now*! The emergency mantra I liked to use was, "I choose power!" because I was always giving up my power. I would say this mantra over and over again and it would make me feel better. I felt myself growing stronger.

DATING AGAIN?

About a year after my divorce, I felt I was emotionally and physically ready to start dating again. I'd lost the 25 pounds, I had a wardrobe makeover by a friend who is a wardrobe consultant, and I felt emotionally stronger.

Where to start? The dating scene was certainly different from when I last dated as a teenager! There are cell phones, computers, instant messaging, text messages, video, online dating, and so many more issues to deal with in today's dating scene!

I hate to admit this, but between the blind dates, a matchmaker, the bar scene and getting onto the online dating websites, I did 20 dates in 30 days and then dated nearly 150 different men in 283 days. I certainly didn't set out to be a dating guinea pig and date this many different men, but I did. It felt like I had another full-time job! The reality was, I did it because I was naïve about the dating process, I didn't know how to pre-screen the men, I didn't know what I wanted in a relationship partner, and I made tons and tons of mistakes.

I also discovered some of my old patterns were still surfacing. I was attracting men who had narcissistic tendencies. I even attracted a new woman friend that was narcissistic. Because I was emotionally healthier, I recognized it quickly and I learned I don't have to keep people in my life that don't make me feel good.

My dating experiences ranged from fun, to boring, to ridiculous, and to potentially life threatening. Although it took me a little longer than it probably should, I eventually stopped myself and asked, "Why am I attracting the men and women I don't want to attract?"

Of course, I had to look within myself to find the answer. What was I thinking to attract them? What was I doing to attract them? What type of man did I want to attract now that I'd gone out with so many different men? And, so many more questions!

As I was ending my marathon dating spree, I started to worry I'd closed my heart off for good. I had gone out with so many different men and I hadn't fall in love with any of them. I tried the friends with benefits thing with a couple of them (As a side note, I couldn't make it work. Ultimately the guys fell in love. This is a subject for perhaps another book?)

I also ended up being 'the other woman' with some men. I didn't know they were in committed relationships (or married) until after we'd dated for a while. Of course, this was when I was ultimately blindsided and fell in love with a guy already in a committed relationship. Patterns! While it took me a little while to get over this toxic relationship, I did. I realized later that he had actually opened my heart again!

I had a rebound guy after falling in love. And, then when I was ready to give dating a serious break, I met a wonderful, kind, genuine man who has the ego I'm attracted to, but it's a healthy ego. He and I met by accident. I was having trouble canceling my online dating subscription. Frustrated, I went online to cancel it again. It was then when he showed up in my list of daily matches. When I saw his picture and read his profile, something spoke to me. I then did something completely unusual for me; I approached *him* with an email.

About a week later, we met for drinks. It didn't take long into our conversation when I felt I'd known this man for a lifetime. Our conversation was easy. We had a lot in common and yet we didn't. This was the beginning of our healthy, loving relationship.

While we've had a couple of bumps in the road because we've both had some old patterns surface in small ways, we're learning the value and the art of communicating without judgment. We're not only lovers— we're best friends!

LEAVE YOUR EMOTIONAL BAGGAGE BEHIND!

Just as a piece of luggage can get heavy if we carry it for too long, so does the emotional baggage we carry throughout our lives. We spiral into victimhood; it becomes our norm, a pattern that's hard for us to break, and eventually, our way of life. If we don't learn to let go of our emotional baggage, it can prevent us from living the life we so richly desire, deserve, and it keeps us from being in healthy, loving relationships.

So park your emotional baggage at the curb…let it go, so you can move forward and enjoy your life and enjoy your relationships after divorce!

For more information about healthy loving dating, relationships and sex go to www.DatingOver40Secrets.com.

About Kathy

Kathy Van Liere is a best-selling author and she's been seen on ABC, NBC, CBS, and Fox.

Ms. Van Liere's won an Editor's Choice Award for her Outstanding Contribution for a Chapter she wrote entitled, "Creating Our Own Rules For Dating Over 40" in the best-selling book *"Trendsetters"* which hit two of Amazon's best seller lists. The book *"Trendsetters"* features top advice from leading entrepreneurs, business owners and marketing experts from around the world. The authors tackle an array of subjects ranging from health, wealth, marketing and business success. She's also co-authoring a book, entitled *"The Success Secret"* with Jack Canfield that will be released in late 2012.

Ms. Van Liere's also a CPA, she's worked as Chief Financial Officer for a variety of companies for more than 20 years. She's also been a highly sought-after business consultant, and a Certified Life Coach through Clarity International.

CHAPTER 11

How to be THE Expert

By Loretta R. Washburn,
REALTOR®, Entrepreneur, Artist, & Photographer

According to The Illustrated Contemporary Dictionary, Encyclopedia Edition, an expert is someone who has special skill or knowledge—a specialist. Skillful as the result of practice.

I think we all know what an expert is. I want *you* to be the expert! Many people believe they are an expert in their field and then there are those who think they are an expert in everything. Here is what I want to have happen: I want all of you out there to believe that you are THE expert. I want you to put yourself head and shoulders above everyone else that you are competing with. No matter what you are doing for a living you can position yourself as THE expert. Whether you are a waitress, plumber, or president of a major company…you can always position yourself above the rest.

What will that do for your career? You will be the one that is sought after. You and your company will be sitting on top of the world, heads and shoulders above the rest! Being different will always rise to the top.

As a Realtor®, I have positioned myself there and it didn't take very long—but it did take effort and a great positive belief system. I got myself on a TV show and it aired on ABC, CBS, NBC & FOX affiliates, and was written up in several major magazines. Following that, I co-authored a #1 Best-selling book. I am milking that and will always have that in my back pocket to use. If I were to change careers, I could still use it for whatever I were to decide to do.

What can you do? Get yourself in the media, do something out of the ordinary, extraordinary and run with it! Do something that will make you stand out among the rest. Get a hold of your local paper or new stations. They are always looking for a new story. Do what the others are not doing. Put together a press release and use it! Send it out to everyone—get into your local newspaper, local magazine or actually write an article and send it off to a magazine or some kind of periodical. If you don't think you can write, get someone to help you with it.

Go to the bookstore or get online and purchase *The Writer's Market Book*. I used it to land a publisher for my first book. It also has information for magazines and can direct you to who publishes the subject matter while guiding you throughout the whole process. It is a very valuable book and could be very helpful to you. Write an article or book about your expertise. Does that give you credibility? You better believe it does. It makes you THE expert in everyone's eyes. Get something written and use it in your marketing and branding. If you feel it is too much to bite off then write a pamphlet and bind it or get the kit to make it a spiral book. Get creative! After you have done this, market it, sell it or give it out to every current and potential client. Clients love to receive something for free. You can sell it on ebay, Craig's List or on your own website.

You do have a website don't you? If you don't, you best get one. If you know nothing about putting one together, have someone do it for you. A website is vital to your business; you can also use different social media to help you promote your website.

When I think about that it just makes me think about what I would rather be doing, selling real estate. Don't worry about the money as when done correctly, the money will be there. You don't have to have someone man it for you daily, just part time if needed.

Don't worry about money. Instead have the intentions of being a winner. When you believe you are a winner and stay optimistic, expect to win, look at the positive angle in all situations, make the intentional decision to excel and rise to any occasion.

Keep in mind that you have more leverage for success when you expect to win. If there is a problem that arises, look at it as an opportunity to turn it into a positive. Make the best of it and often there is opportunity with every problem. Think outside the box!

What happens during and after a recession?

More millionaires are made during that time! Last year my income tripled and I expect the same this year. I expect nothing less. What did I do to make that happen? I got in the media, got my book and spent money in advertising, a lot of money. Why? No one else is, that gives me free reign and everyone else is left out. Now I can use all of my accomplishments in my marketing. What do the winners do different than those that are struggling? Instead of running with the pack because of the belief of lack, they are running into the fire. It will be the best money you could spend because no one else is spending out of fear. Know that the money will be there.

Do you have someone that motivates you? Do you have a coach? If you don't, get one! I have two that I work with and they advise me to be accountable. Both teach me how to become the success that I choose to be by pushing and pushing. They give me advice, which I take and utilize!

My coaches know what works because they have both gone through what has made them the successes they are (and I can avoid the mistakes they made in the past). Having them is like a huge shortcut to great success.

When someone wise and successful gives you advice, listen up and follow through. I give advice and rarely does anyone follow through with it. They say that maybe it works for me, but probably won't for them.

Keep on doing what you do and keep getting what you are getting. Put your blinders on and run into that fire and don't be scared. Are you afraid of failure or afraid of success? I think more people are afraid of success more than they are of failure. Wow! If you make a whole lot of money what will you do with it? Believe it or not, someone actually told me that if they made more money, they would just have to pay more taxes. That just makes no sense to me. I have talked to many people and asked them what they are doing to create more business. The majority of the time they say they have cut back on advertising or are not advertising at all. No one is spending money.

Of course people are spending money. Maybe not everyone, but there are those out there that have the money to spend and you want to find them. So, because hardly anyone else is spending money on marketing and advertising, now is the time to do the opposite. Figure out the way to get the money to advertise, and run with it. That is running into the fire!

I do a lot of mailings to create new business. I let the neighborhoods know when I have a new listing or sale and I don't let my past clients forget me (I send them the mailings as well). I send out 5x8 cards and include that I have been on four major TV networks with a copy of my book stating that I am a #1 Best-selling Author! I also choose neighborhoods that I would like to list homes in with a simple card saying, TALK ABOUT EXPERIENCE! Then follow it with my successes and the logos from the networks. That puts me head and shoulders above everyone else.

With your advertising, do something that no one else is doing. Get creative and run with it. I like to run with it! People like to get something back when doing business…have sales, cash backs, prizes. Just do what others are not doing. I use the fold-over money card. People lose business cards or toss them. Have one made that is unique. I like the fold-over money card. It looks like three one hundred dollar bills folded and fanned a little with your information on the inside. You can find it on the internet. Everyone loves them…they do not get tossed and people show them to others—they are just too cool to get rid of. I have another thing I do which is a coupon that looks like a very large dollar bill with my portrait in the center. It is a coupon for Lowe's for $300.00 to receive after closing. I mail these out to neighborhoods I want to do business in. Often, mailings that are in an envelope don't even get opened so I have a rubber stamp and stamp on the outside, Gift Inside. Everyone wants a gift and often, someone will pass it on to someone else that they know wants to sell their home. Here's the kicker! I will write up a very short letter telling the recipient they should use me as their Realtor® and I will make them money, I staple a dollar bill to the letter. Again, I stamp that there is a gift inside. You will get a call from someone in shock that you sent them money and they will not forget the person that sent them money! You need to capture people's attention and don't let them forget you. These things will work with any business.

The new thing I am doing now are videos. You can make a video and send it to multiple people or send a video to a specific person and talk to them live—it is the hot thing right now. I know, because both my clients and soon-to-be clients are loving it! In this video, discuss your expertise and let them know why they should be using your business. Because you are THE expert, you can also create a webinar. It is very exciting—I have a camera on my laptop and use the video for so many things. I have program templates for any occasion.

I sent out a video for with an Easter scene around me and an ad in the top right-hand corner you find my phone number. On the bottom right, you will find it says *Email me*. The viewer taps that and to send me an email.

I like it better than being on the phone because I can cover a lot with the video. If it's sent to someone you haven't met yet, it gives the client a warm fuzzy. You aren't just another voice on the phone, you are making a personal connection. One of the most important things in business is relationships. You build a relationship with each client or customer. I always tell clients that this business isn't just about selling homes, it is a people business and I think that goes for all businesses. The video builds the relationship often before there even is one.

When I first meet with a buyer or seller, I have a package for them. In the folder or envelope I have a copy of my TV interview, a promotional card, several business cards and a copy of my best-selling book. Maybe you don't have a book or TV show, but you can create something. If it is a seller, I have the coupon for Lowe's in there as well. You can give them to buyers. Whoever your business serves.

Let go of any fears and know that attitude gets you far.

Like Einstein said: *"Imagination is everything. It is the preview of life's coming attraction.*

Reality is simply an illusion, create the illusion that you desire and your imagination will take you everywhere!"

Come on, all of you, run into the fire. Don't be left with the crowd. Stand out, be bold, and show them all who the expert is. It's you!

About Loretta

Loretta Washburn is an author, artist, photographer and Realtor®. She is a Realtor® with Prudential Towne Realty. She is one of the top leading Realtors® in her area of Hampton Roads.

She has been on numerous TV shows and talk shows, hundreds of radio shows, magazines and newspaper articles. You may have seen her on AMERICA'S PREMIER EXPERTS, which aired on ABC, CBS, NBC & FOX affiliates.

Loretta has been a Realtor® for over 15 years and is a member of The Hampton Roads Realtors Association, and The National Association of Realtors. She is also a certified Foreclosure and Short Sale Expert, and is an ABR-Accredited Buyer Representative.

Loretta currently lives in Chesapeake, VA, with her partner, Jacob. When she is not selling real estate she is creating art, behind the camera or writing. She is also a Nutritional Herbalist and teaches people how to live longer and healthier lives.

Her books she is accredited for are: *Mind Travelers; Losing it Naturally, A Holistic Weight Loss Program* and she has co-authored the best-selling book, *WIN-35 Winning Success Strategies from Today's Leading Entrepreneurs.*

Contact info:www.lorettawashburn.com

(757) 288-2247

CHAPTER 12

Beating the System:

Taking Charge of Your Health

By Dr. Mark McCullough

At the end of the day, when you think about getting older, what comes to mind?

Do you dream of spending your days traveling, enjoying new experiences, and sharing life with your spouse, kids, and maybe your grandchildren?

Or do you dream of spending your days confined to a facility for the aged, kept alive by a multi-prescription regime, only getting around by a walker or wheelchair—and spending twelve to twenty thousand dollars every month to live that way?

Your dreams are most likely a lot closer to the first option. So why do so many of us end up forced to settle for the second, spending our older years in suffering and isolation instead of enjoying them with the people we love?

The problem is that we, as a society, have bought into a system focused on easy rewards – answering our bodies' need for nourishment by filling them with the empty calories and preservatives provided by packaged and fast food, and curing the maladies that follow, real and imagined, by popping a pill (or, more likely, several pills).

This approach to health has positioned us to bankrupt our country. We're creating a "health debt" in our society, relying on government agencies and health insurance policies to keep us healthy. In the process, we've become a consumer of disease-management products in the business of "sick-care."

But there is another way. You don't have to become a part of the "sick-care system" in America. You can change your life and your future by simply taking your health back. Your health belongs to you and you alone. Take care of it properly, and you can live the life of your dreams and the life you deserve.

THE HIGH COST OF HIGH WEIGHT

Can you hear it? The sound of whitewater falls roaring? We, as a nation, are like whitewater rafters, floating helplessly downstream, drifting closer and closer to the edge of a fatal drop off a waterfall. But while the roar of the water crashing over the cliffs keeps getting louder and louder, it seems like no one can hear it. Instead, every day there's another pseudo-solution, quick fix or band-aid that's supposed to avert our massive health crises. It won't. Because the voices of the sick care and disease management business, never mind the massive convenience food marketing machine, are louder.

You've heard the expression, "the squeaky wheel gets the grease. " Well in this case, these industries are squeaking the loudest—and robbing us of not only our money, but also our health—the thing they're supposed to be *helping*, not hurting.

Statistics don't lie. According to the 2010 National Health and Nutrition Examination survey, more than one-third of adults and 17% of youth in this country are obese—not just overweight, but obese. Overweight and obesity has been proven to increase the risk of health conditions and diseases including breast cancer, coronary heart disease, type 2 diabetes, sleep apnea, gall bladder disease, osteoarthritis, colon cancer, hypertension, and stroke.

Our national weight problem is so severe that obesity is now *the number two cause of preventable death* in the U.S..

Not only that, but, according to obesity trends among American adults by the CDC's Behavioral Risk Surveillance System, type 2 diabetes has cost America $63.14 billion, osteoporosis comes in at $17.2 billion, hypertension has taken another $3.23 billion, and heart disease has rung up a $6.99 billion tab.

And that's only to date.

Meanwhile, diabetes, hypertension and other obesity-related chronic diseases prevalent among adults have now become more common in youngsters. The percentage of children and adolescents who are over-weight and obese is higher than ever before. In fact, obesity among boys and girls has *quadrupled* in the past 25 years. The combination of inactivity and poor dietary habits is making our children sick.

You can blame it all on the system–but it's not all the system's fault. Because we, as a society, are freely giving in to that system.

The hallmark of any good system is that it keeps you there by continu-ing to "up-sell" you with new and better incentives. There's always a new food product to make you sicker, followed by a new miracle cure to make you feel better. And as you buy in to this system of creating and then resolving symptoms, you begin to break down and disconnect from the most important system of all–your human body.

Deepak Chopra once said that the human body was not designed to be diseased but to function, heal and feel as optimally as possible. Did you know that your system is designed to live and thrive for 120 years? Yet, in our country, men are only making it into their early seventies and women into their late seventies.

Today, the expectation seems to be that we'll live to Medicare age, add ten or more medications to our biochemical regime, and nurse multiple diseases until we finally die. At which point, everyone who knew us will be shocked and remark, "He was so healthy!"

Is that actually true? Are healthy individuals dropping dead without some dysfunction or disease ravaging their body from the inside out?

Not possible.

HOW IS *YOUR* HEALTH?

So how do you make sure you're not one of those "healthy" individuals who suddenly drops dead from years of mismanaging your system?

Think about the things that you're doing right now that may be covering up symptoms of a larger problem. For example, you might buy acid-reducing drugs to hide the symptoms of chronic heartburn caused by being overweight. But the real problem, your weight, will still be there and eventually lead to other symptoms you'll need to "cure" with more drugs.

So ask yourself, have you cured your problem, or are you only hiding it? And what type of long-term effects are these "solutions" having on your health?

If you take shortcuts in life, your life may be cut short.

And it's not just about drugs. If the foods you eat have been preserved and stripped of their life-giving nutrients, what do you think this altered food might do to your body? ADD, ADHD, Type 2 diabetes, heart disease, cancer, Alzheimer's...the list of potential problems goes on and on. And while most of us look at that list and see diseases or conditions that require treatment or a cure, in reality, they are all symptoms of a body that can no longer sustain itself on what it's currently consuming.

THE BUSINESS OF THE BODY

Look at your health as an investment. When you make easy choices for short-term gain–like cheap, low grade foods you don't have to prepare, or prescriptions to mask rather than deal with health problems–you're not just buying into a symptom-based system. You're putting yourself in a position where you will receive low returns on your investment in your body. The results will be a lower quality of life, more dysfunction in terms of health problems and diseases, and ultimately, a shorter lifespan. And even if you live to be eighty years old, the quality of those eighty years will be diminished.

If you are currently living according to this model, you need to understand that you have bought into a bad deal–and you need to get out of that deal NOW. Accept the fact that whatever you might look like on the outside, even if you feel fine, what's underneath your skin has been running on empty for a long time. Your body can seemingly function well...until that day when it doesn't. This is what the sick-care system preys on. Once you get started, you're hooked for life. You're poised and ready for the system's next upsell, the next marketing campaign, the loudest voice.

But you don't get any better. You just get worse.

What you need is a new system to take care of your health. This starts by taking a good, strong look at who is charge of your healthcare right now. Is it an insurance agency? Is it a drug regime? Or are you in charge of your health and dedicated to giving your body the things it needs?

The only way to reclaim your health is to reclaim *control* of your health. Do that, and you'll give yourself the best possible chance of living a long, healthy life.

It starts by taking an honest inventory of where you are right now. What are you eating? How is your weight? What symptoms are you experiencing? How many drugs are you taking, and how often, and why? Once you understand where you are, you can see and where you need to go. You can start to use tools ranging from nutrition and fitness strategies to mindset exercises to get there, plus coaching and accountability to stay on track.

Focus on short-term goals; meet these goals one at a time, in increments to help you achieve more long-term goals. After all, Rome was not built in a day, and neither was your condition. Whether you are overweight, suffering from a chronic illness or even if you're in the best shape of your life, the important thing is to understand how you got to be where you are. Because once you understand what has been keeping you there, you will be able to break through the ceiling you have been hitting and enjoy health and happiness at a higher level.

Different processes, including a food consumption strategy, decisions about supplements, and an exercise and fitness program can be introduced gradually, step by step, depending on your specific situation and condition. And while the accountability and coaching aspect may feel intrusive, once you give yourself over to the system and stop fighting it, your results will be turn-key.

We all thrive on structure. Good structure equals good function. And, once you build and follow through on a new and healthier structure, once it becomes a habit, you will soar to new heights and do things that you would have never done on your own.

Action Steps to a New You!

Our nation has become one of the most overfed, undernourished, inflamed, metabolically deregulated populations in the world. In fact, high energy, nutrient-empty foods are offered in restaurants and grocery stores all over the Westernized world.

In 2001, Dr. Stephen Spindler performed a landmark experiment on rats where he underfed them by 40 percent. Within a month they had a 400% increase in the expression of the anti-aging genes, anti-inflammation genes, antioxidant genes, all of which fight the devastating effects of diabetes.

Eating a live food diet is a natural form of calorie restriction. Cooking foods significantly depletes their enzyme content. According to the Max Planck Institute, 50% of protein is coagulated, as well as 70 to 90% of your vitamins and minerals and as much as 100% of your phytonutrients. A live food diet lets you consume 50% fewer calories than the standard American diet while, at the same time, maintaining a very high level of nutrition.

Consciously choosing foods and their juices, herbs, vitamins, amino acids, minerals, and enzymes, can help you accomplish this. The fastest, most efficient system is to eliminate processed sugar, white flour, processed foods, excitotoxins such as artificial flavorings and colorings, animal fats, trans fats and cooked fats–as well as the bad habits of smoking and watching television.

The following is a list of low-glycemic, low insulin score foods and supplements that are excellent diabetes fighters and can help re-regulate your system.

BASIC ANTIDIABETOGENIC DIET

- All vegetables (except cooked carrots and cooked beets)
- All sea vegetables
- Non-sweet fruits: tomatoes, avocados, cucumber, red pepper, lemons, limes
- Fats and oils: flax oil, hemp oil, sesame oil, walnut, almond, sunflower, and avocado, coconut
- Nuts and seeds except cashews, coconut pulp

- Superfoods: Blue-green algaes, spirulina, chlorella, Green Superfood powder mixes
- Sweeteners: stevia, cardamom, cinnamon
- Salt: Himalayan and Celtic sea salt
- Fruit: fresh, low-glycemic fruits; dehydrated fruits
- Beverages: filtered, blessed, structured water, fresh low-glycemic juices, herbal non-caffeinated teas, green tea

VITAMINS

- B3—good for the functioning of glucose tolerance factor, decreases lipid buildup.
- B6—reverses neuropathy, protects against peripheral nerve degeneration, inhibits glycosylation of proteins and also helps with Magnesium metabolism.
- B12—maintains proper function of the nervous system, reduces oxidative stress
- Biotin—important for carbohydrate, fat, and protein metabolism
- Vitamin C—heals diabetes and reverses complications.
- Vitamin D—can lower blood sugar and boosts the immune system
- Vitamin E—reduces glycosylation, improves insulin sensitivity, and inhibits platelet-clumping.
- Bioflavonoid (quercitin)—promotes insulin secretion and is a potent inhibitor of sorbitol accumulation.

ESSENTIAL FATTY ACIDS (EFA'S)

- Fatty Acid optimization: ALA, GLA, EPA, DHA, and Oleic Acid.
- A balance of Omega 6:3 fatty acid ratios decreases inflammation and increases efficiency at the cellular level.

AMINO ACIDS

- **Acetyl-Carnitine** - improves peripheral nerve function
- **L-Arginine** - boosts insulin sensitivity as well as cardiovascular function.

MINERALS

- **Vanadium**—an important trace mineral in healing diabetes naturally. It seems to keep the blood sugar from rising too high. It supports the absorption of blood sugar into the muscle system and protects against elevated cholesterol, particularly a buildup of cholesterol in the central nervous system. Vanadium has been found to be helpful in protecting against diabetic cataracts and neuropathy. It seems to be associated with modest improvements in fasting glucose and hepatic insulin resistance. Clinical trials have found a significant decrease in insulin requirements in patients with insulin-dependent diabetes after vanadyl sulfate therapy. It has also been found to stimulate glucose uptake and metabolism that leads to glucose normalization. Kelp and sea vegetables are good sources of vanadium.

- **Magnesium**—Magnesium depletion is commonly associated with both type 1 and 2 diabetes, and is one of the most important minerals to replace. Magnesium supplementation may prevent some of the complications of diabetes such as retinopathy and heart disease. Magnesium deficiency has been associated with insulin resistance. Other research has noted that magnesium deficiency resulted in impaired insulin secretion.

  Magnesium is very alkalizing to the body, and helps counter the tendency of the diabetogenic lifestyle and physiology. Its highest concentration is in leafy greens, nuts, whole grains, unpolished rice, and wheat germ. Generally high-magnesium foods include apples, apricots, avocados, beet tops, berries, black walnuts, brazil nuts, cabbage, coconuts, figs, endive, greens, spinach, rye, walnuts, water cress, and yellow corn.

- **Calcium**—an alkalizing mineral that helps neutralize the acidity of diabetes.

- **Zinc**—seems to be important for preventing insulin resistance. It seems to be involved in almost all aspects of insulin metabolism, including synthesis, secretion, and utilization. Zinc seems to have a protective effect against beta cell destruction as well as ant-viral effects.

Foods that contain zinc include legumes, nuts (especially almonds), and seeds (particularly pumpkin and sunflower seeds).

- **Potassium**—helps reduce insulin resistance at post-receptor sites. It seems to improve insulin sensitivity and insulin secretion. High potassium reduces the risk of heart disease and lowers blood pressure. There is some danger with potassium excess, especially with diabetes and kidney disease. Potassium is also alkalizing.

Good sources of potassium are prunes, tomatoes, artichoke, spinach, sunflower seeds, and almonds.

- **Manganese**—an important co-factor in many enzyme systems that are associated with blood sugar control, energy metabolism, and thyroid hormone function. Most diabetics have about half the manganese levels of normal individuals and urinary manganese tended to be slightly higher.

- **Chromium**—an essential nutrient for sugar and fat metabolism. Because chromium appears to enhance the action of insulin and chromium deficiency results in impaired glucose tolerance, chromium insufficiency has been hypothesized to be a contributing factor to the develpment of type 2 diabetes.

HERBS

- **Gymnema**—decreases blood glucose absorption from the intestines; it seems to regenerate the beta cells of the pancreas and improves insulin secretion.

- **Curcumin** (tumeric)—a strong antioxidant associated with treating complications of diabetes. It is also a very good for the liver, which is affected in diabetes.

- **Fenugreek**—has been known to lower blood sugar in type 1 and 2 diabetics. Fenugreek normalizes glucose after meals and improves insulin response in the body, and it lowers total cholesterol and triglycerides.

- **Cinnamon**—a powerful herb for blood sugar. Cinnamon stimulates glucose uptake, increases effectiveness of insulin, and also increases the anti-bacterial anti-viral, and anti-fungal processes.

- **Cayenne**—contains capsaicin which alleviates nerve pain associated with diabetes.

- **Holy Basil**—improves immunity and strengthens the body. It also normalizes triglycerides levels in the blood, lowers cholesterol, and decreases blood pressure and inflammation in the mild to moderate cases of diabetes.

- **Parsley**—excellent for kidney support in diabetics.

- **Banaba**—a natural insulin agent. It balances the blood sugar, transports the blood sugar into the cells, and reduces the conversion of blood sugar into fats. It helps with weight loss and to decrease triglycerides levels. It also transports blood sugar into body cells and helps control carbohydrate cravings.

- **Goat's Rue**—contains guanidine, which is the herbal prototype for the pharmaceutical drug metformin which improves insulin sensitivity in both type 1 and 2 diabetics.

- **Bilberry**-has been being used as a treatment for diabetes for a long time. It has excellent antioxidant properties that helps prevent or reverse damage to cells. It not only has been know to prevent longterm illnesses such as heart disease, cancer, and macular degeneration, it also lowers blood glucose and triglycerides.

- **Milk thistle**-beneficial in a wide range of liver disorders. It has been found to have antioxidant and glucose-regulating properties.

ENZYMES

- **Proteolytic and digestive enzymes**

In addition to these dietary recommendations, it should be noted that exercise does some amazing things for the insulin-resistant, obese and type 2 diabetics. Improvements include improved insulin sensitivity, reduced cholesterol and triglycerides with increased HDL levels, and improved weight loss.

I recommend jumping on a high quality rebounder for up to 16 minutes a day, 4-5 days per week. Other cardiovascular exercises include moderately fast walking, jogging, swimming, cycling, and so on. Exercising at high intensity for short intervals can not only build muscle but also can increase glucose uptake without the use of insulin or other pharmaceuticals.

Stress reduction can also help save your life. It decreases your epineph-rine and corticosteroid production, ultimately leading to improved insu-lin sensitivity. There are many healthy ways to reduce stress. For exam-ple, yoga is good for decreasing physical and mental stress; yoga helps heal internal organs as well as regulates blood glucose levels, reduces stress hormones, and helps control weight.

You don't have to imperil your health and your life with the bad lifestyle and diet habits most of our society embraces. The real "Success Secret" for having a long, happy and healthy life is having the courage to aban-don old habits and putting a new proactive plan in place.

There's no better time to TAKE YOUR HEALTH BACK - and *keep* it for as long as you desire to stay well.

About Mark

Dr. Mark McCullough is a Michigan native who earned his B.S. degree in Chemistry in 1991 and began his career as a bioana-lytical scientist. After five years of Research and Development, Dr. McCullough went back to school to pursue his doctorate degree.

Dr. McCullough established his clinic after graduating from Palmer College of Chiropractic in 1999. Within the first few years of practice, he became one of the largest Chiropractic clinics in the state of Michigan and now operates one of the largest Natural Health Clinics in North America. In addition, he is a nutritional consultant and is a certified specialist in both Youth Fitness and Youth Nutrition by the International Youth Conditioning Association. Dr. Mark is also pursuing a Master's Degree in Herbology.

Dr. McCullough is a contributor to *The New York Times, USA Today,* and *The Wall Street Journal* Bestseller, *"One Minute Wellness."* Dr. McCullough co-founded Next Level Health, a program to help doctors start up and run successful "patient-centered" care to their respective communities. He is founder and CEO of both Pure Health Solutions, LLC, a nutritional consultancy, as well as a Crossfit Affiliate in Battle Creek.

Dr. McCullough also served as the Team Doctor for the 2005 IBL Champion Battle Creek *Dr Mark McCullough Family Chiropractic Battle Creek Michigan Knights* from 2005-2009 and is currently the Team Physician for Team Active Cycling and Multisport Team as well as the Priority Health Cycling and Multisport Team. Dr. McCullough's mission is serving his patients and helping potential students of Natural Whole Body Health realize and achieve their potential as Doctors.

His innovative strategies, inspiration, and passion for helping people are the foundation to his thriving practice in Battle Creek, Michigan as well as the many clinics he consults around the nation. His passionate work began when his own son was diagnosed with autism. And through a customized plan involving numerous lifestyle-enhancing strategies, his son is now a mainstream teenager excelling in music and will be attending Hillsong International Leadership College in Sydney, Australia, in 2012.

Dr. McCullough has hosted weekly radio shows for years. His incredible contributions to his local community of Battle Creek has allowed him to be invited as a guest speaker to many of the schools that teach healthcare around the country. At seminars, conferences, and media appearances throughout North America, he shows people how to apply his Whole Body Wellness Solutions to get you to the Next Level in health, happiness, and life.

In addition to being a devoted to husband to Missy and devoted father to Jake and Macy, Dr. Mark is an outstanding athlete. He was sponsored by a type-1 diabetic team, Triabetes, in 2009 and was not only an Arizona Ironman Finisher, but has been slated as one of the fastest diabetics to do ironman distance triathlon in the world. Other endeavors include the 2009 Huff 50K, 2011 Run Woodstock 50K, 2008 and 2009 Steelhead 70.3. Dr. Mark placed 4th and 3rd in the 2008 and 2009 Bayshore Half Marathon and has achieved National qualifying times in Master's swimming in both 2009 and 2010.

CHAPTER 13

Your Inner Voice – Friend Or Foe?

By Mikkel Pitzner

If you purchased this book, chances are you dream of achieving notice-able results for yourself and wish to become successful. Perhaps you are in employment, but realize the chances of that turning into the lifestyle you always dreamed of is never going to happen; or perhaps you may be among the unfortunate that lost your employment (or maybe your own business) as part of the 2008 financial crisis from which many are still suffering. Or perhaps you are just starting out dreaming about the nice paychecks, grand house, fancy cars and the travels and freedom that money can bring. You may be wondering how to make that dream come true for you. How do you achieve success? What makes some people more successful than others? Do they have special powers, edu-cation, gifts, knowledge, better ideas? Are they more intelligent, more connected or more lucky? What is their secret?

Most people, myself included, tell themselves a plethora of excuses why it would never work for them or why they would not be able to achieve the dream. They say to themselves:
I'm not old enough
I'm just a kid
I had a bad childhood
I'm not popular
I'm not famous
I have no education

I have no experience
I have no money
I don't have time
I'm not pretty enough
There is too much competition
It's already been done before
The economy is too bad
It's too hard
I'm too old
It's too late
My boss is a jerk
My parents are no good...and so on.

We are all what John Addison (formerly CEO of Primerica) call *excuseaholics* or suffer from author Brian Tracy call *excusitis* to some extend. Most of the excuses come from that little voice in your head that keeps talking to you. Authors Bob Allen and Mark Victor Hansen have called this negative voice your *inner whiner*. But if you want to achieve success you will have to overcome this and go beyond the negative inner voice. You will have to find your *inner winner* (as also named by Bob Allen and Mark victor Hansen) voice—the other voice. The one that picks you up, gives you courage and drowns out your fear and excuses (oftentimes pure imaginary fictitious obstacles that your other voice has put in your head).

Chances are you also may have chosen to get this particular book because of it being a book with the world renowned Jack Canfield, who has earned much fame and fortune from the famous Chicken Soup Series of books. He certainly seems to have found the keys to success and has cracked the code for achieving results of really phenomenal scales. Therefore, chances are you may be looking to him and the fellow authors in this book for answers to how you make your dream come to fruition for you and your family. Well, it just so happens Jack Canfield himself is a wonderful example for regarding the voice in your head that tells you all the aforementioned reservations and excuses for why the dream would not work for you, and why it wouldn't even matter if you tried.

You see, when Jack Canfield and Mark Victor Hansen were looking for a publisher to bring *Chicken Soup for the Soul* to the world, they were turned down by one after the other. In fact they received so many No's that most people would have given up.

Believe it or not, the mega-selling series was not an easy sell to publishers. "We were rejected by 123 publishers all told," Canfield told Shareguide.com. "The first time we went to New York, we visited with about a dozen publishers in a two day period with our agent, and nobody wanted it. They all said it was a stupid title, that nobody bought collections of short stories, that there was no edge no sex, no violence. Why would anyone read it?"

In the first month of their efforts to promote the book, they were turned down by 33 of New York's biggest publishing houses, who said: "Anthologies don't sell." "We don't think there is a market for this book." "We just don't get it." "The book is too positive." "It's not topical enough." To top it off, their agent said, "I can't sell this book—I'm giving it back to you guys."

Fortunately Jack Canfield and Mark Victor Hansen did not get deterred, but persisted in their efforts to bring the book to life and to the market. Ultimately, they sold the first *Chicken Soup for the Soul* book to a small press based in Deerfield Beach, Florida, called Health Communications. The rest, as they say, is history. There are currently 80 million copies of the Chicken Soup books in print, with subjects as varied as *Chicken Soup For the Horse Lover's Soul* and *Chicken Soup For the Prisoner's Soul*. Canfield and Hansen ranked as the top-selling authors of 1997 and are multiple New York Times Best Sellers List. Most important of all, the inspirational stories they have gathered in their many volumes have improved the lives of countless readers.

In other words, persistence and perseverance are most certainly traits you need to bring with you in your efforts to achieve success, for seldom will you just find your idea or your work towards your goals come easily and without struggle to overcome.

But let's not get ahead of ourselves, for isn't it often true that we don't even take that first step towards putting our idea into life and press forward? In fact, I would venture to say that the majority of people never even make a move with most of their ideas. Ideas out of which perhaps one or more could be potential million-dollar ideas. Our inner whiner voices list all the aforementioned excuses and probably many more and we quickly come to the conclusion that it is not even worth for us to even try. And so we drop the idea and we stay put at our current position and go on with our lives, probably continuing to complain about the bad economy, the worthless politicians who seem incapable of fixing anything, our lousy boss, unsatisfactory job and our way too small paycheck.

Another way the exact same problem shows itself is through procrastination and contemplation. You may have the best intentions, but intentions alone are not going to get you anywhere—we all know that *the road to hell is paved with good intentions*. Far too many of us do what Joseph McClendon III describes as *Ready Aim, Ready Aim, Ready Aim*—and then nothing. They never pull the trigger. In reality, when procrastination shows up this way, it's really often just another expression of fear, and goes back to that negative inner voice.

However, isn't there often truth in the saying that fear is really just the acronym for *False Expectations Appearing Real*? In other words, your excuses are usually not routed in real reasons why you could not take your idea and move it towards fruition and to a possible successful outcome. Your problem is not that you are too young, too old, have no money or whatever reason your negative inner voice is telling you. Your problem may simply be one of lack of confidence. You are listening too much to your negative inner voice.

So ask yourself: How are you communicating with yourself? What is that inner voice telling you all the time? Is it moving you forward and empowering you, or is it quite the opposite? Do you recognize examples where you are holding yourself back and not taking any action? Do you perhaps see that you are coming up with more excuses for why your idea wouldn't work instead of see all the opportunities that are abundantly available all around you all the time?

Realize that your excuses and self-talk are just self-imposed limitations about who you are and what you are capable of. While I may not be able to quickly eliminate your lack of confidence just by snapping my fingers, allow me to offer you an insight that might help, even though it may feel very awkward and fake in the beginning: *"Fake it until you make it! Act as if you had all the confidence you require until it becomes your reality,"* or as John Addison expresses it; *"Act the way you want to feel and soon you will feel the way you act."*

You are a victim of your negative self-talk. You have to watch out for what your are telling yourself and what you are feeding your mind. Your thinking is determining where you are going. You have to *Feed Your Dreams And Starve Your Nightmares* (line from the movie "A Beautiful Mind"). If you had a nice expensive car in the driveway, you would not be giving the keys to just anyone. But who are you giving the keys to your brain? Be careful who you listen to, be careful what you hear and howyou choose to respond. Don't let other people's wall of fear stop you for making your dream a reality.

There is a famous Cherokee story about two wolves which goes like this:

One evening an old Cherokee Indian told his grandson about a battle that goes on inside people. He said:

"My son, the battle is between two 'wolves' inside us all. One is Evil. It is anger, envy, jealousy, sorrow, regret, greed, arrogance, self-pity, guilt, resentment, inferiority, lies, false pride, superiority, and ego. The other is good. It is joy, peace, love, hope, serenity, humility, kindness, benevolence, empathy, generosity, truth, compassion and faith."

The grandson thought about it for a minute and then asked his grandfather: "Which wolf wins?"

The old Cherokee simply replied: "The one you feed."

What a wonderful and yet simple story. We all have these wolves in our minds forever battling each other. The Evil Wolf or the Good Wolf is fed daily by the choices we make with our thoughts. What you think about and dwell upon will, in a sense, appear in your life and influence your behavior. We have a choice, feed the Good Wolf and it will show up in our character, habits and behavior positively. Or feed the Evil Wolf and our whole world will turn negative: like poison, this will slowly eat away at our soul.

The crucial question is: *which are you feeding today*?

Feed your mind the right things. Read the best books from the many great mentors past and present and stop feeding it all the negatives (which usually includes watching the news and many other TV programs). Hang out with the right people who embody success, find mentors and join mastermind groups.

Yes, you can! Never give up believing in yourself. Whenever you doubt yourself, remember the many amazing stories below of failure turned into fame and success by amazing people we all know and respect. Many have turned their biggest adversities into strengths and have build their successes out of these. Every one of us can make a big difference if we only choose to believe in ourselves and never give up. You don't need to get it right, *you just need to get it going.* You should be your own greatest champion. Be your own biggest cheerleader.

If you already run a small business, then don't let your small business make you small minded. You already have the answer. You already know enough. You already have experience you can put into use to start moving you in the right direction. Don't wait for the perfect time, like many others. There is no perfect time, it is an illusion. You will wait forever for it. There will never be a perfect time to leave your job, move out of state, and start from scratch. Similarly, there will never be a perfect time to get married, have a baby, or have another baby. That's because no matter when you make these choices, they will involve risk—and it's the risk involved that makes choices like these easier to put off until another day. What you often fail to realize is you're not just waiting, you're stagnating. You stop growing, hinder your advancement, and basically become dull as a result of your choice to keep life on pause. If your current job is holding you back, then you should quit. Same with anything else holding you back.

Don't wait for your ship to come in—you have to swim out and meet your ship. Indeed if there is a perfect time, it is now. The perfect time will always be now. There are excuses and there are results. You just have to choose. You have to show up and take action.

When you face your fear head on, you will often find that it shrinks and oftentimes eventually completely disappears. Leaders embrace adversity. Leaders make their adversity their strength. Embrace failures by learning from them, and then get up on that horse again and go and succeed. Change the way you feel about failing. Like John Maxwell tells us *Fail Forward Fast.*

Brian Tracy taught me that the mind can only hold one thought at a time. If you keep your goal in mind and thus think about your goal, you automatically will be thinking on something positive and you cannot at the same time be thinking a negative thought.

In his famous book, *"Eat That Frog,"* Brian Tracy gives us the following advice: Do the one thing that will make the most impact in propelling you towards the goal you have set for yourself. You will find oftentimes it is the same thing that you dread the most, so if you do not know which one of the things on your to do list you really need to get done then look for the one that you really dread the most. It just might be that one. Of course once you have done that one task that would move the needle for you the most, then you go on to the next top task that now will have the biggest impact for your success.

Follow Pareto's law, the law of 20/80, which says that 20% of your tasks accounts for 80% of your results. You will advance yourself and your results greatly if you just do the most important tasks, even if that means you won't be doing half of all the other tasks of minor importance. The problem is that many of us do all the smaller things of little importance. As one of my favorite mentors Jim Rohn used to say *"Learn how to separate the majors and the minors. A lot of people don't do well simply because they major in minors."*

So this chapter is your permission slip. Your permission slip to go out there and state your claim. To take that position and go and succeed.

The worst thing one can do is not to try, to be aware of what one wants and not give in to it, to spend years in silent hurt wondering if something could have materialized - never knowing.

— Jim Rohn

About Mikkel

Mikkel Pitzner is a serial Entrepreneur, investor, professional board member in Denmark, Sweden, and the U.S. (currently sitting on 9 boards), marketing and social media expert and consultant, 'masterminder' and dreamer extraordinaire.

Mikkel received his Bachelor of Science in Economics, with honors, from University College of London, England in 1991. He also completed intense courses in Political Science and Game Theory at Columbia University in New York and a business course for CEOs at Harvard Business School in Massachusetts.

He is a Partner of a unique marketing and trailer rental company called "Freetrailer," as well as a Partner in a promotional marketing company for corporations.

Originally from Denmark, where he used to run what turned into the 4th largest car rental company, he spearheaded efforts that resulted in doubled expansion growth and quadrupled locations. Up until recently, he owned and operated the largest limousine service company in Denmark, in which he grew profits 3200% during the first year of ownership alone. The company served the most discerned clientele including no less than three U.S. presidents. He also successfully ran a scuba diving equipment import & distribution company until it was sold to a German distributor.

Mikkel is also a multiple best-selling author and speaker; he teaches entrepreneurs how to create a business that will provide you with the lifestyle of your choice, taking you off the treadmill of your job, so you can spend your time doing what you love. Mikkel Pitzner has been featured on CNBC, ABC, CNNMONEY.com, Entrepreneur, FOX News, CBS News, *The Wall Street Journal, Fortune, Fast Company, SmartMoney, USA Today* and NBC. Mikkel Pitzner was also recently a guest on the Brian Tracy TV Show.

Mikkel currently resides in Florida with his beautiful wife Olga, 20-month-old son, Gabriel and a baby girl on the way. He is building four new business ventures simultaneously, while helping a local manufacturer in a struggling and challenging economy.

Get your free gift from Mikkel when you visit
www.mikkelpitzner.com/the-success-secret-free-gift

CHAPTER 14

The Success Secrets for Business & 'The Good Life'

By Robert Blair

William Shakespeare stated, "This Above All…to Thine Own Self Be True!" Shakespeare's admonition manifests to the reader that you have Self Worth.

Self worth is what you are, and everything you have is a gift. Self worth puts everyone on a level playing field at birth. What comes next is your ability to make choices and decisions for yourself. This is where your life journey begins; it gives you responsibility for your choices and decisions–you're on your own. Somewhere it begs the question, *Who am I, Truly?*

You decide to have a quiet session with your thoughts and beliefs such as responsibility, self worth, and a level playing field. Then, it hits you– Gifts! What you didn't know is that in the nanosecond after you first asked the question "Who am I, truly?" your subconscious mind started working on your question. Now, your mind is working most of the nightshift to answer your questions–the ones you ask, and the ones that formulate in the background. It could happen overnight, or take several days before coming back with answers.

You may be thinking, "Sweet! So, tell me about these eternal life gifts. How do I get started determining the life gifts I need or want in my life adventure? What is the secret to the gifts? Action, hope, thoughts, belief, they are very similar; however, they do not trump faith!

ACTION IS THE PHYSICAL MANIFESTATION OF FAITH.

You have to attract the secrets to success. You cannot buy them. You cannot run after them and catch them.

Faith is the common denominator, and the eternal life gifts are the ones that give you the secrets. I know it is fashionable to not use the word God when it comes up in conversation, manuscript and other media but God and My Lord and Savior, Jesus Christ, are my story (and my life). I have been blessed more than even I know.

God is *love*, the Alpha and the Omega.

Secret #1: You have to have faith in yourself and God, for He is the one who gave you the eternal life gifts and blessings, or the secrets.

Secret #2: God has told us Pray as though you have already received it and it shall be yours. (Mark 11:22-24)

Many claim they don't believe in faith. If those who have no faith would consider every time they drive down the road, isn't it faith that keeps them driving? You have faith that the person driving in the opposite direction (the oncoming traffic) won't cross the line and create a collision or worse a fatality.

Another physical situation of faith: large airplanes. It appears almost impossible they stay in the air in the illusion of slow motion, when we all know full well they do stay up as needed.

Let's reflect on this last example and use the three legs to discern the difference. The three legs are: faith, knowledge, beliefs.

1. You know the airplane won't fall out of the sky. *A Belief!*

2. From the ground, you can see the airplane lumbering along as such a slow rate that you believe it could fall out of the sky at any given time, but you know it won't. *Knowledge and Belief.*

3. Atmosphere is the unseen element. Your knowledge can make you believe this, as most everyone has traveled on one or more of those lumbering sky buses. You have a belief and some knowledge as to how big the aircraft is, the unbelievable tonnage for

the weight of the air craft and all the cans of freight and luggage, thousands of gallons of fuel, the passengers, and other equipment in the every day flight. *Faith, Knowledge and Belief.*

4. People have a fear of air travel because they cannot see or feel the air/atmosphere. You can feel the wind; you can bask in the warm air, and you can watch the trees sway. But, you cannot see the air that keeps airplanes flying. *Faith.*

As are the secrets buried in this children's poem?

Row - Row - Row, Your Boat.

Gently Down the Stream

Merrily, Merrily, Merrily, Merrily,

Life is But a Dream!

Row, Row, Row…Get it? You have to use *action*. Everything that is needed is not free.

Your Boat: Don't envy other's boats nor lose focus on your journey. You could lose energy, and it is costly to get back on track.

Gently down the stream: Once again, action comes into play. Go with the flow. It's there to help you, as is the hand of God. Gently floating gives you rest between action. Also, it gives you everything you need to teach your children to row their own boats.

Merrily, Merrily, Merrily, Merrily: Have fun; stop and smell the roses; take the path less traveled; watch the scenery; view the wonderful artistry of the creator. Enjoy your trip, love your family, excel at your work, and love your fellow man. Be grateful for every day; carry your gratitude stone.

Life is But a Dream; As in a dream, you can change your journey. Everything you are or have to this point in your life is due to your decisions and choices. That does not make them good or bad, right or wrong, happy or sad. How come you never heard the last part after *Life Is But A Dream*? Because unlike children, you stopped thinking like a child, stopped exploring, stopped asking questions. Now is the chance to explore your dream life.

THE SECRET OF ETERNAL LIFE GIFTS OF THE FATHER

God has an abundance of unbelievably, beautiful baskets, each overflowing with eternal life gifts made of love and woven with bright, vibrant royal colors of silk–the finest in the universe. The baskets put to shame the lovely Faberge Eggs. He has opened the windows of heaven to bestow these life gifts in each and every soul of His children, His obedient and faithful sons and daughters. Everyone receives four, five, sometimes even six God-given, eternal life gifts. The gifts focus on your strengths and help you focus to build your life Journey.

The Secrets of the Gifts

No One Is Left out; Gifts never run out.

No One receives the same gifts each are unique.

None of the gifts are ever taken away.

Never are they taxed. They abide within you.

There is not a limit of the number of Secrets you will receive. Secrets will always be with us even to the end of the world (Matthew 20:28)

God has promised us wealth, health and happiness for everyone who tithes, will receive many times over in return, gifts of the Father." He dares you to prove him wrong. (Malachi 3:10)

This promise is, the more I study the Bible, the more gifts I find. The more you engage the gifts the more they give up there secrets, the wider God opens the windows of heaven to shower you with gifts and blessings beyond my capability of containment.

One of Your Eternal Life Gifts could be that you are an Organizer: the ability to take control and create order stabilizes the process for clients and enables you to move towards the final result. Thus, you are seen as trustworthy, credible and professional in the eyes of your clients. Gifts help you in your business as well as other areas of your life.

The Good Life begins and ends with you. Surprised?

The Good Life" is different for each individual, as his/her journey and adventure here on this planet is unique. I believe being able to have anything you want. Maybe not everything you can think of; but surely, anything you put your mind to. I would put peace of mind and happiness right at the top of my bucket list.

THE PERFECT GAME

If you are offered a gift, take it and say thank you. If you get a rec-ommendation or a suggestion to try something new, or go someplace new, say thanks and have fun. But remember, regardless of the outcome, know that everything was perfect. You and only you can send your re-quest for secret gifts to your "other than conscious" mind. It will have an answer for everything. You can be, have or do anything you want.

Recent groundbreaking research in the field of new biology radically changes our understanding of life. It shows that genes and DNA do not control our biology; instead, DNA is controlled by signals from outside the cell. Signals including the energetic messages emanating *from our positive and negative thoughts*, which shows our bodies can be changed as we retrain our thinking. That is a scientific and physical truth. Science has evolved to a point that we know for certain: "A thought and / or a belief becomes things."

Every person in your life is here for a reason, whether you see it or not. Every person is here to help others or to teach you something. Each per-son has gifts for your soul, family, and your states (*e.g.* your Peace of mind). Everyone reflects some aspect of yourself that needs to be loved, forgiven, embraced or simply accepted. That is the best reason we are here.

Do Not Be conformed to this world, but transform your minds and that you may know that which is real and or of good report (Romans 12:2)

Have a structured system that helps you to have a "Business and The Good Life" in good times, and not so good times. You can refine the Good Life System as your situation and personal growth changes.

I am going to give you a basic structure to get you started. You can start in as quick as five minutes if you want.

First, focus on the most important parts of your life.

Put a Good Life System that, at your pace, will take you from where your life is today to where you want it to be, and by when. This is not hard to do, but it will need to be done consistently and intentional.

Embraced Peace of Mind.

GOALS

Here is a list of the five most important areas of your life that need attention and action. You will find these five areas cover all of your basic structure. This life system will work for anyone who puts it to work for them. As you go along, you will realize one area can effect some of the other areas; also they will have an affect on you.

1. God Spiritual

2. Your Family

3. Your Business: Profession, Career or Work

4. Your Finances: Home Budget

5. Your Physical and Mental states.

6. Fun For You

Take each area and write three goals for each area that have compelling *Why's*. Take a list of your goals everywhere you go, and review them every chance you get. Each time you review each goal, you are sending the request to your "other than conscious mind." The subconscious does not know if your request is happy, sad or strange. It will just answer the thought. Answers come in many shapes, and come from many directions. Remember to write your goals as though you have already received them and they will be yours. Make a "Myths, Untruths & the Secret Keys to Prosper in Your Business & Live The Good Life" written plan to reach your goals. Break it down into detailed, small steps.

DREAM BOARDS

Everyone should have their own Dream Board. A Dream Board is a collection of your goals and wants. Cut out pictures of things you want and attach them to your Dream Board. Dreams truly come true! Study the pictures to send your desire to the father of your Gifts.

JOURNAL DAILY

If your life is worth living, then is it not worth to recording? A Journal is not a diary. Your Journal will not be printed in the newspapers nor ABC, NBC Etc. It will not appear on Oprah or a talk radio show. Each night, journal how your day went, and include your thoughts, feelings, needs and desires. Include a line or two about tomorrow. This is also the time to invoke the Secret to go to work on your "not conscious mind" and deliver the next action to bring you closer to your Goals.

HOME BUDGET

In order to start out on the right foot, construct a home budget and start tracking expenditures. Many clients cringe at this part, but it's not that complicated.

Take your checkbook register(s) and **add up your monthly expenditures.**

Take the total amount of take-home pay and divide it up as follows.

- 70 % Live on this amount it includes car and mortgage
- 10% Save do not use it except for a life or death reason
- 10% To reduce debt. When or If you have no debt this money goes towards savings for investments.
- 10% Give this amount away in tithes or as you want.

Each Business has a mission statement, or an objective to help them stay on track. It works.

So, why don't we do the same for our family life? What is your family mission statement, your Objectives, Family Rituals, or Sayings?

Why not let your children use the 70-10-10-10- formula for their allowance?

Believe in yourself, your neighbors, your work, your ultimate attainment of more complete happiness. It is only the farmer who faithfully plants seeds in the Spring, who reaps a harvest in the Autumn.

– B.C. Forbs

About Robert

Robert Blair, *Americas Premier Senior Expert For Business &The Good Life™,* is a best-selling author of *How to Avoid the F Word! Stop Foreclosure!,* and marketing expert as seen on NBC, CBS, ABC, FOX affiliates as well as in *The Wall Street Journal, USA Today.* Robert is regularly sought out by the media for his opinion on the state of the market and how that affects buyers and sellers in current market trends and other topics.

In 1991, Robert was named "The Best Real Estate Salesperson in Ventura County By Buyers & Sellers,™" in a poll conducted by The Ventura County Star & Jim Woodard (a nationally syndicated, freelance columnist featuring Real Estate News & Trends). Robert became to be known as "Americas Most Wanted Broker© ™" *by his clients and associates.*

At 25, Robert started his first long-term business from scratch. His True Value® hardware store grew to include a janitorial products wholesale business, a manufactured home dealership, a storage company and a contractors supply company. This was during an economy of 22% interest rates. In the mid-80s, he added a Century21 office. Life was Good!

Early in his real estate career, Robert honed his knowledge and skills. He focused on building relationships and coaching others about the foundation of business. The Secrets to The Good Life! Robert found the secret that busted the myth, "You Cannot Have a Prosperous Business & The Good Life." He would like to pass to you The Secrets to The Good Life. And, change your life forever.

To learn about Robert Blair GRI, BKR, CDPE or for more Information, Coaching, Mentoring, please contact him at:
Blairhouse1@gmail.com
Ventura, CA
(805) 407-3366

CHAPTER 15

Personal Characteristics That Make a Difference in Life

By Roopa Makhija

Let me introduce myself and my journey.

I was born in India and came to the United States 23 years ago to earn my master's degree in Pharmacy at Long Island University. Coming to the States with no friends or family was not an easy decision; unlike many others, I didn't grow up dreaming about coming to America.

I grew up in a family with an older sister and younger brother. My father was in sales, but it was not his job that makes me reflect on him today and smile. His attitude, even in the final moments of his life dealing with kidney failure, was something that has stayed with me—and will, for the rest of my life.

During dialysis, he celebrated milestones like they were birthdays: the 50th procedure, the 100th procedure, and even though he was going in for a painful process to clean his blood—something most people dread for hours at a time—he found humor in those moments.

The night before he passed away, he asked me what I wanted out of life and I said, "I want to study."

"Whatever happens to me, make sure you send her [Roopa] abroad, she will reach her true potential in the U.S." he fortuitously told my mother that night.

It was his goal to make sure nothing came in my way. Even though my mother and grandmother wanted to get me married at the time, they honored his request.

When I had second thoughts about coming to the U.S., my mother told me, "I have faith in you, but if you do not have faith in yourself, do not go. But I don't want you to regret it five years later."

So, that is what happened.

I came here to obtain my master's in Pharmacy. To avoid being home-sick, I made sure I had no downtime to reminisce, which often meant working 16-18 hours a day.

I would only talk to my mother for 45 minutes once a month just to let her know I was doing well and adjusting to school. I would tutor and work in the research lab to avoid asking her for money past the initial funds she gave me.

After graduation, I went to work for a pharmaceutical company, then decided to continue my education by getting an MBA at the University of Chicago.

More than 12 years ago, I founded Global eProcure, now GEP, and we have offices all over the world, helping clients save money.

And that about sums it up. '**Happily ever after' right?**

Couldn't be further from the truth. There were so many interesting challenges and heartbreaking moments along the way to success that only the right personal characteristics could have gotten me through.

Before I started my own business, my employer at the time wanted me to fly to California for client projects (something I didn't want to do soon after having my first child). My contributions at the company had been limited up to that point and *letting me go* was easier for the company (though very hard for me).

Next I began working for a pharmaceutical company (as Director of Business Development), looking at opportunities leveraging the Internet boom at the beginning of the century. It was difficult for me to make an impact in six months, and *I was terminated again.*

I lost my job twice in less than one year.

After that experience, I did a lot of soul searching. I decided to start GEP to combine my business background and leverage the power of the Internet. I was fortunate to get the right partners and then cajole angel investors to invest $2.5 million into our ideas.

We worked hard to go live in a record time of 60 days but ran out of funding; we figured we would go back for more. Not so fast—because the very same day we got our initial funding, was the day the market collapsed due to the dot-com burst.

We were only able to rustle up an incremental $600,000 from our existing investors and decided right then and there, we would not go back for money again. Today, I would say our "little" company is very successful.

GEP helps Global 2000 companies transform procurement operations to deliver savings through consulting, technology and outsourcing solutions. We help clients reduce their costs by refining and perfecting their supply chain practices.

A few years ago, we celebrated our 10th company anniversary. Reflecting on this success, I realized there are some characteristics that just don't change over time when trying to build a beautiful company or, more importantly, a beautiful life.

THE CHARACTERISTICS

1. Exude A Positive Attitude.

Earlier, I gave the example of my father on dialysis. Most people in his situation would be counting down to the end of their life; but this man was celebrating each and every moment, and sharing them with others. He also continued to have a positive impact on the people close to him, like me! He wanted to make sure I went abroad to continue my studies because that is what I wanted out of life. *Always try to affect those around you and make their lives better with a positive attitude.*

2. Be Persistent.

I was fired twice in one year. But with my GEP business, failure was not an option. Even when investors were willing to take a tax write off, I was not ready to give up. I am sure that our employees, their families and our investors are glad that we did not give up early on.

My mother instilled in me that giving up is never an option. She learned two languages after the age of 40, so she could improve professionally–I would be no different in my drive.

No matter what challenges you face, you must keep pushing forward.

Asking for help is another aspect of persistence you should not be afraid to use. Back when I was at Pharmacy College, the dean asked, "What can I do for you?" A lot of people shy away from this question and think it shows weakness. I told the dean about my father's passing and said I wanted an assistantship to help my mother with tuition.

I also asked for help to call my mother after I was in America for almost two days, had not spoken to her and wanted to let her know I was safe (you needed a lot of change to call international from the payphone and I had not figured out the currency yet). It might have been a small thing, but the help was invaluable and it's the little things that get us by in life. *Ask for help if you need it and don't hesitate to give that help right back to others.*

3. Be Goal Oriented.
When I was turning 40, the time we all go through our mid-life crisis, I set a goal of completing a marathon. I can't even run a half-mile without taking walking breaks but decided to participate in the Philadelphia Marathon (I not only completed that race, but also completed the New York City marathon a year later in seven hours). When you accomplish a goal you set out for yourself, it is a great feeling that only pushes you onto the next goal.

With my schooling, I needed to set milestones or benchmarks of what I wanted to attain. If you set incremental goals, there is something in plain sight that you can and will finish. You have to have something to work toward, write down your goals and steps you can take to get there. After mapping out your process, take it one small goal at a time and you will eventually reach the finish line.

Also don't forget to take a look back every so often to assess your goals. When I was in graduate school, a professor had me write down my goals at that time in my life. I found that paper a couple years ago. It was funny to see how many of the things I put down actually came true; one of them was starting a business. Also, some goals changed for me, so that was important to see. *Always take a look back to assess what you've accomplished and where you want to go.*

4. Be Open To New Experiences.

I was a Resident Advisor while living in Brooklyn and working on my master's degree. This was a great experience. I discovered the American art of using a coffee machine, and learned how to use the washer/dryer (where to put quarters, where you put soap). I figured out these necessities by watching others.

The first flight I ever took was when I came to the states. You can't be afraid to walk out your door, and you can't listen to horror stories (especially if they entail getting mugged in a subway). You need to take on new challenges and new adventures. *Be curious and get outside your comfort zone. Who knows, you might create a new comfort zone.*

When I was a young girl, I would play cricket with the boys and was often the laughingstock, being the only girl in the team. One day, I hit the ball so hard, it broke a neighbor's windowpane. Needless to say she was mad at me. She yelled and suggested I should help my mother with cooking to be more like the other girls. I can confidently say, that is just not me; I don't go with the flow, and I am a happier mother, happier wife and happier business owner for making my own path!

5. Enjoy The Journey.

I think people get very jaded and only focus on getting from point A to point B—but once they are there, they wonder if that's all there is. Life is about the journey, not just the end result. *If you enjoy the process, the journey, then you can never be disappointed.*

When I had a miscarriage, I was wallowing in self-pity and my husband (who was pursuing an MBA at the University of Chicago at the time) could not pull me out of it. To get myself out of this negative mood permeating throughout my being, I decided to pursue my MBA as well, from the very same school. I would never regain what I had lost, but needed to continue on with my life. This allowed me to not only enhance my skills but also spend quality time with my husband since we both were in the same program.

If you are always waiting for the weather to get better (literally and figuratively), then you lose half your life. If it is raining, I say to myself, "I don't have to water the lawn!" If it is snowing, build a snowman or have a snowball fight with kids, make the best of each and every day.

In addition to savoring life's journey, push back every now and then and challenge the established. Make your mark. I remember a very famous cricket commentator inviting me to his office, where I asked why he didn't support or endorse female players in the sport. The back-and-forth conversation, where I did not give in to what society felt was one that I will cherish always and even helped me to become the strong business woman I am today.

6. Learn To Forgive.

If you hold other people accountable for your mistakes, it really limits your own growth and learning. An eye for an eye, a brick for a brick can feel good momentarily, but does not bring true or lasting happiness. Harboring grudges takes away our peace of mind and these negative thoughts affect our mental and physical health, our success and self-worth. Don't stop believing in the world just because somebody may have taken advantage of you. A positive outlook can lead to positive things, but looking at the world from a negative point of view won't solve anything. *Forgiveness is something we do not for others but for ourselves.*

> *"To forgive is to set a prisoner free and discover that the prisoner was you."* — Lewis B. Smedes

7. Be Grateful.

The most important characteristic of all might be gratitude to all the people who make your dreams a reality. My husband is often critical (in a good way) and expects more from those around him. *A lot of the credit for who I am goes to my husband, because he is always pushing me to do more.* He doesn't let me settle. Even his advice to turn from fiction novels to self-improvement books has made me a better person.

I believe there are no coincidences in life—whatever happens is for a reason and we are better human beings because of those experiences.

About Roopa

Roopa Gandhi Makhija is the Founder and President of GEP, which helps Global 2000 companies transform procurement operations to deliver savings through consulting, technology and outsourcing solutions. GEP, founded more than 12 years ago, helps clients reduce their costs by refining and perfecting their supply chain practices.

Roopa has grown a business that persevered through the dot-com burst in 2001, and seen it expand in the Americas, Europe and Asia. Its home base is still in Clark, NJ.

Resonating on duality, Roopa doubles as a powerful business woman, and a loving wife and mother. Her road to creating GEP is long and distinguished, with a Bachelor's Degree in Pharmacy from the University of Mumbai, a Master's Degree in Pharmacy from Long Island University and finally a Master's in Business Administration from the University of Chicago.

She has been a finalist for E&Y Entrepreneur of the Year and NJ Biz Top 50 Women in Business; nonetheless her philosophy is not about the awards, but enjoying the journey. Roopa is the epitome of the American dream, having faced adversity and pushed through to be the industry leader she is today. She jokes about not knowing how to use a coffee maker or washing machine when she first came to the States. Well, look at her now.

She truly believes a positive and grateful attitude, coupled with hard work, being goal-oriented work and determined (and taking a moment to stop and smell the roses from time to time) will get you exactly where you want to go in this gift called life.

For more information on GEP, visit www.gep.com or call (732) 382-6565.

CHAPTER 16

The Wealthy Cop:
How my Success Can Transform your Life!

By Sunil Tulsiani

Since the age of 14, all I ever wanted was to be was a police officer. I realized my dream—and then some—by serving as a police officer with the Ontario Provincial Police for about 15 years. I had worked my way up to Platoon Commander with a lot of responsibility.

And now I was asking my bosses for a year's leave of absence. Unpaid.

And, oh, one more thing...I told them I intended to make a million dollars in that year's time. Even though I had no idea *how* I would make that million.

Well, of course they laughed at me—wouldn't you?

As you can probably see from the title of this chapter, this story has a happy ending. At the time, however, nobody knew how it would come out. Do you know what it's like to have your father praying *against* your success? My dad thought I was so crazy that he asked God every day for me to fail as a real estate investor so I can go back to the police force.

Instead, I transformed my life and achieved things I never thought I would (and things I even never thought I was capable of).

But let's start by going back to the beginning...and to the years that led up to this pivotal moment.

FAMILY FIRST

It was nine years ago that it happened—the event that triggered the huge changes to follow. My wife was not happy about my long hours at the police department. One night, she told me this wasn't working out for her or our two small children. My mind was always elsewhere and she felt alone as a parent and as a wife. The situation had also started to affect her health and our relationship. She wanted me find another way to make a living.

I loved my family so much that I had to make the change. I had to find a way to work that provided me with enough time and enough money to enjoy our lives. But I was very scared to let my career go. The stress began to take a heavy toll on me, my health, my work performance and my happiness.

That's why, in 2005, I went to see my superiors for that fateful meeting; I wanted an unpaid leave of absence to be able to explore my options. I was lucky to get their approval.

Now, I had to do everything in my power to *not* come back to the job I dearly loved.

FINDING A NEW FIELD MAKING A NEW MINDSET

So, how does an ex-platoon commander go out and make a million dollars in one year? That was literally the million dollar question.

Just like so many other people in my position, I began by evaluating as many businesses and franchise opportunities as I could. The norm for a new business, however, seemed to be a lot of hard work for not a lot of money. This wouldn't work for me; so, I kept hunting.

And then, like magic, it happened.

I saw an ad about making money in real estate and I realized this was the way for me to go. You could make money and still have time to enjoy life. Of course, once again, there were a few "small" obstacles in my way–like the fact that I had absolutely no experience or any contacts in the business.

I started to attend personal growth training sessions, participated in several weekend boot camps and started to read personal growth books, like *Rich Dad, Poor Dad* by Robert Kiyosaki, *Unlimited Power* by Tony Robbins and *Secrets of the Millionaire Mind*, by T. Harv Eker.

But the book that became my "bible" was *Think and Grow Rich*. Using some of its principals, I set my goal of making a million dollars in a year, and I posted that goal all over the walls of my house. I was also bold enough to share it with other people, including some of my friends. Most reacted with disbelief, ready to laugh at my "impossible dreams." They thought I had gone crazy. Real estate pros told me what I intended to do was impossible.

So, it was unanimous. Failure was my certain destination—at least in everyone else's mind.

MAKING MONEY WITHOUT MONEY

You probably already guessed that I *did* succeed in my own personal "Mission: Impossible" scenario. Well, almost...I didn't make a million dollars in my first year. When all was said and done, it turned out I only made $980,000! I thought that was close enough.

But the most amazing thing I accomplished in that year, the thing that people constantly ask me about (and that got the attention of the media who referred to me as "The Wealthy Cop") was that *I bought and sold 77 properties in one year - without any experience, and made (almost) a MILLION doing it!!!*

The questions I get are...

- How could I possibly do 77 real estate deals in one year without any experience?

- How did I find good deals when the market was hot?

- How did I invest in real estate with no money? How did I raise the money from other people?

- How did I make so *much* money?

Well, you are in for a treat—as, for the first time outside one of my seminars or coaching sessions, I'm going to answer those very questions in this chapter. But I warn you, it may sound a bit crazy to you and even too simple. But, as my students will tell you, it works for them. It can work for you as well.

MY FIRST BIG BREAKTHROUGHS

You're probably already aware that there are so many real estate investing seminars out there, all charging good money to teach you how to supposedly make *great* money.

That's where I began learning.

But—and this is a BIG but—*the number one thing I decided to do* was to attend these meetings to find people who were active investors and find people who were looking to make money in real estate but didn't want to work very hard.

The idea became so simple that I said to myself, "Why isn't everyone doing it?" I started to attend more training sessions, real estate seminars and boot camps. The idea was to take away a few good ideas from the trainer but, more importantly, to network with people there.

It is important to understand that the people who had money to be at the training sessions were the type of people I wanted to connect with. I basically found three types of people. One, there were those who were simply "dreamers" and wouldn't act on what they learned. Second, there were passive investors who wouldn't take action because of fear. Third, there were *active* investors who could be my mentors.

I would come to the training sessions about half-hour before the start and find out what the attendees wanted. For example, if an active investor was looking for a down payment partner, I would joint venture with them by lending them *my* money. This way, I got to see them in action, earned real-life experience, made some money and got to know their "power team."

Also, I met many good people who intended to become financially-free but lacked the direction and courage to do it. They became my investors because I got them properties with huge potential to make money for them.

I finally realized that I could take as many advance courses in real estate investments as I wanted, but what it really boiled down to was this:

People were either looking for investors or they were looking for good deals.

Now, I'm not a rocket scientist, but I recognize the formula for success:

Find out what people want and give it to them. It became apparent that I had to become an expert on either finding good properties or finding investors. Ideally, *both*.

As I got further into learning about how real estate worked, I realized the mistake most rookie investors like myself made was that they chased after the money and then tried to find deals. That didn't make sense. Who's going to give you money when you have little experience and nothing to offer? I had to find something to bring to the table. And that's how I learned the biggest lesson of my life...

...you can always find an investor if you have an outstanding deal in place.

Now, most people will say, "I want the investors lined up first."

Trust me, you *will* have investors lined up once you have a track record. But when starting out, put together the deal to buy the property first with the proper escape clauses (like "conditional upon financing" or due diligence). These must be great deals which will make investors really hungry to invest.

The realization that finding an amazing deal was the most important part of becoming wealthy motivated me to do flips, joint ventures, no-money-down deals, rentals, assignments and hard money lending. I needed to establish myself as the trusted source of getting properties that were either way below market value or produced great positive cash flow. Again, the ideal was to do *both*.

How did I find great deals?

Simple.

I replaced the familiar real estate motto of "Location, location, location" with "Relationship, relationship, relationship."

I found these deals from the active investors whom I met at the boot camps and at real estate investment clubs. I even paid thousands of dollars for training just so I could have access to the people who knew about great deals and to find qualified joint venture partners.

So, what was a good deal to me?

I looked for properties that required minor upgrades. These were properties that needed to be painted, minor repairs to the kitchen/washroom, a change of carpet and more "curb appeal." I would buy the property at below-market value and further build equity into it by improving its looks.

Once these homes had their makeovers, I would find good renters and management companies. Then I would prepare an investors' package which had a summary, photos and sample pro forma documents. The idea was to make buying in so simple and easy for investors that they had no reason to pass up the opportunity. Think about it this way: they were getting properties that were fixed-up, cleaned, and already tenanted—like a Christmas present all wrapped up with a big bow on top.

MORE MONEY-MAKING SECRETS

Again, I wanted to make money. A lot of money.

I realized that in order for me to make a lot of money, I had to think like a book author. An author doesn't generate very much income selling *one* book—he or she makes the big bucks by selling *millions* of books. I knew, from the connections I had made, that the most successful real estate investors buy more properties.

As I hired people to do the work on the properties I was buying (I am not a handyman), I had more time to devote to finding more great deals and lining up more investors.

To buy multiple properties, however, I had to have as much money at my immediate disposal as possible, especially since I was finding deals first and getting investors after the fact. Fortunately, I also realized it was easier to get money when you have a job as opposed to when you own your own business.

So, before I left the police department, I went to the banks to set up a line of credit. For the first time in my life, I was able to get close to $200,000 by using several lines of credit. I like lines of credit because you don't need to go back for an approval after a flip or re-financing of a property. You can keep using your money again and again while paying little interest.

OTHER PEOPLE'S MONEY

Yes, it's easy for me today to find real estate investors, because I have a proven track record. In fact, I now have too many people lining up to lend me their money or buy great properties. But back then, being a newbie with little experience, it was a little more difficult. Okay, a *lot* more difficult.

So, how did I find my investors the first year?

Well, in addition to networking at the real estate seminars, I connected with people I already knew. The idea was never to approach them directly for money, but, instead, send out group emails to all the people on my list about a new lucrative deal.

Here is sample email:

"I have an amazing property that is fixed up, rented, managed, and will make you $500 per month. Respond now…"

One important question I often get asked during my coaching sessions is, "How did you build your list?"

The short answer is, through many different sources; training sessions, newspaper ads, social media, giving away free reports and simply networking. It was very important for me to build a "quality" list.

IS IT GOOD TIME TO BUY PROPERTIES TODAY?

Whether you want to help others make lot of money or you want to buy properties for yourself, the time to jump in is NOW!

As I say to my students, when your favorite store is having 50% off sale, what do you do?

Well, real estate is on sale in the U.S. today and you should buy as many properties as possible, especially if you know how to get them with little or no money down.

In my seminars, people tell me they want to become financially-free or they want to make $10,000 per month positive cash flow. My answer to them is, "Why aren't you taking action? Making that $10,000 per month is much easier today than it was in 2007, when the prices were high. Today, I am buying all fixed-up homes with 20% cash-on-cash returns for only 25K. You can buy these houses whether you live in the U.S., Canada or any other part of the world as long as you have a trusted source and a good management company.

So, there you have it. Now, it's *your* time to become wealthy. And to me, being wealthy means having lots of money, having lots of time, being surrounded by true and successful friends, being healthy and being in the position to give back to this world.

Before I sign off, I like to give you my digit book, *Make Big Bucks With Discounted Properties* along with some surprise gifts. You can get it right now by going to: www.PrivateInvestmentClub.ca/dp

I wish you peace, happiness and lots of money.

About Sunil

Sunil Tulsiani is fast becoming a familiar face on TV, newspapers and magazines, gaining fame for the success of his real estate investment company and his work as a real estate investment coach. But Sunil Tulsiani didn't start out as a real estate mogul. In fact, he once lived a very different life–as a Police Officer.

Sunil dreamed of being just like the cops he admired on TV, in movies and in real life. He worked hard to make that dream a reality by finally earning a spot as an officer with the Ontario Provincial Police. There, he expanded his crime-fighting skills by taking criminal, auto theft and drug investigation courses and working his way up the ladder.

Sunil remained on the force for over 15 years, serving as a uniformed officer, a police detective, a police negotiator and finally as a platoon commander. But while he was living out his childhood dream, his family was not exactly sharing the joy. The long hours, involving rotating shifts, meant his wife was basically on her own raising their two young children. When she finally told him, "It's me or the badge," Sunil knew it was time for a change.

That's when this top cop began the transition to real estate mogul.

Within that first year, Sunil invested in 77 properties–and while he didn't make his million-dollar target, he made close to $980,000. Today, he is the first cop in the Toronto area to become a real estate millionaire. And he's using his knowledge of how he–an ordinary person with no real estate background–did it to help others change their own lives financially.

To that end, Sunil has created the elite Real Estate Investment Club, a private investment club in the Toronto area (www.privateinvestmentclub.ca), and serves as a mentor and coach to other aspiring real estate investors, offering them an inside entry to this lucrative world.

Sunil's personal philosophy is, "Money doesn't buy happiness—but it sure does help." His new life has allowed him to work less and spend more time with his family, and also allowed him a completely different perspective of the world, one that comes from the point of view of abundance and positivity. He secretly gives back to the people in India that are in need, and enjoys, in his spare time, watching movies, playing squash, traveling and visiting family whenever possible.

He continues to be dedicated to his own personal development by learning from the most successful people in their fields, and his passion continues to grow for coaching, public speaking and creating incredible real estate deals for himself and his students.

Interesting fact is that Sunil's first book under the famous banner of the *Wealthy Cop* is not yet released, and yet over $25,000 worth of copies have already been pre-sold. If you want to reserve your own copy along with over $500 in bonuses, send an email to CEO@PrivateInvestmentClub.ca immediately.

CHAPTER 17

Success is a State of Mind

By Sylvia Runkle

Everything is energy and that's all there is to it. Match the frequency of the reality you want and you cannot help but get that reality. It can be no other way. This is not philosophy. This is physics.

Quote attributed to Albert Einstein*

Not long ago I had the opportunity to work with a client I will call Alex. Since I do long distance programs, he could be from anywhere in the world. Alex was depressed and was looking for change in his professional life. He had two businesses. Both were reasonably successful. But, both took a lot of time to make an adequate living. He made adequate money but had little time for his family and to enjoy life. He felt he had to choose and expand one business and make it more profitable or to begin another business altogether and in either case find a way to spend less time and make more money. I began to talk to him about energies and beliefs.

I taught him to control his energy field. We searched for limiting beliefs. I introduced the concept of "Quantum Shift" as a new belief that could replace outdated, unuseful beliefs. He was enrolled for a nine-week hypnosis and coaching program. We started with self-esteem and worked on beliefs, particularly the belief that you have to work hard to earn a good living.

As the sessions progressed, he felt less and less depressed but still did not know which direction to go. Due to scheduling conflicts, his final session was put off for two weeks. The third week he had his final coaching session. He expressed how glad he was that the session had been put off. He had not wanted to have to tell me that although he felt better, he still did not have what he was looking for.

A couple of days prior to the final session, he happened to speak with someone who was a part of an investor group he had applied to some years before. He had been turned down at the time. He was told that the group had been planning to contact him regarding the earlier request. The group had continued to follow his progress over the years and had decided they were ready to not only invest but to make his business the largest of its type in the area. But they required he give up the second business.

Shortly after that call he received a second call from someone marginally involved in the second business, wanting to take over that business, for his own purposes. "In a moment," Alex's life had changed. He had his direction, he had support, and already time was freed up. He thanked me and said, "This is the life I have always dreamed of—right now!"

"In a moment." This is the way "quantum" shifts happen and success in business or in life is often a quantum type shift. In this chapter, we will explore what has to happen internally for that "Quantum Shift" to occur; for our energies to align with the energies of that which we desire. You will find step-by-step techniques to move into the "success state of mind." First we need to look at what stops it from happening now. Most commonly it consists of one or more of the following:

- Lack of awareness, training, or opportunity.
- Limiting beliefs
- Fear

All three of these interact. Any one of them can create or contribute to the others. Number one is straightforward. Sometimes it is just a matter of learning where to search. But if we do not believe we could do it when we find it, we either won't bother to search, or we will not recognize an opportunity when it is there. Fear, as well, will keep us from searching or even to attempt it if we find it. All of these are reflected in the energy field.

Beliefs:

"In the province of the mind, what one believes to be true, either is true or becomes true, within certain limits. These limits are to be discovered experimentally or experientially. When so determined, these limits are found to be further beliefs to be transcended."

—John C. Lily, "Programming and Metaprogramming
in the Human Biocomputer"**

Limiting beliefs are huge barriers to success. We can do everything we believe we can do and no more. I visualize my other-than-conscious mind as a little guy (for some unknown reason he is Chinese) at diaphragm level on a computer keyboard. My face is the monitor screen. On the screen is whatever seven plus or minus two bits of information he chooses to direct my attention to at the moment. That is a miniscule bit of information out of all of the reality in and around me. He knows my beliefs and simply will not waste precious screen space on something he knows I will not act on due to a belief I hold.

Once you change a limiting belief, it is as if reality changes around you. Suddenly your attention is being directed to new possibilities. It seems as if the world has changed. Beliefs are the frames you put around your experience. Changing limiting beliefs greatly expands the frame you exist in, allowing for greater and richer experience in your life.

Beliefs are easy to change once you learn to identify them. In my workshop, *"Take the Money and Run – Your Life,"* we identify participant's beliefs and then we change them. Participants consistently report huge changes after the experience. I use the Tarot deck, not for psychic prediction, but because of the rich imagery that helps to elicit beliefs. We focus mainly on the first card in the Major Arcana: the Magician. The Magician, the ability to master physical reality, represents the first lesson in the "Fool's Journey" through life.

Getting a "belief buddy" is a great way to start. Begin listening to each other in casual conversation and point out each time a limiting belief is expressed. Even better, identify and change the belief. Start out with the *"I can't*'s." These are easy and life transforming. When you catch yourself or your buddy saying, "I can't...," stop and change it to "Up until now I haven't been able to....". (Stop right here and repeat those two phrases, even without anything specific at the end, notice how different each feels in your body as you say them. If you can feel the difference, you already know the feeling of the possibility of success; you are already on your way.) When you use the present perfect tense it stops the action just before the present and opens your future to possibility! And the little guy on the keyboard goes, "Cool! Now I can show you all the opportunities where you can." And thus reality shifts around you.

Some common beliefs that inhibit success:

"I have to work hard to have money."

"Poor people are good people, rich people are bad people."

"I don't know how to be rich."

"If I have money I will have to change my lifestyle and friends."

"My identity is tied up with pride in my ability to live well with little money."

"If I have money everyone will start asking for some of it and I won't know how to say, "No."

"I can never be successful."

"I will always be poor."

"I will always struggle for money."

Changing Beliefs:

Once you identify a belief, the next step is to change it to something more useful. Often just bringing a limiting belief into consciousness is enough to shift the belief. If you already have enough evidence that the opposite is true, it changes automatically. There are many great techniques for changing beliefs. Some of my favorites are Robert Dilts' 'Slight of Mouth' patterns, or Connierae Andreas' 'Reversing Presuppositions', or the 'Walk-Through' belief change. I recommend NLP training or one of the excellent belief change books in the field. I have included a simple yet powerful belief change process in the next section for you to use, along with a hypnosis script that you can record and listen to often.

When embracing new beliefs, it is important that you define those that will benefit you. You want to have confidence, but confidence without competence will be useless. A more useful belief is that you have the confidence to obtain the training and skill you will need for success. Know what you can do and what you need to learn.

Fear:

Fear often stops you from moving forward and reaching your goals. Fear of failure, fear of success, fear of ridicule, etc. Those who see auras tell us the fear shows up as dark spots in the energy field. Also, fear causes us to draw the energy field in tightly around us. (When we say we feel 'uptight,' it is literally true.) Sometimes I see the work I do as clearing and expanding the energy field. When the energy field shifts, your experience shifts. I have often demonstrated how when there are internal shifts such as belief change, the aura will change. And, in the converse, when you shift the aura, internal shifts such as belief change occur.

Did you know that words can shift your energy field and change a belief? Going back to the difference in feeling between simply stating, "I can't…" and "Up until now I haven't been able to…," that shift in feeling is accompanied by a sizable shift in the auric field. So the shifts can happen either way. Even though you cannot see the aura, you can still learn to manipulate it. I recommend standing for this exercise:

Put yourself in 'neutral.' Relax and clear your mind.

Remember a time you felt fear or were very stressed or 'uptight' about something. Put yourself back into the memory. See what you were seeing, hear what you were hearing and feel what you were feeling. What do you believe about yourself and your ability to succeed at this moment?

Now, return to the neutral state by remembering what you wore two days ago.

1. Remember a time you felt fear or were very stressed or 'uptight' about something. Put yourself back into the memory. See what you were seeing, hear what you were hearing and feel what you were feeling. What do you believe about yourself and your ability to succeed at this moment?

2. Now take the time to remember what you wore two days ago, and go back into neutral.

3. Remember a time you felt great. You felt 'expanded.' Put yourself back into that experience. Increase the full experience by imagining you are turning up a dial like a thermostat. Build it as strongly as feels right for you. Imagine your energy field expanding beyond the walls of the room.

4. Holding this state, think about what caused the earlier fear or 'uptight' feeling. Notice how different it now is; how much more resourceful you feel. What is it you believe to be true for you now?

5. Take the time to remember what you had for lunch three days ago, and go back into neutral.

6. Imagine an experience in the future that would normally shrink and tighten your aura. Imagine expanding your field and going through the experience.

7. Notice how you are now in control of your experience, or at least how you react to and handle your experience. And that is a new belief, isn't it?

SUMMARY

If you would like to live "the life you have dreamed of," like Alex, first get a "belief buddy". Identify old beliefs and what you would like to believe instead. Change the beliefs using the 7-step process above. Below is a hypnosis process that will reinforce and enhance the changes, setting you on your path to success. Record this, adding anything that would enhance it for you, and listen to it often. (Do not listen to it while driving.)

HYPNOSIS SCRIPT FOR SUCCESS STATE OF MIND.

Remember a time you were deeply relaxed. Move back into that memory of deep relaxation. See what you were seeing, hear what you were hearing and feel what you were feeling. On your next breath, take a deep breath in and hold it to the mental count of three. When you let go, just let go. Let go of all stress, let go of all strain, let go of anything that has been stopping you from accessing all the success that is possible for you at this time.

Allow all limiting beliefs, both conscious and unconscious, to float to the surface and then to float away into the distance. Watch them go and as they go notice a wonderful feeling of lightness as well as a new feeling of excitement and anticipation, an unusual sense of pending possibilities. Know that all things are possible for you, coming at the rate that is just right for you.

Take a moment now to decide on what you want to occur first. Think about what you want and realize what it is you will have when you have that. What will having it get you. And after all, that is really what you want, isn't it?

Make any adjustments that need to be made to get it just right for you. Move your mind into the future when you have had this success for one year. Feel the rhythms and tones of that reality. Resonate with it. Then look back to the moment of change. Become aware of how easy it was. Notice what you did first. How the change happened. This is your blue-print for more change in the future and you will continue to change and attract more success in your life. It is becoming a habit with you.

So once again, resonate with this experience (pause about 30 seconds). Now bring that state of being all the way back to the present moment, taking three deep breaths to fully integrate it into who you are now. Allow that state of being to touch and transform every cell. Allow it to extend beyond the skin into the energy field that surrounds you. And your energy field becomes bigger and brighter and clearer, and more vibrant, and you become more of an attractor in the universe for everything that is just right for you. That's right.

If you are listening to this and it is a time for sleep you will void out all waking suggestions, and drift off into a deep, healing sleep where you will dream the amazing dreams of your bright and successful future and awaken in the morning with the changes in place. Or, if it is a time to be awake, wide wide awake, you will begin the journey back to wakefulness – but you will be able to return back fully wide awake, only as slowly as your unconscious mind fully processes all the suggestions made here today, and generates them into your behavior upon awakening. So, taking all the time you need, returning back, wide, wide awake, looking forward to the changes, the successful changes, you will discover in your life upon awakening.

*This quote appeared on Facebook in the form of a poster, attributed to Albert Einstein, but no specific source was given.

**John C. Lily, <u>Programming and Metaprogramming in the Human Biocomputer</u>, Crown Publishers, Inc., New Your, 1972

About Sylvia

Sylvia Runkle is known as "The hypnotist/coach/trainer who helps people move from where they are now to more than they dreamed." Sylvia has been facilitating generative and transformational change with thousands of clients for over 30 years.

Sylvia is a coach, psychotherapist, master hypnotist, and international NLP (Neurolinguistic Programming) trainer.

Having studied the inner workings of the mind since the sixties, she has trained under some of the premier mind masters alive today; Richard Bandler, John Grinder, Judith DeLozier, Robert Dilts, David Gordon, Patrick Porter, Raymond Aaron and many others. She especially treasures having received a personal blessing from Mother Teresa shortly before her passing.

Giving trainings around the world, Sylvia has particularly enjoyed the opportunity to present Hypnosis and NLP certification trainings in Russia and Kazan. She says, "It is so exciting to introduce change techniques in a country that is already rapidly changing."

No stranger to the media, her work has been the subject of numerous newspaper articles and radio and TV interviews. Sylvia's contributions to the fields of NLP and hypnosis include nine published articles and she was the recipient of the 2001 Positive Changes Hypnosis Porter Award.

Known for her ability to facilitate rapid change in clients, she now offers long-distance hypnosis and coaching programs and is available to clients worldwide.

In addition to Hypnosis and NLP trainings, one of her most popular programs is, "Take the Money and Run – Your Life!" This is an interactive workshop where participants learn to identify and transform limiting beliefs, and to become attractors of success in whatever form they define it.

To learn more about Sylvia Runkle and how you, too can access "more than you dreamed" or sponsor a training in your area, visit www.sylviarunkle.com
or call 309-716-2111.

FREE BONUS: You can download an audio file of the Success Script in Sylvia's voice at: www.sylviarunkle.com

CHAPTER 18

Success Means Adapting Constantly (Without Complaining)

By Tom Foster of Foster Web Marketing

We all have a story to tell—the single woman with three children in the booth next to you at the restaurant; the man with one leg in line in front of you at the dry cleaner; the homeless woman on the street with her trusty dog. We usually are mildly curious at the circumstances, but unless we have similarities, we don't think about them for long.

Everyone has a story that makes them unique and transforms them into who they are today. So, why is my story worth listening to? I will let you be the judge. My story might be similar to yours, or not at all. Either way, there are always nuggets to learn from others' successes and mistakes, and these things are what made me the man I am today.

Like many, my parents divorced when I was in my early teens and I went through a period of confusion and chaos. I got into a lot of trouble—drinking and drugs, getting kicked out of schools and moving from parents and then friends' homes when I overstayed my welcome. No one really wanted my drama and looking back, I can hardly blame them. By my senior year in high school I had no ambition, college plans, or job prospects. Mostly out of desperation and the fact the Marine recruiter was really good at his job, I made a life-changing decision to join the Marines when I was still a senior in high school.

175

Little did I know the following six years I spent in the Marines would teach me so much about life and how people behave. Now, I am no hero, not like Marines of today. I did not see any "action"; I did not shoot anyone or get shot at. My entire tour was during peacetime and I was on my way out into civilian life by the time we invaded Iraq the first time in Desert Storm. What Marines are doing today is not what we did from 1985 to 1991. It was a very complacent time; there were many older Marines I reported to who were living for retirement and liked things to just be status quo. I got a sense of this early on and it frustrated me. But, even so, at a young age, I thought I had my life mapped out. I would make the Marines my career. But, life doesn't always turn out the way you originally plan—it often plays out better.

It didn't take long for me to realize I had a passion for technology, which was cultivated during my days as a Marine. I just wanted to make all these systems I found better. Smarter guys taught me how to do things I was interested in and these little projects would occupy the time. That is when my initial technology skills started, as I was stationed in Top Secret Military Communications Centers around the world. Once I was discharged, my career path took some wild turns.

Can you remember what it was like in the early 90s? It was when technology was evolving, but the Internet was still not widely used. It was before Windows had taken off and DOS-based software ruled, but with no distribution. Except Egghead stores, everything was sold directly by software company representatives over the phone or through catalogs. I got a job selling DOS-based translation software that sold for $1,000 per direction! English to Spanish, $1,000. You want Spanish to English? Another $1,000. I earned 100% commission and made $350 per sale. It was awesome—I went from making $12, 500 per year as a Marine to $50,000. Yay, capitalism! I was a happy kid with a new wife and family.

With a head for technology and a heart for marketing, I embarked in sales within the IT industry. Soon thereafter, Microsoft Windows was born; software retailer distribution was growing. One of my first jobs was in distributing software solutions to retail chains, like Best Buy and CompUSA. As an ambitious twenty-something, I thought I found what I was to do for the rest of my life. However, things happened and that door slammed shut. The retail software boom was a quick one. Here and gone. I made great money, but like so many others, I found myself without an industry and not many prospects. With a family to provide for, I knew I had to adapt or I was going to get left behind.

At some point in life, we all go through those pivotal moments where we have to decide what we are going to do next. Maybe one opportunity disappears or an unwanted change in business pops up—those are the crucial days and weeks you to decide whether you want to be an adapter or a complainer. The adapter takes each crazy twist and turn in life as a chance to do things better and bigger. The complainer laments over the way things used to be and struggles to look at the potential that the future can bring.

When the new millennium arrived, the World Wide Web was being accessed in just about every household and businesses were starting to recognize the opportunity the Internet presented. I saw an opportunity and jumped in by starting a Web development company. My business was anything but sophisticated in the beginning. I was a one-man shop working out of the basement. But boy, did things change fast. Before I knew it, I had a large client database mainly consisting of attorneys who were looking to me to not only develop their websites, but to also help them market. It was another change and another opportunity. As a result, I created a robust content management program, Dynamic Self Syndication (DSS), which is what my company is best known for today. Now, I have a full-fledged Web marketing company with employees spanning the globe (and let's just say I am no longer working in the basement)!

I can't claim I have *always* been an adapter, as there have been times in my life where all I wanted to do was complain about the unwelcome surprises that came my way. Yet in business, I fought hard to adapt, no matter what was thrown my way. I have had the pleasure of working with all kinds of people throughout the years and I have recognized some common traits that separate those who are successful from those who are not. Those who find the most success are able to change their courses when needed and identify opportunities as they arise.

My business revolves around Web marketing—talk about an industry that is constantly changing, where you have to be ready for what the next day will bring. I can't tell you how many people have called my office and complained that the way they approached their business, specifically their marketing, won't work anymore. Some of these individuals spend the whole phone call complaining that Yellow Pages *used* to be a goldmine for them or that television commercials were *once* major lead generators. However, the tides changed and their target audience was no longer listening. These conversations generally go one of two ways: 1. The person recognizes that marketing is no longer the same and is ready to make the shift or 2. The person wants some kind of reassurance that the old way of doing things will once again work. The first group, the adapters as I like to think of them, are the ones who are able to live life to the fullest by recognizing when to change and being proactive.

From my experience and working with so many great businessmen and women, I can tell you that there are three major advantages of taking on the role of an adapter. It doesn't matter your line of work, these benefits apply to any industry.

1. ADAPTING TO CHANGE GIVES YOU A COMPETITIVE ADVANTAGE.

Most people don't like change. In fact, some people despise it—that is why there are so many books, motivational messages and philosophies all wrapped around embracing it. We get comfortable in our ways, like how things are going in our lives, and want nothing more than to know what the next day will bring. That is not real life and it is certainly not the way that business goes. If you are in the business world, you have to learn what it means to truly adapt, but there is a further step you need to take. You need to *understand the importance of being an early adapter* too. Things will change in your industry, especially in how you market. Your competitors might not be ready to alter their course, but if you do, you will have a competitive advantage.

One of my clients is a medical malpractice attorney in New York. Back when video on the Internet was a fairly new concept, he recognized that the way he markets his practice might need to change too. He recognized that the old way of marketing wasn't working for him anymore, so he adapted. This client started producing Web videos that answered questions, explained solutions to problems and otherwise addressed his target audience directly. He was an early adapter. When some of his competitors were still scrambling to create websites, he was out there shooting videos to post on the Internet. The result? He started getting more phone calls from leads than he could have ever imagined. His solo practice turned into a major profit center. He could have sat back and complained that the marketing he had done before wasn't working, but instead he adapted and reaped the benefits.

Did your parents used to reminisce about how the music was better in their day or the cost of gas used to be a quarter? It was so annoying to hear the laments over the "good old days," yet, if you are like me, you now do the same thing to your children! Whether you do it in your personal life or not, you should not have this same mentality in business.

Do you remember when you used to pull out the local telephone book when you needed to hire a plumber? It probably didn't seem long ago that you would only know about the upcoming movies because of the ads in the newspaper or previews on television. Now, you use your iPad to find a plumber and smart phone to look up movies in your area. Things have changed. Your children won't even remember life before the Internet, social media, YouTube and iPhones. Ten to fifteen years ago, no one watched videos online. Now, over 4 billion videos are viewed a day on YouTube. What about social media? Your car is likely older than Facebook, however that social media website now has 845 million active users.

The important lesson is to know when to jump in before your competitors. Most people are slow to change when needed, but you don't have to be one of them. Be an early adapter.

2. ADAPTING TO CHANGE EXPANDS YOUR MARKET REACH.

Ninety-seven percent of consumers are using the Internet to find local businesses. That means only 3 percent are *not* using the Internet to locate products and services in their area. This statistic might be hard to believe, considering it wasn't long ago when everyone was working off of a dial-up modem.

Learning how to adapt in business and the changing marketplace can do wonders for your bottom line. If you were trying to decide where to set up your store, would you pick the location where 97 percent of your customers are located or in an area where there are only about 3 percent? Hopefully, the answer is obvious. Don't make a big mistake by assuming that since the location where 3 percent of your customers are situated used to be an amazing spot, you have to go back. Adapt and go where your clients are. If you can adapt to change, you can expand your market reach.

In the past, if you wanted to reach thousands upon thousands of prospects, you had to be prepared to spend a lot of money. You would have to mortgage your house to simply create a television commercial or two that you hoped would get in front of your target customers. The Internet has changed the landscape for businesses. Companies of all sizes can compete fairly, even on small budgets, to reach clients. You can also spend the same amount of money and reach either a few customers in the neighborhood or thousands of people around the globe. Video marketing, blogging and social media are giving voices and personalities to businesses throughout the world. Videos are going viral and being viewed by millions. Blogging is giving business owners a platform to spread their marketing message. These changes don't seem so bad, do they?

We have clients who have been able to position themselves in the center of breaking news by adapting to the new opportunities that the Internet provides. They have gotten their messages heard on major television shows, radio programs and in newspapers. These clients have been quoted and featured in the *Wall Street Journal*, CNN, *Huffington Post* and other huge media outlets. Instead of complaining about how publicity used to be handled, they used their blogs, videos and social media networks to get in front of the world. They are adapters who recognized how to expand their market reach. You can do the same.

3. ADAPTING TO CHANGE GIVES YOU A BETTER BUSINESS (AND PERSONAL) LIFE.

When we were children, we dreamed about what we wanted to do when we grew up. Our aspirations were usually not small. You may have wanted to become an astronaut, scientist or President of the United States. The sky is the limit when we are young, but somewhere along the way our mindset becomes different. Life throws so many unexpected things our way that we start to question what we can and cannot do. If you can master how to effectively adapt to change, you will have a better business and personal life.

Who said you can't have what you always dreamed of? All you need to do to achieve such a monumental goal is to decide what you want your life to look like and make the changes needed to get there. Be ready to adapt and gain more control over your destiny.

I have witnessed firsthand how some of my clients have done just that. They have made the conscious decision of how many hours they want to work each week, what type of clients they want to work with and how they want their businesses to run. One such client has a DUI defense practice in Virginia. He used to do what he refers to as "random acts of marketing," hoping that his phone would ring. At some point he realized that it was time to adapt to the real world of marketing. He decided whom he wanted as a client, how many hours he was willing to pour in each week and the amount of money he wanted to make each year. Then, he adapted his marketing to his goals. It worked for him and it can work for you. You need to be able to change your mindset, your marketing and your business. Life is just not long enough to sit back and complain that things are not how you want them to be. Do something about it.

You might have noticed that adapting and Web marketing were intermingled throughout these main points. The reason is that they go hand and hand. You have to be in the habit of adapting to your circumstances and going where your clients are. If you are in business, that means you have to embrace the changing wave of Web marketing, as everything revolves around the Internet. That is how you will succeed.

About Tom

Tom Foster is a nationally recognized Internet marketing specialist and founder of Foster Web Marketing. He has authored several books, including *Explode Your Practice Through Internet Marketing: A How-To Guide for Attorneys, Secrets of Social Media for Attorneys Revealed: Mission 101* and *How Smart Lawyers are Using Video on the Web to Get More Cases Without Breaking the Bank.*

Tom entered the world of technology in 1991, after serving a six-year tour in the Marines. Over the past two decades, he has become known as *the* expert in Web marketing. He has been featured on numerous television stations, including affiliates of CBS, NBC, ABC and FOX. In addition, he has been invited to speak for various organizations, such as the American Association for Justice, Great Legal Marketing, Virginia Trial Lawyers Association, Virginia Women Attorneys Association and Top Practices.

Tom has grown Foster Web Marketing from a small Web design company into a large, multi-faceted corporation that now offers a range of services—from website design to Web video production.

CHAPTER 19

Optimism on Purpose

By Troy Singer

"The best way to not feel hopeless is to get up and do something. Don't wait for good things to happen to you. If you go out and make some good things happen, you will fill the world with hope, you will fill yourself with hope."

— President Barack Obama

Optimism is a spring of hope gushing forward, convinced it can become a roaring waterfall. I am not talking the type of optimism that smacks of Utopian sunshine and rainbows—although that has its place too—I am talking about *deliberate optimism*. Deliberate optimists practice their craft daily. They intentionally build their lives around a belief that success and failure are both completely in our control.

I will teach you the steps to deliberate optimism. These are precise steps that you can begin today to change your own life. Do something. Make things happen for yourself.

RE-BIRTH YOURSELF

No matter how dirty your past is, your future is still spotless.

Let's face it: everyone begins life with the baggage of the family, location or economic circumstances into which they were born. The smartest, most successful people decide when and how to trade up to Louis Vuitton bags. The decision to live with deliberate optimism lies within each of us. I am not the most educated or well-read or handsomest man

I know, but people constantly tell me that they want my life. I tell them they can get their own!

The amazing thing about humans is their ability to evolve, re-birth themselves, if you will. You can choose to be a survivor or a 'thriver.' Survivors live with the things that come at them. They weather the storms of life and make it through. Thrivers anticipate the coming storms with enthusiasm; knowing rain produces rainbows. If you have a difficult time envisioning the rainbow because you cannot see past the storm, look to the role models around you. If you see it being done by someone else, then that proves it can be done. Re-birthing yourself puts YOU in control of who you are from your re-birth forward. The power of re-birth can be so strong that I have even known individuals who changed their name to signify the new person they have chosen to become.

You don't need a bad childhood or some horrible life experience to decide to re-birth yourself. You can begin your re-birth with the desire to have more and be more than you are today. Then you need to decide what you want out of this life and why you deserve it.

REVIEW CUSTOMIZED DAILY AFFIRMATIONS

Man's rise or fall, success or failure, happiness or unhappiness depends on his attitude… a man's attitude will create the situation he imagines. –James Lane Allen

Telling yourself who you are or plan to be on a daily basis will keep you focused on the prize. Create a detailed list of daily affirmations, both personal and professional, and read it to yourself every morning. Do not skip this step. Your affirmations might include employment goals such as increasing sales by 25% this quarter, personal goals like losing 10 lbs. this month or life goals such as defining what you desire in a life partner.

When I shared my personal affirmation list, "Troy's Daily Affirmations for an Extraordinary and Purposeful Life" with a few, select, people who I trust, their reaction has been "that sounds just like you!" But, does my list reflect me or do I now embody the list of affirmations of which I remind myself daily? Remember, your attitude creates what you imagine. We become aware of the things we notice or hear every day. Have you ever had the experience where you never noticed a particular type of car on the road until you read an article or see a memorable advertisement; then suddenly you see them everywhere? If you bring attention to what you desire you will find those opportunities all around you.

Lest you think that I am making this stuff up, I want to call your attention to a scientific study Tali Sharot wrote in *Time* magazine May 28, 2011, "The problem with pessimistic expectations, such as those of the clinically depressed, is that they have the power to alter the future; negative expectations shape outcomes in a negative way. How do expectations change reality?"

The answer came from a study which involved student subjects who were primed prior to taking a standardized test. Group A was primed with positive words such as intelligent, clever or smart. Group B was primed with words such as ignorant or stupid in order to induce expectations of failure. The researcher measured brain wave data for the students and found that students responded differently if they were primed with positive words than if they were primed with negative words. In fact, when a mistake was made in the test by a student who had heard the positive words, the student had increased activity in that part of the brain involved in self-reflection or recollection. Conversely, the students who were primed with negative words had NO heightened activity after a wrong answer. It appeared that their brains expected to do poorly and, therefore, creased to react with surprise or conflict when an error was made. If you thought the power of positive thinking is just hype, think again! Your body reacts in a quantifiable way to positive thoughts.

TEACH YOURSELF TO LIVE WITH PURPOSE

You've got to get up every morning with determination if you're going to go to bed with satisfaction — George Lorimer

If you look at the lives of optimists, you will rarely find people for whom life just "happened." It is far easier to remain optimistic when you have a clear idea of where you are going, how to get there, and why you want to get there to begin with.

So I want you to live deliberately, passionately and sincerely. To live deliberately, passionately and sincerely, you must know who you want to be. Take the time to discover what you want out of life and what truly makes you happy. Set some goals for yourself that you can measure. If you think you have heard this many times before, perhaps it is time for you to consider *why* so many people are telling you this. It works!

Your goals are different from your daily affirmations. Your daily affirmations outline what you want, what drives you. Your goals are the plan that will get you there. Living deliberately means living with purpose. It is impossible to live deliberately unless you have goals.

To harness the determination to live deliberately you will also need passion for what you are doing. Passion fuels your drive to succeed. If the desire isn't strong enough, you are setting yourself up for failure. Many personal failures can be attributed to not being "into" whatever it was we were doing.

To live with purpose you must also live sincerely. Being sincere means not only telling the truth to others, but it also means not lying to oneself. Be honest about what you want and need. On your most difficult days, being honest with yourself about why you want to be at work or in your relationships will help guide your actions to success in those areas.

DON'T LET FEAR TAKE THE DRIVER'S SEAT

One who fears failure limits his activities. Failure is only the opportunity to more intelligently begin again. – Henry Ford

I see people everyday who fear failure to the point of paralysis and who make self-deprecation an art form. They are *their own* worst enemy. I have an acquaintance I will call "Rita." Some people might look at Rita and think she has had a tough life. She isn't married, can barely pay her bills and has had health issues. What anyone who saw Rita on the street would not know is that Rita cancelled her last date because she had been burned in relationships before and was afraid to try again, she didn't put in for a promotion at work because she didn't believe she could do the job and didn't want to take a chance, and she is so worried about her health issues returning that she won't even go far from home. Rita's every sentence seems to start with "I can't because…"

Fear of failure can limit you or inspire you. It is said that Thomas Edison failed at creating the light bulb 999 times before succeeding on the 1000th attempt. Each time he failed, he told himself that he had just learned another way to not invent the light bulb. What can Rita, and you, learn from Thomas Edison? Every failure is a chance at greater success the next time. A failed relationship can mean learning what not to look for in your next date. A job that didn't work out can be viewed as a door that closed so that you can open a new and better one. Health fears can better be viewed as reasons to live even more for today.

Do not let fear of failure drive you to be your own worst enemy. Speak to yourself positively and remind yourself of your worth. The only difference between the cowardly lion and the king of the jungle is courage.

BEWARE THE LAW OF SELF-LIMITING BELIEFS

"Argue for your limitations, and sure enough they're yours." – Richard Bach

Imagine for a minute that you are the happy face at the center of the above diagram. That's where you are today; what you have accomplished thus far. The box outlined in black represents the actual boundaries of your capabilities. The larger, gray circle around you represents your self-limiting beliefs. Your self-limiting beliefs are what you think you can accomplish or what you think your boundaries of your capabilities are. The white area between your self-limitations and your actual limitations is your untapped potential.

Even if you only worked to the level of the potential you *think* you have, you still have a huge area in which to improve yourself daily. Your goal is to live more on the outside of your circle of self-limiting beliefs. Expand your sphere daily. You don't have to leave your comfort zone all at once. Expand daily. Today you can start with calling one client who you are convinced will say no. Tomorrow, call two. By being deliberately optimistic, you can expand your sphere, remove some of your self-limiting thought and propel your life into places you once thought were off limits.

BE MINDFUL OF, AND GRATEFUL FOR, WHAT YOU HAVE ACCOMPLISHED

If you count all your assets, you always show a profit. – Robert Quillen

You can't help but smile when you think of wonderful things you have accomplished in your life. You probably just thought of several and you are smiling now! That happy energy you feel when you think about your accomplishments is the same energy you must harness to become purposefully optimistic. If you had success once, you are capable of it again.

Make a formal list of wonderful things you've accomplished in your life. Your list might include something:

- As simple as helping a stranger in need to as formal as earning a high-level award.
- As historic as hitting a little league home run or winning a childhood competition to as recent as accomplishing something at work.
- Like being thankful for family, friends, home, job or material assets.

Why include things for which you are thankful? Being thankful grounds us, while giving us hope of being able to accomplish more. Even if your situation isn't exactly what you want it to be at that moment, there's almost always a way to look at the situation and find something for which to be thankful! The next part of your list should include the following phrase:

When I'm down [or when I remember] I think "I'm so happy and grateful that…" or, I simply look around where I am and say "Thank you." There's always something to be thankful for, it's just that we have to adjust our focus more often than not to recognize what's directly in front of us. Dissatisfaction and unhappiness often find us when we are so intent on pursuing the things we think will make us happy that we ignore the wonderful and deserving items right in front of us. Always be grateful!

Purposeful optimism will change your life. You have it in your power every day when you awake to choose how you will live your day. Will you choose to harness your hope and optimism and guide it to your advantage until success gushes forth a waterfall in your life? Optimism on purpose is a great circle that begins with you and who you plan to be, and ends at being thankful for who you are. Again, it begins and ends with *you*.

If you are unhappy where you are, don't wait for good things to happen to you. Do something. Take action to re-birth yourself and start over. Speak positive affirmations to yourself daily. Teach yourself to live with purpose. Don't let fear take over, and beware the law of self-limiting beliefs. But perhaps most important of all, be grateful of all that you have already accomplished.

About Troy

Troy Singer is a native Ohioan who loves living in Dayton Ohio. His true passions are Real Estate investing, golf, traveling, running and CrossFit. Troy also enjoys serving on committees for the Dayton United Way and the board of the Dayton Habitat for Humanity.

Troy co-authored the Best-selling "The New Masters or Real Estate" with Ron Le-Grand after meeting him in 2007. Since then, Troy has enthusiastically stayed within the wholesaling side of the business as a part-time investment and business venture.

In addition to Real Estate Investing, Troy is a trained sales professional with over 19 years experience in print and packaging sales. He currently works for the Hooven-Dayton Corp in a relationship manager role to the company's single largest customer. The Hooven-Dayton Corp is a label and flexible packaging printer in Dayton, Ohio.

You can contact Troy, visit www.TroySinger.com or call him at (937) 694-4393.

www.TroySinger.com

CHAPTER 20

The Success Secret

By William Jordan

How would you like to be on the annual Forbes list of the wealthiest people in the world? How about being ranked the 164th wealthiest person in the world? Would you feel pretty comfortable with a net worth of six billion dollars?

Well if you are Sean Quinn, once the wealthiest man in Ireland, you wouldn't feel so comfortable today. In November of 2011, Quinn filed for bankruptcy. Shockingly this was only three years after a 2008 Forbes report estimated his personal net worth to be approximately $6,000,000,000 (that's billion with a 'B').

Quinn would have been well served to read *The Success Secret* and apply a few simple steps for creating and preserving wealth. Success, financial or otherwise, depends on effectively analyzing the relationship between risk and reward in a given situation.

For Mr. Quinn, he literally bet the farm on a single investment in an Irish bank. He failed to apply my first rule of financial success, don't gamble with the money you need to live.

SECRETS TO MY SUCCESS

I'm a conservative guy. You should know that about me and perhaps a few other things. I'm a wealth manager who has had the good fortune to own my own firm and to have been featured as a guest on various financial oriented television programs as well as being quoted in everything from *The Wall Street Journal* to *Time* Magazine.

I've been fortunate enough to call the 2000 stock market top (though I was a year early), to advise my clients of the coming real estate disaster of the late 2000s (again almost a year early) and to be one of the few voices calling for a stock market recovery at the beginning of 2009. If I could boil down the secrets to my success, it would come down to a few simple principles.

Take the road less traveled. The majority of wealth managers, wall street firms and individual investors follow the herd and invest in the same investments at the same time. Usually you will do better by doing the opposite of what the herd is doing.

Never lose money. While it's almost impossible to completely avoid losing money, few wealth managers begin their investment evaluation process by asking themselves, how could this investment lose money? It's usually about how much can be made. This rule can be softened depending on your personal goals and comfort with risk.

Always be early. The common theme with my financial warnings to the public has been that I'm always early. No one can pick the absolute top of any market and when it comes to protecting your wealth, as well as striving for success, it is always better to be early than late.

Know where to take risk, and when to avoid it—too often I see risk being taken in the wrong place or with the wrong money. The right investment in the wrong place can be a disaster. This principle led to the creation of my unique investment allocation plan.

THE 7-7-7 SOLUTION

One of the keys to success is to realize that money is emotional. The 7-7-7 plan also recognizes that investments are divided into different categories based on the level of principal risk, income yield, liquidity and the potential for growth. As such, investments can not all be viewed as performing a similar role in a similar time frame for a client's financial plan.

The ultimate purpose of all investing is to create income. The question is, what do you want that income for? Retirement, college for the (grand)kids or increased travel are some of the common goals. Our challenge then is to maximize the eventual income with risk being taken where it is most appropriate (and limited, where it is least appropriate).

The resulting plan is designed to create the highest degree of confidence for our clients while allowing for the maximum income to be taken from their investments once they desire it. In addition, the 7-7-7 plan reduces the effect of unpredictable investment declines by taking only the most appropriate level of risk.

DESIGNING YOUR PLAN

Essentially the 7-7-7 plan divides a client's portfolio into three subaccounts. The Secure Account, the High Yield Account and the Growth Account.

The key to the three accounts is that all of a client's income (planned or unplanned) is designed to come only from one account at a time. The Secure Account is therefore invested only in extremely conservative investments which will cover 100% of the income needs of the client through spending both interest and principal during the next seven years.

The tremendous benefit of the 7-7-7 plan is you can know with certainty where any desired income will come from for the next 21 years. When I say this to my clients some will joke that they don't know if they will be here in 21 years, and yet you can see in every face how comforting it is to know they have a well designed income strategy which will last more than two decades.

At the end of the first seven years if a client was taking income, the Secure Account will have reached a zero balance, while the High Yield and Growth Accounts will have (presumably) grown in value since no income has been taken from them. The excess money in either of those two accounts would be used, depending on where the best performance was, to replenish the Secure Account and the process would repeat.

A SIGNIFICANT DIFFERENCE

For my average retired/retiring client a typical allocation would allow for the portfolio to generate an annual distribution of 5.91% while keeping up with a 3% inflation rate and ensuring the income lasts for more than 35 years.

Most financial advisors have historically suggested spending only 4% of your portfolio per year in retirement. A 5.91% annual distribution is a 48% increase in lifestyle income!

The bottom line with this plan is that you take risk only with money you won't need for 15 years. That is the sort of account where stock market investing and other risk based investments can actually make sense.

THE STOCK MARKET SOLUTION

For fifteen years I have asked clients of my wealth management firm the same simple question based on their financial priorities. Is it more important to you to squeeze out the maximum gains in the good years OR to protect from losing money in the bad years? The odds are 99% it's the same answer you just gave—protect from losing money.

If you had $1,000,000 and lost 50% in one really bad year, what rate of return do you need on the remaining $500,000 to get back to your original million? 100%!

A 50% loss requires a 100% gain to get back to break even. Therefore one of my financial rules of thumb is, *a negative number counts double.* It's not a perfect formula, it just makes a point. Protecting from significant loss is far more important than chasing the greatest gain. Just ask Sean Quinn.

WHEN LESS IS MORE

Here is a slightly more involved scenario. Take that same $1,000,000 and assume a 20% gain for two years, then a 30% loss. How much have you made? If you remember my rule of thumb, you should be pretty close. The answer is just 0.8%.

Instead, what if you made only half (10%) in the good years and didn't lose anything in the bad year? Your return after three years, 21%!

Sound impossible? Think again. We have delivered exactly these kinds of results to our clients for more than a decade. Here is the simple secret to achieving similar results.

SECURE INDEXED INVESTING

How do you avoid losing money in the stock market? The answer lies within the original question and just required approaching the stock market from a different angle. If we don't want to lose money in the stock market, then we can't invest our principal in stocks...but we *can* invest our interest.

This chain of thinking allowed me to rediscover a simple investment strategy which has been almost forgotten in the last two decades. I call it the Secure Indexed Investment and there are only two steps.

REDISCOVERING TIMELESS SECRETS

The first step is to determine how much interest you can make in the next year on a safe fixed income investment. For our discussion here, I'm going to use 7%. Before you scoff, read the following section on the 7% Solution and then you will see why 7% is a reasonable number.

Now invest enough of your funds into the fixed income investment so after one year you will be back to 100%.

Allow me to put numbers to this point. If you invest $934,579 at 7% for one year it grows to $1,000,000.

The second step would be to take the remainder, $65,421, and use it to buy a 12-month call option on the S&P 500 index at the price closest to where the index is currently. If you did this the day I'm writing this book, you would net about 65% of the gain from the stock market over the next 12 months if the market is up, but if the market is down you would not lose a cent.

In summary, the fixed income investment of $934,579 would grow to $1,000,000 after 12 months so even if the stock market went down in value you would not lose principal. If the market is up, the options will have a value which is approximately 65% of the market's gain.

When I bring up the idea of options it is worth noting that options are extremely risky. You can lose all of your investment. In our scenario, since we really invested only the amount of interest we stand to earn in the next year, losing the option money doesn't hurt our original principal, we just end up where we started.

WHAT RISK REALLY COSTS

Before you think this doesn't sound impressive, imagine if you applied this time tested strategy in 2007. The chart below shows the actual stock market returns and what our Secure Indexed Investment would have delivered.

	Actual S&P 500	Hypothetical Secure Index		Results with a $100,000 investment	
				S&P 500	Secure Indexed
2007	5.49%	3.57%	2007	$105,490	$103,569
2008	-38.49%	0.00%	2008	$64,887	$103,569
2009	27.63%	17.96%	2009	$82,815	$122,169
2010	12.60%	8.19%	2010	$93,250	$132,175

If you were thinking a 65% participation sounded lackluster, think again. The actual stock market results from 2007-2010 resulted in losing almost 7% yet the Secure Indexed Investment would have generated better than a 32% increase while taking no principal risk.

If you think this is encouraging then realize I have given you only the simplest and easiest use of this strategy. In the first quarter of 2012 we used this approach to actually generate more return than the S&P 500 while still keeping the principal fully protected.

There is more to the implementation of this strategy and it is one where I stress the need to work with a professional who fully understands what we are doing. Since this strategy, though time tested, depends on a reasonable yield on your safe money, let's take a look at our last success secret.

THE 7% SOLUTION

This leads me to one of my favorite investments—an investment which protects your principal, doesn't require a long-term time commitment and yields 7% or better. In today's environment, I consider it to be the best investment available. Secured trust deeds.

If you have any experience with trust deeds then you probably agree this is an outstanding investment. What you may not realize is 2012 (and the next few years) will be looked back upon as ideal for trust deed investors.

THE GOLDEN AGE OF TRUST DEED INVESTING

The wealth management firm I own is a Registered Investment Advisor, which means I can work with any investment, whether it may be bonds, stocks, annuities or anything else you can think of. For me, it's about finding the best combination of low risk and reasonable returns. At the present, I believe there is no better combination of low risk and high yields than can be found in trust deeds.

Essentially a trust deed is a mortgage funded by a private lender (you, the investor). As with all mortgages, the trust deed is secured by a specific property which would be an investment property, not someone's home. The lower the loan amount relative to the value of the property (referred to as the LTV) the safer the loan. In today's environment I'm seeing first trust deeds paying 7% - 10% with LTVs of 50% - 60%!

Compare this to any investment, and these numbers should jump off the page. With an LTV of 50% the property securing the note would have to decline by 50% from today's values for there to be risk to your principal. That's a 50% decline from values AFTER the 30% +/- which occurred in 2007 – 2009.

EXCEPTIONAL RISK ADJUSTED RETURNS

Consider the interest rate. Fixed income investments paying 7% to 10% annual interest are hard to find, certainly with this level of safety. While trust deeds have been around for decades if not centuries, the level of security is ridiculously high due to the real estate crash of 2007-2009 and the credit crisis of 2008. The combination of these two events left a gaping hole of opportunity to earn very high yields with an incredibly low level of risk.

I would have to say it is possible for something unique to happen with one individual property. There are several ways to reduce or eliminate this risk, which is something we provide to our clients.

In considering the risk of this type of investment, I concluded I would be comfortable using it with a significant portion of a retiree's assets. Just as there are some investors who have all of their money in CDs or government bonds, it is possible to safely construct a portfolio exclusively of trust deeds. If this is considered I would again stress working with a professional.

AAA RATED TRUST DEEDS

Basically I'm saying I would put trust deeds on par with AAA-rated short-term bonds, though there is no rating scale for trust deeds. If there was, I think they would be AAA rated.

Since the real estate market has to decline by more than 40%-50% for there to be principal risk, I'm truly not concerned. From today's prices after the crash we've already experienced, I consider such an occurrence to be impossible.

Once again my goal in this book is not to train you on every facet of implementing this, or any, investment strategy. Instead I am highlighting for you the excellent opportunities which exist around you.

YOUR SUCCESS SECRET

Those who are successful will generally take action which others won't. I have applied this principal in my firm which is why we seek out and offer unique investments and often ignored strategies. Regardless if you apply these principles to your investments, or in your life, you will find your life enriched by taking the road less traveled.

For a more complete discussion of these topics and other wealth management strategies, pick up a copy of my book Strategic Wealth.

About William

William Jordan is a nationally recognized expert in the area of financial planning and wealth management. You may have seen William on NBC, CBS or CNBC, heard him on The Money Hour, or read his financial advice in *Forbes, The Wall Street Journal, Kiplinger's* and many other national and local publications.

A repeat winner of the Five Star Wealth Manager award, author of multiple books and nationally recognized expert, William is a trusted financial resource and members of the media frequently seek his financial wisdom when needing advice phrased in terms that everyone will understand.

As President of William Jordan Associates, Inc. and WJA Wealth Management, LLC, William has worked with and impacted more than ten thousand individuals and families in his 15 years as a wealth manager. His firm has taken wealth management "beyond peace of mind" in allowing investors to increase the lifestyle their wealth allows them while at the same time reducing risk.

William and Tiphanie, his wife of 17 years, reside in Capistrano Beach, California, along with their two daughters. Both are active in their local church and in volunteering their time and expertise. For more information on William or his wealth management firm visit www.WilliamJordanAssociates.com.

William Jordan Associates, Inc.
www.WJAoc.com
(949) 916-8000

CHAPTER 21

Seven Steps To Retrain Your Brain For Success

By Dr. Caroline Manuel
www.thelaughingmonk.com

"First comes thought; then organization of that thought, into ideas and plans; then transformation of those plans into reality. The beginning, as you will observe, is in your imagination." –Napoleon Hill

How can our minds create a viable thought and hold it in focus until it transforms into a plan and a reality? In life, our mind is crowded with many worries. From work frustration, credit card debt, relationship problems, divorce and so on, these stressors clutter the mind like bad seeds. They spur negative thoughts and emotions and sometimes blossom into full-blown anxiety and depression. These conditions are the leading cause of poor quality of life; they are boulders that block the path to success.

The good news is our brain is plastic, which means it can revitalize itself to success as well as remove the blocks to happiness. As Napoleon Hill writes, you can retrain your brain to create empowering thoughts, which like viable seeds produce a bountiful crop for a successful life.

Dr. Caroline has helped thousands of people live their best lives with the well-researched and effective mind retraining success tools she describes in her book, *The Laughing Monk*. As the embodiment of wisdom, her eponymous character, the Laughing Monk, warns:

Like a flowing river, the mind gathers dark thoughts that over years become habits. When one lives in the shadow of those thoughts, feelings of fear deprive one of the sweetness of life.

The Laughing Monk advises the book's protagonist, Meera, a young woman battling the demons of anxiety, that her thoughts are the cause of her fear—which in turn prevent her from experiencing her full potential.

Dr. Caroline counsels that it is not the event that causes our emotions, but how we interpret the event—what thoughts and meaning we give to it—that influences our emotions and behavior. For example, when you make a mistake at work, thinking that "I am a failure" can cause a *feeling* of disappointment and the resultant *action* of avoiding expressing thoughts and opinions during business meetings or with superiors.

Thoughts both guide your feelings and actions. Your thoughts are automatic and not always under your conscious control, but you can learn to become aware of your thinking and reword or reframe your negative thinking and behavior, resulting in a change of feelings and behavior.

For example, a mistake at work can be reframed as a lesson to help you learn and grow. This can make you feel empowered and result in expressing yourself. Let's use the case of David Loveland to illustrate.

David Loveland is a soft-spoken software engineer. He is devoted to his work of fifteen years and has won a few "Employee of the Year" awards for excellence in leading his multinational company to success. He and his wife have been married for sixteen years and have young children. He is a good provider, loyal and dedicated to his family, but he is so busy at work that he is not very present in their lives. At forty-two, he finds his life is starting to crumble around him. Following his promotion to a different department which requires him to manage projects rather than people, he feels overwhelmed by his new manager's demanding tone and aloofness.

David soon begins to realize he prefers managing people to projects. He feels increasingly stressed and unappreciated. His body is tense from the torments of his mind; he suffers from somatic problems such as headaches, nausea and difficulties concentrating, which result in mistakes at work. He tosses and turns at night, unable to sleep, his mind racing with negative thoughts.

Stress, the silent invader, is slowly taking away the pleasures of life.

David telephones the Human Resources manager to talk about his work stress. When he doesn't hear back that day, David thinks that the company he has served for so many years doesn't value him. He feels worthless. "I'm afraid of losing my job, I am a loser as a father," he thinks. His unhelpful negative thoughts ricochet, knocking David into a downward spiral of depression.

It is easy to see how self-talk and thoughts can influence emotions and actions. David's negative thoughts about himself, the future and the world around him made him feel anxious and deflated, causing his actions to change from that of a confident player in life to a defeated soul who now fears people, work and life.

All day, he curls up in a ball, isolating himself from people. They in turn begin to resent him, which David views as personal rejection, increasing his depression. He wants to manage his anxiety, and learn to be successful at work and shore up his relationships with his family and friends.

It's time for David to change his thinking for the better and in turn, feel confident rather than fearful.

The Laughing Monk points out to David the seven steps to achieve success in his work and life:

Step 1. STOP: Practice awareness of your thoughts.

Stop, take a deep breath, and simply observe your feelings, sensations and thoughts. You can become aware of your thoughts by noticing emotions such as anger and sadness as well as sensations in the body such as fatigue, pain, apprehension or nausea.

David learns to notice his emotions and physical sensations and thoughts: "What am I feeling? What sensations do I notice?" He observes distressed feelings of failure, anger, frustration, and anxiety. He scans his body head to toe, feels a pounding in his head, tension in his neck and a tight chest.

Thoughts: What thoughts or images went through David's mind before or at this moment?: "The manager is deliberately ignoring my email. I am not important to him."

Notice the link between thoughts, emotions and the resultant actions or behaviors.

David can see how his feelings of anger, sadness and the sensations of muscle tension and pounding in the head are connected with the associated thoughts: "I am not important to him," and " I have failed" with the resultant behavior of anxiously pacing and then staying in bed all day.

Step 2. Query: Ask is it a helpful or useful thought?

Some of your hurts you have cured,
And the sharpest you still have survived,
But what torments of grief you've endured
From evils that never arrived.
– Ralph Waldo Emerson

In this quote, Emerson wisely refers to the "torments of grief… from evils that never arrived" as merely distorted thoughts with no basis in reality that end up causing so much emotional pain and impede success in life.

David asked himself if the thoughts that 'he was a failure' and that 'his manager didn't care' were useful thoughts. The answer was 'no,' because these thoughts made him feel bad, culminating in wasted time and suffering.

Your thoughts are automatic. That is, they just happen to pop up in your head and often go unnoticed. Thoughts are words, images or memories.

Automatic negative thoughts (known as ANTS) are the limiting thoughts and the silent killers of happiness and success in life.

Thoughts are not necessarily true, accurate or helpful. Thoughts held as true are called beliefs. You tend to automatically believe your thoughts without checking whether or not they are true.

David's thought "Nobody cares for me" was not accurate or helpful to him. It was just a thought–and a limiting thought–like a boulder blocking the path to success. It changed David from feeling like a winner in life to thinking like a loser.

Step 3. Reframe: If a thought is not helpful or useful, then change or reword it until it becomes more useful or helpful.

As you think, so you feel; as you feel so you act. Reframe
your thinking to feel well–and act to create your success.
–The Monk from ***The Laughing Monk***

David changed the unhelpful thought to: "The manager may not have checked his e-mail yet or perhaps he doesn't have a response yet. This does not mean I am a failure."

Step 4. Change Your Behavior: Changing what we normally do can change the way we feel and think.

David took another action. He went up to meet his manager at work and learned from his personal assistant that he was away. This action and his changed thinking resulted in David feeling better–which then helped him focus on a solution to his problem rather than feeling like a victim.

Step 5. Mindful Presence: Often at work and at home, David's mind busied itself at the pace of peak hour traffic, thinking about past distressing work events or worrying about what terrible things might happen in the future. Busy minds get cluttered and go on autopilot, such as when David is at work or home he is unaware of the environment or people around him. He is not present in the moment. Therefore there is very little room left for solutions to his dilemmas.

Meditation and mindful presence can in fact "train" the mind to react to challenges with positive emotions. Dr. Richard Davidson's research using brain imaging found that meditation improves circulation in the regions of the brain that regulate emotion–indicating that the brain can be *retrained* to experience happiness. Psychologist Sarah Lazar used brain imaging to compare the brains of people who practiced meditation every day with those of non-meditators. The scans showed that certain areas of the cortex or outer layer of the brain that regulate our thinking, reasoning, memory and decision-making functions were significantly thicker in the meditators. This means meditation improves brain function.

Fortune 500 companies such as Google teach their employees techniques like mindfulness to augment productivity at work. Mindfulness is simply a practical way to be in the moment by observing details of sound, taste, and smell around you as well as noticing physical sensations and thoughts without judging them. Practicing mindfulness will distract the busy mind of negative thoughts and reduce the tenacity of unhelpful cognitions.

People need to feel heard, listened to and understood. Mindful presence or showing up in your body and soul for the person you are with adds tremendous value to your relationship with them.

For example: David is fully present and in the moment as he listens attentively, stills his mind and directs his gaze on the people he is with both at work and at home. He also calms his busy mind with deep mindful breathing as below. He breathes in deeply to the count of 10 and focuses on counting and noticing the cool air flowing in. Next he breathes out deeply to the count of 10 and notices the warm air streaming out of his nostrils, his abdomen pulling in.

When David notices that his attention has drifted, he simply acknowledges this bringing his awareness back to his breath. Although David found it boring to sit still and focus on breath and other mindful activities, he persisted. After a few months of consistent practice of mindful presence and breathing his busy mind slowly stilled itself, clearing away its clutter. David felt alert and happy at work.

Step 6. Anticipation: "If you fail to plan, you plan to fail."

A longitudinal Harvard study showed that anticipation and planning increase adaptation and resilience in life.

Plan effectively by making lists, prioritizing things by their level of urgency and importance, and getting specific and clear on what you want in different areas of life such as work, relationships, finances and health.

David wrote a clear list of what he wanted in his life. He prioritized and became clear about his goals. This helped him make good decisions, especially about urgent work issues.

Step 7. Reach Out: Reaching out to ask for help and also to serve others are useful strategies for living well.

David reached out to a therapist to help him practice reframing his thinking, make lists, discuss ideas and find clarity regarding his plans. He also joined the Salvation Army to donate a few hours of his time helping out in their kitchen, staying in the moment by focusing on preparing meals for the homeless. This made him feel both rewarded and worthy.

David reached for success strategies by becoming aware of his thoughts, querying his thoughts to see if they were useful, reframing negative and unhelpful thoughts, changing self-sabotaging behaviors and practicing being in the moment. He anticipated and planned effectively, learned to ask for help, and strove to serve others.

Three months later, after amicable discussions with his manager, David received a severance package from his company. He started working in a new business almost immediately. After learning to plan and create realistic goals, he now balances work, charity and life. He is able to spend quality time with his family. David learned to reframe the challenges he faced at work as lessons–which enabled him to retrain his brain for success.

The Laughing Monk urges you to retrain your brain to success with these seven steps:

Step 1. Stop – stop and become aware of your thoughts.

Step 2. Query – the thought whether it is helpful or not.

Step 3. Reframe – change your thinking.

Step 4. Change your behavior or action.

Step 5. Mindful presence.

Step 6. Anticipate and plan.

Step 7. Reach out for help and serve others.

Visit www.thelaughingmonk.com for tools to successful living.

About Caroline

Dr. Caroline Manuel is a Happiness Expert, Psychiatrist, Best-selling Author and Speaker, who is regularly sought out for strategies to overcome stress and optimize happiness.

As an internationally recognized psychiatrist, therapist, author, and speaker, she has appeared as a mental health expert on CBS, NBC, ABC and FOX, and has been featured in *USA Today, The Wall Street Journal, and Newsweek.*

Dr. Caroline's techniques for overcoming adversity and stress management are also featured on her virtual platform, www.thelaughingmonk.com. The website offers readers inspiring ways to transform depression, anxiety and stress into a more vital, joyful life experience.

She began her medical training in India and completed her postgraduate psychiatric training in Texas, USA. Utilizing tools from her training in mental health and from her own personal experience in overcoming adversity, she helps people retrain their brain to achieve success in life.

"Charity and contribution play a significant role in creating authentic happiness," says Dr. Caroline, who is writing her upcoming book, The Laughing Monk, to be published in 2012. To accompany the launch of the book, she is planning to collaborate with charities such as Salvation Army to provide meals for the homeless across Australia and the USA.

Dr. Caroline gratefully acknowledges New York Times Bestselling editor Stacey Donovan, and Kavya Peters, for their editorial help.

For more tips to retrain your brain for success
visit the website: www.thelaughingmonk.com.

CHAPTER 22

Your Company Should Workout!

5 Exercises to Create a Solid, Healthy & Profitable Marketing Platform to Grow Your Business

By William R. Benner Jr. and Justin T. Perry

We all know how important exercise is to maintaining a healthy lifestyle. However, at times we may find certain things get in the way, and prevent us from staying fit. It could be we just don't make the time, or that (in many cases) we don't even know where to begin.

As the authors of this chapter, we are not personal trainers or health gurus. We are businessmen who enjoy the benefits of exercise as well as an active lifestyle, and one thing we have learned is that in the same way people find it hard to fit exercise into their daily lives, many businesses find it hard to develop and incorporate a solid marketing platform into their company work flow. In one way of thinking, marketing is to a business what exercise is to the body. Marketing helps your business develop a strong customer base, grow, and ensure your company remains active so that you can stay in business for many years to come.

So what exactly does proper marketing entail, and how do you know if you are doing the correct "exercises" in order to achieve the desired result? The American Marketing Association (AMA) defines marketing as "the activity, set of institutions, and processes for creating, communicating, delivering, and exchanging offerings that have value for customers, clients, partners, and society at large." While that definition says a lot, it doesn't provide you with any indication of where to get started or what those value-generating activities are.

Our promise to you is that by the end of this chapter, you will learn five solid "exercises" that your business can incorporate, to help you develop a solid marketing platform from which to grow.

Before we get started, we'd like to tell you a little bit about us, and how we've developed our marketing "exercise program." Pangolin has been in business since 1986. We are the world leaders in software and systems for creating laser light shows. If you've ever seen a professional laser show, then you've probably seen our products in action. They are used to create shows at the world's top theme parks and major events like concerts, the Super Bowl and the Olympics. When we began, we did not put much effort into developing a formal marketing platform. Of course we did the basics, such as creating a website, printing brochures and attending a few tradeshows; but for the most part, these three activities comprised our company's entire marketing platform.

It wasn't until a few years ago when we launched a new product called QuickShow, a product aimed at bringing laser shows to the consumer market, that we realized we needed to develop a solid marketing platform.

When we got started, we were just like the person who didn't have the time to go the gym for the last ten years, and really doesn't even know where to begin. So we started attending all kinds of seminars, reading books, and trying different marketing products. We tested everything we could find, and finally identified five solid strategies, which we noticed had a major impact on our business–and by major impact, we mean a 50% growth in sales within one year.

Presented for you below is a new "workout" routine for your business–five proven strategies that form the basis of a solid marketing platform for your business. These strategies are guaranteed to improve the "health" of your company.

1: BUILD A MARKETING DATABASE

As a business owner, you already have your customers' information (name, email address, telephone number, etc.) in some kind of accounting software. Take these existing contacts and import them into a marketing database software. These programs allow you to develop email, text, and in some cases telephone marketing campaigns, to get your message out to existing and potential customers. You can send out different marketing campaigns like monthly newsletters, weekly video email blasts, or other information about products or services you want to sell. In addition, some of these programs can even generate automated systems to follow up with people who showed interest in your various marketing campaigns.

These programs generate very in-depth reports, allowing you to track results of your campaigns and see from where potential sales are coming. There are many different programs to choose from, and most of them come with a free trial. So start playing around with some of these, and find one that you feel comfortable with. We use a program called Campaign Monitor, which meets our needs very well. However, there are other popular ones out there such as Constant Contact and AWebber. So try a few, pick the one you like, then copy your existing customer information into the program, and voila! You have just implemented your first marketing exercise, and have developed a foundation from which to grow.

2: CAPTURE NEW LEADS

The next step in our marketing exercise routine is to develop a system to capture new leads. There are a few great ways to do this, which work regardless of the industry you are in, or the product you sell.

First, on your website (preferably towards the top and in a highly visible area) make sure you have a place for people to enter their name and email address in exchange for something free (basically anything of "value"). This could be a free report about your industry, a free demo of your product or a free consultation for your services–you get the idea. The whole notion is that people may be cautious about providing their personal information if they get nothing in return, so offer them a carrot. And if they're already coming to your website, and interested in your free item, then they are a potential customer. The leads captured in this

211

way are then automatically or manually entered into your marketing database, after which you can begin sending marketing-related messages to them.

Another great way to capture new qualified leads is to start a referral or affiliate program. While these can get very intricate and complex, the basic principle is to give people an incentive for sending you new business. For example, we gave our existing customers a commission for any new sale they sent to us. We uploaded these contacts into our database and developed targeted marketing campaigns for them. Many of these contacts did in fact purchase our product, and in return, we gave the original customer (who sent us the lead) a commission for their effort.

A third way to get new leads is to simply beat the streets. Attend tradeshows and industry events and get business cards. It may sound old-fashioned, but you would be amazed at just how much money can be made simply attending an event, uploading the contacts you make into your database, and sending out targeted marketing campaigns to those individuals.

Adding different exercises like weight training, cardio, and aerobics to your workout helps ensure that you are exercising all of the different parts of your body. And capturing new leads is just like adding different exercises to your work out. It helps ensure that you are marketing to all of the possible customers you possibly could, in an effort to achieve a well-rounded and diverse customer base.

3: GET SOCIAL – HARNESS THE POWER OF SOCIAL MEDIA

After you have been exercising for a while, at a certain point you will hit what is called a plateau. Basically, this is when your body becomes accustomed to the current exercises you have been doing, after which you no longer get the same result. In order to overcome this plateau, you must incorporate new and different exercises, to stimulate your body and muscles in a new way. The same principle applies to marketing. If you do what you've always done, you will reach a point where the results start to diminish.

Whether or not you like it or understand it completely, you should get your business involved with social media sites including Facebook,

Twitter and YouTube. At first, we were fairly skeptical about getting our business up on sites like these, since we didn't believe they offered any real benefit. Well this attitude couldn't have been more wrong! Social media sites are becoming immensely powerful as a marketing tool for businesses.

First, social media sites give you a fun and informal channel to communicate with your existing customers. In addition, they allow you to share photos, videos, and links with your customers, which can further build trust and reinforce the marketing message you are trying to deliver. And finally, and perhaps most importantly, they can be used as a powerful tool to attract new business.

The process is relatively simple. To get started create accounts on Facebook, Twitter, and YouTube, and then just start adding content to these pages (i.e. photos, videos, descriptions, etc). Facebook is especially powerful in attracting new business, because it allows you to create a custom advertisement, and then select the demographic of the customers you want to view the advertisement (i.e. age, interests, geographic area, etc). Facebook will position these ads on the pages of potential customers, and then when they click on the advertisement, it will take them to a website of your choice. We recommend creating a custom landing page that discusses a few of your best selling points and captures their information right away. Once you've got their information, you add it to your marketing database as discussed above.

Using social media is not only a great way to keep existing customers updated on your latest news and offers, but also as a great way of attracting new customers.

4: PEOPLE BUY PEOPLE–HELP YOUR CLIENTS TELL THEIR STORIES

One thing we've learned from doing business all over the world, is that regardless of where you are, people buy people. Just think about it: when a sales person approaches you, there is a natural instinct to go on the defensive and to take what they tell you with a grain of salt. But when you hear another client talking about a product they've used, and when that client tells you about how wonderful it is, you tend to believe them far more than you would a salesman. After all, a client is not trying to sell you anything; they are simply sharing their opinion on a product that they found had a lot of value. And believe it or not, those kinds of stories have a huge impact on the purchasing decision of your future clients. Therefore our next point is for you to incorporate testimonials into your marketing message.

You likely have more than a few reliable clients with whom you have a solid relationship. Reach out to them and ask them to tell you "why" they chose your product, and "what" it is about your product that benefited them. Collect these stories and put them in a place where other potential clients can see them: on your website, within your literature, or in a video email blast to your database. You will be amazed by the results. All of the sudden your clients are doing the selling for you.

Have you ever gone to the gym or watched TV and seen those success stories of people who lost an overwhelming amount of weight? Those stories can be pretty inspiring. The concept is the same regardless of the business you are in. Help your clients to tell their stories, and share their success with potential clients, and you will see more people buying into the product or service you have to offer.

5: BRAND YOURSELF – MEDIA, PR AND YOUR ONLINE PRESENCE

So once you've been going to the gym for a while and start seeing the changes happening to your body, generally one of the first things you want to do is to show off your new physique to the world. And rightfully so! You've worked hard in order to get it. Well, the same thing applies to your business. You need to let the world know about your company and the beneficial products or services you offer. One of the best ways to do this is through media, PR, and building a strong online presence. Now, we are not saying you need to go out and hire an expensive PR firm in order to get started. Actually, what we recommend is something you can do yourself and can produce the same if not better results. We've devised an easy-to-follow system here at Pangolin which has allowed us to get into every major magazine in our industry (for FREE), and to dominate the search engines.

The first step is to begin writing press releases and articles about cool, innovative, or unique things your business is doing. Be sure to incorporate "keywords" and links to your website. (Keywords are words and phrases that you know people in your industry would search for when looking for a product or service you offer). Next, you need to create accounts with online PR and article syndications sites. Some of these sites require you to pay a monthly subscription fee, but there are also free sites, such as like PR Log, Idea Marketers, and Go Articles. Find the ones you like best, and establish accounts with them. After that, start uploading your press releases and articles to these sites. One of the great things about sites like these is that they allow you to target an exact industry, such as entertainment, industrial, or service based.

After you've done these things, it is time to start making friends and contacts with the editors at industry magazines. Start a database in your software solely focused on editors at the magazines you want to target. Then, when you get a cool new press release or article, email it to the editors on your list. Magazine editors always need news and stories. Chances are that if your story is cool or interesting enough, they will use it.

Finally, share these articles and press releases with your existing and potential customers via social media outlets including Facebook and Twitter. By placing valuable and unique information on these sites, it helps position you as a credible and innovate company within field, and also shows your customers that you are a leader in your industry.

So there you have it, five solid exercises with concrete examples you can use to get your very own marketing platform up and running. These exercises are guaranteed to help increase your sales and grow your business for years to come.

Now, go work out! Trust us, you'll like the way it feels!

About William

William R. Benner, Jr. is President and CTO of Pangolin Laser Systems. As President, he sets the general strategic direction for the company and oversees all company operations. As CTO, he is in charge of all hardware and software, as well as research and development on new products. Under the leadership of Mr. Benner, Pangolin Laser Systems has become a multi-national organization with offices in the United States, China and Central Europe.

Mr. Benner holds numerous patents, and has received personal letters of commendation from President Ronal Reagan, and Florida Governor Bob Graham. He has been published in the SMPTE Journal, The Laserist, Laser FX, US Tech magazine, and Motorola's *Embedded* Connection magazine and is co-author of the best selling books *"Game Changers", "WIN"* and *"The Only Business Book You'll Ever Need"*, and was selected as one of America's Premiere Experts as well as having been featured on NBC, ABC, CBS and FOX television affiliates.

In addition to having received more than 20 international awards for technical achievement, Benner's products are currently used by some of the best-known companies in the world, including Walt Disney World, Universal Studios, DreamWorks, Boeing, Samsung, and Lawrence Livermore Labs. Benner's innovative strategies and developments continue to strongly influence both laser- and SMS-display industries.

Beyond his work at Pangolin, Mr. Benner has served as a director on several boards as well as Technical Committee Chairman for the International Laser Display Association. He has also contributed expertise to companies outside of Pangolin including NEOS, Cambridge Technologies, RMB Miniature Bearings, and many others.

Mr. Benner represented the state of Florida and the United States Skill Olympics and represented the U.S. in International Skill Olympics trials, receiving gold medals for each. Benner has also received the International Laser Display Association's highest accolade, the Career Achievement Award.

When he is not working, Mr. Benner enjoys spending time sampling fine wines and cuisine in Napa Valley with his lovely wife Karen of 20 years. Benner also spends time with his son William III who is an avid golfer and basketball player and is currently preparing to embark upon his first year of college.

About Justin

Justin T. Perry is the Chief Operating Officer for Pangolin Laser Systems. Mr. Perry has been in the business and marketing industry since a very early age, starting his first business at the age of 17.

Mr. Perry is a proud alumnus of the University of Central Florida's School of Business Administration, where he focused primarily in the fields of Marketing and Finance. During the course of his studies, Mr. Perry also interned with national automotive firm J & L Marketing, where he traveled across the United States designing, developing and launching several automotive marketing campaigns for some of the world's most widely known automotive manufacturing companies including BMW, Mercedes Benz, Jaguar, Chrysler, and General Motors.

As Chief Operating Officer for Pangolin, Mr. Perry oversees the company's general business, financial, and marketing efforts. In addition, he has assisted in the expansion of the Pangolin's distribution networks, working with clients from around the world to expand the markets served by the laser and text messaging products. Mr. Perry routinely travels around the world meeting with clients from many different countries, outlining, developing and launching strategic partnerships, which have had major impacts for both Pangolin and their clients. Although only 26 years old, Mr. Perry has earned a reputation in the laser business as being one of the foremost experts on how to market and grow their industry.

In addition to his current role at Pangolin, Mr. Perry was elected to the International Laser Display Association's Board of Directors. He has also served on the ILDA Association's marketing department for nearly two years, and was recently also elected Chairman for this department. Mr. Perry also published articles in major industry publications including mondo[dr], *Total Production International, and Lighting & Sound America.*

Mr. Perry has a true passion for marketing and international business strategic partnerships, and enjoys collaborating with companies around the world to help grow the laser industry as a whole. When he is not working, Mr. Perry enjoys spending time with his newlywed wife Saori, engaging in an active outdoor lifestyle in sunny Orlando, Florida.

CHAPTER 23

Four Steps to Conquering Stress

By Catherine Scheers

They say that only two things in life are certain–death and taxes. I would add a third–stress. Regardless of your occupation or your family, stress is almost certain to follow you. Left unchecked, it will kill your career, and very likely kill you. The ability to short-circuit stress is one of the most important secrets of success. Those who acquire this ability will rise above their contemporaries. And, unlike some portents of success–like being born to wealthy parents or having a university degree from an Ivy League school–the ability to handle stressful situations with grace can be learned. I know, because I have lived it, and learned from it–so can you.

The secret to conquering stress lies in four P's–**Perfectionism**, **Patterns**, **Practice** and **Perseverance**.

PERFECTIONISM–ELIMINATE IT

Have you ever had a wake-up call from the universe? I've heard that when God is trying to get your attention, first he whispers, then he taps you on the shoulder, then he nudges you, and finally, if you are still not listening, he will smack you upside the head. Well it seems I'm a little hard of hearing (or more likely too busy to listen to the whispers), so one day I woke up to the sound of a semi-trailer's blaring horn. The problem is that it was 6:30 a.m. and I was driving to work. I was so burned out, even after a full night's sleep, that I had fallen asleep driving and crossed the centre line into the path of an oncoming semi! Talk about a wake-up call! What had brought me to this point in my life, where I was totally exhausted, with blood pressure so high that my doctor said I was in the stroke zone? Perfectionism–that deadly, soul-destroying disease.

I used to think that perfectionism was a good thing – I mean, it has the word "perfect" in it, right? Employers certainly loved seeing the word in my resume. The problem with perfectionism is that it requires the approval of others. Without the validation of others, we simply don't value ourselves or our efforts.

I share my story in the hope that it will help others – that you can either see yourself in my shoes, or you can see that if I can conquer stress, you can too.

My story begins in a busy household, as the seventh out of eight children. In this brood, the only way to get attention was to be really good or really bad, and really bad was already taken. Thus began a life of perfectionism, over-achieving and the desperate need for others' approval.

I was an A student in school, Captain of the cheerleading squad and Winter Carnival Queen. Married at 21 with 3 kids in short order, I still wanted to go to university. After a divorce and remarriage, and adding two stepchildren to our busy home while working full-time, I began my university career part-time. Every Saturday for eight years, I persevered until I had my Bachelor of Arts in Communication, with honours of course. It seems I had something to prove to everyone, including–or rather especially–myself.

Whether working as an entrepreneur or in the corporate world, I kept running into the same challenges – difficult bosses or clients, long hours required to succeed in my career and the stress of balancing all this with a busy family and aging parents. Yet I loved the challenge of planning and executing projects successfully, and was loathe to give up the challenge, the six-figure salary, and my work. It took that wake-up call with the semi to shake me up enough to realize that I was literally killing myself for the approval of others. I chose to leave that career and began to research stress and my response to it. Thus began my training with Jack Canfield.

Through Jack's work, I realized that I was my own biggest problem.

Ouch! My perfectionism demanded feeding with more and more responsibility at work, larger and more complex problems, bigger and bigger budgets to balance, and therefore more accolades and promotions. However the accolades were never enough. The slap on the back or "good work," was never enough to assuage the perfectionist that fed on the approval of others. The more we need it, the less others are apt to give that approval. Some will withhold it simply to control us. Others are too caught up in their own careers to notice us. Ironically, my family was waiting at home to give me unconditional love, but I was too busy and exhausted to be present to receive their love.

Having our locus of control, our need for approval, outside of ourselves and at the mercy of others is a very dangerous place for our egos. We perfectionists will sacrifice almost anything to get it, often at our own peril.

Jack taught me that my needs are as important as others' needs and what others think of me is none of my business. Those simple truths allowed me to break free from the vicious cycle of stress in which I was caught up.

PATTERNS - BREAK THEM

So I'd like to end the story there - I'm fixed! But no, life is a journey and I am a work in progress. Point in fact—as an entrepreneur, I have unconsciously created a too-busy schedule with ambitious goals leading to a stressful environment in my own company. How did this happen? Well, you can take a duck out of water, but she still quacks. The same perfectionist tendencies are lurking under the surface. It took a good deal of soul searching to realize *why* these patterns keep appearing in my life.

Why was I so ambitious? Yup, you guessed it—the need for approval, both my own and others—and low self-esteem. I have never felt "good enough" just as I am, so I am always on some self-improvement program or another. How liberating would it be to just stop the insanity, realize we are okay just as we are, and that we don't have to do anything, just BE?!

The bottom line is that I have to learn to love myself just as I am, regardless of my weight, my age, my income or debts, my accomplishments or lack hereof. When I can love myself completely and unconditionally every day, the frantic chase for more or different will be blissfully over.

Being here, now, as is, will be enough.

Until then, I will keep on the alert for repeating patterns in my life. Patterns serve us by pointing to a deeper story, but their ongoing repetition prevents us from evolving spiritually.

PRACTICE

a.) Practice loving you.

One of the hardest parts of overcoming perfectionism was stopping the daily self-flagellation–to stop beating myself up over every perceived shortcoming. What a relief it is to leave that behind! That doesn't mean that those ugly voices don't try to pipe up all the time–they do; it's a life-long pattern that is not going to be broken overnight. However I am vigilant–when I hear that negative self-talk bubbling up in my brain, I STOP it! I tell myself that I am OK just as I am, and that I am doing the best I can. There are enough people in this world that will try to knock you down–you don't have to join them. Be your own best support system.

Another way to practice self-love and raise your self-esteem is the mirror exercise, taught to me by Jack Canfield: Every night, look yourself in the mirror and acknowledge yourself for what you accomplished that day, disciplines kept, temptations resisted, and say, "I love you." **No one will ever love you or respect you more than you love and respect yourself**. Practicing the mirror exercise daily will raise your self-love and self-esteem. When you change yourself, which is the only thing you can control, the way others respond to you will change as well.

b.) Practice finding space in your life for you.

Do you have breathing space in your daily calendar? How about time for self-care, exercise, getting proper nutrition and fresh air? If you are a busy professional, you may be laughing now–who has time for this? But you cannot be effective if you are burned out. You cannot make good decisions if you are hungry, thirsty, or have a headache from not breathing properly. Schedule time for these things. As Stephen Covey says, "sharpen the saw" before you start trying to cut down the tree. I have been so busy at work that I actually got reprimanded for going to the bathroom. Not the first sign of a problem with my workload, but certainly a bellwether. If you don't have time to pee or breathe, stress is definitely going to be a factor. Remember, your needs are as important as their needs.

Practice fortress time to accomplish your priorities. Have you ever had one of those days with back-to-back meetings all day long? At the end of the day you are stressed, haven't accomplished your objectives for the day, and end up working late to tackle your priorities? What if you booked work periods in your calendar so that others can't fill up your time with their priorities? Most successful people do just this, and have their assistants guard that time fiercely.

c.) Practice stress reduction techniques.
There are as many stress reduction strategies as there are stars in the sky—you can research them and find a few that work for you. Two techniques that have helped me are meditation and the Quick Coherence technique (HeartMath Institute). Check my website (www.empoweringsuccess.ca) for "Stress to Bliss in 60 Seconds" videos–tips from celebrities on how they reduce stress.

PERSEVERANCE

a.) Persevere against resistance.
People and organizations often prefer to maintain the status quo rather than embrace change. When you start setting healthy boundaries and acting differently, you may experience resistance or push back. Do not be deterred. Your quality of life, and quite possibly your life itself, depends on your ability to persevere in your quest for balance and bliss versus the workaholism and stress you have been experiencing. In the long run, you will be happier and more productive, which will translate into better results for the company and you personally.

When you find that *you* are the one resisting change, resisting the implementation of these strategies, take Louise Hay's advice: Go to the mirror, look yourself in the eye, and say, "I release the need for resistance," over and over again, until you feel your heart and mind opening to change. In my experience, you may need to repeat this frequently.

b.) Persevere against inertia.
Like any new skill, practicing effective stress management takes

time. The tighter your work schedule, the more diligent you will need to be to create and **invest** the time and energy to implement these strategies. But unlike most of your daily tasks, these strategies will energize you, reinvigorate you, and give you the physical and mental strength to tackle any project with more grace and vigor. That's why I say the time you take for these techniques is an invest-ment–it will give you more than you invest.

c.) Persevere against patterns and habits.

Your old patterns will draw you into your usual rut like tire tracks in mud. Einstein said that doing the same thing over and over and expecting different results is the definition of insanity. Most of us are not insane but we are certainly creatures of habit. We *hope* that want-ing different results is enough to make it so, but if you want different results you must act differently. Pick at least one of these strategies to implement each week over the next month. Start with one, then add another and another and another.

Give up the pattern of blaming and complaining. Take 100 percent responsibility for your life, your choices, your reactions, your stress. Since you can't control others, try changing your reactions instead. Stop disempowering yourself by blaming others, and take respon-sibility for creating positive change in your life. Read and reread *"The Success Principles,"* by Jack Canfield, and implement those principles in your life to break your old patterns and habits.

d.) Practice perseverance and track your progress.

Journal about the process every night. Learn from your successes and where you could have made better choices. Rate your stress each day at mid-day when you are in the thick of it. See if it is going up or down, and what makes it go up or down.

I applaud you for wanting to improve your life, and taking the necessary steps to do so. Please reach out to me via my website or Facebook and tell me how things are going for you. Are you having success with implementing these tools? What are the challenges you are experiencing? I look forward to celebrating your successes and helping you conquer stress.

About Catherine

Catherine Scheers is the President of Empowering Success, a division of Lariat Communications Inc. She is also the Managing Director of eWomenNetwork's Calgary West chapter and a member of the Evolutionary Business Council. Her background includes entrepreneurial and corporate work, politics and the oil and gas industry. As someone who has held several highly stressful positions, Catherine has a big heart for helping others overcome stress.

She is an alumna of the University of Calgary, 2005, Bachelor of Arts, Communications (Honours). Catherine is a graduate of Jack Canfield's Train the Trainer program, and received her Professional Certified Success Coach designation from the Success Coach Institute.

Catherine is an author, trainer and success coach committed to living her best life and empowering others to do the same, for the highest good of all.

She lives in Cochrane, Alberta, Canada with her husband Chris–they have raised five children and have two grandchildren.

To learn more about Catherine and how you can receive the free Special Report, "Five Ways To Reduce Stress This Week," visit her website at www.empoweringsuccess. ca. Follow her on Facebook, Twitter and LinkedIn.

CHAPTER 24

Catch the Outsourcing Wave

By Dane Christensen

The key to success is to not fight against natural forces, but rather to get out ahead of the waves of societal and economic change and let their power propel you forward. I want to discuss a couple of these inexorable forces of nature that we see happening before our eyes and how you can get out in front of these waves to accomplish your goals.

Massively successful people like Andrew Carnegie, Henry Ford, Bill Gates and Mark Zuckerberg illustrate this concept. Carnegie didn't create the need for steel in a burgeoning industrial era. He just got in front of that wave. Ford didn't invent the car or spur the demand for this marvelous invention—he just found a way to stay out ahead of the demand. Gates didn't drive the computer revolution—he simply put himself at the center of it. And social networks were already primed to explode when Zuckerberg developed Facebook—he was simply in the right place at the right time with the right service.

But you don't have to catch a wave of that magnitude to be successful. Massive societal and economic changes are happening now. We all know this. We see it every day. These changes mean difficulty for some and opportunities for others. Whether you benefit from these changes or not depends on your ability to understand the forces at play objectively and to position yourself strategically in front of them.

So enough of vague generalities, I want to help you understand some of the inexorable shifts we see today and how they provide you with a fantastic opportunity: Outsourcing.

To many 'outsourcing' is a dirty word, evoking images of vacant factories, unemployed Americans and offshore sweatshops—and for good reason, as that is clearly a sign of the times. The flow of manufacturing jobs from affluent populations to emerging economies is inevitable. Any expectation that we can somehow drag high-paying manufacturing jobs back to the U.S. through political pressure is folly. Given the large discrepancy in the cost of production between various locations, it just makes sense that production will move to the lower-cost locations.

This process is as natural as rivers flowing to the ocean. There is little point in bemoaning the situation. It is happening, and it is not going to stop any time soon. Given this reality, you might as well capitalize on the situation. In other words, "if you can't beat 'em, join em."

Another fundamental change we see every day is increasing complexity in terms of technology, the economy, society, and in every aspect of our lives. Dealing with complexity is possibly the single greatest challenge to people who are trying to succeed. The myriad steps involved in developing a product or service and finding the market for it are far more numerous today than they were just a few years ago. And we also know that this trend isn't going away. In fact, it's accelerating.

I was confronted with this challenge when my web development company began taking off and I was getting more projects than I could handle. I have a fairly extensive skill set when it comes to web development and marketing and I'm always tempted to do everything by myself. It always felt more efficient when I went solo and didn't need to coordinate with others to get a job done.

But over time, I found that web technology was advancing faster than my ability to keep up with it. My clients were asking for functionality that I didn't have the skills to deliver. They wanted integrations between ecommerce systems and marketing automation tools. They wanted impressive multimedia presentations. They wanted integration with social media sites. And on and on it went. At a certain point it became clear that I simply wasn't going to be able to keep up.

I never even considered hiring employees. The long-term commitment to significant monthly overhead, including taxes and benefits just didn't make sense for a business that was only doing six figures annually at the time. Besides, with one employee, I would be getting their skill sets and no more. And I was finding I needed a much wider range of skills.

That's when I really got involved in outsourcing and realized what an amazing process it is. Before long, I had a 'virtual team' that ranged from just a few people to as many as 20 people at various points. I had a wide set of skill sets at my disposal, always someone available to do the jobs I needed done, and didn't have to deal with all the overhead that comes with an employee. If I didn't have work for someone to do, it wasn't a problem. I didn't have to come up with tasks for them to justify their pay. I just put them on the bench for a while.

It has never been easier to outsource the work you need done. There are a number of websites dedicated to this concept that provide a vast marketplace for virtually every kind of service your business needs. Among the top outsourcing websites are:

Elance (www.elance.com)

Freelancer (www.freelancer.com)

Guru (www.guru.com)

oDesk (www.odesk.com)

ScriptLance (www.scriptlance.com)

Vworker (www.vworker.com)

The web-based outsourcing industry started out, not surprisingly, with a focus on programmers developing software and web applications. But over the years, the field has expanded to incorporate all the key functions of any business including administrative and business services, sales and marketing, customer service, multimedia, writing and more.

And here is the essential dynamic that you must understand: On all of these sites, the number of people looking for work far exceeds the number of jobs available. For example, at the time of this writing the Vworker website lists 1,929 jobs available and 358,864 workers ready to do the work. That's nearly 200 workers for every project! The proportions are similar on the other sites. Given this lopsided situation, is there any question about which side of the equation you want to be on?

When you post a job on any of these 'freelancer' websites, you will start getting extremely competitive bids on your project almost immediately. You'll be amazed how inexpensive it is to get your work done. I have had projects that my corporate clients paid over $10,000 for (and felt like they got a bargain) that I outsourced entirely at a cost to me of less than $500.

Many people have set up lucrative operations based simply on the concept of arbitraging the difference between labor costs of employment versus outsourcing. What it really boils down to is putting yourself between the people who have more money than time and those people who have more time than money.

If that last sentence didn't make sense to you instantly, re-read it. That is the key. When working with corporate clients, I've found that the people I work with are really short on time. They have an endless mountain of work and they have plenty of corporate funding available to get that work done. They just don't have the time to take the steps that you could easily take to find just the right person who can get that work done for a fraction of what the corporation is willing to pay.

Is it really that simple? Just step into the gap between the people with money and those with the skills and watch the money roll in?

Ah, if only it were. Then everybody would do it. You definitely need to have certain skills and knowledge to play the outsourcing game profitably. That brings me to my Top Ten pointers for outsourcing.

1. UNDERSTAND WHAT YOU ARE OUTSOURCING.

Outsourcing a job because you have no idea how to do it yourself is a recipe for disaster. The reason to outsource a job is not because you aren't capable of doing it yourself, but rather that someone else is willing to do it for much less than your time is worth. I once sourced an integration project to someone else because I didn't know the technologies involved. Though his credentials looked good, this particular vendor turned out to be a flake. Had I really understood what he was working on, I would have realized much sooner that he didn't understand this technology any better than I did and saved myself a lot of headaches.

2. DEVELOP COMPLETE SPECIFICATIONS.

One side benefit of working with contractors is it really forces you to do something you should be doing anyway—creating crystal clear and complete specs for your project. It's one thing to wing it when you are working with your vision, your ideas and your tools. But contractors don't have the benefit of all your knowledge and experience, so without detailed specs to guide them, they are likely to flounder for some time before they acquire all the information they need.

3. DO YOUR DUE DILIGENCE ON SERVICE PROVIDERS.

All of the outsourcing websites mentioned above provide the ability for service providers to complete profiles including their experience, specific skills, and portfolio. There is generally a feedback mechanism so you can see how other employers have rated providers. Many of them even have testing so you can see how providers scored on specific skill sets. And of course, they all provide the ability to communicate with potential vendors before hiring them. So there is no excuse for not doing a thorough job of screening contractors. You will inevitably have numerous prospects to choose from, so for the sake of time, choose the top three based on their experience, portfolio, reviews and test scores. Then send each one of those your completed specs and ask them for comments and questions. More often than not, the responses you get to this will be all you need. But take as much time as the project warrants to communicate with your top prospects through email, chat or via phone (or Skype).

4. CONSIDER FACTORS OTHER THAN PRICE.

Ultimately, the objective of outsourcing is to get work done for less money. But that doesn't mean that price is the only factor to consider. The adage "you get what you pay for" is as applicable in outsourcing as anywhere. Some vendors will actually send ridiculously low bids to every project that comes up. They'll engage with you on that basis knowing that you will inevitably reveal some details that you missed in the original bid (see point point 2 above) and that provides the opening for them to jack up their bids. What other factors should you consider? Beyond the others covered above, (portfolio, reviews, test scores, etc.) consider their location (i.e. their time zone) if you have a project that requires real-time interaction. Another factor I consider heavily is their command of the English language and ability to communicate clearly.

5. START WITH SMALL JOBS.

In order to further evaluate workers, I often try to come up with smaller jobs to test them out with. It's a bit like a baseball farm team. If they do a good job on my smaller jobs then I'll consider them for the more substantial jobs. And I must admit that I do dangle the larger jobs in front of developers to motivate them to do their best work on my smaller projects.

6. CLEAR COMMUNICATIONS.

Clear communication on your part is arguably the most important factor in maximizing the efficiency of your outsourcing arrangements. One well-organized email complete with to-do lists and references to additional information may take you a couple hours to develop. But that is fraction of the time you'll spend responding to a seemingly endless string of questions you'll deal with over time if you just dash off a half-baked explanation of what you want. Not to mention the extra money you'll pay to your provider since they will be wasting their time trying to understand what you want. A fringe benefit of clear communication is that service providers really appreciate it and will be more eager to work on your projects.

7. USE PROJECT MANAGEMENT TOOLS.

While the outsourcing sites provide some basic communication and organizing features, you'll need to get set up with tools to help you keep track of your team's efforts. There are many web-based project management tools. These tools allow you to assign tasks, track progress, exchange information and files and communicate in a structured way. I particularly like the Jira tracking program and Confluence collaboration tool provided by Atlassian. (www.atlassian.com)   and have developed a project collaboration system named WaveCenter (www.wavecenter. com) on the Confluence platform. There are many more such programs that you can find on Google with a quick search on "project management tools."

8. AVOID OTHER BROKERS.

When you post a job on the freelance websites you will often get responses from people representing other people with the skills you need. While there is nothing inherently wrong with this, I tend to avoid these people. Since in a sense I am filling the role of the broker, it seems a bit redundant to go through another broker (who is obviously marking up the cost), especially when there are so many competent people who you can work directly with.

9. HAVE BACK UPS.

My experience with contractors through these sites is that they are generally conscientious and eager to impress. However, occasionally contractors will simply disappear in the middle of a project. Don't get caught flat footed when this occurs. Keep track of the people who applied to your job originally and perhaps ping them from time to time, particularly if you are feeling any uncertainty about the reliability of your current developer.

10. FORM RELATIONSHIPS.

Although there is a seemingly endless supply of skilled contractors available to you through these outsourcing sites, avoid the temptation to continuously play them against each other in order to drive prices down. If you can find a contractor who understands your business, communicates clearly, and is consistently responsive, stick with them--even if they do charge more than some other contractors. It will be more efficient in the long run. Besides, it's more enjoyable to work with someone you have a positive, ongoing working relationship with than some stranger.

Having written these ten tips for outsourcing, I realize how much more there is to say about it. You can learn much more by simply Googling "How to outsource." But ultimately, there's no better way to learn than to break down some of your jobs into manageable tasks and give it a try for yourself. Once you get into it, you'll understand how powerful outsourcing can be.

About Dane

Dane Christensen is a serial entrepreneur and Internet veteran who has developed countless web properties and served in key roles for Silicon Valley companies for over 20 years. He has mastered the art and science of leveraging web-based outsourcing and crowdsourcing networks to accomplish great things on a limited budget. Dane reveals the same techniques he used to develop cool web properties like wavecenter.com and enormal.org.

Dane Christensen
3713 Lynx Court
San Jose, CA 95136
me@danchristensen.com
(408) 781-1767
www.danechristensen.com

CHAPTER 25

Parents As Coaches Program Develops Happy, Healthy Children that are Impervious to Bullying and Negative Peer Pressure

By Gary Schill

Hello, my name is Master Gary A. Schill. I am the creator of the World Renowned "Parents as Coaches" program (www.SuccessfulFamilies. com), and I have some very tough questions for you. Don't worry; I have information for you that will be worth every second you invest in reading this chapter.

How many times have you said to yourself, your spouse, a friend or a business colleague, "I wish I knew that when I was younger, it would have made a huge difference in my success?"

How much time are you spending planning a vacation, the purchase of a car, a nice piece of jewelry, a purse, a dress, a flat panel television or the latest "I" device?How often do you watch reality TV, sports or television in general?

Now, how often do you spend quality time with your child? How much are you investing in your children's education? I am not talking about their elementary, high school or college education. I am talking about their **REAL WORLD EDUCATION!**

Now that the tough questions are out of the way, I guess you are wondering, who is this guy and why should I listen to him? For nearly 25 years I have worked with families just like yours and mine developing proven success secrets that ensure our children are happy, healthy and impervious to bullying and negative peer pressure. I own and operate one of the most successful Martial Arts academies in the country (www. PeakPerformanceMartialArts.com).

The "Parents as Coaches" program was created out of necessity. When we started our Peak Performers Program for the children in our Martial Arts Program, we quickly realized their parents were never taught the same fundamental success secrets that the top 3% of the population possess and use every day. The "Parents as Coaches" program was created to provide the parents of the children in our program with the ability to coach the children the same lessons at home as at the academy. It builds a bridge of congruency between the lessons we teach in our program and the lessons provided at home.

There are some very scary statistics facing our children today. First, we are ranked 26th in Education in the world. Personally, this makes me sick. We live in the greatest country in the world and with the resources we have available to us, there is no way we should be ranked 26th. Our children are facing a national debt that is climbing by nearly a trillion dollars a quarter and there is no end in sight.

What does all this mean? It means we are going to have to take some very proactive steps to ensure our children are properly prepared for when they leave our homes. Frankly, it is your responsibility to ensure they receive the best "Real World" education possible. Listed below are just three of the Success Lessons we teach to our Martial Arts Parents. These parents experience great relationships with their children. Our proven success system motivates the children to be proactive in their responsibilities at home—they clean their room, take care of their chores and are motivated in school. They do it on their own, without the parents having to fuss or argue with them. What a concept!

Before I begin with these simple but effective lessons, I want you to read what a few of my parents have said about our "Parents as Coaches" (PAC) program.

"One of the most surprising things we took away from the PAC was the vision boards and how effective they were. In nine short months, our daughter went from never saving money or getting her chores done to completing her work daily, saving money and purchasing her first iPod Touch with her own money."

—Dawn Marcellis, Professional Computer Programmer

"As an Assistant District Attorney, I see many of our children that are in trouble today. My children have been in Master Schill's Program for 7 years, both of them are black belts. The Parents as Coaches program really outlines the success steps we did not receive from our parents. It is the best investment any parent can make in themselves and their children."

—Mike Waldman, Attorney

These are just a couple of the *thousands* of testimonials to the effectiveness of the program. So the question is, "Are you ready to make a difference in your family's life and ensure they will have the necessary tools to be successful?"

"BEGIN WITH THE END IN MIND"

The first lesson we are going to teach you is to "Begin with the End in Mind." When we had our children, no one came to us and said, "Here is the owners manual, it will provide you all of the answers for raising great kids." We all literally came home from the hospital, scared as hell and wondered "WHAT THE HELL DO WE DO NOW?" All of our personal fears came to the surface and we just took it one day at a time. It is not until they reach the last two years of high school when the mad dash for the finish starts. It is then we realize that we have not properly prepared our children for leaving our homes or for the real world.

Regardless of what stage of life your child is in, you need to ask yourself, "What life skills do I want my child to possess when they leave my home?" The last thing we want them saying is what we have been saying, "I wish I would have known that when I was younger." So, the first exercise that I want you to complete is to sit down and look at your own life and start creating a vision of what you want your child's life to look like at age 18, age 22 and age 25. One of the challenges we have today with our education system is we are not providing our children (from the time they enter Kindergarten to Adulthood) a clear picture of what life skills we want them to have attained, what expectations we have for them and what expectations they should have for themselves. We go from kindergarten to first grade, second grade and so on and so on… just going through the motions with no plan, ultimately setting them up for failure.

You need to develop a road map for every aspect of their lives. Doing so will set them up for success instead of repeated failures.

To clarify, I am not asking you to do everything for them, I am asking you to outline a clear vision of what you want for them. Listed below are the top questions you need to ask when developing your "Begin with the End in Mind" roadmap.

1. Why types of behavior do I want my child to exhibit?
2. What level of Self-Confidence do I want them to have?
3. What level of education do I want them to achieve?
4. What life skills, I know as an adult, do I want them to know much earlier in life?
5. What level of financial education do I want them to possess?
6. What business knowledge do you want them to have attained?
7. Add any other level of knowledge you want them to learn and master.

Once you are done making your list we can move to phase two, establishing a vision board.

"VISION BOARD"

A Vision Board is a very useful and effective tool. It allows you to display your hopes, dreams and desires and then moves them to a manageable goal system. How many times have you been somewhere, even just sitting on the couch and you get a "Million Dollar Idea" that could possibly change your life forever? You never take any action and then sometime later you see your idea on television. A vision board assists you in taking that vision into action steps to ensure you experience the success for which you are capable.

Once you complete the "Begin with the End in Mind" exercise, use the diagram below to start developing your Vision Board. I am also providing you with a valuable resource. Please scan the QR Code below fill out the form and I will send you a package to assist you with this exercise.

SCAN THE CODE AND FINISH THE CHAPTER

Below you will find three columns. We are going to start with the column to the right, "Achieve More." In this column we are going to list the things *you* want to achieve. In the middle "Do More" column, we are going to list the steps we need to take to achieve our desired outcomes. To the far left "Be More" column, we are going to list the type of person we have to "Become" in order to be able to "Do More." As a result this will allow us to "Achieve More" of our hopes, dreams, desires and rewards.

"Be More"	"Do More"	"Achieve More"
Write here what type of **PERSON YOU HAVE TO BECOME** to Do More so **YOU** can Achieve More	Write here what you will have to **DO** to **ACHIEVE MORE**	Write here the things you want to accomplish, **YOUR HOPES, DREAMS, DESIRES, AND REWARDS...**

I know you have heard the phrase, "You do not plan to fail, you fail to plan." The question for you is, "Are you going to keep doing the things that are not providing you with the greatest success or are you ready to build your road map to success?" This is all a Vision Board is. It is the high-level plan that you start breaking down into 90-day, 60-day, 30-day and weekly plans. It provides you a clear direction on where you are going and what steps you need to take to ensure your success.

In the downloadable version I am also including the 90-Day Planners and Weekly focus Sheet along with instructions on how to take it from your Vision Board to implementing a successful plan.

"ROUTINE"

The last topic I want to share with you is about "Routine." One of the top questions we field is: What is the number one thing we can do to eliminate the turmoil in our household? The answer to that question, for many areas of our lives, is simply, "Routine."

For children, I recommend starting with their bed time. Again, "Begin with the End in Mind" and then reverse engineer the rest of the evening based upon the routine you desire. This way the children know exactly what to expect, i.e., what time they need to brush their teeth, what time they need to be reading their books, what time the need to have their clothes and required materials for the next day laid out, what time they need to eat, etc.

Children do very well when they know what to expect. The same can be said for them being at school or extracurricular activities on time. Begin with what time you want or need them to leave and then reverse everything else from there.

The great benefit about routines is when there are any unexpected life challenges or even devastating news, as long as the routine is in place, the children will know and feel that everything will be okay. It provides them a sense of security and reduces anxiety and stress.

For you, a routine is equally important. When you are working on your weekly goal sheets, it is extremely important you fill out what you want to accomplish for next week on the Friday before. It allows your brain to figure the best course of action that needs to take place to ensure your success. Too many times we do not plan properly or we are faced with a challenge that seems overwhelming. We make an emotional and immediate reaction and then later we come up with a plan that would have produced more favorable results.

By working on your weekly sheets the Friday before, your brain has time to process and provide you with a clear vision of the steps needed in order to achieve your goals. It is not an emotional reaction, but a calculated and formulated plan for success.

One of the most obvious mistakes we make as parents is forgetting that everything we learned about parenting we learned from our parents. There were many times all of us said to our parents, "When I have kids of my own I will treat them differently," and for many of us, we are repeating the same mistakes. You have to be proactive as a parent regardless of how tired you are or what information you lack. We have to be a solid example to our children.

In closing I want to share something with you. *Successful people are not successful by accident.* The success people experience is not by accident, or just a coincidence. They are not banking on the lottery or some wealthy relative to give them an inheritance that will provide their lifestyle or retirement. There is a specific set of steps and rules that the 'ultra successful' follow. These steps are completely by design and have been around for thousands of years. They study these steps and follow them every day. These simple but effective rules are why they are always succeeding when others are failing.

These three simple but effective lessons are part of the overall success plan. For purchasing our book, I have a bonus I want to give you. Scan the QR Code below and register for a 4th FREE lesson from our "Parents As Coaches" seminar. This lesson will help you battle one of the greatest challenges facing our children today, "Preventing the Quitting Habit." Quitting has become too easy today and it needs to be avoided at all cost.

www.SuccessfulFamilies.com/ParentsAsCoaches/

To learn more about our programs email us at info@SuccessfulFamilies.com

Best of luck to all of you in your quest for the growth and the success of your children.

About Gary

Master Gary A. Schill is the owner and chief instructor of Peak Performance Training Center, a child, family and professional coaching program that provides personal development and success coaching via the Martial Arts.

Master Schill is married to his beautiful wife Paula, and together they have five children ranging in ages from 4-30. The three oldest boys all have black belts, his daughter will test for her black belt in 2012 and his youngest son is working towards his black belt sometime in the near future.

With more than 38 years of Martial Arts experience, Master Schill has developed a revolutionary development program that is proven to develop a child's emotional, mental, physical and social intelligence. Understanding that most parents were never taught proper success traits or parenting skills, he developed Parents as Coaches, or "PAC." The PAC program provides parents with a new set of success secrets that will ensure their children posses life skills found only in the top 3% of the world's population.

Master Schill works with the local school districts teaching anti-bullying, anti-negative peer pressure and abduction prevention techniques to more than 25,000 children annually. In addition, he provides parenting clases to local parents and various organizations.

CHAPTER 26

Initiating Change to Achieve Fulfillment

By Grace Daly

As we strive to accomplish the constant stream of goals to grow our careers and businesses, it's not uncommon to get sidetracked from our own true definitions of bliss. Suddenly one day it dawns on us that what we're currently doing—and what we originally thought we wanted to achieve—has somehow grown vastly apart from our day-to-day enjoyment. It's at this point we seek a greater purpose to all of "this."

Promotions, larger salaries and bonuses are fine goals to strive for; however, these things will always come and go—always. The question is, what remains with you at the end of each day? Fulfillment is what many people seek, especially once they've come to the realization it's missing. They ask themselves: is this really it? There's a longing for purpose, for a greater good in their everyday roles. What may have been a life of accumulating and drive shifts to a life of fulfillment and purpose.

Although change is necessary for growth, embracing change is still difficult for many people. After all, change is about seeing, learning and doing things from a different perspective. Everyone handles change in their own ways and I break this down into three groups of people. The first group does not like change and constantly resists it. The second group is those who adapt to change; recognizing this flexibility brings improvement to business, career and life. Taking this one step further would lead us to the third and last group. This group is the minority in number, yet the most powerful and impactful. They initiate the change. Events are not happening to these people–these people make the events happen. They take full responsibility for creating their own destiny. These are the creative thinkers; those who retort: "Says who?" and "Why not?" when their ambitions are questioned. The reason they are so successful in thinking outside the box is because they've never been inside one. They are daredevils, playing by their own rules and taking risks in order to fulfill not only personal gain but also a greater purpose. It is in this greater purpose they achieve this fulfillment in their lives. This is how I initiated the change in my life—to live my purpose and achieve fulfillment, operating from a platform to reach and serve others.

I look back in disbelief at the blind ambition during the youth of my career. I accepted an incredible amount of stress during the years of what I used to define as "success." Sure, there were moments of massive achievement and pure fun that I shared with my loved ones, but I remember few moments of serenity and times of reflection. There was just no stillness during those years of my life. My mother would fondly validate how I've lived up to my fire horse sign on the Chinese horoscope. The fire horse spirit of unleashed determination and hard work fueled my relentless pursuit and achievement of career goals to reach certain successes by milestone birthdays. I did clearly see most of these successes were material gain or even ego driven for some public recognition of a leadership role. At that time, that was the only way I knew how to soothe a pressing need from my childhood of scarcity and an obligation to prove self worth. As I've done very well in my career, I've also shared everything I've had with family and close friends. The irony was this continued track created a growing, unquenchable need to accumulate more to share more, which may not have been the right reason for doing something with such zeal. Shouldn't we accomplish something out of pure enjoyment?

This reminded me of an experience I once had at a professional race track. For a considerable fee, after signing several releases and disclaimers, I suited up and watched a half hour training video with an instructor. I was then led out to the raceway pit to wait for my turn to drive a race car several times around a professional race course. Now because I didn't drive a stick, I did a ride along with a professional driver. He easily whipped up to 195 mph in no time flat. Going that warp speed made everything outside just a continuous blur, the only thing in focus was the endless blacktop track that effortlessly disappeared under the car. There was an adrenaline high to go faster; and that was easy for me to shout over the roaring engine—especially since I was not the one driving, "Faster, faster!! Woohoo! We're flying!" Well, in many ways my career in corporate America was much like that. With more curiosity than hesitation, some basic tools, and invaluable mentors, I jumped right into a ride that lasted decades. At times because I was going so fast–it didn't feel like I was driving, in fact at that speed you don't think about who's steering–you just go with the flow; as if you're on a ride along.

Going 195 mph was the norm in corporate America and anything slower than that would be frowned upon. Also because everyone was going that speed we actually fed off each other's energies and egos. Because I remained true to my own promise- to play as hard as I worked, I honestly did not miss or crave any moments of stillness. I was zooming through my days, with the sunsets that quickly rushed in after each dawn. The hours in between became a monotonous stream of meetings in windowless and cold conference rooms, managing damage control on escalations and working with team members to get through another day. The travel days would start at 4 a.m., leaving to the airport to catch the first flight out. Eating on the run and milling about airport terminals for electrical outlets to recharge my blackberry became routine. Those days were filled with long store tours with field partners, entertaining them with the proper corporate protocol of evening dinners and positive discussions. Followed with a late check in to the hotel; unpacking, ironing if necessary and finally firing up the laptop to reply to those emails that required further attention than a quick blackberry response. These trips would end with a mad dash to the airport, rushing through security to catch the last flight out. When you're living this pace with everyone else, no one is there to say: "Hey quit driving so fast, everything's blurring right by." This was the common bond amongst us in our retail development industry; trading war stories with a look, a meaningful nod, half jokingly and half seriously, we'd silently admit: I don't know why we're doing this.

Although I was proud of my work and accomplishments, I always felt I was predefined by the positions I held with these large corporations. In some ways, I allowed and encouraged this to happen. This was a home for me, a successful place. Later on I found I was identified too closely by the companies I worked for and the positions I held. And after time,

I was always referred to as Grace Daly, Senior Director of this, or VP of that–opening over 100 stores a year or managing a fleet of 900+ stores nationwide. I became defined by how big my budget was—whether it was 10M, 20M or 30M-and how much work I had to award a contractor or supplier. I was constantly approached by the masses with the products and services they had to sell me. That was the industry game which we all agreed to play.

After having my full of the grind, I decided to leave this "successful" and lucrative 25-year retail career to pursue my ultimate dream as a writer and coach. After all, coaching and writing had always been an innate and passionate part of me–showing in my work and how I led my teams or wrote SOPs, RFPs and contracts. This audacious move during the worst economic climate sprung various reactions with raised eyebrows: "You're what? Why are you leaving your job?" "Were you really laid off?" "If you're bored don't leave yet, just find a new retailer to build with." "Are you sure you want to do this?" "Why don't you sleep on it some more?"

Ironically that last comment confirmed how I felt–as if I've been asleep all this time–by not pursuing my true purpose. You see, when you wake up to live your life on purpose, you get it and can never go back. It's like seeing everything in vivid 3D high definition color when all you ever saw before was the static on the black-and-white television with adjustable rabbit ears for 25 years. Now this is not to discredit my past career, because all those experiences brought me here to this point. It's just a matter of seeing with distinct clarity and understanding what fulfillment meant to me.

It proved to be a karmic decision because shortly after I initiated this change in my career, many more people than usual reached out to me for guidance. Some were colleagues in my retail development industry, some were partners from retail ops, finance or loss prevention. Once I launched my website, I started to reach people beyond my industry. Many were either unemployed or extremely unhappy in their current jobs. The following are some examples.

At his last job, John was a project manager directing several build outs in the southeast region. When the economy took a turn for the worse with development at a standstill, John was let go in the first round of layoffs.

When the unemployment benefits ran out, their savings were tapped into. Eventually John, his wife and two kids moved into his mother-in-law's home. His wife tutored whenever possible for extra cash and John worked various jobs assisting local businesses with repairs and maintenance.

Now for the people still employed, a majority of them felt the same sense of lost hope. Jane was overworked and stressed out from endless rounds of layoffs and cutbacks at her workplace. One time Jane even described how it felt like a jail term to serve, a punishment to endure every time Sunday night rolled around. It became increasingly difficult for her to go into work.

Both John and Jane had entirely different situations when it came to employment yet they were both missing fulfillment and the sense of purpose in their lives. Consciously seeking a healthier lifestyle–by eliminating certain stresses, giving up control of that which you have no power over, learning to let go and forgive and also finding beauty and appreciation in life–comes only with a deep understanding and internal perspective of one self. With John's case, this lull of being out of work gave him the stillness to re-evaluate what he really wanted to do. It gave him a desire to pursue a long forgotten dream.

"I would be a soccer coach, coaching the kids. I would see so much more of my own kids, especially since I've missed their earlier years from working so much."

"I'd leave this place where they mistreat their employees. I'd start my own boutique design company, create a nourishing culture for my associates to thrive in."

"I would be a personal trainer, the ideal healthy lifestyle I want and need. And the best part is I can help other people get healthy, too."

"I would go back for my nursing degree and then work part time, per diem. I'll be helping my patients heal and have more time with my family."

"I would grow to a leadership role in this company so that I can implement positive change that would support the employees to do their best job possible."

I felt their eyes light up and a genuine excitement rose in their voice as they elaborated on their dreams. Just speaking of it was as if they un-buried and shared with me a long-lost treasure. Now, embracing these possibilities, they were on route to claiming and sharing their purpose. They applied this sense of fulfillment into every part of their lives. You can do the same. You can discover how to live your purpose and add fulfillment to your life. Too many people trade their dreams for their fears, ironically mostly fears that do not ever happen.

With each client I coached, I immediately saw the greater impact each of these people would have on others. This shared adrenaline high val-idated my own purpose and fulfillment in my coaching and writing, which spurred me to coach more people, organizations and businesses. After coaching thousands of people in multiple industries, I noticed a pattern, a set road we all go through. Sometimes we just need to recog-nize all the different paths that truly exist for each of us before moving forward. Whether it is Providence revealing a bit more and more of our path each day or it is learning to trust our own intuition–it is all the same path. It takes courage, passion and unconditional love to propel you to take full responsibility and seek fulfillment. As we are living our pur-pose, we will find everything else great follows.

Here are four keys to help you initiate change and achieve your fulfill-ment

1. **See past the pain.** Many people are so fixated in the current situation, they cannot get past their own pain. You must have such a crystal clear focus of the future that you can feel it in-stantly in all five of your senses. When you dream in this level of detail, you are creating your future.

2. **Go where you are loved.** Too often folks tend to stay in envi-ronments and situations they are familiar with, even though it may not be healthy or supportive. You are ultimately respon-sible for your own happiness, so you must seek loving envi-ronments that will help you flourish.

3. **Recognize the greater good.** There is a purpose for you to ful-fill in your life. It is commendable to excel in your career and enjoy reaping those benefits; however, your ultimate greatness still lies dormant in you. It will not be released until you come to the self realization that there is a greater good, a greater pur-pose to contribute to that is bigger and beyond you.

4. **Be centered and true to yourself.** Have the conviction & perseverance to march to the beat of your own drum. Believe in yourself, seeking only your own approval and trusting your intuition. When you walk in faith, Providence comes to your aid and you will not fail in achieving fulfillment in your life.

About Grace

How do you achieve fulfillment and happiness in your life? Ask Grace.

Grace Daly, bestselling and award winning author, inspirational speaker and certified coach, has helped thousands of people design their blueprint to fulfillment by harnessing the power of their innate strengths and aligning it to their life's purpose. With more than 25 years in the retail industry, Grace is a passionate advocate for the advancement of the retail and restaurant development industry. Grace's expertise is regularly sought after through her column in the leading industry magazines: Retail Facility Business® and Restaurant Facility Business®. Her talks on leadership, service and inspiration moves her audiences to take positive action. Her clients include: The First Step, Women's Unlimited, InterFace Retail & Restaurant Facility & Construction Exchanges, Chick-Fil-A, Verizon Wireless and Chipotle. Her engaging interviews include leaders from Aeropostale, Apple, The Body Shop, Charming Shoppes, Chick-Fil-A, Del Taco, Gap, IKEA, Pandora Jewelry, Target, Verizon Wireless and Whataburger.

Grace is the author of *The Seven Success Keys for the Retail Facilities Professional* and *Everyday Inspiration.* Her bestsellers include: *Win, 35 Winning Strategies from Today's Leading Entrepreneurs* and *The Only Business Book You'll Ever Need* co-authored with legendary business leader Brian Tracy. Her latest books include: *It's All Up To You - The Top 10 Things You Should Know to Have the Best Life Possible*, co-authored with best-selling author, speaker and promotions powerhouse Paul Edgewater and also her industry book: *Inspiring Leadership in Retail & Restaurant Development.*

Grace is the recipient of the Editor's Choice Awards for her published work and has been inducted into the National Academy of Best-Selling Authors™. She is a member of the American Society of Journalist & Authors and the Retail Design Institute. Grace is an honored recipient to the 2012/2013 NAPW Professional Women of the Year. Grace is dedicated to paying it forward to her community and working with those who courageously pursue the life of their dreams. To learn more about Grace Daly, the leading authority on fulfillment and inspiration, please visit www.GraceDaly.com. Get Ready, Get Inspired!™

CHAPTER 27

Why You Must Have a Powerful Unique Selling Proposition (USP)

By JW Dicks, Esq. and Nick Nanton, Esq.

Miller Lite. Tastes Great, Less Filling.

Burger King. Have It Your Way.

Domino's. Your Pizza in 30 Minutes or Less.

Above, as you probably already know, are three of the most famous advertising slogans of the past thirty or forty years.

What you might not know is the real genius of each of those slogans, (besides being memorable), is that they each contain the product's **Unique Selling Proposition**, or **"USP."** In each case, the slogans neatly capture the advantage of that particular brand over the competition in a compelling way.

Let's briefly review them all to see how they accomplish this impressive feat. Miller, for example, came up with "Tastes Great, Less Filling" when light beer was relatively new. Diet food has a connotation of not tasting as good as "regular" food–so the brewer needed to reassure consumers their light beer did, in fact, taste great even though it didn't have as many calories. Even cleverer, by the way, is the fact that the copy doesn't allude to calories or weight–instead, it says "less *filling*," so manly men didn't have to seem like they were worried about their waistlines.

As for Burger King, the franchise was, for a long time, the only fast food provider that allowed you to custom-order a burger without making you wait a half-hour. That's because McDonalds and the rest of the pack prepared all their burgers in advance; special orders disrupted their assembly line service. "Have It Your Way" delivered that message quickly and effectively.

Finally, Domino's knew they could never make amazing claims about the taste of their pizza; it couldn't stand the scrutiny next to a real neighborhood pizza place. So what was their advantage? They could get one to you fast. Thus, "30 Minutes or Less" became their catch-phrase (backed up by a claim at the time that they would refund your money if they were late, until too many car accidents resulting from overanxious delivery drivers caused a multitude of lawsuits). That catchphrase is still top-of-mind as ever, by the way, with a summer movie comedy of the same name being released in 2011.

In each of the above cases, the USP gave the products their full-on identity and also controlled how the public perceived them. That perception, naturally, tilted in the company's favor. And that's the ultimate value of a successful USP—it defines a product or service in such a way that it creates a winning advantage in potential customers' minds, thus driving sales.

When it comes to marketing (or even creating) a business, the all-important first step is to determine what your own USP is. Everything else— strategy, campaigns, price points, website design, even business cards and letterhead—can and should spring from this one essential point: *how do you benefit your customers in a way that your competition doesn't?*

And, by the way, if you can't answer that simple question, you might want to go back and rethink your business until you can.

USP PRELIMINARIES

But first, before you go back and rethink, you need to understand just what factors can go into creating a powerful USP. Who knows? You may already have one lurking in your business model that you have been unaware of until this point.

Here are a few points to consider before you get started on your USP:

- **Your Brand vs. Your USP**

  If you are already a well known expert in your field, your personal brand may be your USP. The reason being, if who you are is the reason people want to do business with you, then that is what is unique and that should be emphasized. On the other hand, if you are building your personal brand as an expert in your field, then using another USP gives you additional ammunition to position yourself in the light most attractive to the market you are going after. Using a separate Unique Selling Proposition gives you an opportunity to describe you and your company's greatest benefit to your ideal customers. Your USP should answer the question customers all wonder: "What's in it for me?"

  The more compelling and targeted your answer, the more likely you will get the desired response. For example, if you are a dentist, simply listing your services and credentials puts you in the same category as everyone else. Creating a USP such as, "we guarantee you a painless visit with our exclusive Sedation Relax Care treatment," separates you from other dentists and offers the patient prospect a unique alternative to what he may be expecting. Continue to look for the unique benefit you offer that others do not and target that message as hard as you can to the specific demographic market looking for that result.

- **Look for What's Missing**

  One of the most important features of a compelling USP is that it *fills a void*. If there is an obvious shortcoming in the current competition—or if you think you can create a convincing *perception* of a shortcoming—it's a good direction to take.

  And don't overlook the power of creating that perception. Let's return to Domino's. Before they started pushing the idea that you should have a pizza in your hands in thirty minutes or less, do you think this was ever a serious issue to most people? No one ever really worried about how long it would take to get a pizza delivered, they just knew it would come eventually. Suddenly, Domino's created a whole new speed standard which caught on in people's minds. Sure, the competition tried to emulate that standard, but it was too late. People now associated Domino's with "30 Minutes or Less."

Look around. What *isn't* your competition capitalizing on? There's always something you can use to differentiate yourself from them. Just make sure it's the *right* something. And the way you do that is to ask one simple question….

- **Who Cares?**
  No, we're not being sarcastic. The answer to "Who cares?" is crucial to determining whether you have, in fact, latched onto the right "something" for your USP. That's because, if the bulk of your potential customers end up reacting to your USP with a mighty shrug of their shoulders, then your USP isn't going to be an effective one.

Whatever your primary claim about your business is going to be, it has to be a statement that either already matters or you can *make* matter to your prospects. Let's go back to the Burger King USP. When that was formulated, the true "Burger King" was, of course, McDonalds. Their business model revolutionized the restaurant business and created the fast food franchise as we know it today.

The genius (and resulting fortune) of the Golden Arches' business approach was their system of preparing the burgers in advance so you could get your order quickly. BK flipped that approach by tapping into the downside—the fact that it's not easy to "hold the pickles" when the burger is already wrapped up and waiting in the heated holding area. "Have It Your Way" even quietly pointed out another advantage to their set-up. A customer is guaranteed a fresher burger when they're making it right in front of you, as the Burger King system ensured.

In both cases—freshness and ability to control what's on the burger – BK hit on issues that customers cared about a great deal. They could get the same food at pretty much the same speed and price, but also enjoy those additional advantages. BK discovered what was lacking in their overpowering competition and successfully exploited that weakness by making their customers *care* about that weakness. They still didn't overtake Mickey D's, but they did carve out a very profitable niche for themselves.

In our dental example, one thing we know is that people don't like pain and some simply will not go to the dentist because they believe they will feel pain. The sedation dentist takes away that that problem and in our example makes the prospect feel more comfortable that they are telling the truth by guaranteeing their offer.

The lawyer or CPA that offers flat rate billing changes the game for their service to the people who hate hourly billing. In this case, a professional, by changing the process of their business, does the same thing Burger King did to win over their customers. The offer in both cases, gave the prospect exactly what they wanted, in a way they wanted it.

- **Make a Promise You Can Keep**
Above all, whatever you decide your USP is, make sure it's something you can actually *fulfill*. People are already prone to distrust marketing and advertising—they're bombarded with it 24/7 and know most of it is a deliberate attempt to 'overhype' and manipulate.

Anyone who's seen a movie trailer filled with excitement and explosions, only to go to the movie and discover they're watching an unintelligible, unmemorable and just plain dull cinematic disaster, knows how deep an impression deceptive advertising can make. Movies can get away with that; they're in and out of theatres in a few weeks at most and don't have to concern themselves with the long-term damage misleading marketing can incur.

Professionals and businesses in for the long haul are in an entirely different position. This is where the old expression, "Fooled me once, shame on you, fooled me twice, shame on me," really comes into play. If your main advertising ploy is a blatant lie or misrepresentation, then you begin losing customers not just for one-time sales, but for *life*. No one wants to be seen as a sucker— and very, very few will come back to you if they feel you sold them a bill of goods.

While this trust factor has always been important, it is even more important today because of social media. Prospects now have the ability to review your company with their friends or various services they trust. There can now be no question that what you offer can actually be delivered and it must be delivered in the manner your customer perceives what you promised. There is no time for hedging or equivocating about what you can do. If you say you can do it, you better do it. Word travels faster than ever before and you will get branded in a negative way if you can't back up your promises.

Create a USP that squares firmly with your reality of who you are, what you do and what you deliver.

USP PRINCIPLES

Let's switch gears from the broader criteria we discussed above to some more specific guidelines, in order to focus on the actual content of a USP.

What aspects of a business transaction do customers care about enough that would swing their business your way? There are an almost unlimited number of such aspects to choose from, depending on what you're selling, but we're going to break them down into some major categories that can help any business pick and choose to find what might (or already does...) work for them.

- **Lower Price**
  This is a pretty obvious one. You're offering the same product or service as others, but you charge less money. A great example of that is Wal-Mart's famous tagline, "Every Day Low Prices." Along these lines, there are also businesses where that type of USP is actually built into the name, such as "The 99¢ Store!"

  Many people try to take on this category, but we don't recommend it. Fighting prices is a slippery slope because there is always someone who will try to beat you and there are many emerging companies that offer to do things for free just to get the prospect in the door. Free is definitely a strategy, but you have to have big bucks to carry the negative cash flow while you are waiting for the customer to buy something else that makes you money.

  Instead of the free or discount price model, we recommend value based pricing. In other words, when you set a price for your service, think about the value that the buyer is going to get in exchange for their money. The higher value, the higher you can charge. But it is very important that you take the time to help your prospect understand this value, or you won't be doing much selling!

In our running example of the sedation dentist, the value of his work without pain is very high to the person who can't tolerate pain. This person will always be willing to pay more for sedation dentistry because the value they are getting is more than just the cleaning of teeth or filling of a cavity.

- **Higher Quality**
  A higher quality product is another way of creating more value for a specific category of customers willing to pay more for quality. An example of this is a handmade suit tailored to fit. The quality can also be matched with personalization or comfort, because both bring a higher value. Whatever your product or service might be, if you believe there is enough of a customer base that will pay more for a higher standard of quality, this could be a way to go. No one expects to pay Hyundai prices for a Mercedes Benz, after all. You just have to make an effective case for that higher standard. Read some of these companies' ads to see exactly how they do it and you can adapt their strategies to your business.

- **Demographics**
  Back in the 1960s, Pepsi made a splash in the soda marketplace by advertising their soft drinks to "The Pepsi Generation." They successfully defined themselves demographically by appealing to the younger side of the then-growing generation gap.

Most large corporations since then have continued to target younger consumers, but, in truth, you can successfully go after any group of people—seniors, Latinos, African-Americans, and the affluent are just a few examples. Or you might want to sell specifically to those who work in a certain industry—doctors, lawyers, accountants, etc. Whatever the case, when you identify a large group with money to spend (that's being under-served by a particular product or service you can provide), you could have a very effective USP on your hands.

By the way, in many cases, the group doesn't even have to be particularly large to create a terrific customer base for you. They just have to be very targeted and have strong feelings about their positions. This is how many companies have gained success in the "Green" field of products, from organic foods to baby clothes.

- **Service with a Smile**
  When you're coming up against the mammoth bureaucracy of a huge company, the advantages of an average mom-and-pop business can seem awfully inviting. For example, you can quickly get an actual human on the phone without going through a half-hour of pre-recorded options. Turn your individuality into an attractive USP by selling your hands-on service—this is an area in which people *do* care a lot.

We all hate getting put on hold and listening to endless phone options without ever being able to get to a real person who can help you. This is why personalized, "Done for You" services are so successful. Not only do you work with a company who is there to answer your questions, they will do the work for you to your satisfaction. This kind of service is a growing trend and particularly attractive to the affluent market who has the money but wants more time. This market is very willing to pay someone to give them more time by taking the work and burden off of their hands.

- **No-Cost Education**
  In many business sectors, the pros don't take the time to explain why they're doing what they're doing for you—they just do it (providing you pay them to, of course). If you can provide no-cost materials to educate your potential customers about your particular industry, it creates added value to your product or services, especially if you offer free help with that product or service.

For example, think about the effective Home Depot commercial campaign that showed the store personnel teaching their customers about how to do simple home improvement tasks. Education may be an intangible that might only resonate for certain businesses such as that one, but, when used appropriately, it can make for a solid USP.

- **...or Your Money Back**
One of the quickest ways to build new customer trust, especially if you're a relatively unknown commodity, is to offer rock-solid guarantees, warranties and assurances that surpass the competition's promises. By knowing that if they take a chance on you, their bet is covered by your policies, they're much more likely to go ahead and give you a try.

The strongest statement you can make along these lines is to guarantee something the competition either won't or can't. Just using a tagline that says something like, "We Guarantee X, Y & Z–Our Competition Won't" gives you an instant one-up that any prospect can quickly comprehend.

- **Bonus Time**
Many kids used to buy a box of Cracker Jack not because of the popcorn snack itself, but for the free toy contained in the box. Having a consistent giveaway component in your brand can work similarly to bring in sales.

On the adult side, the beauty products company Clinique makes it a point several times a year to promote "Clinique Bonus Time" at all the major department stores. If you spend a certain amount of money on their products, you get a bonus. This has become an important long-term marketing tool for their company as well as a vital part of their USP.

Offering bonuses, reward programs, gift certificates and other incentives for good customers can also be an important aspect of your USP, as well as good business. Everyone loves to feel like they're getting something for nothing–even if, paradoxically, they're spending money to make it happen!

- **Wide Variety**
There used to be a commercial for a phone directory that always made us chuckle. A character in the ad would say that the directory not only covered a wider area than a rival directory, but it

also contained more listings. Well, if you thought about that for a moment, the one benefit kind of makes the other thing happen automatically!

Nevertheless, offering more choices than the primary competition can be a definite selling point for your business, especially if the customer still isn't quite sure what he or she wants to buy. Knowing you can provide a wide array of choices is reassuring and makes prospects feel they can make a more educated decision if they know everything that's available.

- **Batteries Included**
  Most of us can identify with the childhood memory of getting a brand new toy, excitedly opening it up and then completely deflating when it was obvious that toy needed batteries to run—and there were none in the house at the moment.

  That's why packaging your product or service with everything a customer needs can make for an effective USP. People are busy, and this is another example where offering a solid "Done-For-You" approach resonates with people who have hectic schedules or simply don't want to be bothered with taking a few extra steps. "One Stop Shopping" always has a certain appeal.

- **Nowhere Else**
  The ultimate USP is when you're *the only one* who can deliver a certain product or service. "Not available anywhere else" is a strong statement and can obviously only be used in certain situations. When you are selling a unique product, however, remember that education must be a part of the USP. If potential customers aren't familiar with what you're selling, they may be hesitant to buy it!

  As we noted at the top of this list, there are theoretically an infinite number of USP's that can be crafted, because there are an infinite number of possibilities to the marketplace. You can also create a potentially powerful combination of two or more of these ideas (for example, "Same Price - Superior Quality"). While the above list hits on the strongest elements a USP can contain, there may be still others more suitable to selling your business or service.

PUTTING YOUR USP INTO ACTION

Once you've settled on a potential USP, first test it out on some business associates you trust —and even some potential customers—to get their reactions. Remember, the primary question you want answered is *will this help sway a customer in my direction?* Also, is it strong enough, memorable enough and does it offer enough of a benefit to my potential target group?

Make sure the opinions you get on these questions are informed and from people you respect. If your budget allows, you might even want to hire a firm to do some market research. Remember that the USP is *one of the most important decisions you will make* when it comes to your business, so it shouldn't be undertaken lightly.

When you've made the final decision to move forward with a USP, you must make sure that it carries through in every aspect of your business. We're not just talking about marketing, although, obviously, that's critical. We're talking about how your receptionist answers the phone, what you put in your email signature, how you approach customers about sales and how you think about your business. As we noted at the beginning of this report, *everything* should spring from your USP.

And always make sure you and your staff can adequately communicate your USP quickly and effectively to anyone being introduced to your business. If you can't, you've got the wrong USP.

Finally, remember that times change and so do marketplaces. The Pepsi Generation couldn't last forever and neither can your USP. Don't stubbornly cling to something that no longer has the effectiveness it once had; you'll find that a new and improved USP that fits the current moment in time can reenergize your company and make it seem brand new.

About JW

JW Dicks, Esq., is America's foremost authority on using personal branding for business development. He has created some of the most successful brand and marketing campaigns for business and professional clients to make them the Credible Celebrity Expert in their field and build multi-million dollar businesses using their recognized status.

JW Dicks has started, bought, built, and sold a large number of businesses over his 39-year career and developed a loyal international following as a business attorney, author, speaker, consultant, and business expert's coach. He not only practices what he preaches by using his strategies to build his own businesses, he also applies those same concepts to help clients grow their business or professional practice the ways he does.

 JW has been extensively quoted in such national media as *USA Today, The Wall Street Journal, Newsweek, Inc. Magazine*, Forbes.com, CNBC.Com, and Fortune Small business. His television appearances include ABC, NBC, CBS and FOX affiliate stations around the country. He is the resident branding expert for Fast Company's internationally syndicated blog and is the publisher of Celebrity Expert Insider, a monthly newsletter targeting business and brand building strategies.

JW has written over 22 books, including numerous best sellers, and has been inducted into the National Academy of Best-Selling Authors. JW is married to Linda, his wife of 39 years, and they have two daughters, two granddaughters and two Yorkies. JW is a 6th generation Floridian and splits time between his home in Orlando and beach house on the Florida west coast.

About Nick

An Emmy Award Winning Director and Producer, Nick Nanton, Esq., is known as the Top Agent to Celebrity Experts around the world for his role in developing and marketing business and professional experts, through personal branding, media, marketing and PR to help them gain credibility and recognition for their accomplishments. Nick is recognized as the nation's leading expert on personal branding as Fast Company Magazine's Expert Blogger on the subject and lectures regularly on the topic at at major universities around the world. His book *Celebrity Branding You®* has also been used as the textbook on personal branding for University student.

The CEO of The Dicks + Nanton Celebrity Branding Agency, an international agency with more than 1000 clients in 26 countries, Nick is an award winning director, producer and songwriter who has worked on everything from large scale events to television shows with the likes of Bill Cosby, President George H.W. Bush, Brian Tracy, Michael Gerber and many more.

Nick is recognized as one of the top thought-leaders in the business world and has co-authored 16 best-selling books alongside Brian Tracy, Jack Canfield (creator of the *Chicken Soup for the Soul* Series), Dan Kennedy, Robert Allen, Dr. Ivan Misner (Founder of BNI), Jay Conrad Levinson (Author of the *Guerilla Marketing* Series), Leigh Steinberg and many others, including the breakthrough hit *Celebrity Branding You!®*.

Nick has published books by Brian Tracy, Mari Smith, Jack Canfield, Dan Kennedy and many other celebrity experts and Nick has led the marketing and PR campaigns that have driven more than 600 authors to Best-Seller status. Nick has been seen in *USA Today*, The *Wall St. Journal*, *Newsweek*, Inc. Magazine, *The New York Times, Entrepreneur®* Magazine, FastCompany.com. and has appeared on ABC, NBC, CBS, and FOX television affiliates around the country, as well as CNN, FOX News, CNBC, and MSNBC from coast to coast speaking on subjects ranging from branding, marketing and law, to American Idol.

Nick is a member of the Florida Bar, holds a JD from the University of Florida Levin College of Law, as well as a BSBA in Finance from the University of Florida's Warrington College of Business. Nick is a voting member of The National Academy of Recording Arts & Sciences (NARAS, Home to The GRAMMYs), a member of The National Academy of Television Arts & Sciences (Home to the Emmy Awards) co-founder of the National Academy of Best-Selling Authors, an 11-time Telly Award winner, and spends his spare time working with Young Life and Downtown Credo Orlando and rooting for the Florida Gators with his wife Kristina and their three children, Brock, Bowen and Addison.

CHAPTER 28

How To Create A Success Driven Core Message

By Greg Rollett

A business's success lies in its ability to communicate how their products and services will impact the lives of their prospects and customers.

The words, the images and the vision in your messaging will help you strike the minds, hearts and souls of your market and make lasting change in your customer's lives.

Getting this message right is everything in today's media driven business landscape. With every turn, your prospects and customers are being infiltrated with advertising, marketing, branding, videos, music, movies, games and anything else that lives within a smartphone, tablet, laptop, office, car or home these days.

How your market hears and experiences your messaging has everything to do with how they do (or don't) do business with you.

When we first started the ProductPros, we knew we needed to create a core message, and sync this messaging up through every medium imaginable to attract the best clients for our business and truly make the sales process effortless and enjoyable for everyone.

The message we have today was not created overnight, nor will it forever remain the way it is now—it is constantly changing and evolving, just as we are in the business, and just as our customers are, while going through their experience with our business.

The core message we have been using in our messaging has focused on helping entrepreneurs, experts and professionals create highly valuable and financially rewarding information products. As we have built our company, this has changed and evolved to helping entrepreneurs, experts and professionals find highly valuable ways to package information to educate and profit from their marketplace.

Similar message, but not entirely the same. It attracts a different type of client—a client that is helping us grow our business exponentially and going to make the best use of the resources and experiences we provide.

Let's talk about how you can begin to craft your core message.

TALKING DIRECTLY TO YOUR IDEAL CLIENT

Knowing who you want to hear your message is the foundation of a successful business. While the optimist in you wants to help everyone, you need to put a strong focus on talking to one specific person and pouring your heart out to him or her in a way that no one else can.

At the end of the day, although *you* are cashing in the checks and giving yourself a paycheck, it is *the customers* that provide you with your lifestyle.

Find more of the best ones, and your life can change dramatically. But first, you need to know who the best ones are; sadly, many business owners, experts and professionals do not know who this person is, what they look like or where to find them.

To illustrate this point, I want you to think of your favorite TV character. Jot his or her name down on a piece of paper and then write down 3-5 characteristics about that character.

I always use Homer Simpson in this scenario. When I start thinking about Homer Simpson, I know that he is:

- Married to Marge
- Has three children: Bart, Lisa and Maggie
- Works at the Power Plant and his boss is Mr. Burns
- He loves his Duff Beer and heads to Moe's to kick back a few with Barney
- His neighbor is Ned Flanders

- He wears blue pants and a white shirt.
- He is probably in his 40s, a bit overweight

And I can go on and on and on about Homer Simpson. But think about this.

Homer Simpson is a fictional character—a cartoon character, in fact. One that has no bearing on how much money I make or how I can keep food on the table. But yet, I know just about every detail about him and his life.

Most businesses owners and experts cannot do the same for their ideal clients. Try the same exercise now, but give *your ideal client or customer* a name. Then write down 3-5 things that will tell you about them, their needs and their personality that makes them ideal to your business.

When I first started creating information products, I marketed to the indie musician industry and performed a similar exercise. I knew that I couldn't create a sales message to every musician, from every genre, but I could find one musician who was more likely than the others to buy my products and learn from the things I was selling.

Here is what my ideal customer looked like:

- They are between the ages of 24-30 and are likely to have just gotten out of college and not yet entered the "real world"
- They worked as a server, in fast food or another hospitality-driven job
- They wore a backwards baseball cap, a t-shirt with a silly slogan, khaki shorts and flip-flops
- They played local dive bars and earned about $100-150 per show, yet spent about $100-150 at the bar
- They wanted more than anything to quit their job and play music for a living
- They didn't care about MTV or platinum records, just wanted to do what they loved for a living

And again, I could go on and on and one about my ideal customers.

Do you see now, with the information I provided above, that I could speak directly to that person, their needs and how our business can help them get the things they wanted from their life?

I hope that you have created this same type of profile for your customers as well.

FINDING YOUR MARKET'S CORE PROBLEMS

As a business owner or expert, your profits and success depend on how well you solve your market's problems. In fact, that is really the only reason that you are in business.

Think about the businesses around you. If you walk into your garage and see some unwanted bugs, you have a bug problem. When you have this problem, you call the local exterminator. He solves your problem.

If you run out of paper in your printer, your local office supply store solves your paper problem.

When you are hungry, a restaurant or supermarket solves your problem. Some better than others.

And that is why you truly need to know the core problem that you solve, before crafting your core message. (If someone is on the road and only has 5-10 minutes to eat, the local steak house is not going to be the problem solver.)

You also want to break past the surface level problems your customers have. You want to find the deep root of the problem and the emotions tied to that problem.

Think about someone who wants to lose weight. On the surface they want to lose a few pounds, or whatever that number might be. But their real problem isn't losing weight.

Maybe it's a health issue. Or it could be that they are going on a beach vacation in a few weeks or a high school or family reunion. Maybe they are training for an event.

All of those reasons are vastly different and require different marketing, different programs and different levels of service, even though they are all rooted back to losing weight.

In your business it is no different. People have different, deep-down reasons for needing help in their lives and in their business. It's up to you to find those reasons.

An easy way to find the core problems of your ideal customer is to simply ask them. Engage in online conversations, send out surveys or even jump on the phone with them to see why they joined your business or what they are looking to get out of the relationship. You will be surprised by the stories you hear and the information you learn about your market.

Another way to see the core problems, needs and desires of your market is to look at user-generated reviews online. Services like Yelp and Amazon are great places to see customer feedback. Look at the 2-, 3- and 4-star reviews and notice the things they were looking to experience (and what fell short). This is very powerful and can help you in your marketing and the creation of your message.

A final way is to leverage the conversations happening on social media. Perform searches for Facebook Groups, look for Twitter posts and even LinkedIn Groups to see what people are talking about and the help they need in their life and in business. This is a wealth of information that can help you fully understand what exactly your market wants.

Now that you know who your market is and what they need, it's time to craft your message and share it with your marketplace.

CRAFTING YOUR CORE MESSAGE

This is actually a very challenging step for many experts and entrepreneurs; it becomes even more increasingly difficult if you are in a commodity industry, or have many competitors that offer similar products or services.

The first step in drafting your 'Core Message' is to clarify your USP, or unique selling proposition. How does your product or service differ in the marketplace? Why is it superior? Why should I choose to spend my hard-earned money with you and not someone else?

These are all difficult questions to answer if you have not gone through the first two steps I laid out. If you do not know who your core customers are, nor there needs and desires, how can you tell them what you have to offer is going to help them?

But since I know you are a massive action taker, you can take the steps to draft your USP. At the ProductPros, our USP is simple. We take the ideas that you have for information products, get them out of your head and turn them into highly valuable products for you in 30 days.

Most companies in our space will only tell you "how to" create the products. Our philosophy is that, yes you can create your own, but if you don't know where to start, or you do not have the time or the resources, we will take the load off your plate and create the product for you, in a done-for-you services model.

The reason we do this is because we know who our market is and what they desire. We know that affluent experts and professionals want to continue to educate their clientele and prospects, but are too busy providing great services to take the time and energy to build out a product framework, record video or audio, edit the files, create manuals and Action Guides, find designers and then package the materials in a way their customers and prospects will consume and enjoy.

Your USP should be similar.

Once you have your USP, you need to get deeper and really connect that USP to your audience. Some questions to ask yourself may include:

- How can I back up my USP with proof?
- Will my customer understand the key benefits of what we do without asking any follow-up questions?
- Is my core message focused on the outcome my prospect wants and not solely focused on the solution I provide?
- Does your core message position you as the Celebrity Expert in your marketplace?
- Does it have qualities others will want to share on your behalf (this could be your sales team, your partners and affiliates or it could be your customers)?

Think about your core message like this: If you were at a conference, tradeshow or event and told a few people about what you do, what will happen when they go off and converse with others at the event, without you there? Will they tell people about you and what you do in a way that is easy to understand, and in a way that excites others so they will have to hunt you down to learn more?

That is the power of a great core message.

WHAT TO DO WITH YOUR CORE MESSAGE

Once you have your core message, it's time to share it with the world. Every piece of content, education and marketing needs to include your core message, and then you need to use evidence, proof and credibility to back up your core message.

In videos, you can talk about your core message and then share success stories of how others have gotten the benefits that you talk about in your core message.

In blog posts or articles, you want to spend your time writing about how your core message is changing people's businesses and lives.

In your advertising or marketing, you want to ingrain your core message and back it up with testimonials or proof to give your core message meaning and believability.

When you educate clients or prospects, you need to build upon your core message and educate them on why that message is vital to their success in business and in life.

With our core message, we back it up by showing how our clients have benefited from our system. We show the products we created, we show the results our clients have achieved in their business through these products and we even share the results their clients and customers have had after buying the products we created for our own customers.

We share the stories of how easy our process is and how fun it is to work with us.

Everything we do supports our core message and continues to position us as the Celebrity Experts in our marketplace.

Once you begin to leverage your core message, share it with the world and get others to experience it, your business will never be the same.

About Greg

Greg Rollett, the ProductPro, is a best-selling author and online marketing expert who works with authors, experts, entertainers, entrepreneurs and business owners all over the world to help them share their knowledge and change the lives and businesses of others. After creating a successful string of his own educational products, Greg began helping others in the production and marketing of their own products.

Greg is a front-runner in utilizing the power of social media, direct response marketing and customer education to drive new leads and convert those leads into long-standing customers and advocates.

Previous clients include Coca-Cola, Miller Lite, Warner Bros and Cash Money Records, as well as hundreds of entrepreneurs and small-business owners. Greg's work has been featured on FOX News, ABC, and the Daily Buzz. Greg has written for Mashable, the Huffington Post, AOL, AMEX's Open Forum and more.

Greg loves to challenge the current business environments that constrain people to working 12-hour days during the best portions of their lives. By teaching them to leverage technology and the power of information, Greg loves helping others create freedom businesses that allow them to generate income, make the world a better place and live a radically ambitious lifestyle in the process.

A former touring musician, Greg is highly sought after as a speaker, having appeared on stages with former Florida Gov. Charlie Crist, best-selling authors Chris Brogan and Nick Nanton, as well as at events such as Affiliate Summit.

If you would like to learn more about Greg and how he can help your business, please contact him directly at greg@productprosystems.com or by calling his office at 877.897.4611.

You can also download a free report on how to create your own educational products at www.productprosystems.com.

CHAPTER 29

The Secret to Success Seldom Discovered

By James Ballidis

She walked into the room, and the entire assembly of one hundred attendees stood, clapping their hands. Feeling a little embarrassed and overwhelmed, she took her seat. Such a distinguished group had never greeted her. She did not consider herself a polished, professional speaker and was concerned she would disappoint them.

She had a message to deliver, but could she be a convincing messenger?

To calm her nerves, she recalled a Sunday sermon she had heard several weeks prior, in which God asked Moses to deliver his people from the Pharaoh. She had been moved by the courage Moses summoned to overcome his fears and doubts and act. She had a problem to solve, but nothing as formidable as Moses' departure from Egypt and the mighty Pharaoh. The sermon's message, "God will help you because you are promoting his will," comforted her—but, as is often the case, only momentarily.

As the meeting commenced, several important people spoke of great needs and causes. While the group was attentive and polite, no one was really listening to the speakers' appeals for action. They eagerly awaited the opportunity to hear the woman from Oklahoma, the woman with a bold promise to reveal the secret to enlightenment and success, the woman they had just greeted.

A small, frail woman, she began to taste the nervousness rising from her upset stomach. As several of the people surrounding her smiled warmly, she fiddled with her hands under the table.

Could she express herself effectively? Could she convince them of the need she had come to convey?

Her tension escalated as the third and final speaker arose and took the podium. Knowing she would be next and that this first speech, this first opportunity to express the need, would arrive all too quickly, she wondered whether she could muster the courage to take it. Instead of succumbing to the urge to politely excuse herself to the lobby, she remained seated.

As the speaker before her was delivering a passionate plea for action, she tried to focus on his message and not her anxiety. She marveled at his delivery, so polished and practiced. She felt it lulling her, convincing her, compelling her to agree. Although later she did not recall his point, she wished for such oratory skill.

The next few minutes were a blur: she heard her name called and a description of her life. Although she noted the absence of what many would consider grand achievements, she was proud when it was announced she had raised a family and been married to her husband for 40 years until his recent death. Suddenly, she was asked to come forward.

As she made her way forward, the master of ceremony, whom she had never met, reached to shake her hand, turning her to pose for a photo with him in an attempt to preserve the moment for himself.

She stood at the podium, her slight frame hidden behind it and her glasses in need of adjusting. Nervously, she smoothed her neatly pulled back hair, her fingers brushing absently rearward from just above her ear. Lacking any papers or notes, she now wished she had written some thoughts down. She stared at them in total silence for more than a minute, maybe two. No one stirred. No one left. No one even coughed, a noise common to large gatherings. The hall was arrested by the eerie silence of anticipation.

"I want to start by thanking you all for such a warm welcome, but that is not why I am here," she said. "I am quite desperate for your help on a project near and very dear to me. Without your assistance, I will not be able to accomplish it."

"You see, I am without means, but this need must be met," she continued. "I will explain later what you can do to help, but for now I hope you will honor my request with generosity and spirit. Please sign up at the back table." She smiled, smoothed her hair again, and began to leave the stage. She had said almost the same thing to smaller groups and was proud of the commitments she had received.

Murmurs echoed throughout the great hall. People stirred in their seats. Soon their questions were discernible. "What is this about?" they asked. "We were promised a life-changing secret." Once at her seat, she surveyed the nine other members of her table; their expressions reflected the sentiments of the audience: confusion and bewilderment.

A handsome gentleman sitting to her left touched her hand. He looked to be 25, far younger than the rest in attendance. He gazed into her dark hazel eyes, worn with experience and age, and said: "We are here because we were told you had a very special message, one that only you could deliver. Look at the flyer in front of me. It clearly states, 'Come learn of a very special need. Once fulfilled, you will discover the secret to being enlightened and rewarded for the rest of your life.'"

Calmly, yet a bit overwhelmed, the woman asked, "Did I not offer those things to you? I very much need all of your help, and I asked for it, didn't I? Would it not be rewarding to help someone in need such as myself? As for the promise of the secret to a rewarding life, it only applies to those who agree to help."

"Yes," replied the young man, "but you have not told of the problem you wish to solve. The promotional literature only said that you were an amazing, lifesaving person and that you would be making a special request. We heard nothing specific about this request."

Others around the table nodded in agreement, one woman expressing anger at the waste of her time.

Apologetically, the woman stood and, with all eyes in the room focused on her, said, "I am sorry that you are disappointed. I made no promise that my need was of interest to you, but it is very much of importance to me. I have asked for help. Isn't that enough? I do not claim to be an amazing, lifesaving person. That is the opinion of others who have agreed to help me."

The young man, seemingly the only one in the room with a voice, said, "It is not that we do not want to help, but what is the cause? Without an understanding of the cause, we are naturally reluctant to help."

She realized little help would be coming. "I wish I was a better presenter, like the speaker before me," she said. "I could have persuaded you all to join me as he did." However, she suddenly realized she could not recall the need he spoke of.

"I simply asked for help," she continued. "I need the help desperately, so you see the cause is unimportant. I will leave all of you to your afternoon. Thank you for your time." She began to leave.

As she made her way to the empty signup sheet and the rear door, first one person, then another, and then several approached her. "We want to help, but please tell us the cause you seek to champion," they said.

To each of them she said, "I am sorry to have troubled you."

As she left, consternation smothered the initial excitement of the day. The room fell completely silent, each person reflecting on the unexpected turn of events, questioning the impetus for her behavior:

Does she need financial help? Is she too proud to ask? Maybe she needed help for another in her family? Why would others agree to help her? Have we missed something?

Eventually the young man asked, "Does anyone want to help her? I sure do."

There was a resounding, "Yes, but what is it she is trying to accomplish?"

"I promise to find out this secret cause that she needs help with and return to tell you about it," he volunteered. "Wait here! Please do not leave."

He ran after this interesting but perplexing woman. As he exited the large hotel, he saw her getting into an old but well-maintained car. "Wait, wait," he called out, "I need to speak to you."

As she heard his call, she turned. She asked the valet to hold her car. She took several steps toward the approaching man. Out of breath, he stopped in front of her, holding up his right palm to give himself a second or two to think and catch his breath. She waited patiently.

"I ran out to catch you because nearly everyone in that room may be willing to help you," he said. "I beg you to tell us the cause that compelled you to come here. Without an explanation, we cannot evaluate its merit. We need to know that you are not simply squandering our hard-earned money or time. We need to judge and believe in the cause ourselves before we can commit. I promised the others to find out your secret cause and report back to them."

The woman looked at him with kind eyes. She wanted to tell him everything would be okay, but she had failed; she knew that now. "What you seek is before us all," she said.

"So many in the world plead for help every day," she said. "Unless it is a cause that we have assessed, analyzed, and approved, we refuse them. We listen not to the request but only the cause. Popular causes may elicit attention, but all requests for help deserve to be heard."

"Those around us ask for help, but we do not pay attention," she continued. "Family members request help, but we ignore them. We are so busy tending to our lives, our concerns, and our needs that we do not hear the pleas of the desperate. Yet these people still stand before us. I stood before this group in need, but rather than be heard, I was asked to justify my request."

The woman realized that she too failed to listen to the request of the prior speaker. Focused so intently on her insecurities and lack of confidence in her pending speech, she had missed the message. Embarrassed and angry with herself, she vowed to avoid that mistake in the future.

She grabbed the young man's hand while she squeezed her eyes shut, frustrated by her own shortcomings. "I need help to persuade others to hear the call for help," she said. "They must hear the call, not the cause, in their professional and personal lives. I need each to listen and take action. You see, the cause is really not a cause at all, but a call for help."

Opening her eyes to look deeply at and empower this young man, she emphasized, "Your success will be dependant upon your willingness to focus on the needs of others and not your own. If people learned that simple secret, they would enjoy a full, rich, and rewarding life. Causes are popular or unpopular at any given moment, but fulfilling the needs of others is always rewarding." With that, she turned and walked to her car. The man never saw her again.

He did, however, help the woman with her need. He returned with her message to the great hall. Thereafter, he listened intently to the requests of others and experienced the joy and reward of fulfilling their needs. He intently listened to the needs of others, and captured the joy and reward of fulfilling their requests. He prospered because each story of need was resolved, and that success led to another need, until his list of successes was too large to catalogue.

On the wall of his office he has mounted that flyer from so long ago.

"Come learn of a very special need. Once fulfilled, you will discover the secret to being enlightened and rewarded for the rest of your life."

He has vowed to deliver that message every day.

About James

James Ballidis is the managing partner for the California law firm of Allen, Flatt, Ballidis & Leslie Inc. He graduated from Southwestern Law School in Los Angeles in 1985 and that same summer, he was admitted to the California State Bar. He is licensed to appear before the California Supreme Court and the District Courts of California.

James is a practicing trial attorney, author and State Bar Committee member for the Administration of Justice. He has been granted an AV® Preeminent™ designation for outstanding achievement and professional ethics as awarded by Martindale-Hubbell, an independent rating organization of lawyers in the United States. He has also been featured in "88-lawyers" and nominated to "Superlawyers" (both organizations dedicated to identifying and recognizing superior lawyers in their field).

His firm specializes in personal injury claims arising from motorized and non-motorized accidents, including bicycle, automobile, truck and pedestrian collisions. He has successfully tried and settled hundreds of personal injury claims, including multimillion dollar verdicts for product defects and personal injuries. The firm has also won several important appeals addressing the bad faith conduct of insurance companies in the handling of injury, product and wrongful death claims.

The law firm of Allen, Flatt, Ballidis & Leslie Inc. has served clients since 1974 in Newport Beach, California. For more information on Mr. Ballidis, and the law firm of Allen, Flatt, Ballidis & Leslie Inc., including our track record and client testimonials, please visit the following websites:
www.ca-personalinjuryattorney.com or
www.thecaliforniainjurylawyer.com

If you know a California resident that was injured in an accident, and you would like to send a helpful books or information to that person about their rights, call 1-888-752-7474 or (949) 752-7474. Our firm specializes in significant personal injury cases. If you would like our office to consider representing you, please call us immediately.

CHAPTER 30

How to Go from Zero Dollars and Zero Customers to a Multimillion Dollar Business—Fast!

By Jimmy Vee and Travis Miller,
Band geeks who expose how you
can naturally attract customers at will...

(Warning: these ideas are unconventional...but they really work)

This one time at band camp, we met and became friends. We flunked calculus and switched our majors to marketing. After college, we worked together at an advertising agency. Six years later, we started our own business. We had no customers, no prospects and no leads. Travis' wedding was six weeks away. Jim's was six months away and there was no way either of our fiancées wanted to marry a broke loser.

We had just left the comfort and security of our high-paying jobs to strike out on our own and try to make it as entrepreneurs. We started our company with $200. We bought a phone and the bank charged us a fee to have the account. We were fast on our way to losing money.

We knew we had to do something (and do it fast) with less than $200.

You may be in a similar position now or remember when you were. It's do-or-die, gun-to-the-head, make-it-or-break-it marketing in its purest form. You need to attract customers immediately or fail. There is no in between.

THE MOST FRIGHTENING TIME IN YOUR LIFE

It can be the most frightening time in a business owner's life. When you have to come home in the evening and face your family then wake up in the morning and face yourself in the mirror…knowing that tomorrow will be the same as today. No new opportunities, no new prospects and no money at the end of the week. Sometimes it feels like the entire weight of the world is on your shoulders.

If you're working on starting your own business—maybe even quitting your job like we did—you may be hesitating or waiting until you get your new venture going before you walk the plank. Your dislike for your job grows bigger by the day and your desire to perform goes down, but you just can't seem to gain traction with your new project.

YOUR FUTURE

Today we own a multimillion dollar customer attraction agency and help business owners and entrepreneurs all over the world create lives and businesses that are **ESP**—Enjoyable, Simple & Prosperous. We work out of an office we own; we personally designed it from scratch. With a vibrant orange and green color scheme and entire walls painted with a special dry erase "Idea Paint," the environment allows our staff of 20 to collaborate and be creative. The office is less than five minutes from our homes, our children's schools and popular stores and restaurants.

We have a long list of clients who love us and fly from all over the country to learn from us. We each vacation over eight weeks every year. We are frequently written about in magazines and newspapers (including our dream, Ripley's Believe It Or Not) for our quirky and outrageous marketing, and we consistently win awards for running an innovative and vibrant growing business.

We're not telling you this to brag. Not at all. We're telling you this because you can do it too. You can build and live your own dream. It all comes from being able to naturally attract a steady stream of your perfect clients.

EASILY & EFFORTLESSLY ATTRACT CLIENTS

Thankfully, when we began, we already knew a thing or two about effective marketing. In our careers as marketing executives, we had worked together to create campaigns and systems for our clients that made many business owners instant successes. In total, we had invested $96 million of our clients' money and with that generated more than $10 billion in sales. It wasn't our money to spend or keep so we didn't get rich. But we did learn an awful lot in the process about how to attract customers and make them buy.

Armed with that knowledge, experience and just less than $200, we went to work creating our dream and our fortune. We asked, "How can we duplicate the results we created for our clients and cause people to come to us but without spending a lot of money?"

So we locked ourselves in our office, which happened to be a 10x10 room in one of our houses. Everyday for months and months we would hole away in that office and shut the door and try to solve the problem.

We tried different ideas and we tested different techniques and we presented different theories. And then one day it all came to us at once.

THE 'EUREKA' MOMENT

This simple, little idea would truly make people quickly, easily and naturally come to you and identify themselves, almost waving their hands saying, "I want what you have to sell." Then you could put all of your focus, energy, budget and time marketing directly to those people who have already told you that they *want* what you have to offer — these ideal clients *want* the benefit you offer and they've given you permission to tell them about it.

That sale has almost no friction, a higher closing ratio and typically is more enjoyable to make. It also provides you a customer with a longer relationship span who has a higher degree of respect for you and your company, which is very important, and a greater level of profitability to your company, which is extremely important.

This process, which we called Gravitational Marketing®, causes potential customers to raise their hands and say, "Market to me because this is something I'm interested in." That is a powerful thing.

THE POWER OF GRAVITATIONAL MARKETING®

Gravitational Marketing® is based on the principle that all bodies exhibit an inherent force called gravity that naturally attracts other bodies. Following that analogy, every business has a natural tendency, however large or small, to attract customers. This force is created by several factors such as a company's general existence, location, signage, current marketing and advertising efforts and word-of-mouth advertising. As the force grows, it builds momentum and allows you to attract exactly the right group of prospects and customers without wasting tons of money.

Our method levels the playing field and gives businesses that have limited marketing and sales resources an opportunity to increase their gravitational potential without drastically increasing their marketing costs or the size of their company.

Gravitational Marketing® is the process of motivating prospects to ask for your marketing messages, forging emotional relationships with them, getting your newly formed friends to buy, motivating existing customers to return and ultimately motivating all of your customers to tell others, thereby harnessing the power of word-of-mouth advertising, which we all know is the best and cheapest form of marketing.

Once you fully understand and learn how to use Gravitational Marketing®, you will spend less on advertising, have better relationships with your potential and existing customers and have a virtual sales force working day and night for you for free.

HOW GRAVITATIONAL MARKETING® WORKS

The process of Gravitational Marketing® is broken down into four primary components: Gravitate, Captivate, Invigorate and Motivate.

Gravitate

The Gravitate process begins first by either choosing who it is that your existing product or service would be right for, or finding the 'who' first and then determining what they want. We call this targeting.

Next you find out what problems they're having, what difficulties and challenges they face or what they really want but have to live without. And you offer the solution to that problem, whatever it is.

For instance, if you are a financial planner, then the people that you're going to help want security, they want to retire wealthy and they want to retire early. They don't know how to accomplish these things. That's their problem.

If you're a real estate agent, the clients you will help want to sell their homes as quickly as possible for as much as possible or own as much home as possible for the lowest payment possible. That's what they want from you. Nothing else.

If you're a car dealer, the people you want to help are afraid of getting taken advantage of when buying a car. They want to make sure that they get the best deal possible.

If you're a marketing consultant, the people that you are going to help want to get new business and they need to know how they can do that.

The list goes on and on.

So you offer a very simple initial solution that only requires a small step, a small type of action with little commitment and zero risk.

It's almost like a piece of bait. It's like saying, "I've got the answer to your problem—come to me and I'll explain."

At first glance, this may seem like regular advertising, but indeed, it is very different.

Captivate

The Captivate phase happens once you've gotten your prospects' attention. They've asked for more information about the solution that you're offering and you have a chance to present yourself to them. But you have to present yourself in a way that is unforgettable. You can't just be another "me too" service or a commodity product. You've got to be sensational. You've got to be memorable. You've got to be unique. You must captivate your audience in order to hold their attention, arouse child-like curiosity in them and cause them to be intrigued and to want to know more.

Invigorate

You Invigorate your prospects by helping them understand how bad the problem actually is that they're facing now and how wonderful the solution really could be. You must get them to visualize themselves living the dream.

You need to involve their emotions in the process and help them understand the depth of their problem but also the true availability of the solution and the wonderful things that will come with the solution.

Motivate

Finally, you have to Motivate your prospects to take the action you want them to take. That means you have to know ahead of time what that action should be. You can't just willy-nilly get to the Motivate phase and not know how to proceed and let the prospect direct the transaction.

With a clear vision of the desired action you can overwhelm the prospect with benefits, bonuses, offers and value that make doing business with you irresistible.

Each step of this process is critical. If you fail to attract prospects (Gravitate) in the first place nothing will happen. But once you've attracted the prospect, if you don't capture their attention (Captivate) you will become invisible and the sale will be lost. Even if you have captured their attention, if you don't involve their emotions and get them excited (Invigorate) about the possibility and potential of working together, the game is over. Finally, if everything has come together but you don't cause the prospect to take the final action (Motivate), if you don't ask them to spend money, all of your efforts will have been wasted.

WHAT TO DO TODAY TO MAKE MONEY TOMORROW

All this sounds great, but we know that action is what creates success. So we're going to give you a down and dirty, step-by-step action plan for creating your own Gravitational Marketing® campaign.

Step 1. Be Sensational

The first step is to learn to be unforgettable. Be the kind of person and the kind of business people want to get more of. Same Is Lame. Boring is invisible. Average companies get average results. Sensational people and businesses attract more than their fair share of the business.

How can you be sensational? Simple. Be interested in other people. Be unique enough to remember. Be fun to be around and do business with. Be willing to take risks and try new things. Be visible to the right people as frequently as you can. Be credible, by doing what you say you're going to do and get testimonials from past clients that prove your credibility. Be spreadable—that is, be worth talking about and worth recommending.

Step 2: Position Yourself As An Expert

Let's face it, people don't like to be sold. But they love to buy things. And who do people most want to do business with? Experts. It's the difference between being a specialist and a generalist. People will pay more for a specialist, they'll feel more comfortable during a transaction with a specialist and they are more receptive to doing business in the first place with a specialist. In the end, people are more satisfied after working with an expert and more likely to tell others.

How can you become an expert? Understand that you know more about your business than most other people in the world. That alone makes you an expert. Then all you have to do is share what you know with others who are seeking your knowledge and advice.

Step 3: Determine Who You Want To Attract

You can't do business with everyone, so determine who wants what you have to sell most and target them specifically. Your marketing dollars will go further if you narrow your efforts to a specific group of people. You can be a big fish in a small pond instead of being lost in the sea of media clutter.

You'll be able to hone your message to match your target's wants, needs and desires. You'll be able to increase your visibility and credibility with a small group much more quickly than you can a large group.

Step 4: Know What Sets You Apart

Determine what unique emotional appeals and benefits your product or service delivers to your target. Create your marketing message around this uniqueness and stick to it. Don't get caught up with features or image or pricing. Instead, lock on to your target's emotional desires and craft a message around it.

Step 5: Take Baby Steps

The biggest marketing mistake people make is they ask their advertising to do too much. Very rarely can you make a sale in a single ad. Instead, offer your potential prospects a simple, no risk, no cost, intermediate step that separates the ad from the sale. This will cause your ads to generate more leads—people who are interested in what you have to of-fer—and give you a chance to build a persuasive case with those people.

Jimmy Vee

About Jimmy & Travis

Jimmy Vee & Travis Miller are the nation's leading experts on attracting customers, and the authors of the best-selling book *Gravitational Marketing: The Science of Attracting Customers* and *Invasion of the Profit Snatchers: A Practical Guide to Increase Sales without Cutting Prices & Protecting your Dealership from Looters, Moochers, & Vendors Gone Wild.*

Travis Miller

Called "The Penn & Teller of Marketing," Jim & Travis have been helping business owners differentiate themselves, attract customers and increase sales for over a decade. In 2004 they created Gravitational Marketing®, an exclusive customer attraction agency for busy entrepreneurs who want to stand out and sell more without spending more in advertising.

Jim & Travis also own and operate Rich Dealers® International, one of the largest retail automotive advertising agencies in the world.

Collectively, their campaigns have resulted in over 12 billion dollars in sales. Every month they create record shattering promotions and bring together some of the brightest and most successful entrepreneurs and business people to participate in fun and insanely profitable think-tank, mastermind experiences.

Jim and Travis have spoken all over the world on their special brand of customer attraction, known as Gravitational Marketing®, and have been seen on or in *Entrepreneur* Magazine, *Investor's Business Daily,* Ripley's Believe It Or Not, Forbes, CNBC, Fox Business, *Advertising Age, Direct Marketing News, BusinessWeek, Brandweek* and many other publications and media outlets.

Jimmy Vee & Travis Miller believe that life and business should be ESP—Enjoyable, Simple & Prosperous. They help make this a reality through their work at Gravitational Marketing®, freeing business owners from tedious tasks that keep them bound to the business, worried about profitability and unable to live their lives to the fullest.

Jim and Travis both reside in Orlando, Florida, each married with two young children.

CHAPTER 31

The Social Media Success Secret: Myths and Must-Dos

By Lindsay Dicks

The evolution of social media has presented a sort of "good news/bad news" scenario for small businesspeople and entrepreneurs around the world.

The good news is, Twitter, Facebook, LinkedIn and the rest have provided us with all of these new and exciting possibilities for connecting with customers, forming relationships and building our brands.

And the bad news?

Well, when it comes to actually using social media, most of us still don't exactly know what we're doing. Sure, anyone can post a Facebook status, but very few of us understand exactly what we *should* and *can* be doing with social media to accomplish our goals. And with new platforms popping up every few months (Pinterest, anyone?), whatever we do master is almost certain to change in the near future.

So how do we get the most out of the current social media trends, while developing a plan that will be easily adaptable to new platforms, new products and new audiences in the future?

Let's start by poking a few holes into conventional social media wisdom..

SOCIAL MEDIA MYTHS

Before you can fully grasp what *to* do with social media, it's also important you know what *not* to do. Because social media is so new and, at the same time, so pervasive, there is a lot of misinformation out there about who it's for, what it does and how it works. So let's take a few moments to tackle some of the misinformation that may be holding your social media strategy back—or just pointing you in the wrong direction.

Myth #1: Social media is FREE (or at least extremely cheap!).
It's true, membership in sites like Facebook and Twitter won't cost you a cent. But using them effectively takes time and expertise–time and expertise most of us just don't have. Bringing in a paid expert may not be free, but it may very well be the best way to insure your social media presence receives the time and guidance necessary to succeed.

Myth #2: Social media is EASY.
We all know mastering the basic tools and broadcasting information on social media isn't complicated–how else could all our grandmas be using it? However, the tools that may offer the most benefit to your business are a bit more complex than the ones granny uses–and more and more of them are appearing every day. Figuring out which of these tools will benefit your business *and how to use them the most effectively for your particular niche* takes time and patience you may not have, but a social media expert will get you going in no time flat.

Myth #3: Social media is just a fad.
Just like the Hula Hoop and Rubik's Cube, many believe social media is just another craze that will soon die down. Well, the fact is, while fads may happen *on* social media (like flash mobs on Twitter), the platform itself is not going anywhere.

The Internet gives individuals and companies a place to freely exchange ideas and information with people down the block and around the world. That's a complete paradigm shift just as newspapers, radio and television were in their time. Until something even more groundbreaking comes along that facilitates this in an even easier way, social media is here to stay and will only get bigger. Hang on to those antiquated beliefs that social media will simply run its course and you're asking to be left out of the most lucrative and growing market on the planet.

Myth #4: Social media is for kids.

If you've seen "The Social Network," you're no doubt aware that Facebook was launched by a college student. But are you aware that today, almost half of Facebook profiles belong to people aged 35 and up? Facebook is no longer just about "hanging out," it's about doing business–which is why adults with buying power are fast emerging as a powerful online target market.

Myth #5: Facebook Ads are the best way to use social media marketing.

Most of us are marketed to from the moment we wake up to the moment we go to bed at night. So we become immune to much advertising. The beauty of social media is that it offers a chance to reach people in a *different* way, because social media channels are fundamentally all about communication. So start by listening. Contribute to some conversations, and eventually start some of your own. Take time to build relationships and establish trust, then those people who have gotten to know and like you won't view messages about your business as just another ad. And when you finally do advertise, keep it subtle and low-key.

Myth #6: Anyone can market successfully using social media.

As I've already pointed out, using social media in a business context is complicated and time consuming. To get the most out of it, you need to understand the tools available to you and your business, your target market, and what works and what doesn't work when it comes to reaching them. You may not have the time or expertise for that, but a professional social media specialist (or team of specialists) will. Social media experts are uniquely suited to bring your existing branding message into the social media world; they'll work closely with you or someone on your team to gain insight into your product or service offering, and combine that with their knowledge of the online landscape to give you and your company maximum online exposure.

Myth #7: Social media marketing success can't be measured.

Most people who worry that they can't measure their social media marketing efforts also don't know what to expect from social media marketing, so they don't start out with clearly defined objectives. If you set concrete goals (things like increased traffic, sign-ups for a newsletter or other measurable activities), systems can be set up to accurately measure your progress. Define what success means first, then set up systems to determine how close you are getting to that definition.

Myth #8: Social media is a world without rules.

Entering a new social media platform is like entering a new culture; as the various platforms have evolved and become more sophisticated, each has developed its own system of etiquette and its own set of rules. Some basic rules, like not over-promoting yourself or your business and not attacking other people or groups, are common to most platforms. However, the diversity and constant change associated with social media means that each platform's "unwritten rules" are different; they also tend to evolve and change. If you don't know what these rules are, your best bet may be to team up with someone who does to guide you through the initial phases and possibly give you valuable ongoing advice.

Myth #9: The more "friends" you add, the more successful you are.

Boasting a long list of Twitter followers is not a guarantee of business success. You need to look more closely at *who those people actually are*. They need to be people who are interested in your product and in a position to support your brand, not necessarily your nine year-old niece who's posting a video of her piano recital on your wall!

Focus on connecting with people who care about what you have to offer and with whom you can also form a clear communication channel. The sheer numbers of random strangers, family members and people you went to school with may look impressive, but when it comes to increasing business, the *quality* of your connections counts. Seeking out and engaging with the right kind of people takes skill and knowledge of consumer behavior.

SOCIAL MEDIA SUCCESS SECRETS

Okay, now that we've talked about what *doesn't* work, let's move on to the positive and what you can start focusing on TODAY to start elevating your social media efforts. Here are eight surefire ways you can utilize your social media presence to establish yourself (and your brand) as the go-to guru within your market.

1) Tweet your analysis of breaking news in your field.
Keeping your audience updated with all the latest breaking news in your industry helps keep them apprised of what's going on. Providing your own thoughtful analysis of the story or event helps keep *you* at the top of your audience's minds as an expert in your field. For example, if you are a tax lawyer, don't just report that a new law is making its way through Congress…take the time to add your own, expert analysis of how the new law might affect your audience and what they can and/or should do about it.

2) Post pictures on Facebook and Twitter of yourself "in action."
Anyone on my Facebook friend list knows that I get around. One day I'm at the Grammys, the next filming on location in Washington, D.C., the next riding a scooter in beautiful Bermuda. However, I don't post those pictures simply because I like to share the fun of the places I get to see, but because, in most of those pictures, I'm also working hard helping my clients boost their celebrity status (I know, it's a tough job, but somebody's gotta do it!). Any opportunity you have to show yourself doing what you do makes your work seem that much more real and relatable to your clients and customers–so don't be shy…post those pics!

3) Post video tips on YouTube and then pin them on Pinterest.
Whatever you're an expert at; take a moment to share what you know via a YouTube video and then pin that video on Pinterest! Video tips are a great way to connect with your audience–people feel closer to you when they can see and hear you, rather than simply reading your status updates or Twitter posts. If you produce these videos well, they act like your own personal commer-

cials. You'll be amazed at how much mileage you can get out of a collection of well-produced video tips. And you won't just reap the branding benefits; you'll also score with the search engines!

4) Share your blog entries and articles across Facebook, Twitter, Google+ and LinkedIn.

If you've been listening to me (and if not, why not?), you should be regularly publishing blog entries and articles. Now is your chance to let those blogs and articles do double-duty for you by posting them to your social media accounts. This not only drives traffic back to your website, it also reminds your audience of what an expert you are in your industry!

5) Answer questions your followers and connections may have.

One of the best aspects of social media platforms like Facebook and Twitter is the fact that they allow you to interact with your audience in real time. When you pay attention to the conversations going on in cyberspace, chances are you'll run across people who are asking questions or looking for advice. If they happen to be asking a question you know the answer to, chime in! You won't just help the person who asked the question, but also everyone else out there who might have a similar question. And at the same time, you'll be subtly demonstrating your expertise to your audience, reminding them that you are THE go-to person in your industry.

6) Get personal… but not TOO personal.

I like to think of the social media world as a giant cocktail party– a place to interact with interesting people, have fun, relax and tell jokes…all while networking and getting my brand out there. I firmly believe that social media doesn't have to be all business, all the time. By letting my audience know what I'm up to–traveling, eating, shopping or just hanging out with my friends–I get to share a little piece of myself they can connect with that actually helps me build my brand. So don't be afraid to be yourself and talk about your family, your pets, your hobbies and whatever makes you *you*. Just remember not to drop your guard *too* much when mixing business with pleasure (think classy cocktail party, not drunken fraternity bash)!

7) Share actionable tips for your customers and prospects.

There's nothing wrong with sharing information with your audience, but sharing advice on how to do something is even better. In the business realm, we call this *actionable content*, and it's incredibly powerful. Whether you're a real estate broker sharing inexpensive ways to add value to your home, or an accountant providing a checklist of things to take care of before tax time, providing your audience with actionable, easily digestible tips is an ideal way to show that you really know your stuff.

8) Post valuable content from authoritative sources... and add your commentary.

Have you ever seen a piece of content by a celebrity or fellow expert that struck you as something your audience might find valuable? Go ahead and share it. You don't want to promote the competition, but posting content from big names in your field or related industry shows your audience that you're "in the loop" and looking out for them. Add your own analysis and you'll definitely cement that expert status in their minds.

The endless possibilities offered by the social media universe can be confusing–especially when it comes to using it to promote your business. But at the end of the day, the most important thing is to be able to say "Yes" to the crucial question, "Am I providing value to my audience?"

If you aren't working to give your audience information they can use, they'll likely pass over your messages and focus on those that will make their lives easier. And even if you have a whole army of Twitter followers, it won't do you much good if none of them are listening or looking forward to what you have to say.

So remember, in the social media universe, it's *not* all about you. Your goal should be to bring something to the table–to make them smile, to help them out, to keep them up to date on the latest news in your industry, and/or to shed light on new developments they might find scary or confusing.

Act like the knowledgeable, helpful expert you are and your audience can't help but pay attention to each and every interaction–and to turn to *you* as the true celebrity expert in your field.

About Lindsay

Lindsay Dicks helps her clients tell their stories in the online world. Being brought up around a family of marketers, but a product of Generation Y, Lindsay naturally gravitated to the new world of on-line marketing. Lindsay began freelance writing in 2000 and soon after launched her own PR firm that thrived by offering an in-your-face "Guaranteed PR" that was one of the first of its type in the nation.

Lindsay's new media career is centered on her philosophy that "people buy people." Her goal is to help her clients build a relationship with their prospects and customers. Once that relationship is built and they learn to trust them as the expert in their field, then they will do business with them. Lindsay also built a patent-pending process that utilizes social media marketing, content marketing and search engine optimiza-tion to create online "buzz" for her clients that helps them to convey their business and personal story. Lindsay's clientele span the entire business map and range from doctors and small business owners to Inc 500 CEOs.

Lindsay is a graduate of the University of Florida. She is the CEO of CelebritySites™, an online marketing company specializing in social media and online personal brand-ing. Lindsay is also a multi-best-selling author including the best-selling book "*Power Principles for Success*" which she co-authored with Brian Tracy. She was also se-lected as one of America's PremierExperts™ and has been quoted in *Newsweek*, the *Wall Street Journal, USA Today, Inc Magazine* as well as featured on NBC, ABC, and CBS television affiliates speaking on social media, search engine optimization and making more money online. Lindsay was also recently brought on FOX 35 News as their Online Marketing Expert.

Lindsay, a national speaker, has shared the stage with some of the top speakers in the world such as Brian Tracy, Lee Milteer, Ron LeGrand, Arielle Ford, David Bullock, Brian Horn, Peter Shankman and many others. Lindsay was also a Producer on the Emmy-nominated film Jacob's Turn.

You can connect with Lindsay at:
Lindsay@CelebritySites.com
www.twitter.com/LindsayMDicks
www.facebook.com/LindsayDicks

CHAPTER 32

A Prescription for Working Toward a Worry-Free Financial Life

By Lorie A. L. Nicholas

"I'm sorry Ms. Nicholas, but we are unable to help you. Your credit scores are too low, and your debt to income ratio is too high. Since you do not have any money, you do not qualify for our loan modification program."

I must have heard this statement over a thousand times as I searched for help. I had been contacting banks and mortgage companies to get my mortgage loan locked into a fixed rate with a low interest. I was one of the millions of victims of the subprime mortgage economic downturn. I never imagined my life would be so upside down financially and truly didn't see it coming. I was living paycheck to paycheck, not realizing I was heading for trouble. As long as the bills were paid, I thought everything was good. Then it just seemed that everything hit the fan at once. I experienced some personal setbacks that I had been trying to resolve, but now realized they were beyond my control. Just when things could not get any worse, I received the letter from my mortgage company that my interest rate would increase in the next month. I had to read the letter twice to understand the technical language. My payment would increase by approximately $700. Where was I going to get $700 by next month?

As I was dealing with my own dilemma, I began to hear of other people whose payments increased by extraordinary leaps. Families were losing their homes, or just walking away from their homes, due to the jump in their interest rates and payments. I tried desperately to get help and refinance for a fixed rate. I may have had low self-esteem and a lack of confidence before, but with all that was happening to me, I began to fall into a deep depression. I felt as if everything was hopeless. I heard the response stated in the opening "we are not able to help you" from almost all the banks and mortgage companies. I had one banker tell me to stop paying my bills then "maybe" I might be able to get some assistance, but it was not a guarantee. Another mortgage program told me with my debt to income ratio being at 95%, I needed to apply for food stamps so that I could eat. As time moved on, and the increase hit, I struggled every month to make payment. During the process, I encountered a problem with one of my mortgage payments. My delayed payment created a trickle effect on my credit card payments. This was around the time that the credit card companies had instituted new rules. Under these new guidelines, the credit card companies practiced the authority to double payments and increase interest rates for a person defaulting or missing a payment on another creditors account. With this new policy, my interest rates went from 12% and 15% to 25.99% and 39.99%. No matter how much I called the credit card companies requesting assistance from the representatives and supervisors, no matter how long I had been a loyal paying customer, I did not receive any help directly from the creditors. Similar to the message I received at the opening of this chapter from the mortgage companies and banks, I received the same response from the creditors "we cannot help you…" Eventually my persistence with one creditor came to the decision that they would close my account, stop additional interest from accumulating and I would just need to pay off my balances. The other creditors remained inflexible.

I contemplated walking away from my apartment. I contemplated applying for bankruptcy. Bankruptcy was something I didn't want to consider, yet on the other hand, I had heard how filing bankruptcy had helped some people. As I conducted my research, the thought of a bankruptcy filing remaining on my credit for 7-10 years disturbed me. I decided I would utilize this strategy as a last resort, if there were no other means available.

After several more rejection phone calls, I eventually reignited strength in my faith. I became determined that I was not going to let debt beat me, but *I was going to beat debt*. I was also saddened of the stories of families who had physically lost their homes and wondered how we could all be of help to each other. I could understand and relate to their plight. Their stories hit so close to home. I first wondered what got us all into this mess. Although there were several places to point the blame, the bottom line was that we were all now in a financial crisis and needed to recover.

The steps I utilized to overcome my financial crisis, were believe it or not, very basic, and are steps that everyone can follow. However, of more importance is your belief that things will work out, and your commitment and determination to succeed and not give up on yourself, no matter what obstacles or roadblocks fall onto your path. The following was my six-step approach of working toward a successful worry free financial life:

STEP 1: PEOPLE DO NOT PLAN TO FAIL, THEY FAIL TO PLAN

In my 20 years of counseling clients, I have never met anyone who intentionally planned to fail at life. I like to be optimistic and believe everyone attempts to make something of their life. However, when obstacles fall in their path, or when they are surrounded by people who tell them they will never amount to anything or laugh at their dreams, people stop dreaming and believing in themselves.

When it comes to financial matters, we must learn to plan and budget. As the first action step, write down all of your current monthly financial obligations. I made a list of every single expense. For credit card bills, I wrote down the total balance and minimum monthly payment due. I calculated given the current payments, how long it would take me to pay off all my expenses.

STEP 2: BREAKING THROUGH YOUR BARRIERS

In order to overcome the obstacles in your path (i.e. your debt or financial situation) you have to be determined and committed to making a change in your life. We did not fall into debt overnight. It was a gradual process. Therefore, we need to realize, our debt will not go away overnight either, unless by some miracle we win the Mega millions or Powerball.

Step 2 of my debt recovery involved looking at all of my incoming sources of funds obtained each month. Write down all your sources of income that you obtain each month. Be sure to include all paychecks you receive as well as alimony, child support, money received from retirement funds, investments, etc.

STEP 3: BE CONSCIOUS ABOUT WHERE YOUR MONEY GOES

How many of you have ever left home with $10 or $20 dollars, then upon returning home, was unable to account for where the money went? It is very easy for money to slip away from us. It is important to be aware of how we are spending our money and what we are spending our money on. With this in mind, calculate the differences between step 1 (your current monthly financial obligations) and step 2 (all incoming monthly funds). If your monthly income is equal to or more than your financial obligations, then you should have enough money to cover your expenses. If your financial obligations are more than your current monthly income, then there are some additional steps that need to be considered. Depending on the amount of difference between the two monthly figures, determine whether there are resources that you can tap into to make up for this difference (i.e. borrow money from family or friends, reduce interest rates on credit cards, work out payments of smaller amounts with the company, obtain additional work to help increase incoming funds.)

You want to begin to develop a budget in which your income is able to equal and eventually surpass your expenditures. In order to do this, determine how to reduce your expenditures (Refer to step 4.)

STEP 4: STEPPING OUT OF YOUR COMFORT ZONE

At times, we may find it hard to break from our normal routines. We get comfortable keeping things the way they are. This may not always be a healthy or adaptive way of coping with things. Depending on the situation, it may require us to step out of our comfort zone and get a little uncomfortable with the changes we need to make in our lives.

Make a log of your daily expenses for one or two months. Carefully review your expenditures and determine what types of things you can cut back on. As stated earlier, it is important to track your cash flow, and know where your money goes. When it comes to our finances, we may need to temporarily cut back on things we may have overindulged on for internal gratification. I reviewed all of my expenses just to assess whether there were any expenses that could be reduced or eliminated. I reduced what I could, but for the most part, since there were no excess expenses of lattes or eating out, I did not have many expenses to cut back or eliminate. My bills were my living expenses. It is important to track your cash flow, and know where your money goes.

STEP 5: TRANSFORMING NEGATIVE THINKING INTO POSITIVE ENERGY

It is not unusual to think negatively when faced with a crisis or unpleasant situation. I stated earlier how my situation left me feeling hopeless with a low self-esteem and lack of confidence. I acknowledged my feelings and understood what was making me feel the way I did, but like I tell my clients, you have to get back up. *It's when you do not get back up that you are throwing in the towel of defeat.* I began transforming my negative thoughts into positive words and energy. I realized I was not alone in this situation; there were other resources I could utilize to help.

I reviewed my resources of people I knew and companies I was connected to, and ended up consulting with lawyers from a Legal Program I belonged to. As one of the services, the lawyers will write letters on your behalf. I had the lawyer write letters on my behalf to the creditors. The results I received gratified me; yet, at the same time it was disheartening that something I had been trying to do for months' (trying to work something out directly with my creditors) required the intervention of legal action. My interest rates of 25.99% and 39.99% were dramatically reduced to 5.5% and 6%. When my interest rates first increased, I was barely covering the payment for the interest because I was not able to make all the minimum payments on my bills with my current income. So, along with the inability to cover my expenses, came penalty fees and late fees, ballooning my expenses and balances even further. With my new interest rates in effect, I recalculated how long it would take for me to pay off my revised current expenses. I was beginning to feel more confident and a sense of hope. I strategized a plan to decide which bills I should pay off first. I looked at the following factors:

I assessed whether the balance would be something that I could pay off within a few months, and if so, how much I would have to pay to meet this payoff, while still being able to take care of my other bills? I reviewed the following scenarios and determined which scenario would work best for my situation in terms of what I should pay off first:

1. High Interest Rates-High Balance

2. High Interest Rates-Low Balance

3. Low Interest Rates-High Balance

4. Low Interest Rates-Low Balance

In some cases, if I did not have much remaining in the balance, I opted to pay off that credit card first. Once that card was paid off, I then used the money from that payment and added it to the money I was paying on the next credit card, paying down the balance on another card. I am continuing to do this strategy and this has been working out great. Throughout the process, I continue to review my income and have continued to monitor closely how I am spending money and how I am allocating my funds toward my bill payments. As I stay on track with my plan, the balances continue to reduce drastically. As I complete paying off each bill, I gratefully celebrate my blessings, not by spending money, but by being proud that I continued to stay the course and am accomplishing improving my financial situation.

STEP 6: OCEANS OF PROSPERITY-PROGRAMMING YOUR MIND FOR SUCCESS

As I continued to successfully recover from debt, I decided it was time for me to take heed to other financial lessons which aligned with my values. They were 1. Pay yourself first and 2. Tithings/Charity.

Many financial advisors emphasize paying yourself first, no matter what your circumstances. They suggest 10% of your monthly income. If you are feeling overwhelmed with your current financial situation, try to at least save a certain amount of money, even as little as $5 a week or a month to start. Then increase this amount as you are able. Whatever amount you decide on, make sure it is an amount that you can be consistent with on a regular weekly or monthly basis.

I reviewed my income and expenses and determined what I should give in each area that I would be able to maintain on a monthly basis, without disrupting my current payment schedule. I decided for each area, I would give $50/month. Something I considered to be "doable" without breaking my bank, yet keeping me on track with my debt reduction payment plan. At this present time, I remain faithfully on the road to debt recovery. I hope that by sharing these first six steps, , I have inspired you into realizing that you too can successfully succeed in your financial recovery. As you start this process, you will be able to reduce your financial stress, and work toward creating a worry free financial life.

About Lorie

Lorie A. L. Nicholas, Ph.D., is a Staff Psychologist in the Federal Bureau of Prisons. She is part of a team of Psychologists, responsible for conducting suicide risk assessments, acute crisis interventions, and monitoring the overall mental health services to both male and female federal inmates. Dr. Nicholas also serves as an Adjunct Professor in the Department of Law & Police Science and Criminal Justice Administration at John Jay College of Criminal Justice (CUNY). She holds a doctorate in Clinical-Community Psychology.

Dr. Nicholas has presented at many conferences and conducted workshops and trainings on topics which include stress management, race-related concerns, the criminal justice system, substance abuse, violence, incarcerated mothers and their children, and financial stress/financial literacy. Dr. Nicholas has an extensive background working with children, youth and adults. She has been involved with numerous research projects as well.

Dr. Nicholas is the CEO of Dream Builders United, and is known as the Financial Recovery Doctor. Dream Builders United was created to empower distressed families/home owners through financial education, so that families can pursue their dream of living debt-free, owning and maintaining a home, and reaching other financial goals. Dr. Nicholas' invested interest in providing financial education to families came as a result of a personal experience when she fell victim to the subprime economic downsizing (refer to Dr. Nicholas chapter as a co-author in the book The Law of Business Attraction.)

In addition to her own personal experiences, Dr. Nicholas has incorporated counseling clients on basic financial problems, which were causing severe stress and creating a domino effect in other areas of their lives. Dr. Nicholas also volunteers, providing financial education to youth aging out of the foster care system, and builds homes and restores communities for Habitat for Humanity. Dr. Nicholas has been actively involved as an instructor for Habitat For Humanity's Loan Ranger Program. As a Loan Ranger, Dr. Nicholas educates communities about understanding credit and debt. As a result of her commitment to community, and making a difference in the lives of people, Dream Builders United strives to help to educate individuals and families around financial literacy, while building a legacy of financial freedom.

Dr. Nicholas is available for speaking engagements and trainings, and can be reached at info@dreambuildersunited.com.

CHAPTER 33

Blockages to Success: Faith Filters & Spiritual Constipation

By Lynne Marchant, M.Div

I HAVE MADE UP MY MIND!

With that said, picture a three-year-old child with arms crossed, feet firmly planted and the ensuing tantrum that will take place if a nearby adult thinks differently.

Why is it that we start out in life with a clean slate, no baggage, and yet by the time we reach adulthood we are often confused and even paralyzed with regard to what we want to do in life?

My dear friend Rick, recently wrote this poem called 'Indecision.'

I've made a decision.
What is it?
I've decided not to decide.
Is it wise?
I think so.
Perhaps a re-think?
Not necessary.
Are you being hasty?
How should I know?
What if?
What if what?
Does it matter?
Doesn't it?

Could be worse?
Could be better?
Remember the last time?
Ok.......OK
Leave it with me.

Now picture *yourself* trying to make a decision. Are you more like the three-year-old child or more like the majority of adults depicted in this poem who had that incorrigible child persuaded or disciplined out of you?

What happened to that determined little kid? Where did she/he go? If I were a dream doctor, I would diagnose this problem as a 'faith blockage.' The debris of your life journey has gathered in your mind and is causing a blockage of faith in THE most important person in your life—you! Here ends the dream (or hopefully begins the clearing), of the blockage so you can open up to faith, hope and dreams of new possibilities!

Martin Luther King Jr. said "Faith is taking the first step even when you can't see the whole staircase." Faith means having confident belief in the truth, value, or trustworthiness of a person *[insert your name here]*, thing or idea, and belief does not rest on logical proof or material evidence. Having faith in YOU means holding on to a confident belief that your instincts are right! Trust in yourself and your instincts so that you can set out on the journey of your life and fulfill all your dreams.

Lao Tzu said, "a journey of a thousand miles begins with a single step,' but the first step in every journey is always the dream. It is the dream or goal that passes through our minds and how we respond to those thoughts that makes the difference between ordinary and extraordinary, between possible and impossible, and between success and failure. Our minds become the 'faith filter' that each dream must pass through before it is accepted or rejected. When our faith filter is full of doubts, past failures, and negative thoughts, is it any wonder that our dreams sadly end up sitting on the shelf of "what if" or "what might have been?"

As human beings we all come in varied packages, shapes and sizes, abilities and interests; however, we all have many similarities. We were all born, and one day we will all die.

Sadly, many of us will go to the grave with our song unsung. Why?

Simply because often times we don't follow our dreams—they get stuck in the faith filter of our minds. We don't take the first step. We wait for the elusive 'perfect time!'

I will [live my dream] when the kids grow up, when I get a better job, when I move, when I...

If not now, WHEN?

A few years ago, a friend and I were leading a group on a tour of Greece, Israel and Egypt. I was excited to have an opportunity to climb Mount Sinai (7500') to watch the sunrise, so I invited everyone on the trip to join me one night for this—likely once in a lifetime—challenge. Of the 20 people, about half were interested, even keen at the outset. When the time came to go, suddenly people began changing their minds. The talk at the dinner table was peppered with "I don't want to get up at midnight and be up all night," "I don't think I can do it," "I'll slow you down," and, "It's cold."

It became clear to me that in the moment an opportunity arises (in this case a short climb), if our mind says, "I'd like to do that," then you are capable of it, and you will do it. But if your mind says, "No way Jose, not interested," then you are right; you can't or won't do it.

It is the mind that gets in the way of your quest, not money, abilities, or anything else! Trust your instincts as they are rarely wrong unless your 'faith in you filter' is blocked! For those who did find the idea of climbing Mount Sinai appealing, why do you think they were backing out and finding all kinds of reasons not to face the challenge?

Fear of failure is always the biggest killer of dreams, so sometimes it is easier never to begin. Squash that dangerous idea before it kindles into a passionate fire! Whether the dream/goal/idea is large or small, the process is the same. We reject or accept the first thought as it crosses our mind. If we feed the thought like a seed it will grow. If we make a plan, do the preparations, and then live the dream, we will make it a reality. By the way, the five people who accepted the challenge to climb with me that night all watched the sunrise at the top of Mount Sinai!

W. Clement Stone said, "whatever the mind can conceive and believe, it can achieve." That has been a mantra of mine for many years and I have found it to be true for my life. The obstacles of life are first overcome in the mind.

"I have made up my mind!" is another mantra of mine, knowing that first my thoughts have managed to clear the 'faith in me' filter, allowing the dream to take hold and become a reality. My packaging might be different from yours, but we are the same as far as hopes and dreams are concerned. Some of my family and close friends would describe me as incorrigible while I would say I am a strong-minded woman with great determination! The fact of the matter is I have never —well, rarely— had trouble deciding I want to do something and then finding a way to achieve that goal.

My adventurous spirit has found me sitting in a classroom at age 39, beginning a Masters Degree as part of a career change.

Asking a simple question about the meaning of some scallop shells on a church wall led to a 900-kilometer adventure on the Camino de Santiago seven years later. Who knew this would be a life changing question? The Way of St. James takes about one month minimum to walk and offers many challenges and lessons for those who are willing to learn. Both of these goals were seven years in the making from initial idea to fruition. Not necessarily smooth sailing but when "I have made up my mind!" there really is no stopping me. I could begin to describe the long school days and nights of study and handling long distance travel while raising two teenage girls or the ugly blisters I earned on The Way. But the important lesson is not the lack of sleep or discomfort and pain that will stop you—it is the mind. The Faith Filter comes into play again.

On my adventure journeys I have met many fellow travelers along the way. We are all there on that particular path for different reasons and yet we all have something in common. No matter what age we are, or what country we are from, or what we do for a living, at that particular moment in time we are all on a quest that is physical, mental and spiritual. Focused. Present. No where else to be. Only walking and talking, resting, refueling, literally moving one step at a time towards a goal.

In a book about success secrets, obviously much will be written about achieving success. In my line of work, it is easy to see that THE most important thing in life, more than wealth and the toys that it will buy, is health. No matter how much money you have, if you don't have good health you have nothing. Much has been written about diets and exercise for physical health, and mental health. The latter is also enhanced by exercise and eating right. Looking after our bodies is a great stress reliever. Not much thought is given to spiritual health. In this day and time many people describe themselves as spiritual but not religious. I can work with that, as it can actually be helpful in crossing all faiths, as long as we begin with an agreement that there is a higher power outside ourselves which calls us to live with purpose and to help others. I call that higher power God, some would say Allah, some Yahweh, the universe...whatever you call your higher power, most of the major religions in the world from Jainism to Zoroastrianism agree with The Golden Rule. *Do unto others as you would have others do unto you.*

If we agree at this point that a blockage in our success in life can come from the 'Faith in you Filter' that can prevent us from ever getting started on living our dream, why is it that we all know people who seem to have it all and yet they are very unhappy? We can look to the lives of famous people who have had great success in life in movies or music, and yet they die too early, often tragically and very unhappy. Somehow in the midst of the outward signs and symbols of success, the needs of their own souls have been lost and buried. This can be caused by blockage of another kind!

The law of gravity says that what goes up must come down. It would make sense then that what goes in, must come out. Allow me to be indelicate for a moment—think of your own body on a daily basis. It is a remarkable piece of machinery that needs to receive from you its daily fuel, in the form of food and drink. We don't always make wise choices, but regardless of that we take in some form of food and liquids and we eat. Our bodies have remarkable systems that break down this food into the many nutrients we need to make our bodies tick, sending it into the blood stream to be delivered to our brain and organs so they can keep us going and help us to perform well in our day.

There are days when we take in a little too much food which the body cannot use or deal with and so it is stored for later use. However, the food that is used and processed through our system also produces waste; that waste needs to pass through our systems too, making its way out of the body. If you have ever had trouble in that department, you will quickly relate to the discomfort, headache, pain, and how unwell you feel. In a word, constipation!

Our God is a generous God who bestows many gifts upon us daily. We can take all we need, use what we want, sometimes we have more than we need and we store it up for later use. God also calls us to give back and when we are not being generous from our bounty, we will find our lives blocked by spiritual constipation! Makes sense to me. All that we give out into the lives of others comes back to us tenfold. Spiritual constipation can also be blocking us from our dreams. If we have it all and yet still feel unhappy, despondent, unfulfilled, it might be time to check for spiritual constipation. Giving to others, helping out and helping up is the fastest track to recovery from all kinds of ills. Don't let spiritual constipation keep you from living your dreams. Listen carefully to the voice of your own soul, it speaks to you in whispers and with subtle suggestions, but it will have its voice heard and it will keep you healthy in body, mind and soul.

The number seven is thought to be the number of wholeness, completion. For a daily health check up of body, mind and soul follow these seven simple steps on your journey to success:

1. **Check your 'Faith in You Filter' daily**

2. **Trust your instincts**

3. **Believe (have faith) in yourself and in your dreams**

4. **Love yourself; be kind to you and do nice things for you**

5. **Love others; be kind and generous with your time, talent and treasure**

6. **Laugh - a lot!**

7. **Give thanks for each new day and the opportunity to begin again!**

About Lynne

Lynne Marchant, Faith Expert. When audiences are listening to Lynne they often wonder where is she from...Australia? Ireland? Liverpool, England? None of the above! She was born and raised in Yorkshire, in the North East of England and emigrated to Canada when she was 19 to begin an adventure that is ongoing. Lynne describes her accent as "British Allsorts," having learned to slow down her speech, but the lilt is still there, making her pleasant to hear.

Lynne spent time earlier in life raising her two daughters and then re-entered the work force in the field of Human Resources. During the seven years in that industry, God was calling her to something else! The best-kept secret about Lynne is that she is an ordained priest in the Anglican Church of Canada (Episcopalian). She was ordained in 1997 and has spent her time serving two different congregations in the Diocese of Niagara, Ontario, Canada. Her sense of humor and down to earth style make her in much demand in her parish, the wider church, and as a conference speaker.

Lynne's daily life and work puts her in touch with many people who may be joyfully celebrating the birth of a child, wish to be married, or may be struggling through life dealing with illness, divorce, or death. Sharing their stories with her makes the struggles more bearable. Lynne's compassion for others and passion for life make her a good listener; and a trouble shared is a trouble halved! Being honored and privileged to enter into sacred space and sacred journeys with people feeds Lynne's soul and has provided her with a plethora of stories and insights about life and living in the moment that adds to her ability to inspire and teach others—one on one, in workshops, or in large groups as a motivational speaker for both business and church land.

Vivian Green said, "Life isn't about waiting for the storm to pass, it's about learning to dance in the rain." And that is just what Lynne did when her life took an unexpected twist, She learned to ballroom dance! You name it—waltz, tango, foxtrot, quickstep, cha cha, rhumba, mambo, jive. Dancing with the Stars, here she comes! Just put on some music and watch her wind up and go! If she is not on the dance floor you will find her out on the trails, hiking.

Did I mention that she is also a Personal Trainer with CanFitPro? Lynne's zest for life, adventure and travel have taken her to the rooftop of Africa, climbing all 19, 350' of Mount Kilimanjaro; she has walked the famous El Camino de Santiago in Spain – twice; she has trekked to Base Camp Everest in Nepal and walked Coast to Coast across England following A. Wainwright's path.

If you would like to track Lynne down, you can reach her on LinkedIn, Facebook, Twitter, at stjohnsniagarafalls.ca or via The Diocese of Niagara.

"One should always have a definite objective, in a walk as in life. It is so much more satisfying to reach a target by personal effort than to wander aimlessly....life without ambition is...well, aimless wandering."

- A. Wainwright, *A Coast to Coast Walk*

CHAPTER 34

Set the Target BEFORE You Try to Hit it!

By Michael Conduff

The souvenir shop at Silver Dollar City in Branson, Missouri, was an Aladdin's Cave for my two boys. Eyes alight with the innocent joy of their late adolescent years, they were scavenging through glittering treasure in every aisle. In true "practice what you preach" boundary-setting style, I had provided their parameters before we even arrived at the frontier park that morning.

"You may each have one souvenir, not to exceed $25, and purchased when we get ready to leave for the day—and not a moment earlier," I explained.

I've been down this path before, and knew that if they didn't have a numerical or dollar limit, they would want everything they saw all day long (and without the time frame boundary, I would end up lugging whatever they got for the remainder of the day).

"*Okay, Dad,*" they agreed.

It was a magnificent day, and everyone had a fabulous time. The riders in the family rode, the 'watchers' of us watched, the gamers gamed and the eaters ate. Everyone knew what they liked, what they were good at, and accommodated the others in the party accordingly. Now it was time to head back to the larger family gathering waiting at the rented condo.

True to my commitment, as we went through the exit into the final sou-vie shop, I handed them each $25 and now only supervised for safety's sake. Because they knew they could only have one souvenir, they did not spend a lot of time looking at trinkets; instead going right to the really good stuff. As boys and brothers, they naturally engaged in animated conversation, each trying to influence the other's behavior. I laughed silently as I watched this recurring dynamic. One was mercurial and gifted athletically and the other much more thoughtful and intellectual, so they each argued for what they wanted, trying to convince the other to get the same thing.

They headed to the checkout and I edged closer to make sure that all went well. Only then did I see both boys had chosen a wooden bow and arrow set. I immediately had a Christmas Story flashback, and "You'll shoot your eye out!" came unbidden to my lips. Fortunately I was not quite close enough for them to hear me and I had an extra moment to realize that I could not change the rules now. I had said, "One, $25 and at exit" with no other criteria. So instead, I congratulated them on the expeditiousness and lack of drama in their selection process, and we headed back to the condo, and this interlude gave me a bit of time to regroup.

"Boys, those are some awesome bows and arrows," I said. "I know you guys are great archers, so we will have to set up some targets for you when we get back to the condo."

"Great idea, Dad!" they chimed in unison.

As soon as the SUV braked to a halt, they rushed out the backseat and ran through the condo door.

"Look what we have!" they hollered to the assembled family members, proudly opening their boxes. I grinned as I heard the aunts say, "Be careful, you'll shoot your eye out!" and their indignant response, "No, we won't!"

Before I could get situated, arrows were flying. They were shooting as fast as they could reload and everything in bow range was fair game. Remembering my condo damage deposit I hollered, "Quick!! Everyone to the patio for an exhibition of bow shooting!"

Racing out first, I grabbed a marker, masking tape and a piece of cardboard. With an exaggerated flair I drew a bull's-eye, propped the target against a lawn chair, stepped off five yards and put a piece of masking tape on the patio floor.

"Okay boys, this is an official shooting range. You each get three shots to hit the target. You must stay behind the line and shoot by age, with the youngest going first."

"Aunts and uncles, your job is to be the official judges. If the arrow hits the target you get to cheer loudly, clap and holler good shot. If the arrow misses the target you get to cheer and say, 'good try!'"

Since it was official, everyone was excited and ready to go. The first, the athlete, hit the target on his first shot and the family responded with enthusiasm and accolades. The oldest was next and while his shot was just off the target, it was close, and the family encouraged him with great shouts of "good try!"

After alternating a few more times both boys were hitting the target with regularity. Quickly grabbing my masking tape I stepped off three more yards. Now there were two ranges, five yards and eight yards. Again, they alternated shots, and with applause and whistles encouraging them they were quite focused on hitting the target.

When this range became comfortable, I put down two more strips of tape; one at ten yards and one at twelve. Now, ten yards with a toy bow is quite a distance and neither boy was hitting from it with regularity, and twelve yards was downright difficult. Rather than let them get discouraged, I added a new wrinkle.

"Okay, now that practice is over we are going to have a points contest," I announced. "Each range is worth a different amount of points. Five yards is one point, eight yards is two, ten yards is three and twelve yards is five. Each boy will shoot three arrows and we will add up all the points."

Selecting an uncle as official score keeper and handing him the marker and a piece of paper I asked, "Which boy wants to go first?"

While they were arguing, I snuck over to the uncle and said, "Keep the total number of points, not the points of each one." Eyes twinkling, he nodded and got ready.

Sure enough the youngest jumped up and went to the two point line. First shot–a hit! Hoots and hollers from the aunts and uncles! A big "2" was written on the score sheet.

Beaming he stepped back to the three point line. Second shot–barely missed. "Great shot, very close, way to go!" encouraged the assembly.

Only slightly crestfallen, he now had to think about strategy. Did he go for the big five, try the three again, go back to the two or even take the easy 'gimme' shot? You could practically see the wheels turning.

Hesitating slightly, he notched his last arrow and went to the one-point line. Another hit! More hoots and hollers. High fives, woo-hoo! A "1" appeared on the score sheet.

"That's three for me! Beat that" he crowed to his brother.

Moving deliberately, the oldest went right for the one-point line. A hit! The audience responded enthusiastically. A "1" appeared below the "2" and the other "1." He moved back to the two point line. A hit! More applause. Another "2" on the score sheet!

Next he went all the way to the five point line. Assured of what he assumed was at least a tie he was going for the gold. Aiming carefully, he launched his arrow and it was so close! The audience loved it and everyone was laughing and clapping and yelling, "Good Job!"

"I tied," he hollered above the noise of the celebration.

"Whoa," I said. "This is a family total contest. Let's add up our results. Two plus one plus one plus two equals what?"

"Duh, Dad," they said together. "Six!"

"Exactly! Now that is our new record! Together you all shot six, now do you think you can break that?"

"Sure!" they hollered together.

"Super," I said. "What is the most points you can score together?"

The youngest shrugged. Math held no interest for him. He was ready to shoot again. In a minute the oldest ventured a guess, "Thirty?" he said tentatively.

"Excellent!" I applauded. "Now, the current record is six, and the maximum record is thirty. Why don't you guys practice and we will go in and get the dinner ready. You can put on another exhibition afterwards and see if you have improved."

The balance of the vacation was spent with at least a little time each day trying to get to thirty. They both got really good at hitting threes, but the five pointers remained elusive. On the final day they decided to go for the gold, shooting only from the five-point line. They each got two, for a total of twenty points. Their misses were just barely.

"How do you guys feel about twenty?" I asked. "That's a really good score!"

"Oh Dad, it's horrible. We wanted a thirty!"

"Well, it's not a thirty, I agree with that. Do you remember what your first record was?"

"Six," they said.

"Is twenty a lot more than six?"

"Duh!"

"Well, is twenty closer to thirty or to six?"

"It's only ten from thirty and fourteen from six," said the mathematician. "It is closer to thirty!"

"Right!" I smiled. "So, at first the record was six and now it is twenty. That is a lot of progress for one week. It is only two shots away from perfect. Do you think with more practice you could get to twenty five or even maybe the whole thirty?"

"Sure!"

THE LEARNINGS:

Set Targets
Before the boys had a target, they were shooting at anything that moved (and sometimes even each other). Once they had a target, they could focus. This sounds elementary, but I am amazed when I ask my clients what a bull's-eye is for them, and they do not know or cannot articulate

it succinctly. Worse yet, different folks (from the same team) often give contradictory answers!

Spend some time together as a team and agree on the target! Set it BEFORE your team starts shooting.

Start Easy to Go Far
If you want folks to keep trying they must experience success. Make sure there is a way to reinforce behaviors you want. At the beginning, applause for earnest attempts was valuable. The audience reinforced good tries as much as they did hits. Punishing less than perfect results (while folks are learning the process) prevents future progress.

Keep a team score
Teams win together or lose together. If one component of your organization is competing against the other, bad stuff happens. With a combined score the boys rooted for– not against– each other! They put their heads together on strategy, taking advantage of each other's strengths. The "contest" was against the best of the team score, not against their teammate.

All too often I watch one team member given a raise or an accolade they never could have won on their own without team support. Management always seems surprised when other members of the team do not support that member (sometimes the team even tries sabotaging the member's success). Everyone has a role to play, and some folks are better in some aspects. But at the end of the day we all have to cross the finish line together!

Keep it Challenging – but not Impossible!
At first, the twelve-yard shot was nearly impossible–almost no chance. After practice and positive reinforcement for trying, twelve became doable, but not routine. Your folks need significant targets they believe they can achieve. If at any point it becomes too easy, they lose interest. If they believe it is impossible, they quit trying.

Reward the Hail Mary
For your team to get to excellent or best practice, they have to stretch and push their comfort zone. The first really long/big/difficult tries must be rewarded. If the team in any way feels punished for trying they will never throw for the end zone. Early on the boys chose easy shots in or-

der to get rewards, but as they learned that the applause was just as loud (or louder) for a near miss at the longer distances as for the easy shots, they began trying more and more of the long shots. The other advantage of trying the long shots is that it makes the short ones a whole lot easier.

Control Behaviors via Boundaries

I did not tell my boys what they could do. There was no way I was smart enough to anticipate all of the possibilities. Nor did I act as judge of their choices; that would have taken them off the hook for the consequences. Rather I set simple, easy to follow boundaries and encouraged them to make their own choices within their boundaries.

In my early CEO years I played a lot of "Mother, may I" with my staff and with my board bosses. The staff would bring me alternatives, and I would choose one for them. If it worked they had the satisfaction of knowing they developed it, and if it didn't they had the cover that I had chosen it. It did not take me long to realize I was not only the bottleneck, I was playing the scapegoat.

Then I saw that I was doing the same thing with my board. I would take them a recommended course of action, they would ask a bunch of questions and ninety-nine percent of the time they would go with my recommendation. When it worked I could smile knowing I was so great. When it didn't (fortunately not too often!), I could shrug and say, "Well, I was just doing what the board directed."

Know Your Role and Honor it

I love to shoot a bow and could certainly have jumped in to the archery contest. Instead I was setting the target ranges, defining success and being a cheerleader. Having a cheering squad of aunts and uncles was huge. Their reinforcing claps and shouts kept the boys on target. The scorekeeper made sure the results were evident.

If your governing board or executive team tries to jump into the activities of the organization, or conversely if staff starts trying to govern, role violation occurs and mayhem is often the result.

Tie it Together!

The very best organizations routinely follow these behaviors. They set targets and develop boundaries. They reward *team* behavior that stays within the boundaries and approaches the targets. They start with reasonable expectations and increase those as competence increases. They reward good tries at long shots as well as success at the normal ones. They know their role and fulfill it to the best of their ability. They celebrate successes and even throw a few Hail Marys.

The very best teams do this–does *your* team??

About Michael

Michael A. (Mike) Conduff is the President and CEO of The Elim Group–*Your Governance Experts*, a governance, leadership, speaking and consulting firm. Mike has 35+ years of leadership, management and governance experience, having served as the City Manager of four highly acclaimed University communities in the United States.

Mike earned his B.S. in civil engineering at the University of New Hampshire, graduating Cum Laude. His M.B.A. is from Pittsburg State University. He is also a charter graduate of the Carver Policy Governance® Academy and is a Past Chair of the Board of Directors of the International Policy Governance® Association. Mike has a number of national and international not-for-profit, for-profit and local government clients. His success in dealing with Boards has earned him the reputation of being the "Go-To Guy" for council retreats and corporate governance.

In addition Mike is a best-selling author, and has written or co-authored numerous books, including *Pushing to the Front,* with Brian Tracy, *Democracy at the Doorstep – True Stories from the Green Berets of Public Administrators, Bottom Line Green – How America's Cities are Saving the Planet (And Money Too!)* with Jim Hunt, *The OnTarget Board Member – 8 Indisputable Behaviors,* soon to be in its third edition, and *The Policy Governance® Fieldbook,* a book on the practical applications of Policy Governance. He writes a regular column in the internationally distributed *Public Manager* magazine, and is a contributing author for the internationally acclaimed "Green Book" series for ICMA.

As a much sought after and frequent keynote speaker at national and international events, Mike regularly receives "best of the conference" accolades from attendees and conference planners.

Mike is a Fellow in the prestigious National Academy of Public Administration. He has been honored with the 2006 TCMA Mentoring Award in memory of Gary Gwyn, the 2004 International Award for Career Development in Memory of L. P. (Perry) Cookingham from ICMA, and the especially meaningful Joy Sansom Mentor Award from the Urban Management Assistants of North Texas for his commitment to helping others achieve their potential. The Center for Digital Government awarded Mike their coveted "Best of Texas Visionary Award."

A fourth generation Native American, Mike grew up on stories of his Cherokee ancestry, and attributes his love of motivational speaking and telling stories to his grandmothers. He is a Past President of both the Texas City Management Association and Kansas City Management Association. He was one of the original cohort of fully credentialed members of the International City/County Management Association, and is a past member of its Executive Board, where he chaired the Finance Committee. He still serves ICMA as their Senior Advisor for Governance.

To learn more about Mike or to engage him for your corporate, non-profit or local government event, call The Elim Group at (940) 382-3945
or visit www.TheElimGroup.com.

CHAPTER 35

The Five Biggest Mistakes Retirees Routinely Make That Can Easily Threaten Their Financial Security

By Michael Reese, CFP®

If you are retired (or plan to retire soon), chances are you take income from your retirement savings to support your lifestyle.

You may be wondering how you can protect that savings against too much risk, not to mention against healthcare and other surprise expenses that sometimes come with age–or life in general.

Chances are also good you'd like to pass on your taxable IRA to your spouse and/or children and grandchildren, tax-free–not to mention avoid paying the IRS more than your legal minimum obligation.

If any of that sounds like you, keep reading. Because chances are that no matter who you are, you're making some common mistakes that could be costing you money.

WHO AM I AND WHY SHOULD YOU LISTEN TO ME?

My name is Michael Reese, and I'm a Certified Financial Planner™ who has specialized in helping retirees enjoy a safe and secure retirement over the past 15-plus years, regardless of the economy's ups and downs.

I'm not just any financial planner–I've taught thousands of financial advisors throughout the country techniques I've developed over the years. I'm regularly asked to speak at industry events and I'm recognized as one of the financial industry's thought leaders.

I'm also a Registered Investment Advisor with over a dozen licenses and designations under my belt, and an alphabet soup of initials after my name including CFP®, CLU, and ChFC.

What does all this mean for you?

When it comes to retirement advice, I know what I'm talking about, and the advice most consumers are getting from big Wall Street firms and financial media is just plain bad.

Hence why I'm writing this article–to explain how you can avoid the *five biggest mistakes* people make with their retirement funds.

MISTAKE #1: NO CLEAR RETIREMENT INCOME PLAN

Most of the people who come into our office do not have a clearly defined income plan for their retirement, which makes sense, since most people don't even know exactly what a "clearly defined retirement income plan" is!

It's really pretty simple. You should have a plan for retirement accounts that are:

- Guaranteed to last as long as you do (and your spouse, if you're married).

- Designed to have automatic step-ups to fight the impact of inflation.

- Flexible enough to handle things like increased healthcare expenses, periodic lump sum expenses like a new car or home repair, and the occasional "bucket list" expense like a trip to Europe.

- Bulletproof against market downturns, meaning that your income won't go down when the markets do.

Do you have that kind of plan? If you're like most people, chances are you don't.

What most people do have are traditionally "balanced" portfolios made up of roughly 50% stocks and 50% bonds. Income taken is usually around 4% of the initial portfolio value.

With portfolios like these:

- Income may come from a combination of stock dividends, bond interest, and limited partnership distributions.

- Shortfalls are often made up by selling whatever in the portfolio seems to make sense at the time.

- Inflation protection is accomplished through capital gains in the value of the stock positions in the portfolio–which only works when markets are rising.

- Portfolio values fluctuate significantly–which is great when markets go up, but potentially devastating when they go down.

- There's no defined plan for healthcare protection or other extra expenses.

In other words, if you have what most people have, chances are you don't have a clear retirement income plan you can count on to provide for you and your spouse for the rest of your life.

MISTAKE #2: TOO MUCH PORTFOLIO RISK

One of the biggest mistakes retirees make is keeping too much money in the stock market after they retire. Once you retire, ideally you should be at the point where you no longer have to take any risk with your money.

I've created a simple model to help you match up where you should put your money based on where you are in life. I call it the "Three Stages of Money."

- **Stage 1: Youth / Savings**
  When you were a child, chances are you kept your money in a basic savings account. Why? Banks provide a **SAFE** (meaning

you don't have to worry about losing it) and **LIQUID** (meaning you can get it when you need it) place for your money. Which, when you're a kid, is all you need.

You will still need banks for a range of different things as you get older. However, a mistake that I often see retirees make is that they tend to keep *way* too much money in the bank. I advise keeping 6 to 12 months of income at the bank for emergencies (retirees tend to need emergency money more often than non-retirees) along with any money you've earmarked for a big purchase you'll be making in the near future, like a new car, a new home or a child or grandchild's college tuition. But beyond that, more is too much. In the financial industry, we call it "going broke safely," because the interest you earn on money at the bank–in CDs or a traditional savings account–is normally less than inflation.

- **Stage 2: Adult / Investments**
Once you start working, you should start investing a portion of your earnings in order to **GROW** and **ACCUMULATE** a nest egg. This is the stage of risk and return, when you'll be working with Wall Street brokerage firms and money managers. Some years you will make money–sometimes a lot of money. That's the return part. And some years, you will lose money–again, sometimes a *lot* of money. That's the risk part.

Over time, the goal is for your gains to be larger and more frequent than your losses so that you earn a positive rate of return. The idea is to put together an asset allocation of stocks, bonds, and mutual funds with the objective of maximizing your growth potential, while limiting your down years.

So what money should you have in brokerage or Wall Street accounts? Money you don't expect to need for income for the next ten years. While you are working, other money belongs at Stage 1, in the bank, where it is **SAFE** and **LIQUID.**

- **Stage 3: Maturity / Preservation and Income**
Once you've accumulated enough money to achieve financial security, it's time to transition from **GROWTH** and **ACCU-MULATION** to **PRESERVATION** and **INCOME.**

Experts–not Wall Street experts, but impartial financial experts–say you should have just 5% to 25% of your post-retirement money in the stock market. The reason is that once you retire, your days of taking risk should be over, and the goal should be holding on to all of that money you earned by taking risks in Stage 2.

In Stage 3, I recommend working with legal reserve life insurance companies. From a financial perspective, nobody does a better job of preserving your assets and providing contractually guaranteed lifetime income.

Specifically, I advise utilizing insurance accounts to contractually guarantee your base income. There are a variety of different insurance accounts that can do that for you, and many of them have eliminated the problem of "if you die too soon the insurance company ends up with your money." Obviously, those are the plans you want to focus on.

This does not mean you should put all of your money in insurance. For a well-diversified retirement portfolio, you need money in all three stages we've covered to enjoy the best of all worlds.

MISTAKE #3: NO TAX PLAN

If your advisors aren't reviewing your tax return in detail each year, how in the world can you expect to be minimizing your tax liability? You can't.

At a minimum, your financial advisor, your accountant and any investment advisors you work with should meet annually to discuss your return. And no, unless you are a CPA who specializes in 1040 returns, you don't count as an accountant! Without these types of review meetings, you can easily end up unnecessarily paying the IRS $1,000 or more each year. In our office, we've seen retirees paying well over $5,000 more than necessary to the IRS each year, all because their tax advisors and financial advisors were not on the same page.

But that stuff is peanuts compared to another tax problem you have. Think about these two questions:

- What is your largest tax liability?
- And what are you doing about it?

If you are like most retirees, you have substantial amounts of money in your retirement plan. This could be a 401k, 403b, 457, IRA, etc. You benefit over the years by not paying tax as your money grows in these accounts, but guess what happens when you withdraw the funds during retirement?

That's right–you pay tax.

Not only do you pay tax on your withdrawal, but you also will often owe more tax on your Social Security income because of that withdrawal. Most people don't know about that little trap. Your retirement plan is also 100% exposed to tax increases in the future. That means that the moment tax rates go up, which is a very likely scenario, your retirement plan's value to you will immediately go down.

For example, say you have $500,000 in your 401k, 403b, IRA, etc., and your current tax rate is 15%. The value of that account to you is actually the $500,000 *minus* the 15% that goes to the IRS. Meaning your $500,000 account is really worth $425,000 to you.

If tax rates increase by 5%, from 15% to 20%, your real account value will go down another $25,000. This is the same thing as a market loss, except in this case, it's permanent.

Adding to the trap is the fact that the more money you withdraw, the higher the tax rates go. And since withdrawals often impact how much of your Social Security is subject to tax, you often end up not only paying more tax on your retirement plan withdrawals, but you also pay more tax on your Social Security income–a double whammy!

Since we know taxes are likely to go up in the future, it's crucial that you talk with your advisors about how to protect yourself against those expected increases.

MISTAKE #4: NO HEALTHCARE STRATEGY

You can't do a very good job planning for your retirement if you ignore potential healthcare costs. No one likes to think about it, but depending on the study you read, somewhere between 40% and 60% of us will need long-term care at some point in our lives. And this type of care is expensive.

How expensive? Well, when you think about long-term care, you might think about a nursing home. In Michigan, where I live, the cost of nursing home care is currently $80,000-$85,000 per year. At-home care costs over $40,000 a year. So–how long will your money last when you have to spend an additional $40,000 to $80,000 per year on healthcare, with prices going up every year? Especially when you consider that Medicare covers almost none of this.

I'm not going to tell you to rush out and buy a traditional long-term care insurance plan. Instead, I advise the following:

1. Identify the impact that the costs of care would have on your portfolio. (Your financial advisor should be able to easily help you with that.) If your portfolio can handle it, feel free to self-insure.

2. If you don't like the results you see in step 1, consider various ways to protect yourself. The insurance industry offers three options:

   a. Traditional long-term care insurance

   b. Long-term care riders on annuities

   c. Long-term care riders on life insurance

3. Make a decision and **TAKE ACTION**. Once you've taken action, you never have to worry about this boring topic again.

From my point of view, I strongly advise you to check out life insurance options, as we are currently finding them to be some of the most attractive options in today's environment.

MISTAKE #5: USING CLASSIC ESTATE PLANS WHEN YOU HAVE IRAS (OR 401K, 403B, ETC.)

What does a classic estate plan look like? It's simple and straightforward and goes something like this:

- The surviving spouse gets everything.

- After both spouses are gone, everything goes to the children equally.

- If a child does not survive the parents, then that child's share goes to that child's children equally, if they have children. Otherwise, it goes to the other siblings equally.

Obviously, if you are in a second or third (or more!) marriage, things get a bit more complicated.

Now, all of this works out well with most assets. But retirement plans are different animals. How you manage these plans can either create or eliminate potentially hundreds of thousands of dollars in taxation.

This is where something called a "Protected Retirement Trust," or PRT, can help. A PRT is designed to transfer your retirement plan to your family completely free of taxation utilizing the rules found in IRS Publication 525. It's set up by an estate planning attorney, and you "fund" it by transferring 2% to 5% of your retirement plan into the trust each year, depending on your circumstances, goals, etc. You do have to pay a small amount of tax as you transfer the money each year, but once the transfer is made, that money is tax-free forever.

In other words, you pay pennies now, to save dollars later.

If your current advisors are not talking to you about this aspect of your estate planning, I suggest a conversation sooner rather than later.

SUMMARY

If you're like most people planning for retirement, chances are you're making one or more of the five mistakes I talked about in this chapter. And the thing is, it's not really your fault. Most financial advisors don't have the necessary knowledge base in these areas–and you can't blame yourself for not knowing what your advisors don't know.

However, now that you *do* know, it's time to stop doing what you have been doing and take action to correct those mistakes so you can improve your financial security. Once you do, you will be able to fully enjoy your retirement, free of financial stress, knowing that you've made the right choices with your money for you and your family.

For more information about a stress-free financial future, please contact me at [**MIKE@CEN-WEALTH.COM**].

About Michael

Michael Reese, CFP®, CLU, ChFC is the founder and principal of Centennial Wealth Advisory, LLC based in Traverse City, Michigan. He is a Certified Financial Planner™, Chartered Financial Consultant, and a Chartered Life Underwriter.

Michael's vision is to help American retirees "re-think" how they manage their financial portfolios during their retirement years. His focus is to help retirees enjoy financial security in any economy, something that he believes is sorely lacking in today's financial world. Specifically, Michael fully addresses the five key areas of retirement planning that are essential for providing your retirement security: income, investment, tax, healthcare, and estate planning. He finds most retirees rarely have a coordinated retirement plan in any one of those core areas, much less all five.

Due to his thought leadership, Mr. Reese has been widely quoted in multiple publications including Yahoo! Finance, Bankrate, Kiplinger's, and *US News & World Report.* He is a frequent speaker at industry events, and is the featured presenter at Advisor Excel's IRA College where he has trained over 1,000 financial advisors throughout the country on his planning techniques.

He is the host of "The Michael Reese Show," which airs on the local NBC affiliate on Saturday mornings, where he shares financial planning tips to members of his community.

Michael lives in Traverse City, Michigan, with his wife Becky, their five children, and his dog Charlie.

If you are retired, or retiring soon, and you want to learn more about how you can truly enjoy a safe and secure retirement in any economy, go to Michael's website, www.michael-reese.com and request a copy of Michael's free special report titled: "The Five Biggest Mistakes Retirees Routinely Make That Can Easily Threaten Their Financial Security."

www.michael-reese.com

CHAPTER 36

The Secret To Successfully Finding The Right Financial Advisor

By Radon Stancil, CFP®

You may ask yourself, "Is it really possible to know if you have found the right financial advisor?" You may know things like their name, office location, and even their family. But if you are going to be successful in this endeavor, there are other key factors you should know upfront. For instance, you should know exactly how your advisor gets paid. and what their responsibility is to you. Is your advisor held to a fiduciary standard? Do they have a system in place to communicate with you regularly? Do you have a written document called an Investment Policy Statement? These are just a few questions we will consider in this chapter.

COMMISSIONS AND FEES

Individuals come into my office all the time and tell me they have been with a certain advisor for a few years whom they like and trust. When I ask how their advisor gets paid, most do not know—they assume their advisor gets paid by the mutual fund or the annuity company. Some say they pay their advisor a fee, and others say their advisors receive some combination of commission and fees. However, most do not know what that fee entails! You should always ask and (always know the answer) to the question, "How does my advisor get paid?"

Understanding exactly how your advisor is compensated is very important. Consider this: If your advisor only receives a commission when they sell you something or change your mutual funds, how much can you trust their recommendations? If they are paid by fee only, that makes it important to understand what the fee is and how they charge it.

If you are interviewing a new advisor, make sure you ask about their compensation upfront. If the advisor is trying to sell you a product that is on a commission basis, you should know. By no means am I saying that commissions are wrong. What I am saying is that you should understand how your advisor gets paid. If you know how they are getting paid you can then ask why a particular product or service is being recommended. You could also ask if the advisor shopped around for the best, lowest cost product or if they chose a product that pays the highest commission.

Knowing how your advisor gets paid will help you tremendously. If your current advisor—or an advisor you are considering hiring—does not want to clearly answer questions about their compensation, that could be a sign they are trying to hide something. It may be an indication that they are not thinking of your best interest, but possibly of their own best interest. If this is the case, I encourage you to consider a different advisor.

IS YOUR ADVISOR HELD TO A FIDUCIARY STANDARD?

In the financial services industry, there are brokers and there are advisors. There are people who sell products and people who sell knowledge. There are people who look out for their commissions and people who look out for you. The difference is a fiduciary standard. Merriam-Webster's defines fiduciary as "held or founded in trust or confidence." A fiduciary standard is about your interests, goals, and well-being. Do you know if your financial advisor is held to a fiduciary standard? I think they should be, to protect you and your financial livelihood. Do you expect your doctor or lawyer to put your interests first? Of course you do; doctors and lawyers are held to a fiduciary standard. As for financial advisors, the fact is many are not held to this high standard. If you currently have an advisor, ask them if they are required by law to put your interests first. If you are interviewing an advisor, make sure they are held to a fiduciary standard before you do business with them.

A Registered Investment Advisor (RIA) is a person or company registered with the U.S. Securities and Exchange Commission (SEC) or with a State Securities Division. This registration does not mean the SEC approves, sanctions, or attests to the merits of the person or company. It simply indicates the person or entity is registered and has agreed to abide by certain fiduciary standards. An RIA may be registered with a State Securities Division as well as with the SEC. The RIA and Investment Advisor (IA) designations came about from the Investment Advisors Act of 1940. The fiduciary standard is based on the laws put in place by this act and means that an advisor is required to act only in the best interest of his or her client. This is true even if the interest conflicts with the advisor's financial interests. An advisor held to this standard is required to report any conflicts or potential conflicts of interest before and during the time the advisor is engaged by the client. Additionally, RIAs and IAs must disclose how they are compensated and agree to abide by a code of ethics.

Very few who claim to be financial advisors are actually federally- or state-registered. Most are considered to be broker-dealers, which are held to lower and non-regulated standards. Federal law requires broker-dealers to act in the best interest of their employer—not their clients. This does not mean they are unethical or plan to harm their clients. In fact, I feel confident most are ethical and do not intend harm to their clients. The scary thing is that they are not required by law to act in their client's best interest. If your advisor is not required to act in your best interest, then this limits your recourse if you feel you have been taken advantage of.

To guard against unethical violations, the SEC requires broker-dealers to include the following disclosure in their client agreements. Read this disclosure. Is this the type of relationship you want with your advisor?

"Your account is a brokerage account and not an advisory account. Our interests may not always be the same as yours. Please ask us questions to make sure you understand your rights and our obligations to you, including the extent of our obligations to disclose conflicts of interest and to act in your best interest. We are paid both by you and, sometimes, by people who compensate us based on what you buy. Therefore, our profits, and our salespersons' compensation, may vary by product and over time."

If you have signed an agreement with an advisor, go look at it. Is this disclaimer in there? If so, ask your advisor for more details. Decide if the relationship is in your best interest.

WHAT IS AN INVESTMENT POLICY STATEMENT?

Do you have an Investment Policy Statement (IPS)? An IPS is a written statement detailing the policies, procedures, and goals you and your advisor have agreed to in regards to managing your investments. This type of document is required when a fiduciary relationship exists. An IPS outlines a systematic approach for making decisions. It establishes a way to tackle difficult issues related to your investment choices. Having a plan provides clarity as you work with your advisor to meet certain expectations and goals. A well-thought-out statement helps your advisor understand what you expect. It also demonstrates your advisor's willingness to meet your investment needs and help you meet your goals.

What should an IPS include? It is advisable to include the following sections in the IPS:

- **Objectives**: In clearly defined language, the IPS should describe expectations, risk tolerance, return decisions, and guidelines for investments.

- **Asset allocation policy**: This section will categorize the asset classes you want in your portfolio and define how those assets are best allocated to meet your goals.

- **Management procedures**: This should outline how you want your investments monitored and evaluated. It should detail how and when changes should be managed.

- **Communication procedures**: Good communication is essential when it comes to your investments. This section should detail communication processes and objectives for the client and advisor. It should also assign responsibility for implementation.

Here are the steps needed to establish an investment policy:

1. Identify what your financial goals and needs are so you can determine your financial situation.

2. Establish your risk tolerance and your investment time horizon.

3. Set long-term investment goals.

4. Decide what restrictions you have for your portfolio and assets.

5. Determine the asset classes and allocation that will maximize the likelihood of achieving your investment objectives at the lowest level of risk.

6. Decide how you want to handle investment selection, rebalancing, buy-sell principles, portfolio reviews, reporting, and so on.

7. Implement the decisions and review as necessary.

Lack of information and forethought causes investors to make inappropriate decisions. Emotions also factor into poor decision making. An IPS will provide investors with a written statement that can guide them to make prudent and rational decisions.

CERTIFIED FINANCIAL PLANNER™ PRACTITIONER

Should your advisor be a Certified Financial Planner™ Practitioner? Most likely the only one who would say no to this is an advisor who has not achieved the designation. Why should your advisor be one? When people hear the term "financial planner," they believe that person to have some sort of certification or to have undergone some level of training—that is not the case. Nearly anyone can get away with calling themselves a financial planner. However, it is only those who have fulfilled the requirements of the Certified Financial Planner Board of Standards who may use the CFP® certification mark. This mark can provide you with a sense of security knowing the person has met a baseline of training preparation. The requirements, outlined in detail below, are a combination of education, exams, years of experience, and adherence to an ethical code.

- **Education**: A CFP® practitioner must have a bachelor's degree from an accredited U.S. college or university, or an equivalent foreign university. Their studies must have included financial planning subject areas outlined by the CFP Board as necessary to become a competent financial planner. The subject areas encompass investment planning, income tax planning, insurance planning, employee benefits planning, risk management, as well as retirement and estate planning.

- **Examination**: To earn the CFP® certification, the person must pass a comprehensive 10-hour exam (taken over two days). The exam includes scenarios and case studies that determine one's ability to diagnose issues related to financial planning and apply their learned knowledge to real-world circumstances.

- **Experience**: To become a CFP® practitioner, the person must have a minimum of three years of full-time financial planning experience. This must equate to 2,000 hours per year.

- **Ethics**: The CFP Board has developed documents that detail the ethical and practice standards to be followed by CFP® professionals. Those with the CFP® designation agree to follow the Board's Standards of Professional Conduct.

After becoming certified, their training is not over. To continue using the CFP® designation, individuals must complete ongoing education and ethics training. This includes 30 hours of continuing education every two years. Two of those hours must be on the Code of Ethics and other parts of Standards of Professional Conduct. This training is intended to ensure that these professionals stay abreast of developments in the financial planning field. Furthermore, CFP® professionals have to renew their agreement to abide by the Standards of Professional Conduct. A major aspect of this agreement requires that CFP® professionals provide financial planning services at a fiduciary standard of care. They must offer financial planning services that align with the best interests of their clients.

CFP® professionals who fail to meet these requirements can be suspended or have their certification permanently revoked. When choosing a financial advisor, I recommend you consider working with a Certified Financial Planner™ Practitioner to provide you with added confidence in their abilities.

ACT IN YOUR OWN BEST INTEREST

There are other things to consider when choosing an advisor, but looking at the topics detailed in this chapter can be a great start. Choosing a competent financial advisor whom you trust may be one of the most important decisions you make. Not only can your choice impact you, it can also impact your loved ones. Choose your advisor wisely—the right advisor can be a guide to you and your family throughout your life as you address specific financial concerns. They can help you find financial peace of mind and assist you in achieving your life goals. Never let an advisor scare you into becoming a client or make you feel guilty in order to keep you as a client. Take the time to get complete answers to all of your questions. Above all, act in your own best interest. By following these careful steps you can—and will—be successful in finding the right financial advisor for you.

About Radon

Radon Stancil is a CERTIFIED FINANCIAL PLANNER™ in Raleigh, NC. His specialty is working with individuals who are close to, or already in, retirement, as well as high income business owners. His goal is to make sure his clients have the best understanding of their financial situation. He created the Peace of Mind Retirement Process™ to help his clients develop a systematic approach to retirement planning. He then created the Peace of Mind Retirement Map™ to help his clients track their progress. This unique approach removes the stress from retirement planning and gives an increased level of financial security.

Radon is the author of *Take Control Of Your Retirement Plan* and is regularly sought out by the media for his opinions and expertise. Radon has been seen on CBS, NBC, ABC and FOX affiliates as well as in *The Wall Street Journal, USA Today* and *Newsweek.* He says, "I love helping my clients with their most pressing concerns. I like taking complicated topics and breaking them down in an easy to understand way. It brings me great satisfaction when a client says, 'OK, now I get it.'"

To learn more about Radon and his Peace of Mind Retirement Strategies™ visit www. FinancialPlanStrategies.com or call (919) 787-8866.

CHAPTER 37

Attract & Convert:

The Six-Step System to a Mammoth Marketing ROI

By Richard Seppala

Imagine spending millions of dollars on Super Bowl ads—and having them not only flop, but actively cause viewers to *hate* you.

That's what happened with the internet powerhouse Groupon in 2011. For their first TV campaign ever, they made a series of commercials with stars like Timothy Hutton, Elizabeth Hurley and Cuba Gooding Jr. that seemed to poke fun at charitable endeavors like the rainforest and saving the whales. Problem was that viewers thought the commercials were making fun of these kinds of causes, and that Groupon was a cold and cruel company.

The commercials soon vanished without a trace.

It just goes to show you that a huge company can just as easily make a huge marketing blunder as a single entrepreneur. Of course, it is a lot more embarrassing (not to mention expensive!) when you have an epic fail in front of the entire Super Bowl audience.

The truth is that marketing *never* has to crash and burn. Your marketing ROI should soar and score every time—as long as you stick to the basics. I should know. For over a decade, I've helped companies big and small, national and local, online and offline, boost their marketing ROI as well as their conversion rates. In my professional guise as "The ROI Guy," I specialize in supplying the systems and tools that help businesses grow consistently, even when times are tough.

In this chapter, I'd like to share some of the wisdom I've gained over the years and provide a six-step system to ensure *your* marketing is bulletproof and does everything you want it to do. You don't have to reinvent the wheel when it comes to selling your products and services. You just have to play by the rules. But first you have to know them...so here they are.

STEP 1: SET YOUR GOAL

Your goal for your marketing campaign is the starting point for everything that follows; that's why it's all-important to be as specific as possible when you determine that goal. You might say, "Well, my goal is pretty obvious—I want more people to buy what I'm selling." But try to drill deeper.

For example, are you rolling out a new product or service that you want to introduce or do you just want to find a way to reframe what you're already selling in a new and exciting way? Are you out to boost your retention of existing customers, or do you want to try and get customers who used to buy from you back in the fold?

Large "one-size-fits-all" campaigns usually only work for large companies with the budgets to continually hammer consumers until their brands are burned in their brains. For smaller businesses and entrepreneurs, it's usually smarter and a whole lot more cost-effective to create specific campaigns aimed at very specific goals. You'll find it easier to zero in on the niche market that will be the most responsive and to craft a message that will be the most effective for that niche market.

Answer these Key Questions to successfully complete this step:

Question #1: What do I want to achieve with this campaign?

Question #2: How realistic is this goal?

Question #3: Do I need to reevaluate this goal and make it more specific or narrow to attain it?

STEP 2: DETERMINE YOUR TARGET GROUP

If you're happy with the goal you've set for your campaign, your next step is to determine your target group. In some cases, this might be easy to determine. For example, in the previous step, we talked about campaigns where the goal is to retain current customers or get former customers to buy from you again. In the first case, your target group is the people already buying from you, in the second, it's the people who stopped buying from you.

If you keep a well-organized database of all your customers, clients or patients (and if you don't—well, that's a whole other problem!), targeting both of those groups is a snap. You have all the contact info you need at your fingertips (or, probably more accurately, in your hard drive or server).

If you're after new customers, that's when this step gets a little more hairy, because you must determine exactly *who* is most likely to buy what you're trying to sell in your campaign.

Again, this still might be a simple matter. Maybe you're a dentist who wants to expand his dental implant business—in which case, you obviously want to target seniors, since that group has the biggest problem with tooth loss. If you're a dentist who wants to promote whitening procedures, however, you can see where it gets more difficult.

You might want to check out the people who currently buy the product or service you want to feature in the new campaign. Review what they might have in common—age, income, gender, any important demographic information that might correlate. If you are going to purchase a list to market to, take those common demographic qualities into account.

Just like your initial campaign goal, the more specific you can get with your target group, the more cost-efficient and the more effective your marketing will be. You don't want to waste time and money selling to people who are not likely to buy. And they don't want to waste time *dealing* with your marketing.

Answer these Key Questions to successfully complete this step:

Question #1: Why would someone want what I'm selling in this campaign?

Question #2: What kinds of people buy this particular/product or service?

Question #3: What's the best way to generate a reliable list of these kinds of people?

STEP 3: MANUFACTURE YOUR MESSAGE

You know what you want to accomplish. You know who you want to reach. Now...what are you going to actually *say* to reach your marketing goals and generate enthusiastic leads?

In some cases, you may want to focus on **educating** your target group about your product. Let's go back to our example of the dentist who wants to have more implant patients; many seniors simply don't *know* very much about implants and how dramatically they can improve their quality of life. In that case, free educational materials with the dentist's branding prominently featured might be the best course of action.

Or you might want to focus on a **special offer**. The dentist may want to just get more potential patients in for appointments, so offering a free whitening procedure with each cleaning might be attractive enough to get a few "dental chickens" to roost in his or her chair.

Your product or service may offer a distinct **competitive advantage** from other companies that can be spotlighted in an impactful way. This can be effective in steering people away from other similar businesses or bringing first-time buyers of that product your way.

Whatever your message, **make it as simple as possible**. When you try to say too many things at once, people get lost. Your marketing is your priority, not theirs, so you only have a few seconds to gain their attention before they decide to give you a try, or at least explore the possibility. You can combine a couple of messages—say, a competitive advantage with a special offer—but make sure what your saying is clear and concise.

Answer these Key Questions to successfully complete this step:

Question #1: How can you best appeal to your target group?

Question #2: What kind of language will be most effective?

Question #3: How can you make it as simple as possible, yet as powerful as possible?

STEP 4: DECIDE HOW TO DEPLOY

You have your goal, your target group and your message in place. Now you'll have to take all those factors into account as you decide what marketing channels will be best suited to what you want to accomplish.

This means matching the *right* media with the *right* message. There are all kinds of ways to market, some more conventional than others. What you have to determine is which ways best suit both your target audience and your message.

Let's go back to our dentist who wants to sell more implants. If *education* is the best method to accomplish this, and the target group is seniors who are wary of a hard sell, the dentist may decide holding free presentations or seminars at senior communities is the most effective way to sell himself personally while discussing the many benefits of implants. He can end the seminars with some type of free consultation offer.

A new dry cleaner in the neighborhood, in contrast, doesn't need to educate anyone about dry cleaning—they just need people to give them a try. Getting a coupon in a local Val-U-Pak with a special introductory offer, or even going door-to-door with a special coupon book. is more the kind of direct marketing that's going to encourage sampling.

A plastic surgeon looking to grow his practice would have an entirely different approach—possibly a direct mail campaign targeted at older, upper-income households in the area that both educates and sells the various services available at his clinic.

The online marketing revolution, of course, has made available many incredible low to no-cost alternatives to traditional marketing placements. Social media and email are great ways to both reach out as well as keep in touch with your existing and past clients, and don't underestimate the power of a website that you customize to rank high on Google searches.

Answer these Key Questions to successfully complete this step:

Question #1: Where is the best place to reach your target group?

Question #2: What is the best "delivery system" to get your message across?

Question #3: Does your chosen marketing method align with your initial marketing goal?

STEP 5: TRACK, MEASURE AND ANALYZE

Well, if you've completed the first four steps I've described here, you must feel a wonderful sense of accomplishment. You're all done!

But if that's true...how come you've still got two more steps to go?

The reason is that you are very far from done if you want to consistently and effectively market your business. Everything you've done so far is probably based mostly on guesswork and research *within* your business. Me, I'm a numbers guy—which is why I make sure my clients have the tools to scientifically assess exactly which of their marketing campaign worked the best—and, more importantly, which campaigns made the most money.

You can only do that by *tracking, measuring and analyzing*. Hopefully, you used special phone tracking numbers in your marketing materials that allowed you to see which campaigns generated the most leads. Hopefully, you also had in place systems to automatically grab lead contact information and add it to your database for future marketing. The cherry on the top of this sundae would be you having the ability to actually *keep track* of how much money each campaign brought in vs. the cost of that campaign, as that's the only true way to really measure your marketing ROI.

The reason your marketing ROI is such an important number is because it's what defines the actual financial success of your marketing campaign. You may have made a lot from a campaign, but you also may have spent more money implementing that campaign, making it a net loss. On the other hand, you may have not generated a ton of money from another campaign—but, since you did it for free through social media, everything you made was pure profit.

You should also review the conversion rates of each campaign. You may have generated a lot of leads, but you may not have generated a lot of *sales*—which could mean your target group was interested, but maybe didn't have the available money to spend with you. Or it could mean you didn't have the right conversion tools in place, such as a trained staff that knows how to handle incoming sales calls from generated leads.

The point is, if the campaign worked, you want to figure out *why* it worked. If it didn't work, you want to figure out where you went wrong. Numbers don't lie and the more you crunch them, the more information you have for the next campaign and the more you improve your chances of success.

Answer these Key Questions to successfully complete this step:

Question #1: What was the response rate to your campaign and how does it compare to other campaigns?

Question #2: What was the conversion rate for the leads you generated and howdoes it compare to other campaigns?

Question #3: What was the campaign's ROI and how might you improve its profitability next time around?

STEP 6: DON'T FAIL TO FOLLOW UP!

Here's a fact you may not be aware of—most sales aren't made on the first try or even the second. The shocker? Most sales are made on the 5th to 8th contact!

That's why, even if the generated leads didn't buy the first time around, it's no time to give up. It may not have been a good time for them when your campaign first reached them or they may have needed to think about it (especially if you're selling a big ticket product or service).

There's nothing like a friendly reminder, either through an email, a phone call or a postcard, that you're there and want their business.

You spent a lot of time, effort and probably money to generate those leads. It takes a lot less of each of those ingredients to follow up with them, especially if you set up an automated follow-up marketing system. Letting go of leads, especially ones that have already displayed in an interest in what you're selling, is like leaving money on the table—and no business wants to do that if it doesn't have to.

Answer these Key Questions to successfully complete this step:

Question #1: Are generated leads' contact information being consistently added to your marketing database (even if they don't buy at first)?

Question #2: What's the easiest way to follow up with leads so that it gets done as automatically as possible?

Question #3: How can you overcome their initial reluctance to commit to buying from you?

These six steps, as I said, can mean the difference between marketing success and throwing money out the window. Ongoing success with marketing campaigns means having a top-to-bottom marketing system in place that addresses all these steps and makes sure each is given the attention they deserve.

I provide my clients with The ROI Matrix, an automated system that does just that–while offering other sales and marketing tools to help them collect and analyze the necessary marketing data.

Marketing is no different than any other business discipline. The more you do it, the better you get at it. But that comes with a caveat—you must pay attention to the numbers, analyze your results and understand how to keep improving your marketing ROI. In the end that saves you a ton of money; and, because your marketing becomes so much more effective, it also makes you a ton of money.

And that's what I call a win-win.

Contact me at Richard@TheROIMatrix if you'd like more information on how to "market to the max."

About Richard

Richard Seppala, also known as "The ROI Guy™," is a marketing expert, business consultant and best-selling author who helps companies maximize their profits by accurately measuring the ROI (Return on Investment) of their marketing efforts. His latest revolutionary tracking system, "The ROI Matrix," measures to the penny just how much revenue each specific marketing placement generates for a client.

Richard founded his "ROI Guy" company in 2005. In addition to his acclaimed marketing tracking systems, called "The Holy Grail of Marketing," he also supplies businesses and medical practices with cutting-edge sales solutions designed to facilitate the conversion of generated leads to cash-paying customers.

By identifying marketing strengths and weakness, The ROI Guy™ is able to substantially boost his clients' bottom lines by eliminating wasteful spending on ineffective marketing, as well as leveraging advertising campaigns that prove the most profitable. By providing "all-in-one" automated systems that allow for the real-time tracking of each generated lead, a business can easily access valuable marketing data with just a few keystrokes.

Richard's marketing expertise is regularly sought out by the media, which he's shared on NBC, CBS, ABC and FOX affiliates, as well as in *The Wall Street Journal, USA Today* and *Newsweek.* He's also launched his own television show, "ROI TV," which features interviews with other top marketing specialists.

To learn more about Richard Seppala, The ROI Guy™, and how you can receive free special reports and other invaluable marketing information from one of the country's leading experts, visit www.YourROIGuy.com or call Toll-Free 1-800-647-1909.

CHAPTER 38

Finding Good Advice About Money Matters

By Rick Parkes

Please stop me if you've heard this one:

When the engine of a giant ship failed, the owners of the shipping company tried one engineer after another, in an effort to get the big engine running again. As a last resort, they brought in an elderly mechanic with decades of experience fixing ship engines. The old man was not impressive by appearance. He shuffled when he walked, and he carried with him only a small flash light and a wooden toolbox. The old man moved slowly around the large engine, examining every inch, occasionally stopping to utter a knowing, "Hmmm."

With the owners of the ship looking on, the old man reached into his tool box and pulled out a small hammer. He gave something a gentle tap and instantly the engine came to life. He carefully put away the hammer. His work was done.

A week later, the owners received a bill from the old man for $15,000.

"What!?" they exclaimed. "He just tapped something with a hammer!"

So they wrote the old mechanic a note saying, "Please send us an itemized bill."

The man sent back a bill that read:

Tapping with a hammer: **$ 10.00**

Knowing where to tap: **$14,990.00**

It's an old story, but it well illustrates the value of knowledge and experience in any specialty. That is especially relevant today because 70 million baby boomers (those born during the birthrate surge following World War II) are now on the verge of retirement. Statistically, those born between 1944 and 1964 will live longer than any generation before it. One of the side effects of this blessing, however, is the fear among many that they will run out of money in retirement. Longevity is great. Outliving your resources is not.

The recession of 2008 was a wake-up call for many baby boomers. Some saw as much as 40% of their retirement nest egg vanish like smoke in the wind. Perhaps the worst day of that period was September 29, 2008, when the Dow lost almost 778 points in one day. It was the largest single-day point loss ever recorded, and it represented approximately $1.2 trillion in market value. The following day, I was scheduled to speak at a financial planning workshop. My topic was supposed to be "How Inflation Affects Retirement." But when I observed how stunned and worried my audience appeared to be because of what had happened the day before, I scrapped my speech and simply opened it up for questions. They had plenty of them.

"Why didn't my broker see it coming?"

"Will the market go any lower?"

"Is the market going to recover?"

"When will this happen next?

Because I am neither fortune-teller nor soothsayer, I had to say, "I don't know" to questions like that. The answer, although truthful, felt hollow to me, and I knew it was of little consolation to these people whose faith in what they had perceived to be a relatively sound economy had been severely shaken. In the days to follow, they would learn the unsettling truth of what was behind the crash. They would become painfully acquainted with such phrases as "too big to fail," "housing bubble" and "corporate bailouts." They were discovering the rotten timbers in their financial house, and they felt rightly betrayed. Standing before them, I remember wishing that I could press the rewind button and help them all begin again. As a proponent of safe money investing, I am a big believer in the "Rule of 100"—a financial philosophy that uses age to gauge appropriate market risk. Subtract your age from 100, and that's the percent you should have at risk. Many of those in my audience were approaching retirement. From their tales of woe, it was apparent that they had not heard of such a rule and now it was too late. Some who yesterday were making plans for an imminent retirement were now postponing it indefinitely.

GETTING A SECOND OPINION

What happened in 2008 was the first clear sign for many in the boom generation that the investing advice they had been given was lacking. Many among them reasoned that any investing strategy, or any financial planning philosophy, that would allow them to lose almost half of their savings in so short a time, just had to be faulty. Many were interested in getting second opinions.

Getting opinions about investing these days is certainly no problem. All you have to do is turn on the television or pick up a magazine. The problem is there are too many opinions. The talking heads on the money channels bicker like children in a sandbox, while authors, journalists and ideologues battle it out in the print media. They can't all be right, can they?

It is possible to receive conflicting medical advice. I woke up one morning with severe back pain. My doctor prescribed muscle relaxers. My chiropractor recommended treatment that did not involve medication. I am not a doctor, but it's my back. I took advantage of both opinions, and the pain disappeared the next day. Which doctor was right? Perhaps they were both right. Opinions about investing may be just as diametrically opposite as the ones I received from the two doctors. And both opinions may originate from individuals who are registered, licensed, certified and well educated, as were my family practitioner and my chiropractor. But is it possible for financial professionals to be motivated by greed? One would be naïve not to acknowledge that such a thing can exist in the financial world. Anyone familiar with the Bernie Madoff scandal? But I believe such things are rare. I know both my internist and my chiropractor, and I am confident that neither one of them would place fees over the safety of one of their patients. Similarly, differing opinions from financial advisors are most likely a reflection the advisor's training and experience and are merely the lens through which he or she sees the investing world. That is why one group of advisors, because of their training and experience may recommend equities for every solution. It's what they know best. Whereas another group may exclude any use of equities and only recommend insurance solutions, such as annuities and life insurance, because those solutions are tightly within his or her sphere of knowledge. Usually, when there are extreme poles, the reality often lies in the sizable middle ground between them. Both in life and money matters, some opposing points of view are neither right nor wrong. They are just different points of view of the same overall scene. So where does that leave us?

THE BEST PROFESSIONALS ARE GOOD LISTENERS

A wise doctor once reminded me, "It's your body. You live in it, not me." I gave that a lot of thought. The doctor was right, of course. I may not have medical training, but I know when something hurts far better than the doctor does. The same is true when it comes to handling your money. It's your money. If the advice you are given doesn't fit you, don't be afraid to say so. If it isn't clear to you, don't hesitate to stand up, hold your hand out like a traffic cop, and say, "Hold it. I don't understand that!"

Let's say you walk into a store to buy a pair of shoes, and for some odd reason, the salesperson tries to convince you that you should buy a pair that is one size too small. You squeeze your feet into the shoes, but your toes hurt. You can barely stand up in them, much less walk. Would you buy those shoes? Of course not. Why? Because they hurt your feet. You know your shoe size. While there may be instruments and measuring tools to help determine your appropriate shoe size, in the end you will go with what feels most comfortable.

When it comes to planning income for retirement, for example, you may be interested in guarantees and not projections. Then tell the doctor...I mean your financial professional, that. And if the answer comes back that there are no guarantees, then you know you are talking to the wrong financial professional. On the other hand, you may have a pension that will provide you with more than enough income in retirement. You are interested in taking on the measure of acceptable risk that will allow your money to see the most gain. If the answer is, "We have no such investments available," then perhaps you should look elsewhere for financial advice. There is no "one size fits all" here. So much depends on your unique situation.

Over the years, I have observed that good doctors spend much more time in the examination phase than they do in the diagnosis and prescription phase. And the more serious they think a problem may be, the more time they spend listening and asking questions before prescribing remedy. Being a good listener is the most important quality a financial advisor can have. Yes, credentials and training are important. But if the financial advisor is a poor listener, then letters after the name on the business card are just alphabet soup.

It is always wise to ask yourself, "If I implement this decision, how will I feel about it ten minutes from now, ten days from now, or ten years from now?" If the answer to that question is "good," then it's probably okay to say "yes." But only do so after gathering all the information you need to make that determination. When it comes to your money, an uninformed decision is nearly always a bad one.

EVERY SITUATION IS UNIQUE

The reason why detectives dust for fingerprints at a crime scene is because no two fingerprints are exactly alike. Each individual's financial picture is like a fingerprint. No two are alike. Even if two people worked at the same job for 30 years, and they both retired with exactly the same amount of money in their pension, or 401(k), and their debts and net worth are exactly the same, each would still feel differently about their finances. Each would have different goals, desires and risk tolerances. This means that any financial plan that was truly suitable for them would have to be tailored to fit them. No cookie-cutter program would work.

In 2007, a man walked into my office seeking financial advice, telling me that he had been up all night, pacing the floor. I instinctively took out my notepad and began listening to his story. My visitor was tall and distinguished looking, though casually dressed. He was intelligent, although not necessarily about money. Until this week, he had worked as an engineer for a computer programming firm, which had suddenly declared bankruptcy and closed its doors. The man, who was in his early

70s, showed me where his 401(k) plan was worth more than a half million dollars. He explained that he had expected to retire on a generous pension his company had provided, and that he intended to pass the 401(k) on to his children. But the pension was now gone.

The more I listened, the more it occurred to me that the man was unknowingly sitting on another potential time bomb. His 401(k) money was nearly all invested in mutual funds. His portfolio was more than 90 percent at risk, so we took steps to reallocate his portfolio to accommodate the proper safe/risk ratio appropriate for his age. What neither of us knew, or had any way of knowing, was that within a year the housing bubble would burst, precipitating the most dramatic stock market freefall since the great depression. Happily, when the crash occurred, he was insulated from a devastating loss. One of the most personally fulfilling moments of my career up to that point came when I received a phone call from the man thanking me. He told me that he and his daughter had just returned from a tour of China, something that they both had always dreamed of doing. He also told me that it was something that would have been impossible had we not performed emergency surgery on his 401(k) the year before enabling him to have a worry-free retirement.

"Now, at least I can sleep well at night," he told me.

That remark played on my thinking for the rest of the day. Having lost a daughter to leukemia 20 years ago, I know what sleeplessness is. Unfortunately, there was no cure available for my daughter, and my sleepless nights lasted until she ultimately lost her battle with her disease. But on that day in 2007, it felt good knowing I knew where to "hit with my hammer," so to speak, and cure this man's case of insomnia.

SLEEP WELL AT NIGHT

Years ago, a farmer owned land along the Atlantic seacoast and advertised for hired hands. There were few applicants. Many were reluctant to work on farms along the coast because of the frequent storms that could wreak havoc on the buildings and crops. Just when the farmer thought he wouldn't be able to hire anyone for the job, a short, thin man, well past middle age, approached him and asked about the position.

"What makes you a good farm hand?" the farmer asked him.

"I can sleep on a stormy night," the man answered.

Although puzzled by this answer, the farmer, desperate for help, hired him. The little man worked well around the farm, busy from dawn to dusk, and the farmer felt satisfied with the man's work. Then one night the wind howled loudly from an offshore storm. Jumping out of bed, the farmer grabbed a lantern and rushed next door to the hired hand's sleeping quarters. He shook the new man and yelled, "Get up! A storm is coming! Tie things down before they blow away!" The little man rolled over in bed and said firmly, "No, sir. I told you, I can sleep through a stormy night."

Enraged by the response, the farmer was tempted to fire him on the spot. Instead, he hurried outside to prepare for the storm. To his amazement, he discovered that all of the haystacks had been covered with tarpaulins. The cows were in the barn, the chickens were in the coops, and the doors were barred. The shutters were tightly secured. Everything was tied down. **Nothing could blow away**. The farmer then understood what his hired hand had meant, so he returned to his own bed to sleep while the wind blew.

The hired hand in the story was able to sleep because he had secured against the storm. He had anticipated uncertainty and had prepared for it.

Nothing is more certain than uncertainty. That's why we hope for the best, always. But we plan for the worst…just in case.

About Rick

Rick Parkes has been changing lives as a financial advisor for over three decades. He helps people who have money keep their money, and create a plan that will ensure they do not outlive their money but live a comfortable life in retirement. He wants his clients to have a real plan instead of wishful thinking so they can Sleep Well At Night both when they are planning for, and when they reach, retirement. He calls it S.W.A.N. planning. Rick has been interviewed on ABC, NBC, Fox and CBS explaining the strategies that he has designed to help people weather the financial storms that lie ahead. History proves we see, on average, a bear market (a drop of 20% or more) every 4 ½ years but we just can't pinpoint when they will hit. So we have to have a real plan so as not to fumble the ball in the red zone just before retiring. Many of these strategies are described in his new book, *Help I'm Retiring!*, released by Amazon publishing.

CHAPTER 39

The Success Secrets for Dentists

By Dr. Scott Schumann

What did dentists like me focus on before we started practicing dentistry?

Well, we focused on...dentistry. Because once we decided on that career path, we had to spend years of higher education learning how to be the best we could be at it.

Let's face the truth, though—what we *didn't* learn how to be is business-people.

And yet, we *are* running small businesses, because each and every one of us who heads up a practice. That was the missing component from most of our educations—and a vitally important one. You can be an amazing dentist and still run a lousy business; in the long term, this will hurt your ability to serve your patients, as well as your potential to have the best possible life you can have.

That's why, in this chapter, I'd like to share with my fellow colleagues, and really anyone with a small business, the lessons I've learned and implemented over the years as I built an amazingly successful dental practice.

The sad part is that it took the threat of dying to really make me give my practice a hard look and see what was missing.

GETTING MY GROOVE ON

I did okay in my first decade as a dentist with a small practice. Then in 2003, I was setting up a new practice with two other guys in Grove City in south Columbus, Ohio, when a routine gall bladder operation turned into the nightmare of my life.

And one fateful night, two surgeon friends came and said I needed to call my lawyer in *that night* to sign some final papers. Why? Because I was probably going to die before morning.

I made it through that night, but the prognosis still hadn't changed. I asked my pastor to come in the next day and requested he lead a prayer session with me–that was the turning point. That night, I overcame a lot of the negative emotions that had previously held me back—and I got motivated. I was suddenly determined to take charge of my life and *do well*. As I recovered, I was suddenly open to learning and changing. I attended business coaching courses and mastermind groups. I sought out people above me for advice and I would ask them, what can I do to be better?

In June of 2004, I finally returned to the practice I had begun to set up. In the next six months, I did more business than I did in all of 2003. Why? Because I changed my approach and attitude. Before, I was lazy about marketing and running a business properly. Now, I knew that if you didn't tell people about your practice, they wouldn't come; if you didn't work with your staff to provide the best overall patient experience, you wouldn't build strong customer loyalty; and if you didn't do what it took to create a high-profit business, you wouldn't grow profits.

And that's how I went from being a small-town dentist with a below average practice to developing one of the best dental teams in the nation and being on the Inc. 5000 list of fastest growing private companies in America the last two years.

Here are 12 of my Success Secrets that allowed me to make that awesome transition and will also allow you to create the business of *your* dreams.

SECRET #1: IT'S A *BUSINESS!*

As I mentioned, when I went into dentistry, nobody really told me I had to be a businessman too—that's why I ended up thinking I could provide free dental work to my pals all day and somehow pay the bills. Well, the number one goal of any business is to make money. If you don't make money, it doesn't do you or your patients any good—because, sooner or later, you'll be too broke to help anybody.

I put some basic principles in place for my practice. Number one was to fill my chair, get my money and show my patients some love. Number two was to improve my attitude and my willingness to work. I could no longer say I was too tired to do a treatment when it was added to the schedule; that's like turning away opportunity. And number three, I realized you can't be successful by yourself - you need to hire and train the right team to back you up.

SECRET #2: SHARE YOUR BUSINESS VISION

You probably carry your business vision around in your head. But that vision would do a lot more good if you got it out of your skull and shared it with your staff and patients. For example, my vision for my practice is "100% healthy mouths with the best option long-term care and the most gorgeous smiles."

So what inspires you to do what you do? Do you think that vision will also inspire the people who work for you as well as your customers?

For example: I believe what we do can change lives. We can help people move past pain, embarrassment and dental difficulties to live fuller and more enjoyable lives. I make sure everyone I come into contact with at my practice knows what I'm really all about. That makes everyone feel better about being there and more motivated to give their best—even if all they have to do is sit in my dental chair!

SECRET #3: CREATE THE RIGHT CULTURE

My one-on-one patient treatments are only a small part of the overall interaction with my practice at Grove City Dental. That's why having a strong staff culture in place is vital; your staff is representing *you* to your patients, and they need to reflect your personality and your approach. That culture also unifies your staff and keeps them on the right track.

That's why I give my staff specific goals to fulfill whenever they encounter a patient. Those goals include:

- Greet them and make them feel at home
- Make sure you are wearing your nametag, so they don't have to ask your name
- Introduce yourself with a firm handshake and a "Texas-size" smile. Make eye contact.
- Hang up their coat/purse for them, no matter what they say
- Offer the use of the restroom
- Let them know how long their appointment will be, what we will be doing, and how much their co-pay will be.
- Let new patients know about all the procedures and services we offer as you give them a quick tour of the office.
- Always try to make their day
- Make them feel like they made *your* day by simply talking to you.

When you put certain standards like these in place, they become part of the normal routine. Your patients will appreciate the consideration every time they come in (because, if you are considerate, they WILL come in again)!

SECRET #4: TRAIN AND INVEST IN YOUR STAFF

The choice is yours. Do you want a bunch of random employees doing random things? Or do you want to build a strong, effective team that gets things done the way *you* want them done?

If you're willing to put forth the time, effort and expense, you can build a winning team that provides the high level of support and service that both you and your patients want out of your practice. It also gives you back more time *and* money—because it's the ideal way to multiply yourself and open a whole lot of doors to more diversification and more profit streams.

In my case, I train my staff to do things the "Grove City Dental Way." That means we calibrate the office so that everyone knows how *we* do it, not how some other place does it or how one particular person does it. That means we put standard operating procedures in writing so everyone is on the same page.

It also means we measure performance to make sure everyone is giving 100%. We avoid office "drama." And we help each other to be their absolute best. Most of all, we keep a positive mindset in place. We say "can" instead of "can't."

SECRET #5: KNOW WHAT YOU DO

Sounds easy, right? You're a dentist. Well, think bigger than that. What's the *result* of what you do? You make good-looking people better-looking by improving their smiles. You provide sedation dentistry to help people catch up with ten years of neglecting their teeth in as few as one to two visits. You change lives and make people feel good again about their appearance.

When you think about what you do, think about it in terms of the benefits you deliver to your patients. And be able to state those benefits in about thirty seconds or less (make it your own personal commercial)!

SECRET #6: KEEP ADDING BULLETS TO YOUR BELT

In the last secret, I asked you to "know what you do." In contrast, this secret is about looking at what you *don't* do.

What *aren't* you delivering to your patients that you could be? What do they want that you don't provide? Do you offer Sedation Dentistry? How about implants? Certain dental niches lead to riches—and give your patients a fuller range of options to choose from. That's a big win-win for everybody. So routinely *ask* your patients what else they might like from you, then act on the answers!

SECRET #7: PUMP UP YOUR SERVICE

As dentists, we aren't changing oil filters or rotating tires—we're working with real live people who want to be treated like people. Make sure their experience is all that it can be.

Examples: If you spot a problem during a routine check-up, see if you can handle it the same day so the person doesn't have to go to the trouble of coming in for another appointment. Take the time to explain dental issues and procedures in terms the patient can understand. Also take the time to break down treatment costs and explain what can happen if they don't attend to their dental health.

Your focus should be on them, not on you. Help them to make the best possible decisions for their oral (and overall) health. Make sure your staff has scripts to help them make those decisions as well. Remember your vision for your practice and put it into practice!

SECRET #8: MAKE IT EASY TO PAY

Most patients want to make the best dental care decisions , so they simply find it hard to pay for them in this day and age. Help them out as best as you can. If your cash flow is good, offer them in-house solutions. Use credit solutions such as Care Credit, CreditWell and Springstone. They'll appreciate you going the extra mile for them to help them work out the cost on their terms.

SECRET #9: SYSTEMS WILL SET YOU FREE

When you set up the right systems at your office and document them correctly, you'll find that everyone knows what they're supposed to be doing at any given time in any given situation. You'll also find that temp help can fit in a lot faster, when all they have to do is consult the proper checklists to see if they're following through on a task in the right way.

You want these systems to be as "stupid-proof" as possible. Start the day and end it at ground zero and make sure that, in between, everything has a place and everything *is* in its place.

Finally, make sure your staff is held accountable and responsible. Good is the enemy of great —but with the proper project management, you don't have to settle for *less* than great. Your employees are either making you money or costing you money, so make sure it's the former and not the latter!

SECRET #10: MORE PATIENTS SOLVE MOST PROBLEMS

So how do you get more patients? Simple. Marketing. Just as dentists have to be businesspeople, they also have to be *marketers.* Sooner or later, your current patients will either leave or die—which means you have to continually look for new ones. Marketing is how you do that.

Now, going through all the marketing do's and don'ts could fill up a whole row of books, so I'm not going to have time to talk about everything here. But here are a few "musts:"

Know who you're marketing to. Some campaigns work for women, some for men, some for older people, some for younger. Your campaign presentation must fit your audience.

Train your staff to "sell" when answering incoming sales calls. There is an art to handling these calls; your staff must engage with the caller, rather than just give out "yes" and "no" answers. Converting a lead to a sale is a skill that everyone needs to learn.

Capture lead contact info and follow up on it. When someone does email or call, make sure you get the person's name and contact info. Use it for your next marketing campaign (with their permission, of course). Offer them free information about the service they're interested in. NEVER let go of a "warm" lead (someone already interested in buying from you)!

"Celebrity Brand" yourself. Make yourself the leading dental authority in your area so new patients are drawn to you.

Make your office experience match your marketing. If you fail to deliver on what your marketing promises, the result is a letdown for the consumer.

SECRET #11: NUMBERS DON'T LIE AND NEITHER DOES THE MIRROR

Set benchmarks and targets for you and your staff. And "play 'till the whistle blows," because most games are won in the last few minutes of the game. You want to set in place real-life practical ways to measure progress and success periodically to make sure you're heading in the right direction. Always include your staff in the effort to reach those goals.

SECRET #12: SHARE THE WEALTH

Or, as I like to say to my basketball buddies, "Hook a brother up." I like to reward my staff when they attain certain performance benchmarks. Some dentists think, "Hey, that's what they get paid for," but I think that's a little short-sighted. A bonus, grab pull, a trip or even a simple thank you is an easy way to reward performance—and it's an incentive for those who *don't* get the bonus to try harder next time.

I can't possibly get all of my secrets in one single chapter, which is why I've built a website, www.TheSuccessSecretsForDentists.com. When you go there, opt into getting my FREE The Success Secrets for Dentists newsletter and put in code word SMILE to get an additional bonus

EBook for free Titled *7 Mistakes Most Dentists Make & How You Can Avoid Them* devoted to helping fellow dentists achieve all their goals for their practices. I hope you'll check it out find success with *your* practice.

About Scott

Dr Scott Schumann, America's PremierExperts® Cosmetic and Sedation dentist, is a celebrated 5-Time Best-selling Author. He has featured chapters in *Oral-Facial Emergencies, The 21 Principles of Smile Design, Shift Happens, Power Principles of Success, ROI Marketing Secrets Revealed, More Than a Mouthful, Game Changers the World's Leading Entrepreneurs, How they're Changing the Game & You Can Too!* Dr. Schumann has been nominated for an EMMY Award, won a TELLY award and has been quoted in *USA Today, The The Wall Street Journal,* and *Newsweek.* Scott has made guest appearances on radio and TV including the radio show the Next Big Thing® and America's PremierExperts® TV show which airs on NBC, CBS, ABC and FOX TV. Dr Scott Schumann's company, Grove City Dental, was recently recognized by the **Inc. 500/5000** 2010 and 2011 List for America's Fastest-Growing private companies. Scott is also a speaker presenting at various conferences and mentoring groups helping other business owners take their businesses to the next level.

Dr. Schumann started his career in Ohio teaching in the Advanced Dentistry Clinic at the Ohio State University, teaching dental residents advance cosmetic, implant, hospital, and sedation dentistry for ten years. Dr Scott Schumann is a dentist in Grove City Ohio, a suburb located just eight minutes south of downtown Columbus, Ohio. He is one of America's leading dentists, yet he is still grounded which is evidenced by his patients often describing him as "fun" and "cool."

Scott is proud of his staff, which won "Best Team in the Nation" honors out of 1200 dental offices. He said they won because they are well known for their love of helping their patients achieve the smile they always dreamed of. His highly trained professional team and office, with amazing new technological advancements, makes each patient visit as fun as possible without guilt or embarrassment. Dr Scott Schumann and Grove City Dental is the home of phenomenal sedation dentistry. "This very safe technique will take you to **'La La Land'** and let us take care of your issues in as little as one afternoon while not caring or remembering very little, while time flies by. Whether it is fear & anxiety or you're just too busy with work and you want all your work done in one visit—sedation dentistry will solve your problem."

Recently one of Dr. Scott Schumann's patients, Karen S., shared her story regarding her wonderful experience with Dr. Schumann and sedation dentistry: "I really don't remember much about the appointment... Felt no pain... Was totally comfortable... I am so grateful to Dr. Schumann and his entire staff who could not be any nicer, more sincere or friendly. They made me feel so much better about myself. My smile now reflects the confidence of my heart and the joy of my laugh. I'm a woman who loves to smile and laugh and can do it now without having to hide behind my hands."

For more information, and my FREE "The Success Secrets for Dentists" newsletter, please visit: www.TheSuccessSecretsForDentists.com
www.GroveCityDentists.com
888-496-1250

CHAPTER 40

Don't Panic!
It's Only a Little Turbulence

By Tinka Milinovic

My story is a true American story about a young teenage girl who came from another country, worked her butt off, built a business from the ground up with nothing handed to her. I learned it all in America and have been taking it with me everywhere I go, ever since.

My amazing journey begins in pre-war Yugoslavia—where as a teenager living in Sarajevo, I wanted to travel the world. At age 16, I was chosen for the American foreign exchange student program and found myself attending high school in rural Louisiana.

Soon after landing in the States, war broke out in my homeland and when it reached Sarajevo, Bosnia and Herzegovina, I was cut off from my family, not knowing if they were dead or alive for many years. In the blink of an eye I lost everything. At age 17 I was alone, without the family love and security I was used to, broke and stranded in the rural countryside of the Deep South. The city girl with everything found herself in the boonies with swamps, gators, and road kill. With only a student visa in hand, I was ineligible to a work or obtain student loans. For years I had no money and counted on the kindness of new friends and opportunities I had to make to survive.

I threw myself into the situation with creative determination to overcome any obstacle I encountered and a series of remarkable things happened. Armed with boundless ingenuity, I found a way to graduate from

Louisiana College *Cum Laude* with a Bachelor of Music degree despite having no money to pay for college and the hardship of having to survive on as little as two dollars a day. My music talent and academics earned me a full assistantship to the University of Louisiana at Lafayette and I received a Masters Degree in Opera/Vocal Performance. Eventually I performed roles in different operas both in the States and Sarajevo, as well as musicals, recitals and solo concerts.

But my biggest challenge came when I was 18. I began acting as my own lawyer to navigate the difficult U.S. immigration system, and my resourcefulness was rewarded when I became a U.S. Citizen. People tell me I am the poster child for overcoming adversities and now I see that it was determination, inner strength and intense persistence that led to the next phase of my adventure—international stardom and become a brand.

I knew no one would help me unless I helped myself first. I was too young and proud to ask people for real help (seeing that as a sign of desperation and need), and could not bring myself to tell them that I'm hungry and have no money. I thought shortcuts in life don't happen to people like me, and I have to fight for and earn everything I want; I took the road less traveled and did everything on my own.

Now I know better: showing rational vulnerability, asking politely for things you need doesn't have to be a bad thing. People want to help. You are not alone. Have your pride but conduct the need for help with your loyalty and gratefulness for things you do have. On my own, I created opportunities, possibilities and threw myself into the unknown. Physicists say to every action there's a reaction, and indeed it is so. You will always see it clearly, but the more you do and put yourself out there, the more you will have come back to you. That's just how it is. Change your thought process and start acting now.

I've listed below the top 5 fundamental values that helped shape my success and "a warrior never quits" mindset:

1. Know your values. Ask yourself 'What do I believe in?', 'What makes me different?', and 'What do I have to offer?' That will become your brand and people will be drawn to you because of that.

2. Find a mentor AND form an advisory board. Befriend someone who will be your protector when the going gets rough. Not everyone is lucky to have a father/brother/family member in a high

position whose one phone call will help you deal with trouble. A mentor will open the door for you just as you will open it for someone else who will need your help in the future. Pay it forward. Mentoring comes naturally to maturing men, as they already receive backing from already established, successful men. Women generally don't do this. We are still dealing with jealousy issues and fighting for our own place to toughen up our position in a men's world.

3. Be persistent and tenacious. Identify the goal and keep the focus. Keep looking for ways to accomplish what you want. The essence of innovation is continuing the experiment of solving the problem and accomplishing a goal.

4. Invest your time wisely. When you want to invest money, any financial professional will first ask you about your short terms and long term goals that investing the money is meant to accomplish. So why treat your time any differently? Your time is the most precious thing anyone can take away from you, because it can never be returned. Take care of your time and not be lazy or afraid to dismiss people who are not contributing to your development and life.

5. Explore and experience. Never turn down an opportunity to try and learn something new. Recognize the moment when it's presenting and happening to you. Ultimately it all happens when you enroll other people in your cause. Create everything else that is missing.

It's crucial that you start making success happen instead of waiting for it to happen. Practice creating a momentum. There are no fairy godmothers out there; it's all based on your actions. Take opportunities with a gusto, take control and never give up. Persistence is what will get you to the finish line. My life story is the platform for my brand. I survived and made it happen by throwing myself into the unknown and learning how to swim as hurdles and opportunities arose. Sometimes you'll make a bad decision, but remember, it's not how many times you fall, it's how quick you pick yourself up, dust yourself off, and start all over again. What can you do to learn from the experience, turn it around, and turn this downfall into *an opportunity*? If you lose the fight, don't lose the lesson. That also is an opportunity.

So, just when you think you've experienced it all, life can still take a turn and face you with the unexpected.

"DON'T PANIC!... IT'S ONLY A LITTLE TURBULENCE"

The bubbles from the champagne were starting to go to my head as the pilot announced our private jet was about to land in Tripoli. I could see the outline of Libya capital's lights (or the lack there of) as we made our night descent into the ancient city. It all looked so peaceful, yet little did I know that in less than 24 hours I'd become the center of a global tabloid media frenzy. Such is the jet setting lifestyle.

As in life, there are many different types of landings: some are smooth, some bumpy, some are crash landings, and many times it's all together— a missed approach. I've experienced all of these and one thing is certain—don't panic. A little turbulence is okay! It's how you handle it that determines whether you land on your feet, ready for another adventure.

At the time I was a popular TV host arriving in Tripoli for a television shoot. It was going to be another adventurous trip in and out, but before I could accomplish the task at hand, I was swept into a tabloid drama with none other than French President Nicolas Sarkozy! The French President was rumored to be quite a womanizer and it was just my luck that we were staying at the same hotel. Our presence was recorded by the French media traveling with him as well as the gossipy hotel staff, and suddenly I was his "secret love" and "the reason behind the break-up of his marriage with Cecilia Sarkozy." Now this was more than a buckle-up-for-a-few-bumps type of turbulence... this was prepare-for-crash-landing scary! By the time I flew back home, the story had blown up and my phone was exploding with calls from media around the world. I can laugh about it now, but at the time I got really scared. The one positive thing in all this—after weeks of hell and despite all my confusion—was that my brand was affiliated with another powerful brand.

What was happening behind this curtain on my side was a comic-drama. This reported romance tantalized readers with the prospect of a daughter of the Balkan state becoming the next First Lady of France. I had people from my past crawling out of nowhere excited to have a friend about to move in the Élysée Palace in Paris, official residence of the President of the French Republic. I had people laughing at me. I had people assuming I am just another woman who got with the man because of his power. I had people admiring and congratulating me, calling me their hero. I even received emails from people of different backgrounds and nationalities living in France asking me to help them with their immigration statuses!

Then there were those who were disappointed to read weeks later that I denied I was involved with Sarkozy, and the bunch of red roses delivered to my room had been sent by another suitor. I also received inquiries and large amounts of money offered from major publications and news from all over the world just to share my "night of passion with the Frenchman" story. Curiosity requests did not stop there. Many offered fortune to find out about Sarkozy's manhood size and lovemaking skills. Even if I would lie!

I did what any jet setter in the know does when the turbulence gets to be too much...I flew under the radar. Yes, ladies, it is okay to lay low. I went far away, switched my phone off, and surrounded myself with strictly the most loyal and loving people in my life.

When things get rough and out of your control it is best to take a breather and find a quiet port to ride out the storm and see which way the wind is blowing. Evaluate the situation. Choose your battles. Sometimes inaction is the best course of action. I was coy but honest when I finally did grant an interview to tell my side of the story (soon after the French President had moved on to someone else and I was in the clear).

What I learned from this situation:

1. Everybody wants to claim a piece of public property
2. When the whole world is screaming loader than you, wait for the storm to pass and then react
3. People care about the screaming headlines as a way to get out of their own worries. Their escape is more important than the truth of the headline
4. You become reminded who your real friends are
5. Be appreciative of the new life's lesson/experience
6. Learn not to take yourself too seriously

Getting from one destination to another can be rocky and as any traveler knows, turbulence is a momentary inconvenience. It may scare you, make you spill your drink, (or if you are lucky, throw you into the lap of the handsome guy seated next to you)! But one thing is for sure; you eventually land on solid ground. If I have learned anything it is that surviving a bumpy ride requires faith, confidence, inner strength, and a cool head, all mixed with a healthy doze of humor! Don't forget to find reasons to laugh, no matter what you are going through at the moment.

My success secret is inner perseverance, being driven, persistent, resilient, and not be afraid to throw myself into the unknown and make the most of the experiences life has to offer. The great secret is that the more stuff you do and the more confident you become, the less things you take personally, the easier it becomes to deal with rejections, shocks, unexpected endeavors. Life is a stage, and only you can determine what role you will be playing. It's not going to be easy but with time it gets easier and easier. Remember that no matter what you do in life, stay true to yourself and who you are. I've made my brand by seizing the opportunities that have been given to me, and creating everything else that I have not been given. I've never ignored an opportunity, I took it all like a warrior. I am a pro when it comes to overcoming adversity. My experiences give me strength when I am faced with new hurdles in life, and wherever I am, they allow me to overcome them.

You are always representing yourself—your brand!

About Tinka

Tinka Milinovic (born November 27, 1973) is a Bosnia-Herzegovinian television and radio star and personality, opera singer, recording artist, entrepreneur, philanthropist, actress and model who has appeared on the covers of numerous magazines in Europe.

Starting at age 18, without the assistance of professional legal counsel, Milinovic represented herself before the U.S. immigration system and became a U.S. citizen, a process that took Milinovic several years.

Milinovic's music and tv career was chronicled in a stream of magazine covers, performances and TV appearances in Europe, Middle East, Africa and the United States where she expanded her fan base to international circles. Tinka is a contributing author for the No. 1 lifestyle and fashion magazine in the Middle East, and several others in Europe. Her prolific writings cover topics related to relationships, love, lifestyle and travel.

Presently residing in West Hollywood, New York City and Europe, Milinovic is working on *The Tinka Show* targeting the US audience and international television markets. Milinovic's forthcoming book aims to give a glimpse into the international celebrity lifestyle. She is developing a reality show based on her life story, with all the battles and betrayals, thrills and chills, hardships and triumphs, and how she handles it all with her signature *joie de vivre.*

Milinovic has commented on her perspective on life. "My life is a tapestry of interesting episodes and decisions, some good, some not so good. But it's all been worth it," says Milinovic. "I've seen things, I've experienced things, I made it to the top by throwing myself into the unknown and not being afraid to experience what life has to offer. Now I have a lot to share and inspire others."

Milinovic has returned to the US to further her American market commercial interests, tell her story and find a forum in which to share her brand, and to empower women on their journey to discover themselves and follow their heart's desire.

www.TheTinkaShow.com

CHAPTER 41

Black Belt Personal Development:

Three Key Steps to Take Yourself and Your Business to the Next Level

By Tommy Lee

In the summer of 1992, I realized something was missing in my life. I seemed to have everything going for me, with many friends, a great job and the recognition of being one of the top producers. What I realized was that my career path didn't match my passion.

I started reading books and listening to tapes, and then the light bulb went off. I listened to tape after tape and read book after book. It was almost as if the pages were turning themselves. I could relate to the words, the questions and was gaining clarity.

What I realized is that I had unfulfilled goals and dreams. Two years later, I made the decision to open my own Martial Arts Studio. More than just committing to opening the studio, I set a goal of generating more students and driving more revenue in my first year than any other martial arts studio in the U.S.

I was clear on my goal. I was driven to achieve it. I was laser focused. And I had a plan. In the first six months in business, I had built a studio that was in the top three percent of my industry. I had exceeded my goals in half the time.

I had other studio owners reaching out to me wanting to know my secret formula. The National Association of Professional Martial Artists took note of my achievements and asked me to be a guest speaker at their national conference. I had a proven sales system and a solid plan. But more importantly, I realized that the same principles it took to be a Black Belt applied to running a successful business.

In the following years, I was blessed with the continued growth of my business and impacting the lives of my students. I also gained many honors along the way; I was inducted into the National and International Martial Arts Hall of Fame, personally accepted an award from Chuck Norris, and was recognized multiple times by my peers as one of the top contributors in the Martial Arts Business.

I am not sharing these accolades to impress you, but rather to impress upon you the importance of the Black Belt Success System. I know the secret formula of what it takes to exceed your goals and achieve more than you ever thought possible.

If you are ready to learn the secrets and are committed to applying them, then read on.

BLACK BELT PERSONAL DEVELOPMENT

Let's start by defining what we're talking about a little more specifically—personal development is the study and practice of improving aspects of one's life, including one's career, education, relationships, health, happiness, productivity and spirituality.

People naturally want to improve their lives in all those areas, but they have to improve *themselves* to bring in those very real benefits. That's why personal development is a *choice,* not an automatic gift. I made a choice to make a change in my life, and then opened my first studio.

Many people use personal development tools such as books, CDs, DVDs, webinars, workshops, seminars, conferences and personal coaching. Some people find success, while others say it doesn't work for them. We find that the successful people took action and the others that said it didn't work, didn't actually complete the courses and take action.

How can someone say something doesn't work if they don't use it? Personal development does work. When learned and applied, it can help you achieve better and faster results if you commit to fully implementing the skills and tools in your life. It's just like people who say a diet doesn't work because they can't stop themselves from eating ice cream or fatty fast food. Well, the diet works...they're just not following it!

Personal development is not about a single book, CD, DVD or workshop. It's about committing oneself to learning from these materials and taking action. Feeding your mind with the proper positive mental stimuli is just as important as feeding your body with the right nutrients.

All of this means nothing if you don't act on the information and knowledge you have gained. Success Principles + Knowledge x ("Zero" Effort) = "Zero" Results.

It is like reading everything you can about how to drive safely, but never actually getting behind the wheel and *doing* it. It means nothing to know everything about personal development when you're not actually using that information in your day-to-day life.

It starts with being really clear with what you want to accomplish. As Brian Tracy (multiple NY Times Best-Selling Author) says in his book *Eat that Frog,* "Clarity is perhaps the most important concept in personal productivity." You can't get what you want if you don't *know* what you want.

You also can't get what you want if you allow others to hold you back. Sometimes it's not just internal mental roadblocks in between you and success, it's also your environment. (By environment, I mean who you hang out with most of the time.) The five people you associate with the most are the five people who are going to determine how far you go (indirectly or directly). The saying goes like this, you will become the average of the five people you hang around the most. If they're negative, have excuses for never progressing with their lives, or really don't care about succeeding, that all rubs off on the people they hang with, which means you, if they are in your circle. Negative people hold you down—and positive people propel you forward.

Is your entire circle of influence a negative drain on you or a catalyst for your success?

Take a moment to think about the messages the closest people in your life deliver to you on a daily basis. Consider how many of those messages are positive versus how many of them are discouraging and judgmental. Then ponder how those messages are affecting you *without you even knowing it*. Then take action and do something about it.

A strong support team and coach are paramount for ultimate success. I have personally made the decision to surround myself with people that have a Black Belt Attitude and Mindset. I surround myself with coaches and mentors that challenge me continually to achieve more.

THE BLACK BELT 3-STEP PLAN TO SUCCESS

When it comes to following through on a personal development plan, these three steps have proven to be powerful for myself, my students and clients. Whatever your personal development goal may be, take it through these three sequential stages and you're bound to experience more success.

Step 1: Have the Right Mindset
Having coached over 150 students to Black Belt, and over 100 AAU National and Junior Olympic Champions, I have also mentored hundreds of entrepreneurs to meet and exceed their business goals resulting in championship results. Each champion and highly successful professional I have coached knows the first secret to success is an unshakable self confidence and unwavering belief in one's ability. Whether you believe you can do something or not, YOU'RE RIGHT.

Step 2: Have the Right Skill Set
Black belts and National Champions master each skill necessary to achieve their desired outcome. For them, it's about executing technique in a quick, smooth and effective manner that actually hits the target and gets the result. In order for them to do this, they understand that preparation and practice will help them perform. When the day arrives, they get in the ring, they don't have to think about what they are going to do, they are programmed to perform.

This again translates to our everyday life and business goals. You must master whatever skills necessary to get you to the next stage of your development—whether it be something as simple as thinking positive or mastering the art of influence so you can make more sales.

Just as with the Black Belts and National Champions I have trained, I always recommend finding the experts who can help you master these skills. Experts know what it takes to create championship results and what you have to do to become proficient at what you want to achieve. Never be afraid to solicit expert advice and admit what you *don't* know. How else will you learn?

Step 3: TAKE ACTION!
Albert Einstein once said, "Nothing happens until something moves."

In this case, the something that needs to move is *you*. When you have your mindset and skill set honed, it's time to take action to move toward your goal. Kemmons Wilson, the late founder of the Holiday Inn hotel chain, often said, "I believe, to be successful, that you have to work at least a half day—it doesn't make any difference which half, the first twelve hours or the last twelve hours."

Yes, he was joking, but he was also being serious about the amount of time, effort and action he took to build a successful business.

And here's a final saying to complete our quote trilogy: Thomas Edison, the guy who came up with the light bulb, said, "Opportunity is missed by most people because it is dressed in overalls and looks like work."

Unless you're the luckiest person in the world, no one is going to open the door and hand you the success you want. As our three quotes indicate, *you* have to open the door that leads to that success—and, after you walk through it, you have to take action and work hard to attain it and keep it.

That's why it's important to remember that Step 3 isn't about waiting for your ship to come in, it's about swimming out to meet the ship. Put your dreams into action or they will remain only dreams.

Are you ready to make those dreams reality?

BLACK BELT THINKING

Many people think success is unreachable or unattainable. The good news is the skills needed to succeed in Martial Arts and business are learnable. Success is predictable; you simply have to pay the price, learn from the experts and make the right moves. Admittedly, it's not quite that simple, but I know you have everything you need to go from where you are now to where you want to be.

With that in mind, here are a few other ways you can fine tune your mindset to reach that potential.

- Make sure you choose to be a person who is proactive, not reactive. Proactive people don't defend where they are in life, they take steps to improve it.

- In Martial Arts we can learn by personal experience or by our coach's personal experience. It is much faster and less painful to follow our coach's advice instead of learning the hard way. Don't guess, get a mentor. Find an expert and use his experience instead of wasting precious time on your own learning curve.

- You can do whatever you set your mind to. Make the commitment and move forward. Understand what you need to accomplish your goal and just START.

- Persistent people begin their success where most others quit. Setbacks don't stop them. This is a simple key to success in any area of your life, so become known as a person of persistence and endurance. One person with commitment, persistence and endurance will accomplish more than a thousand people with interest alone. Persistence is a habit—unfortunately, so is quitting. In Martial Arts we say get knocked down seven times and get up eight.

- Never worry about the limited amount of money or resources you have when you begin. Just begin with a million dollars worth of determination. Remember, it's not what you have; it's what you *do* with what you have that makes all the difference. Consider the postage stamp—its usefulness consists in its ability *to stick to one thing until it gets there*. We can all learn a lot from that little ol' stamp.

- Nobody can ever make you feel average without your permission. Ungratefulness and criticism are going to come and it will hurt. They are simply part of the price you pay for moving beyond mediocrity.

Finally, I'd like to ask you to read the following questions and then reflect on this chapter. Ponder your answers. Then, write down your answers. If you take the time to answer each question fully and honestly, you'll find out more about how you can reach the dreams that have so far eluded you.

- What one decision would I make if I knew there would be no consequences?

- Am I currently running *from* something—or *to* something?

- What can I do to make better use of my time?

- What is the main thing I could eliminate from my life to help me fulfill my potential?

- What outside influences and daily habits are causing me to be better? And which are causing me to be worse?

- Based on what I've read so far, what is the one thing I will do to move closer to my goal? When will I have it completed?

Whether you achieve your goals or not is solely up to you. No one can do it for you. There are no promises or guarantees of what level of success you will or will not have. However, if you apply the tips I have shared in this chapter, you will have a better chance of meeting and/or exceeding your goals. You CAN do it, but you need to START.

It takes the same traits to succeed as a Black Belt and National Champion as it does to succeed in business, so be a champion! Empower yourself and your team.

GET AN **EDGE**, MAKE AN **IMPACT**. Follow the Black Belt Success and Champion Principles and take yourself and your business to the next level.

To help you on your journey, I have decided to give you a free gift.

Log on to www.TommyLeeInternational.com and enjoy 30 days of free access to "Black Belt Success Strategies."

About Tommy

Tommy Lee is proud to globally launch his 'Black Belt Peak Performance Business Program' in 2012, which will be accompanied by an elite mastermind series unlike any other in the industry. In the past 16 years, he has coached literally hundreds of entrepreneurs. He has appeared on the Brian Tracy Show featured on NBC and CBS and has been recognized in *USA Today* as one of America's Emerging Business Leaders. He will also have two additional books published in 2012: *Cracking the Success Code*, co-authored by Brian Tracy and Tommy Lee's **Black Belt Selling:** *How to Sell with Respect and Integrity and still get the knockout.*

CHAPTER 42

How Enhancing Your Integrity Can Increase Your Profits

By Tracy E. Myers, CMD

In the heat of a moment or the excitement of a good business deal, it can sometimes be too easy to relax our normal standards of honesty and integrity.

For example, as you conclude a sale to a new customer, you may even think you are doing the right thing—but it's what the customer believes that matters.

As Uncle Frank says, "Lack of integrity is NOT the problem. The problem is that we can't see how badly we lack it."

If you want that customer to keep coming back—and to send their friends—you can't afford to let the perception of your integrity slide, or allow it to appear your moral values have relaxed even a little. Any benefits from letting things slip are likely to be short-lived while the damage can be long lasting.

When people question our integrity, they are not likely to favor us with their business.

Whether it's fair or not, the auto industry doesn't always have a great reputation for integrity. But that's all the more reason why you can benefit from paying attention to enhancing integrity.

However, it's far easier to talk about integrity than to demonstrate it in every aspect of our lives.

So let's pause for a moment to think about what exactly integrity is, why it's important and what we can do to ensure we use it to make ourselves more successful.

According to dictionary.com, integrity means, "Adherence to moral and ethical principles; soundness of moral character; honesty."

When a customer buys from you, they trust you will deliver what you promise. When you place an order with a supplier and they make a commitment to you, you rely on that and make commitments to others based on that promise. At that level, some element of integrity is essential for business to operate.

Integrity is not just about basic honesty.

Your customer may trust you not to abscond with their money but that's not the same as them having confidence that you will deliver great value for money and go the extra mile to make them happy.

In other words, integrity is not just about the big issues; it's about the small factors as well.

There are many different ways that operating with high standards of integrity can have an impact in your business and your life and here are some examples of the benefits of enhancing your integrity.

- **It helps us make big decisions:** Integrity acts as a moral compass to guide your choices. Knowing your boundaries, and knowing when a proposed action is in alignment with the way you want to work and live your life, allows you to choose between different options more easily in all areas of your life.

- **It makes us feel better about ourselves:** When you know you are operating with integrity, you feel confident and comfortable about the way you work. Stress most often comes from trying to live in a way that is not congruent with what's really important to you. If you are saying and doing one thing but thinking and feeling something different, you are storing up problems for yourself.

- **It leads to improved relationships with others:** When you have integrity in the way you deal with people, you will find that others are more likely to behave in that way towards you. If you treat employees and suppliers properly, this will flow through to the way you behave with your customers and will help your business.

- **It helps us make more money:** In the long run, if you are seen to operate with integrity, your customers will come back and will recommend you to their friends. While it may sometimes seem people who cut corners get the benefit, the individuals and companies that sustain success are usually those with a reputation for integrity. Most people are more likely to build long-term relationships with businesses that operate with integrity than with competitors whose ethics are more dubious.

WHERE INTEGRITY MATTERS MOST

Integrity manifests itself in all areas of our lives. If people perceive you lack integrity in one area of your life, they will believe that you are the same in other areas.

Often the areas where we face the greatest temptation to weaken our integrity also give us the greatest opportunity to enhance it. Here are some examples of the different ways integrity can be a factor in different areas of life:

Self: Integrity often begins with being true to yourself. If you don't take time to reflect on what is important to you and what kind of person you want to be, you will end up uncomfortable in your own skin and unhappy with life.

Family and Friends: Your integrity is largely shaped by your relationship with family and friends. If you have people in your life who don't match the standards you want for yourself, you may need to set clear boundaries with them for what is acceptable behavior and what is not. Depending on the relationship, that may mean having an honest conversation with them and discussing your concerns. You may even conclude that you don't want to have certain people in your circle if they are not willing to make appropriate changes. As a person of integrity, you sometimes have to carry out an "audit" and remove relationships from your life that do not fit with your standards.

Business Relationships: The next area where integrity is important is in your business relationships and the commitments you make to the different groups of people in your business circle–including customers, suppliers, business partners and employees. These are all relationships where you want to be known as someone who can be completely trusted. If you do not keep promises to customers, they will not come back. If you fail to stick to commitments to employees, you can't expect to rely on them. So, when you say you will do something, make sure you do it. Keep the promises you make and fulfill agreed-upon commitments. This is the recipe for creating long-lasting relationships in all areas.

Money: The fourth key area where integrity is vital is the way you deal with money. If you are casual about money, this will lead to problems in your financial life. It's just as important to look after money in your personal life as it is in your business. For example, taking action to protect and enhance your credit rating will save you money as well as avoid problems. In business, you must be extremely careful in the way you deal with others on financial matters. Financing is such an important part of the auto business these days that your reputation for handling money and personal details is crucial. If you are entrusted with other people's money or financial information, respect it as if it were your own.

7 KEYS TO MEASURING YOUR INTEGRITY

So it's clear that integrity is important in many areas of our lives. Most of us think of ourselves as good people, but do we know how good we are?

Remember, Uncle Frank says that the problem isn't lack of integrity. The problem is that we can't see how badly we lack it.

That really means we need to have some way we can monitor what we say and do in order to be sure that we really do operate with integrity.

Here are seven different factors you can consider to help you decide whether you measure up as the person of integrity you believe you are.

Honesty: One of the keys to integrity is that you can't really be honest with others if you are not first honest with yourself. That means taking time to reflect on what is important to you. That can sometimes mean facing up to unwelcome truths and making changes in the way you live and work.

Reputation: You may think you are a good person but it's more important what other people think. Your personal and business reputation depend on it. It's one of the crucial factors that will determine whether people call you and come back. Your reputation for integrity takes time to build but it can be lost quickly and a poor reputation can be hard to change. People typically rank integrity and honesty among the top factors when deciding who to do business with. Even when someone has an advantage such as better product or price, they will miss out on sales if potential customers feel they have less integrity and honesty.

Quality of Work: One of the most obvious manifestations of integrity is the quality of work you deliver. Do you just do the minimum necessary or do you always go the extra mile? A person with high standards of integrity believes that what you put into your work is a statement about who you are as a person. They will often demonstrate integrity by starting earlier, staying later and putting more effort into the small details. This is one obvious way your employees and customers can judge your true level of integrity.

Personal Priorities: All of your thoughts and behaviors are driven by your values and beliefs. Your values determine what is important to you and define the kind of person you really are. Your beliefs shape your character and your actions. We are often not consciously aware of these influences, so it's a good idea to think about the factors that motivate you to take action or to refuse to do something. This will reveal an enormous amount about you and your personal priorities. A person with integrity lives a life which is consistent with their most important values and this is obvious for others to see. Integrity is the guiding force that holds you true to your values.

Daily Behavior: Your small behaviors and everyday thoughts are a good indication of your true integrity. Think about your reactions to the inevitable ups and downs of life or to the behavior of other people. These small interactions give you an indication of the type of person you really are. When you reflect on what you do on a day-to-day basis–especially the choices you make when you are rushed or stressed–that gives you a picture of what is really in your heart. Take a moment to reflect on how you behave when driving or when you are a customer in someone else's business. Do you behave in these situations in the way you would want others to behave? Would you act differently if your best customers could see you at that moment?

Your Influences: Another way to reflect on the type of person you really are is to consider what people (living or dead) you admire and see as positive influences. Why do you admire them? What virtues do they have that you look up to? This will give you a good picture of your true character.

Example to Others: If you are in a position of leadership, the way your behavior is seen by others is a crucial element of integrity. Do you behave in the way you ask others to behave? Are you consistent so that people know what to expect of you? Are you seen as someone who keeps their word? All relationships are based on trust, and trust is based on integrity.

HOW TO BECOME A PERSON OF INTEGRITY

So we've talked about integrity and why it's important in many areas of your life. But what happens if, on reflection, you've not always lived up to the standards of integrity you want to hold yourself to?

Well, the good news is that integrity is something you can (and should) always work on improving.

When you recognize how important this is to your life and your business, you can see that taking time to reflect on your integrity and develop your character is time well spent.

Achieving this is partly about disciplining yourself to do more of those things that a person with high integrity would do. But that's not always easy to identify.

So to help the process, here are some actions you can take to move faster towards being the kind of person you know you should be.

STEP 1: DECIDE YOUR MOST IMPORTANT VALUES

As I mentioned earlier, your values are what drive you to operate with integrity. So a good first step is to identify your five most important values in life. You can do this by asking yourself the question, "What is most important to me?"

Sometimes this works best if you identify your values separately for each of the main areas of your life such as your business, your family and your health.

Your values should always be consistent across the areas of your life but they may vary slightly between different parts. For example, your top value in business may not be the same as your top family value.

When coming up with your list, identify as many ideas as you think are appropriate. Then, list them in order of priority and focus on the top five or so. Values are usually described using one or two words but you might find it helpful to write a sentence or two defining what each of those values means to you.

When you rank your values in order of importance, the highest value is the one thing you want above all others. So, for example, if you are forced to make a choice which cannot meet two different values, the choice you make will always be the one that satisfies the value that is the higher in your list. Listing your values in this way helps you define your own character and gives you standards to help identify when you are in alignment with your most important beliefs and convictions.

As well as doing this exercise for yourself, you can do it for your business and involve others in the process. If you are the owner, you naturally want your business to be in alignment with your personal values. But you also need to ensure that everybody in your business knows how you want to operate and is willing to align themselves with these values.

STEP 2: ASK FOR FEEDBACK

While self-reflection is important, it's often a good idea to find out what others such as your partners, employees or customers think. This could simply be a few discreet conversations where you ask some people how they see you. Or you could ask them to complete confidential questionnaires to give you a good insight into how others see you or your business.

STEP 3: IDENTIFY POSITIVE ROLE MODELS

Another step in the process of enhancing your integrity is to study people of great character or successful businesses you admire.

As I mentioned earlier, the people you choose as your role models say a lot about you. So try to choose people that reflect the kind of person you want to be. It could be characters from history such as George Washington, Abraham Lincoln or Winston Churchill. People you admire from the present day work just as well.

Study them and think about why you chose them. Find out how they operated, how they thought and how they achieved success. Then, when faced with decisions and challenges, reflect on how they would behave if they were facing that situation.

Some people even create an imaginary "board" of personal advisors made up of people they admire. Then, whenever they have to make a decision, they close their eyes and imagine the advice and guidance they would get from this group in a real live meeting.

Others simply ask themselves the question, "What would xxx do about this?" when faced with a challenge (replacing xxx with whoever they want to emulate).

STEP 4: TAKE CONSCIOUS ACTION

We learn from psychology that we act in a way that is consistent with how we feel. If you feel happy, you act positively and if you feel angry, you will act negatively. However, we can also change our feelings by acting differently. If you are feeling negative, laughing can change your mood.

This means you can change the kind of person you are by acting in a way that is consistent with the way you want to be. Some people call this "faking it till you make it" but I prefer to think of it as practicing the new approach until the new behavior becomes your regular habit.

Taking deliberate and conscious action is the first step towards making the same behavior unconscious.

Gradually, as the habit becomes embedded, the new way of acting will become the way you are and you will create a personality and behaviors that are in alignment with what you want.

CONTINUING THE PROCESS

As you start thinking and acting in a way that is consistent with your values, you will feel better within yourself and others will see you in a different light. You will become seen as a person of integrity.

Living with integrity will then become the way you work and will strengthen your character. It will also change the way people see you for the better.

As with everything else, practice makes perfect, so you need to focus on enhancing your integrity all the time no matter where you are or what you are doing.

When you do this, you'll become a better person and you'll see positive results in many areas of your life. When your business operates with integrity, it will go from strength to strength.

At that stage, even Uncle Frank will admit that integrity is working to your advantage and is definitely not a problem.

About Tracy

Tracy E. Myers, CMD, is commonly referred to as The Nations Premier Automotive Solutions Provider. Best-selling author and legendary speaker Brian Tracy called him "a visionary...a Walt Disney for a new generation."

He is also a Certified Master Dealer and was the youngest ever recipient of the National Quality Dealer of the Year award by the NIADA, which is the highest obtainable honor in the used car industry. His car dealership, Frank Myers Auto Maxx, was recently recognized as the No. 1 Small Business in NC by *Business Leader* Magazine, one of the Top 3 dealerships to work for in the country by *The Dealer Business Journal* and one of the Top 22 Independent Automotive Retailers in the United States by *Auto Dealer Monthly.*

Myers has been a guest business correspondent on FOX News, appeared on NBC, ABC and CBS affiliates across the country, been featured in *USA Today* and written for *Fast Company.* His inspirational stories and strategies for success are in demand across the country, which has given him the opportunity to share the stage with the likes of with Zig Ziglar, James Malinchak, Brian Tracy, Mike Koenig, Bob Burg and Tom Hopkins...just to name a few. His best-selling books help people become better consumers as well as inspire industry leaders to become "game changers." He was also the star of the Telly Award winning film "Car Men."

As the founder of his own marketing and branding academy, Tracy teaches ambitious business owners, professionals and entrepreneurs how to get noticed, gain instant credibility, make millions and dominate their competition.

For more information about Tracy Myers, please visit http://www.TracyMyers.com.

CHAPTER 43

A Matter of Mind and Heart:
The Balance of Surrender and Action

By J.L. Ashmore

Eighteen years ago, I regularly attended a church in Marin County (where I lived at the time), across the Golden Gate Bridge from San Francisco. The minister of the church, Reverend Marcia, announced in our Sunday service that she was offering a baptism the end of that week which fell on Good Friday—the Friday before Easter.

I felt a guidance within me to go, but was mentally puzzled, as I had been baptized as an infant at my family's local Methodist church where I grew up in Colorado. "Why should I go to be baptized again?" I thought. I asked Reverend Marcia about the evening she had planned and my simultaneous pull and confusion about attending. Marcia said, "If you feel called to come, honor that. You can come as an observer if you wish, or participate. That is your choice."

So, I followed the pull within to go and in continuing to follow that pull, found myself participating rather than observing. As the evening began, Marcia led us through a guided meditation in which we were to ask for inner guidance on our purpose in this life. I openly followed her instructions and felt myself relaxed and enjoying the process without really expecting anything profound to happen. Well, guess again on that one!

As I went inside myself and asked Spirit what I had come here (in this life) to do, I heard in a blaring, powerful voice, "Minister." I was shocked by the clearly audible voice that came from a place unlike any internal dialogue I'd ever heard. When I say internal dialogue, I mean that voice we hear in our heads when we're making decisions. Or the one inside you right now that may be saying, "What is she talking about? I don't ever hear a voice!" However, the one I heard that night in the meditation was different. It felt like it came from outside of me.

I was so shocked by the clarity and strength of what I heard. I opened my eyes and looked around to see if anyone else might have heard the same voice and was also shocked into opening their eyes. What I saw was everyone else sitting quietly and calmly with their eyes closed. The realization made my experience even more unsettling; the message appeared to have been only for my ears to hear.

Although I had been what some might call a 'spiritual seeker' as long as I can remember, I had never seen myself as someone who would or could be a minister delivering a service in a church every Sunday to the same group of people. Although the thought had entered my mind to consider, it just never felt like a fit. Yet here I was sitting in a church receiving this message consisting of the word "minister" on a holy day, after asking Spirit for guidance on what I'd come to do in this life.

At the end of the meditation we were to come to Reverend Marcia in the front of the room one by one. She asked us each what we had received in asking for our purpose before she baptized us. She did so with a rose dipped in water she'd brought back from one of her trips to the River Jordan. My time came, and I found myself face to face with Reverend Marcia as she waited for me to respond to the question. Still shaken by my experience in the meditation, I couldn't bring myself to say the word "minister." So, the only words that squeaked from my quiet, shaking voice were, "I've come to speak God's words."

The space Reverend Marcia had created that evening was both physically beautiful and spiritually life altering for me. But, the profundity of the experience, and my inability at that time to fully receive it, had me quickly slip out of the church as soon as the ritual ended.

After Easter service that next Sunday, our congregation held a potluck brunch. Following brunch, I was talking to a fellow member of the church when Reverend Marcia came to us and put her arms around the two of us. As she did, she said, "This is an ominous moment. This is one future minister talking to another future minister." Now, mind you, I had not told anyone of my experience the Friday before. So, I was stunned by the feeling of confirmation that I was receiving this message once again. I was speechless, and as the Reverend walked away, I excused myself from my friend and quickly made my way to the restroom as tears began rolling down my face. It's not easy for some to understand how these two events catapulted me into a process of moving emotions, clearing limiting beliefs, expanding my trust and faith, and opening my heart to love, all of which would take years to complete. You might think church would be the perfect place to work this out, but I found it difficult to return for some time while I was deep in my process.

For many years, I spent much time wondering why such a message came to me, how to interpret it and what to do about it. During part of that time, I was leading workshops for a training company who had developed a communications program for businesses who were interested in improving their customer relations. Although it was incased in business terms, the workshop had many aspects teaching people to be kinder, more tolerant, and more aware in their interactions with customers and fellow workers, i.e. to be a better person. Isn't that what is at the basis of all religions, to be a better person? This was pointed out to me by a pastor, who happened to attend one of the workshops I was facilitating at a VA hospital in St. Louis. On one of the breaks, I had an opportunity to have a conversation with the pastor. I felt drawn to tell her of my experience on that fate-filled Good Friday and my challenge in understanding the meaning. She was comforting in sharing with me her perspective that there are many ways to "minister," and I was already ministering, with the communications course I was teaching. Her words began to appease the part of my mind that was so intensely looking for the meaning in that message.

Many years later, I felt a strong pull to take myself on a three-day retreat to the beautiful old monastery and grounds of the Immaculate Heart Retreat Center in Montecito, California, near Santa Barbara. The main building on the grounds looks and feels like an old monastery you might find in the countryside of France or Italy. Its thick stone walls and lush fruitful gardens provide a haven for those looking to find peace, solace and beauty. As I've experienced in many cathedrals, mosques, and temples around the world, the years of prayer, meditation and seeking that has been contained in such walls create a feeling of Spirit that is palpable to me.

At Immaculate Heart it is customary for guests to eat breakfast and lunch by themselves at their leisure; however, the evening meal is shared with all the other guests together, around a large mahogany dining table in the great room. At dinner my first evening, I sat next to a genuinely lovely lady named Saral. As often happens when people first meet, the question of "So what do you do?" was quick to arise. Saral began to explain to me how she had officiated weddings in Santa Barbara for the past 12 years. She talked of her passion to connect with the couples in a way that allowed her to create and deliver ceremonies uniquely written to represent the individuals and who they were coming together as a couple. Suddenly, a light sparked within me that quickly filled my entire being. In that moment I knew, without a doubt, that officiating weddings was how I'd fulfill my calling as a minister.

The mystery of the minister message so many years earlier finally made sense to me. Saral became my teacher; she showed me how to open myself to write and perform wedding ceremonies that are not only meaningful to the couple, but inspiring to the guests as well. I used my mind to take action immediately. I obtained my license, created my website and brochures, and devoted time to finding opportunities to create and officiate ceremonies. For the last eight years, I have officiated weddings and found this to be one of my passions. I followed the guidance that came to me over those years which led me to find one of my most treasured ways to express in my life.

In life, it has become a practice for me to find the balance between using the mind and listening to the heart. They are each of value and gifts from God; however, with a balance of both, we can realize clarity in the mind and fulfillment in the heart through *inspired living*. The mind can process information and analyze the pros and cons of any decision. When I speak of the heart, I am referring to the higher heart, the highest part of ourselves, not the emotional heart associated more with romantic love. The higher heart is our connection to Source, a place from which our human personality can receive guidance and inspiration–coming from the word inspire or "in Spirit."

There are many ways one can receive the kind of guidance that comes from a higher Source. Some hear words, as I did in my meditation on Good Friday. Some have a visceral feeling like intuition in the pit of their stomach, as I did to attend the Sacred Heart retreat. Some even get chills down their spine, one side of their body or all over. Some see pictures in their minds eye. Some hear, see, and/or feel a message in their dreams. And if we are all truly children of God, doesn't it make sense that sometimes we hear what we need to hear from our friends, family, or even read it in print? The trick is discerning whether it is information coming from the ego/mind or inspiration coming from the heart.

It is only practice, reflection, contemplation, and learning from experience that allows us to develop our antenna that tunes us into the frequency of the heart, just like tuning into your favorite radio station. Two questions you can ask yourself throughout the day are: 1) Is what I am about to do in alignment with my highest purpose in life? And 2) Is this what my higher heart/Spirit wants me to do?

My commitment to follow the guidance I receive within has taken me to cathedrals in Europe, temples in Egypt and mosques in India. It has taken me to places within myself that were deep and dark as well as places that were filled with light and love. It has allowed me to experience the deeply moving moments of loved ones in transition to the afterlife and the ecstasy of witnessing the miracle of the birth of my eldest granddaughter. I live in profound gratitude for the gifts I have been given in my life and for the senses–the eyes, ears, and feelings to know when to turn to the left or the right in order to receive these beautiful gifts. Life continues to unfold, and I surrender to the next step that allows me to see the next door that opens and beckons me to walk through to see what lies ahead.

May you too find within you the words, feelings, or pictures that will guide you to inspired action and ways of living your life. Once we receive guidance through our desires and dreams, we can use our minds to manifest those dreams into reality. The key is finding the balance in using the mind to fulfill the expressions of the heart. Many blessings on your journey...

J. L. (Jani) Ashmore

In addition to the motto "Follow the guidance from within," Jani has another motto, "Variety is the spice of life!" Along with her passion for creating and officiating wedding ceremonies, Jani has continued her corporate work as a speaker, coach and consultant. She also has a passion for studying alternative health care.

She has traveled to over 30 countries discovering and experiencing different cultures and religions. She has tested her ability to stretch herself throughout her adult life and has, among other things, earned a black belt in karate, walked on fire, ran marathons, hiked the Grand Canyon from rim to rim, and swam with dolphins in the wild.

Jani has had the good fortune to study closely with the likes of Tony Robbins, Byron Katie, Jack Canfield, and James Malinchak, as well as other impactful teachers. Her commitment to her own personal and spiritual growth is innate in her and continues to broaden her life experiences. Jani's proudest accomplishment in her life, however, is seeing the beautiful, responsible, loving woman her daughter, Tamara, has grown to be and now her two blossoming granddaughters, Laurel and Calli.

She was raised on a dairy farm in Colorado and does not hold herself as an expert or guru. What she does claim to have done is to live her life to the fullest using the resources and gifts innate in her and developed by her through her varied areas of interest. She values her time coaching and helping others find their passions and live fulfilling lives.

For more information about Jani and her offerings, please visit her websites at www.ceremoniesoftheheart.org and www.JLAshmore.com.

CHAPTER 44

Celebrate Them! The Secrets to Increasing Customer Loyalty and Employee Retention with Successful Events

By Darren Johnson

As I sit by myself starting to write this story (in our family's newly acquired motor home at Disney's Fort Wilderness Campground), I find myself staring out the window watching a squirrel hanging upside down, doing some variation of forest yoga.

I am truly in awe thinking what a truly blessed and lucky man I am to have such a great life, awesome wife, four amazing daughters, and yes, the perfect career for a guy like me. I know it's a strange place to be writing a book but I only live 40 minutes away and my daughters are at dance practice, my wife is at home waiting for the girls and their friends to return to Fort Wilderness when practice is over. The reality is, this is an incredibly tranquil and peaceful place to write this story and lesson on "Celebrate Them," since our family is here doing just that. We are having a weekend celebration.

The truth of the matter is, when I talk about special events, it's really a function we do almost every day of our lives, and it's as basic as having a meal with your family. The Italians have truly made the simple meal a celebration—great food, wine, and music; it's probably why I like Italy so much. In most cases, we generally think of a live event, or special event, as an act of hospitality usually purposed at celebrating some achievement, milestone, anniversary or holiday. I would dare guess if you are reading this book, then you have produced or organized one or more special events, such as birthday parties, anniversary parties, graduations, Super Bowl parties (and the list goes on forever for all the reasons you can have a celebration).

Have you ever asked yourself, "why do we put ourselves through so much stress planning, worrying, funding, and executing these things?" The answer is very simple: it makes people feel good and appreciated. I am sure you have a friend or relative who always hosts great family gatherings, big meals, or parties, and it seems so easy for them. Those people who are passionate about enjoying their friends and family, and celebrating life and living it to the fullest are the ones who create those most special events and parties, whether private or not. Even corporate events qualify because it makes the people planning them feel good seeing everyone else enjoying themselves. I have never really analyzed this before this moment and now I realize that that is me... I really enjoy watching everyone else have a good time. I absolutely love producing special events, that's probably why I have been doing it for 30 years. There is always this great feeling of personal gratification seeing other people enjoying themselves and having a good time (especially when there are so many things today in our lives that are *not* fun). Be it a relationship, a job, health, family, finances, or the other gazillion things out there–there are so many potential "downers."

I am a firm believer you need no special reason to have a party or celebration, whether it's dinner with a couple of friends on a Wednesday, a backyard BBQ for a 100 on any random Saturday, or a big family meal on Sunday. People love attending get-togethers. So if you want to be the "hub," become *that* person; you'll be amazed how many people you will make happy. You may screw it up a few times, but it gets easier (and better) the more you do it.

If you want to make your customers and employees feel special in the world of corporate events, whether it's a small dentist office, medium-sized building material company, or a Fortune 500 company, "celebrate them!" Don't call them, don't email them, and don't give them a gift card or frozen turkey, CELEBRATE THEM! You know exactly what that feeling is when someone celebrates *you* and makes you feel appreciated. It works exactly the same way for employees as it does for customers. People want to buy from people they like and employees want to work at a place that appreciates them. It's not just about money; it's about feeling the love. We all want to feel the love. Now, don't get me wrong, money definitely helps, but if you struggle with customer loyalty or employee retention, then you may want to read on.

What I am about to share with you may not solve all your problems, but I will tell you this—it's a great place to start. In my 30 years as a professional event producer, I have been hired by some of the most successful companies in the world to either celebrate their employees' achievements or thank their customers for their ongoing loyalty and patronage. When was the last time you did either of these two things?

There are several ways to accomplish this, and I want to make sure I clearly define this message. There is a very deliberate plan and execution that goes into a successful special event; it's not just throwing a bash and everyone has a big time. That's what we did in the '80s and '90s. In the 2000s, companies determined they needed to get some type of ROI (Return on Investment). Today, it's not only about ROI but more importantly, face-time. I am saying face-*time* not Face*book*. "Face-time" is the act of creating a disarming casual environment by which ownership/management can have one-on-one, face-to-face conversations and talk with people about their families, hobbies, pets, sports, or whatever. Customers and employees want to know you genuinely care. They want you to look them in the eye and not be distracted with phones, emails, or texting during the conversation. I see this formula of success work every time; the strategy of "personal face time" is priceless, and even better, it's *free*.

So the seven fundamental key tips in producing a successful event are the same whether you are in the backyard or the ballroom. I use the word "producing or producer," which is an industry term, but basically the "producer" is like the general contractor. He or she is the person who plans and coordinates all of the vendors, locations, music, timing, logistics, and even invites the guests. In the social world, this person is called a wedding planner or wedding coordinator. In the corporate world, this person is an event planner, coordinator, or producer. I personally prefer event producer.

THE GOAL: WHY ARE YOU HAVING THIS EVENT?

This may seem obvious, but if you don't know why or have an end-result (something you are trying to achieve), you may just be wasting your time and money. Don't get me wrong, it is perfectly fine to have a party with no purpose, as long as you know that going in. Events have a lot more continuity when the purpose and the goal are clearly visible from beginning to end.

BUDGET: HOW MUCH MONEY ARE YOU GOING TO SPEND ON THIS EVENT?

This is usually a very difficult thing to determine if you are a small business. What typically happens is you don't have a budget and you try and skimp along during the planning process and the day before (or day of) you realize all of the things you *don't* have and didn't want to spend money on, so instead of being embarrassed or looking like a cheapskate, you rush out and get all those things anyway. Then you usually end up with inferior products and spend the same (or more) money than what the original budget should have been. Larger companies are much better at budgeting and usually get their budget from previous events. So here is your tip: if you don't know how much to budget for your event, I suggest you create a detailed list of all the items (food, beverage, entertainment, rentals, etc.) you would like to have and collect those costs. Add all those items up, and determine if you can live with that number. If you can't live with that number, separate the must-have items from the nice-to-have items and work it from there. You are always better off having fewer nice things than many cheap things.

LOCATION: WHERE ARE WE GOING TO HOST THIS EVENT?

This can, and surely will, impact the budget. You can usually narrow down your location options after you have determined your goal and the budget for the event. It is rather difficult to host an event at Donald Trump's place if your budget is $20 per person. You don't want to have an event at a location that is not conducive to your goal. If the goal is for your sales people to interact with customers, you don't want to be in a loud or noisy place. If you are having an employee recognition event, then you don't want to be in a venue that is chopped up where everyone cannot sit together to see the whole group. I see people battle this the most when it comes to office parties. They want to show off their 5th floor office space, but it typically has no open spaces for people to mingle. The space is usually chopped up into 20 smaller offices and conference rooms, making it impossible to create the right vibe for interaction. Instead, give a lot of consideration to your location *after* you have determined your goal. If you choose a location that is not right for what you are trying to achieve, it is the fastest way to completely undermine your event goal.

STYLE: IS THIS EVENT GOING TO BE FUN, EDUCATIONAL, THEMED, AUDIENCE PARTICIPATORY, CASUAL OR FORMAL?

This item is usually defined when you are addressing the goal. Just make sure that the goal and the style of the event are compatible. Outdoor venues are not typically conducive to formal events. Think about it— women hate sweating, having their hair messed up and wearing heels in grass. Fun events that include audience participation aren't typically held in places like offices, museums, or historical venues; awards dinners aren't typically in barns or airplane hangars. There's a reason for this. Technically speaking you can pull off any type of event in any venue if you are a professional event producer.

FOOD: CATERED OR NOT?

Are you cooking? Is it pot luck, sit down, stand-up, or a plated and served dinner? All these things are tied together and every one of them is determined by your goal. The first item to decide is the timing of the event, because this determines the type and quantity of food. If you have an event from 11 a.m. - 1 p.m., then you better have a real lunch, and not just cheese and crackers. If your event is from 6 p.m. - 9 p.m., then you better plan on having enough food for dinner. I see this mistake made all the time; people have an event during a meal time and only serve light snacks or hors d'oeuvres. Two things happen: (1) everyone gets drunk because they didn't eat or (2) they leave early to get a meal.

It is also very important to serve the right type of food with the right event. If you are having a mixer where people are standing and mingling, don't serve food that requires cutting with a knife. Have you ever tried cutting into a piece of steak while holding your plate, drink, and fork? Of course you have, and you didn't like it, did you? Well, other people don't either! Don't serve BBQ (a.k.a. messy food) at formal events, and lastly, make sure you have non-meat or non- seafood options, after all, people have dietary needs and limitations.

BEVERAGE: IS THERE GOING TO BE ALCOHOL SERVED?

Does it fit with your goal? Are you hosting the bar (a.k.a. paying for it) and if so, is it beer and wine or full open bar? Is it well brands, call brands, or premiums? Are you willing to take responsibility for the consequences if someone is over served? Pay attention to how much your guests are drinking and it is always my recommendation to have a responsible party serve the drinks versus allowing your guests to self-serve.

ENTERTAINMENT: HOW DOES THIS FIT INTO THE GOAL?

If you are having a bunch of guys at an event, a dance band probably isn't the right choice. Entertainment is not only driven by the goal, but also by matching the right entertainment with your audience. Whether it is gender specific, young, not young, sales, operations people, or so forth, you need to know their likes and dislikes. It is extremely uncomfortable to see your entertainment completely flop because your audience did not connect. Some groups want to sit and be entertained; some groups want to blow the roof off. Know who your audience is.

Needless to say, entertainment is the one item that can severely impact your budget. The one single biggest mistake people make is not having some type of music at their event. If you can't budget for live entertainment or a deejay, then at least get your iPod and a small sound system to have some background music. It is very difficult to get a good vibe going without some type of music. It can be done for free and still have the same effect; the radio is better than silence.

Conclusion:

Goal: Clearly define your purpose of having the event.

Budget: Make a list of the nice-to-have and the must-have items.

Location: Pick a location that is conducive to the goal.

Style: Make sure the style of the event matches the goal.

Food: Select food appropriate with the timing and style of event.

Beverage: Determine if alcohol is appropriate for the goal, and if so, use a professional to serve it.

Entertainment: Understand your audience and make sure the entertainment fits the goal.

If you address these items, then you will have the most fundamental and impactful secrets to event success. Just remember everyone wants to feel the love, so just celebrate them!

About Darren

Darren W Johnson, CSEP, a United States Marine and seasoned veteran in the special event industry, has more than three decades of experience in producing live events throughout North America and the Caribbean. Darren has been seen on FOX, ABC, CBS, and NBC affiliates, has written several articles for a national magazine on the topic of tailgating. Darren's second book *"What They Never Taught You About Corporate Event Production"* will be released in the fall of 2012. Darren speaks at the University of Central Florida, Rosen Center on the topic of Event Management.

He is founder and executive producer of Darren W. Johnson Productions, Inc. Darren manages a number of companies under his brand including Creative Services Event Co. (CSEC), Tailgateville and The Extreme Party Truck (XPT). CSEC is a full service event management and production company specializing in strategic planning, design and execution of corporate events, sporting event hospitalities, and public events. Tailgateville provides professional tailgating services at major sporting events and concerts for corporate customers and individuals. The Extreme Party Truck is the world's first mobile entertainment complex; complete with 16 flat panel TV's, a giant 14' big screen, monster sound system with DJ/Karaoke, meat smoker, wine cellar, kegoraters and much, much more.

Darren has produced events for the Fortune 1000 including industry giants such as Disney, Shell Oil, Universal Studios, Pepsi, Frito Lay, Coors Light, Anheuser-Busch, IBM, American Express, Abbott Labs, Merck, Chrysler, Cadillac, Coca Cola, Microsoft, American Express, Sun Micro, Alliance, Prudential and hundreds of others.

With over 4,000 events produced in practically every location type imaginable, ranging from deserts to tropical islands, ballrooms to cruise ships, tents to airplane hangars and race tracks to stadiums, he is a well-seasoned industry expert. Darren's work at major sporting events include the Daytona 500, Pepsi 400, Super Bowl, PGA golf tournaments, NBA all-stars, Capitol One Bowl and the Orange Bowl.

To learn more about Darren W Johnson and receive a free special report on "Celebrate Them: How to Increase Customer Loyalty and Employee Retention with Successful Events" visit www.DarrenWJohnson.com, email Darren@dwj-p.com or call (352) 242-3870.

CHAPTER 45

Entrepreneurial F.R.E.E.D.O.M.™

By Deb Farrell

Have you ever had a nudging feeling you 'should' be doing something different than what you are doing, but you simply couldn't quite put your finger on what that was? Or, have you ever felt a little restless 'knowing' that you can do more than what you were doing, but you just didn't know what that was (or even how to find out)?

I can relate, because that's what happened to me in 2006 and it's been a wonderful journey ever since. What I didn't know at the time was these little nudges and feelings were "awakening" me to find out who I really was. After working in Corporate America for 30+ years, I was slowly feeling like I should be doing something different but I couldn't quite put my finger on it.

At the time I first recall receiving a 'nudge' to do something more, I was working in a Human Resources (HR) Director role. I was in heaven when I first got the J.O.B. (just over broke) role because I was hired in to create an HR department from the ground up–how fun! After all, this was the topic I wrote my thesis paper on in my master's program. Since the time of graduating, I had been strategically planning my career path to take on this ideal role.

It seemed as though everything was going great! I was making a nice six-figure income (which included many perks), I lived in a nice house where we (I was married at the time) could walk across the street and hop in our 35' boat, we adopted our wonderful loving son, Brandon, from Russia (at 9 months), and on and on. I THOUGHT I was happy...up until I heard my friend and mentor, Jack Canfield, co-creator of *Chicken Soup for the Soul* and *The Success Principles* speak at a large network marketing company event. That day changed my life.

If you are familiar with Jack's work, you know there are 64 principles in Jack's book, *The Success Principles, How to Get from Where You Are to Where You Want to Be* (which by the way, I finished reading the last page walking down the aisle to get off the plane before seeing him speak). The one question that changed my life was "what are you pretending not to know?" Wow —what an eye opener for me! I almost fell over!

Have you ever experienced someone asking you a question where the answer changed your life? Well, I was pretending not to know that deep down inside, I was unhappy in almost all areas in my life (i.e., relationships, financial, spiritual, personal – not having fun, etc.). This was very shocking to me because I had always been a very upbeat, positive person and I was always inspiring others to take the next step to be more, do more and have more.

This led me into a full-blown exploration of my entire life. What I found was, I didn't have a healthy marriage (an alcoholic husband), I wanted to make a bigger difference at work, but as you know when you work for someone else inside a company or corporation you can only help as much as the "top" will allow. I simply didn't feel like I had the freedom, time or money to do what I wanted to do or grow into who I wanted to be.

It was from that moment forward that I "jumped" into learning all about Jack's work as well as other successful gurus, and how I could change my life. Since I'm a sponge for knowledge and information, it wasn't hard to take the next steps from there. I studied his books, listened to his CDs on *The Success Principles, How to Get from Where You Are to Where You Want to Be* (over and over again), enrolled and became one of the first 100 graduates from his year-long intensive professional Train-the-Trainer (TTT) program. The program focused on how to 'experientially teach the principles of success and the facilitation of individual and group transformation.'

I share all this, not to impress you, but to impress upon you that we all have the ability to choose what we do with our lives and how we show up in the world. I'm just like you–if I can do it, so can you! However, to do so, we must first decide what that is and what that looks like for us and prepare ourselves for that next step.

To find out what that looks like for you, ask yourself: "am I doing what I love to do? Am I living the life I 'dreamed' I would live when I grew up? Am I surrounding myself with positive, upbeat people who will support me as I take action in making my dreams become a reality?"

If you answered 'no' to any of these questions, first of all, please avoid beating yourself up that you haven't done this as yet. Simply start recognizing what is showing up for you in your life, as I did in the example that I shared earlier. I invite you to take a deeper look and ask yourself "what do I want in my life?" The more clear you become in what it is that you want (and dream big!) the easier and faster it is for you to achieve. After all, it is YOUR life and *only* you can choose what you want to do with it! So why not make it the best life ever by dreaming big??

When I received the nudge to do something greater in helping many more people than what I was doing, I made a conscious decision to prepare myself for my next endeavor. I did this by getting the training I needed and then practiced my skills as a woman's business coach, speaker and best-selling author. I honestly didn't know where to begin, but once I got really, really clear on what it was that I "wanted" to do, God, the Universe, the Divine, Spirit or whatever you call the higher power, was right there to back me up by providing the "next step" (or resource) that I needed to succeed.

I'd like to share an important *Success Secret* with you that is worth mentioning here. Keep in mind once you make a decision to do something and start taking action toward what it is that you want, remember to let go of the "old" (both physical and mental) to get in the new. For example, if you want to get a new wardrobe, you must first clean out the old clothes in order to receive the new. Think of it this way, if you didn't do this cleaning where would you put the new ones? You wouldn't have any room to put them and you also would be telling the Universe that you are not really serious about getting a new wardrobe.

Something similar happened to me with my "old" role as an HR Director and my "new" role as a new woman entrepreneur desiring to have my own business and be my own boss. I went into work on a Friday and I was presented with the "opportunity" to work more hours or I probably should entertain finding another "opportunity" elsewhere. It was a most interesting experience at best, so I took in the information and *decided* to think about this over the weekend.

Hmm, let me think, my son was already in a 'before and after' school latch-key program (6:30 am to 6:00 pm). I was already missing out on his life as it was, and then it dawned on me—the Universe had been helping me prepare to jump into my own business. How divine! God's timing was perfect! I returned on Monday, took a leap of faith and gave my resignation. I extended an offer to stay to help interview and train my replacement, but it was time to let go of the 'old' as this was the 'opportunity' I had been preparing for.

Here's another *Success Secret* for you to know. If you are not familiar with the Laws of the Universe (which also includes the Law of Attraction – i.e. LOA), you may want to educate yourself on how they work. When you get to know the "how" they work, you can better "play" the game of life. Please do not fool yourself thinking that just because you may not know what they are or how they work that they are not working.

Just like all the Universal Laws: the Law of Gravity, Law of Electricity, or the LOA (just to name a few), just because you can't see them doesn't mean they are not there working—all the time. So in the case of me "letting go" of my old job for my new role the LOA "was working." You bring about what you think about and what you repeatedly send out in a vibration. So everything we have in our life is a direct result of what "we asked for"–either way…positive or negative.

So let's tie this back to "letting go" of the old to receive the new, if you feel that you are "losing" something (old job in this case), try taking a new perspective on it and see if you are really losing something or making way for the new thing you have been asking for. I believe you may be happily delighted and grateful–to have asked, believed and received the gift you were asking for.

Similar to a road map that offers you many routes to get to your destination, there are *many* paths that will lead you to what you desire. Do not get hung up (or stuck) on thinking you can only receive the 'thing' you are asking for in the exact way you are "asking." Since the Universe is set up to say "yes" and it wants the best for you, at times you may find that what you receive is much better than what you had originally asked for.

One of the first *Success Secrets* is to find out what you are passionate about and do what you love! As a successful woman entrepreneur who has worked in both the corporate and the entrepreneurial world, I've put together a 5-Step System that you can immediately use to become a successful entrepreneur. I call this the F.R.E.E.D.O.M.™ System (the seven letters in FREEDOM are combined into five steps). These are the exact same steps I share with my clients and they were designed to show YOU a simple step-by-step method to take if you are pursuing the entrepreneurial path to F.R.E.E.D.O.M.™

F. = **F**ocus on living and fulfilling your passions & purpose to do what you love and create your niche so you can make a profit doing it!

- What do you love to do?
- What's important to you?
- What brings meaning into your life and why?

R. = **R**eprogram your 'old' negative unconscious limiting beliefs into new, positive fulfilling & successful ones

- Identify and eliminate what has been unconsciously sabotaging you from moving forward to accomplish your dreams (and it's not your fault!)
- Eliminate the fear & doubt and replace it with balance, harmony & fun!

E. = **E**mpower yourself by using all your S.T.A.K.E.'s (skills, talents, attributes, knowledge, and experiences)

- What are you good at doing (your strengths)?
- What unique talents and attributes do you bring to the table?
- What knowledge and experiences have you gained that the world is waiting to hear?

E. = **E**nrich the lives of others in service to make a difference

- When you help others, you naturally help yourself
- Create your target market, niche and branding around 'how' you want to help others

D. = **D**esign your life around your dreams, desires and goals

- What are your dreams and desires?
- Are your goals in alignment with your dreams?

O. = **O**ptimize all your opportunities–online and offline

- Discover how to get clients and keep them
- Apply your own personal communication style to grow your business – while having fun!
- Discover the 'right tools' and resources to use to keep you on track (from websites, blogs & social media to building your team)

M. = **M**onetize and market your passions

- Apply the right promotional strategies to get the buzz going to grow your business – enthusiastically
- Proven strategies to get clients and increase your audience (and list) quickly
- Simple branding strategies to grow your business consistently
- Create systems & products to produce ongoing passive & time leveraging income

Whatever path you choose, embrace your power and take your strengths out into the world to shine! Avoid the worry about "thinking" or doubting yourself if you could achieve it or not. You wouldn't have had the desire to begin with if you did not already have the capability to accomplish it. **Take action TODAY** to do something toward creating your dream life! As Martin Luther King Jr. says,

> *"Faith is taking the first step, even though*
> *you don't see the whole staircase."*

If you don't know what the first step is, start there to define it and dream big! Don't let anyone 'steal' your dreams. You will come across many 'nay-sayers' telling you that you cannot do something. Simply remember, this is one of the most important times to follow your intuition.

"If you can dream it, you can do it." – Walt Disney

Another critical *Success Secret* strategy to remember is that it's important for you to find a coach or a mentor to help you stay on track throughout your journey. Look for someone who has done what you are wanting to do, and who is successfully still doing it. When you do, you cut your learning curve by up to 90%! I don't know about you, but that's huge to me! I'm not one to recreate the wheel when I can take a huge shortcut. If you are reading this book, than you are ready for a change. Contact me for a FREE complimentary 30-minute Getting Acquainted Breakthrough Session with me personally at:www.womensfreedomauthority.com/get-acquainted-session/ so you can get what you need to excel!

All successful people, from athletes to Politicians, have coaches to guide them. You deserve to have one too. As a successful business coach myself, the greatest piece of advice I could offer you is to find someone who resonates with *you* and what you are trying to accomplish. You want someone to support your ideas and thoughts throughout your process as well as hold you accountable for achieving results.

All the chapters in this book have provided you with a lot of valuable information to use toward achieving your success. Choose the two or three ideas that resonate with you the most to implement immediately. Avoid trying to take on all of them and end up with "analysis paralysis" (having too much info and not knowing which one to act on first).

The most important *Success Secret* for you to take away is to get into the game today by taking action so you can enjoy more F.R.E.E.D.O.M.™, time and wealth in your life. You are worth it and you deserve it!

So, now that you know the *Success Secrets*, "What action are you going to do within the next 15 minutes to get started?"

About Deb

Deb Farrell, also known as "*The* Entrepreneurial Women's F.R.E.E.D.O.M.™ Authority" teaches entrepreneurial women how to jump-start their business from 'Start to Profit' by designing, building and growing a profitable business. She teaches her clients a simple 5-step process to get them up and running as quickly as possible with a system to make a profit through her coaching, speaking and products. She is known for successfully engaging her clients by utilizing her F.R.E.E.D.O.M.™ Model, principles and techniques, designed around a 'woman's' needs...with elegance, grace and ease.

Deb is one of the first 100 graduates from Jack Canfield's, co-creator of *Chicken Soup for the Soul* and author of *The Success Principles, How to Get from Where You Are to Where You Want to Be* year-long intensive Train-The-Trainer (TTT) program which focused on how to experientially teach the principles of success and the facilitation of individual and group transformation. She is a successful women's business coach and certified Dream Coach through Marcia Wieder's Dream Coach University program.

Her purpose and passion is to inspire and teach other women entrepreneurs how to discover their purpose and passions so they can do what they love and prosper! Her mission is to help new, aspiring and struggling women entrepreneurs to make a profit in 30 days or less when moving from a corporate role into an entrepreneurial role–so they can experience more F.R.E.E.D.O.M.™, time and wealth in their life... with elegance, grace and ease.

Deb is the author of *P-A-T-H (Passion Awakens The Heart)...with Purpose, How to Be, Do and Have Anything You Desire in Alignment with Who You Are* and is honored to have Jack Canfield write the Foreword and Marcia Wieder write the Afterword to her book. She is a co-contributing author to the Best Selling Book, *The Gratitude Project Book, Celebrating 365 Days of Gratitude.* She is also featured in the movie documentary *"The Ultimate Business Mastery"* to be released in April 2012 to inspire new entrepreneurs entering the entrepreneurial world.

To learn more about Deb Farrell, The Ultimate Women's F.R.E.E.D.O.M.™ Authority and how you can receive her three free gifts, visit www.WomensFreedomAuthority.com, email her at Deb@WomensFreedomAuthority.com or call (734) 308-9132.

And, be sure to connect with Deb on her social media sites (@DebFarellCoach) on Facebook, LinkedIn, Twitter, Pinterest and Google+.

CHAPTER 46

Empowering Your Child:

Why Every Kid Should be a radKid

By Gary Martin Hays and Diena Thompson

"Safety and security don't just happen, they are the result of collective consensus and public investment.
We owe our children, the most vulnerable citizens in our society, a life free of violence and fear."

—Nelson Mandela, former president of South Africa

THE TRAGIC STORY OF SOMER THOMPSON

At approximately 2:45 p.m. on October 19, 2009, seven-year-old Somer Thompson left her elementary school in Orange Park, Florida. She met up with her twin brother, Samuel, and their older sister, Abigail, for the mile walk home. Somer became separated from her siblings and she stopped to talk to Jarred Harrell, one of 161 registered sex offenders that lived within a five mile radius of Somer's home. He lured Somer into his home to see his dog. Once she was inside, he raped and asphyxiated her.

When Somer did not make it home, an investigation was launched. The local Child Abduction Response Team (CART) was activated. This is a team of local and state law enforcement agencies with specialized training to respond to a missing or abducted child. Unfortunately, the search and recovery efforts were to no avail. Two days later, her body was found when a garbage truck that carried a load of trash from her neighborhood spilled its load in a Georgia landfill nearly 50 miles away.

On February 3, 2012, Harrell entered a plea of guilty and agreed not to appeal any of his convictions to avoid the death penalty. He was sentenced to life in prison with no possibility of parole. At the sentencing hearing, Somer's twin brother, Samuel, told Harrell from the witness stand "[Y]ou know you did this, and now you are going to jail."

DIENA THOMPSON

Diena Thompson is the surviving mother of Somer. Having your child abducted is certainly a parent's worst nightmare, and it unfortunately came true for Diena. As a surviving parent, no one could blame her if she chose to deal with this horrific tragedy in private. Yet, Diena has taken the opposite approach and has made it her life's mission to make sure no other parent has to suffer. She formed The Somer Thompson Foundation in 2010 with the purpose to "provide education in the form of awareness and prevention to both parents and children to avoid the tragedy of experiencing the loss of a child." Diena believes every child should have the opportunity to be a radKID.

WHAT CAN WE DO TO PREVENT THIS TRAGEDY FROM EVER HAPPENING AGAIN?

There are countless books available to adults on so many subjects involving self-improvement—everything from how to be a better communicator to how to be more confident, whether we are speaking to one person or an audience of thousands. The other chapters in this book all deal with "Success Secrets" we, as adults, can use to help us achieve greater success in life. But there are few books or other resources written specifically with children in mind.

What can we as parents do to help insure our child's success in life?

We need to empower our children

to be able to stand up for themselves

and to be able to protect themselves.

We want to be with our children 24/7. We want to put them in protective headgear and bubble wrap every time they walk out the door. But author Anne Cassidy writes in her book, *Parents Who Think Too Much*, "[T]he suits of armor we provide them are as dangerous as the world we're protecting them from." We can not become so obsessed with our children's safety that our worry becomes debilitating paranoia.

Are there reasons we should be concerned about our children's safety? Let's debunk some common misconceptions:

- *"These 'predators' do not live in my neighborhood."*
  The U.S. Department of Justice estimates there is one registered sex offender per square mile in the United States.

- *"My children are too young to be exposed to threats from sexual predators."*
  The average age at which sexual abuse begins is 3 years old. 1 of every 3 reports of sexual abuse to law enforcement are children under 12 years of age. 1 of every 7 are under age 6.

- *"My child would never fall for the lost puppy trick."*
  85% of the time a child is abducted it involves the use of physical force where the predator grabs the child.

- *"I never leave my child alone with strangers."*
  90% of sexual assault/abuse victims knew their offender. 59% were within the family; 37% were acquaintances of the victim or the victim's family.

What are the success principles we need to give to our children? What can we do to prepare our children to strike back against what Stephen M. Daley, M.Ed., the founder and executive director of radKIDS, calls the "ABC'S of Child Victimization"?

<u>A</u>bduction

<u>B</u>ullying

<u>C</u>hild abuse and Neglect

<u>S</u>exual Assault

RADKIDS

We think the best program available to our children is **radKIDS,** the national leader in children's safety education. Stephen Daley left law enforcement after a distinguished 20-year career. Since starting radKIDS, he has trained and certified over 4,000 instructors across the nation.

The "rad" in radKIDS stands for "Resisting Aggression Defensively." Or as Daley likes to put it in children's terms: "**A radKID is a cool kid who doesn't let anyone hurt them**."

radKIDS is making a difference. More than 250,000 children have been trained in the program. More than 80 children threatened with abduction have used their radKIDS skills and returned safely to their families. There have been over 5,000 documented disclosures of sexual abuse, and the program has empowered these children to speak up and get the help they needed to stop the violence in their lives.

radKIDS has 3 guiding principles for all kids, and we believe these are three "SUCCESS PRINCIPLES" every child should learn. Please understand - these are merely words. When coupled with the addition of realistic physical resistance to violence skills (hands-on drills) that train the brain to react - this radKIDS program empowers the child - and gives them the ability and potential to never be a victim.

RADKIDS RULE #1:
NO ONE HAS THE RIGHT TO HURT ME BECAUSE I AM SPECIAL.

Children need to know they "matter." All human beings have this inherent desire, as it is a key to our existence, just as important as air, food and water. We need to guide our kids in a direction that they know, feel and believe that they are important—to us as parents, and to themselves. If a child has a healthy self-esteem, they are better prepared to address all of the challenges they are going to face in this world. If they feel good about themselves—if they know they are special—they will have an easier time handling conflicts and issues as they arise, will resist negative peer pressure, and will stand up for themselves if anyone tries to hurt them.

This feeling of self-value, self worth is also critical in teaching the child that he or she does not have the right to hurt him or herself. Why? Because they are special. This is extremely important when dealing with issues such as drug or alcohol abuse. "You should not try cocaine or crystal meth as you will be hurting yourself" and "No one has the right to hurt me—including myself—because I am special."

Further, kids with a healthy self-esteem enjoy interacting with others, are comfortable in social settings, yet feel capable of working independently. They are not intimidated by challenges and can work towards solutions. These children do not give up easily nor wait for someone to step in to help.

When confronted by a predator and grabbed, a radKID is trained to react and is empowered to protect themselves. The radKID learns to replace the fear, confusion, and panic of a dangerous situation with confidence, personal safety skills, and self-esteem. When grabbed, a radKID thinks and says "How dare you touch me" versus "Help me, help me."

Here are some tips parents can use to help build healthy self-esteem in our children:

- Show consistent love and affection to your child: Hugs and spontaneous affection are great boosters.

- <u>Compliment your child</u>! Mothers were asked in a survey to keep track of how many times they made negative comments versus positive comments to their children. They admitted that the ratio was 10 negative comments to only 1 positive comment. A three year survey in one city's school found that the teachers' comments were 75% negative. In addition, it takes four (4) positive statements to offset the effects of one negative statement to a child. Institute of Family Relations in *Homemade*, December 1986.

- <u>Be proud of your child and talk positively about your child</u>! Tell him or her how proud you are to be their parent! And let them hear you speak positively about them to your friends and to theirs.

- <u>Be a Role Model</u>! Lead by example. Do not be excessively harsh on yourself, or have a negative attitude all of the time. Nurture your own self-esteem, and give your child a positive image to mirror.

RADKIDS RULE #2:
I DON'T HAVE THE RIGHT TO HURT ANYONE ELSE UNLESS THEY ARE TRYING TO HURT ME AND THEN I HAVE EVERY RIGHT TO STOP THEM.

Some parents and educators immediately hear about radKIDS and think "This program is teaching kids how to fight." Nothing could be further from the truth. When children go through the course, they are taught the rules of context; i.e., when the use of physical resistance is appropriate, and when it is not. As Daley points out, "They must understand that their responses must be in proportion to the aggression they are facing. We don't want our students to use excessive force when it is not warranted, nor do we want them to be afraid to physically resist when they are in real jeopardy."

He refers to these as the "When you can and When You can't" rules. In a situation where the child is being teased or threatened with harm or physical violence, radKIDS are taught:

- If it's someone you know, leave immediately and advise a parent.
- If it's someone you don't know, run to escape.
- If you cannot run, PEPPER, HAMMER, KICK to escape. (These are defense skills taught to students).
- Use your radKIDS skills to avoid being carried off or dragged into a vehicle.
- In radKIDS, Physical Resistance means stopping someone from hurting you):

YELL LOUD! HIT HARD! RUN FAST!
(All taught defensively)

Think about Rule #2 for a moment and its application to the problem of bullying in our schools. Bullying happens when someone tries to hurt others by:

- making them feel threatened;
- hurting them by kicking, hitting, pushing, tripping;
- name-calling;
- spreading nasty rumors.

The person that is being bullied often times feels helpless, like he or she can't do anything to stop it. The victims of bullying, the children most prone to being picked on, tend to have the following characteristics:

- low self-esteem (remember radKIDS rule #1!)
- insecure
- lack social skills
- cry or become emotionally distraught easily
- unable to defend or stand up for themselves.

Here are some disturbing statistics on bullying:
Every 7 minutes a child is bullied. In those situations, an adult only intervened in 4% of them. 85% of the time, there was no intervention on behalf of the child being bullied by anyone—adults, friends, other children.

- 90% of all students in grades 4-8 reported being threatened and bullied in school.
- About 22% of students in grades 4-8 reported academic difficulties as a result of bullying.
- 864,000 students report staying home at least one day a month because they fear for their safety in school.

Too many schools have employed a "Zero Tolerance" rule when dealing with bullying. "Zero tolerance" means that any violation of the rules, no matter how minuscule or what the circumstances, will be punished severely. The aggressor and the person being attacked - if they fight back - are punished the same way. It is more of a political response than an educationally sound solution. It sounds impressive for school officials to say that we are taking a tough stand on bullying. "Zero tolerance" makes "Zero sense." Empowering children can, and will, create a partnership and a more powerful learning climate and culture in our schools, one founded on a "Zero Victimization" environment where everyone knows "No one" gets hurt here.

Steve Daley often asks this rhetorical question: "How many times should your child's head be slammed against the bathroom floor at school before you allow him the opportunity to strike back? Or while he waits for an adult to intervene?"

It defies common sense that you are going to punish a child for trying to protect him or herself when being attacked. Recent studies by the federal government find that prevention programs that focus on changing the overall school culture, by taking such steps as having the entire student body involved in bully prevention, are better at reducing school violence. radKIDS changes the culture of the school—not from the top down—but from *within* the student body when the kids realize they are all subject to the 3 radKIDS Rules.

RADKIDS RULE #3:
IF ANYONE TRIES TO HURT ME, TRICK ME, OR MAKE ME FEEL BAD INSIDE OR OUT, IT'S NOT MY FAULT — SO I CAN TELL.

So many kids need to hear those words, especially in the case of sexual abuse. Sherryl Kraizer, Ph.D., writes in *The Safe Child Book*, "[O]ne of the most important elements in a child's recovery is the placing of responsibility where it lies—with the perpetrator." A professional trained in counseling children who are victims in abuse can help the child understand that what happened to them was not their fault, and they did not do anything wrong.

Children also need to know if they are being bulled, abused, or are threatened in any way, it is okay to tell you. radKIDS also adds this advice. "It's important to let your child know they can tell you anything. But also tell them if you get mad or upset, you are not mad at them, but you are angry at the person who hurt them." You don't want your child shutting down the dialogue with you because they feel they have disappointed you or hurt you in some way.

In cases of sexual abuse, children are very hesitant to tell their parents what has happened for several reasons, including:

- fear of what may happen to them;
- fear of what may happen to the abuser;
- fear of disappointment for their parents;
- fear they will not be believed.

If children are not empowered to tell, then parents can look for some nonverbal signs that abuse may be occurring, including:

- the child does not want to be alone with someone known to them or the family;
- sleep difficulties and nightmares;
- acting out or experiencing problems at school;
- using sexual terms or explicit names for body parts;
- displaying inappropriate physical affection.

And thanks to radKIDS, thousands of empowered children have spoken up and received the help the needed to stop the abuse in their lives.

SO WHAT HAPPENS NOW?

So what can you do to help empower your children or the children in your life? Together, we can make a difference One Child and One Community at a Time. The long-term, lasting solution is to have the radKIDS curriculum incorporated into the elementary school's physical education department. It meets curriculum and education standards in all 50 states. As Diena likes to say, "Every child deserves an opportunity to feel safe and be safer in their world today. Is it not our children's right to this type of education and empowerment and, in fact, our responsibility as parents, educators and citizens to make it happen? Together, we can make sure EVERY child becomes empowered through radKIDS and it will help break the potential cycle of violence in our children's lives, and therefore, in all our futures." Bring radKIDS to your community by getting yourself trained as an instructor. You can teach the course after school or during the summer. To learn more about this personal empowerment safety education program, please visit www.radKIDS.org.

About Gary

Gary Martin Hays is not only a successful lawyer, but is a nationally recognized safety advocate who works tirelessly to educate our families and children on issues ranging from bullying to internet safety to abduction prevention. He currently serves on the Board of Directors of the Elizabeth Smart Foundation. Gary has been seen on countless television stations, including ABC, CBS, NBC and FOX affiliates. He has appeared on over 110 radio stations, including the Georgia News Network, discussing legal topics and providing safety tips to families. He hosts "Georgia Behind The Scenes" on the CW Atlanta TV Network and has been quoted in *USA Today, The Wall Street Journal*, and featured on over 250 online sites including Morningstar.com, CBS News's MoneyWatch.com, the *Boston Globe, The New York Daily News and The Miami Herald.*

He is also co-author of the best-selling books *"TRENDSETTERS - The World's Leading Experts Reveal Top Trends To Help You Achieve Health, Wealth and Success," "CHAMPIONS - Knockout Strategies For Health, Wealth and Success" "SOLD - The World's Leading Real Estate Experts Reveal The Secrets To Selling Your Home For Top Dollar In Record Time"* and *"Protect And Defend."*

Gary graduated from Emory University in 1986 with a B.A. degree in Political Science and a minor in Afro-American and African Studies. In 1989, he received his law degree from the Walter F. George School of Law of Mercer University, Macon, Georgia. His outstanding academic achievements landed him a position on Mercer's Law Review. He also served the school as Vice President of the Student Bar Association.

His legal accomplishments include being a member of the prestigious Multi Million Dollar Advocate's Forum, a society limited to those attorneys who have received a settlement or verdict of at least $2 Million Dollars. He has been recognized in *Atlanta Magazine* as one of Georgia's top workers' compensation lawyers. Gary frequently lectures to other attorneys in Georgia on continuing education topics. He has been recognized as one of the Top 100 Trial Lawyers in Georgia since 2007 by the American Trial Lawyers Association, and recognized by *Lawdragon* as one of the leading Plaintiffs' Lawyers in America. His firm specializes in personal injury, wrongful death, workers' compensation, and pharmaceutical claims. Since 1993, his firm has helped over 27,000 victims and their families recover over $235 Million dollars.

In 2008, Gary started the non-profit organization **Keep Georgia Safe** with the mission to provide safety education and crime prevention training in Georgia. Keep Georgia Safe has trained over 80 state and local law enforcement officers in CART (Child

Abduction Response Teams) so our first responders will know what to do in the event a child is abducted in Georgia. Gary has completed Child Abduction Response Team training with the National AMBER Alert program through the U.S. Department of Justice and Fox Valley Technical College. He is a certified instructor in the radKIDS curriculum. His law firm has given away 1,000 bicycle helmets and 14 college scholarships.

To learn more about Gary Martin Hays, visit www.GaryMartinHays.com. To find out more about Keep Georgia Safe, please visit www.KeepGeorgiaSafe.org or call (770) 934-8000.

About Diena

Diena Thompson is a mother of five who was thrust into a mission to protect our children from the threat of predators when she lost the "Sunshine of her life," 7-year-old Somer Thompson, on October 19, 2009 to a pedophile. Diena has made it her mission to draw attention to the dangers that none of us believed could happen in an American neighborhood on a walk home from school. It is now her passion to make sure NO family ever has to experience the pains she continues to feel, and has dedicated herself to bringing awareness to the importance of safety education.

Diena, with the help of a friend, Bobby Ingram, of the band Molly Hatchet, launched **The Somer Thompson Foundation** in the Spring of 2010 in an effort to shed a bright light on the darkness that is the life of those who would prey upon our children. Diena has been tireless in bringing the message of childhood safety through her numerous appearances on *The Today Show,* Jane Velez-Mitchell and Doctor Drew, to name just a few. Diena has also successfully lobbied the Florida legislature when proposed cuts to the Cyber Crimes Division were being considered. By putting her face and story before the legislators, those budget cuts were averted and hopefully, many of Florida's children are now safer because of her efforts.

Diena joined the United States Air Force after high school to serve in the Security Police force. Her service was cut short by the birth of her first child and until October 19, 2009, she served as a mother and provider for her children. After October 19, 2009, Diena assumed her current role as a voice against predators and pedophiles and an advocate for empowering our children to recognize and combat these evil forces that would harm them. Diena has been trained in the RadKids program as a certified instructor to empower our children against the demons who walk among them.

Diena's life's work is in its' infancy and she realizes that achievement of that work will be hard to measure since stopping tragic events don't make the headlines as the unstopped events do. Her goals fuel her to continue in a quest to secure the future for a child but hopefully, many children. To find out more about Diena and her foundation, visit www.TheSomerThompsonFoundation.org.

CHAPTER 47

Success Happens When You're Having Fun

By Genevieve Kohn

"When you change the way you look at things,
the things you look at change."

– Dr. Wayne Dyer

When I was younger, I had the same belief that is instilled is so many: work was supposed to be hard, exhausting, and even downright torturous. If you have ever felt or currently feel that way, this chapter is dedicated to you. The incredible news here is that you absolutely *can* find success by doing work that you love. My story is proof of that.

From 1996 to 2003, I worked as a Medical Technologist at a large Boston hospital. At first it was a great opportunity for a 25-year-old: the pay was more than I had ever earned up to that point, the health-insurance benefits were amazing and it was only two miles from my home. Being a former scrappy kid from Brooklyn, New York, I thought I had officially arrived at adulthood.

However, within two months, I began to feel as if I was in over my head. The job was extremely fast-paced, and to call it stressful would be an understatement. I definitely had a lot to learn and not much time in which to do so. Most of the laboratory testing that was required was on samples from patients that were extremely sick. Results were due in a range of three to sixty minutes.

I wanted to leave this job so badly, but I needed to make a living. Also, I didn't want my education to be a waste of time and money. So I knew I had to stick it out (or so I thought). Someday, I told myself, something better will come along. I didn't know how, but I had to hold out hope.

I began down a more spiritual path to seek answers from the Spirit (or whatever you'd like to call it); I started learning to trust that I would be taken care of. There was a deep-seated knowledge that I was Loved and Cherished, and that I would somehow be happy and successful in all areas. When I would doubt, forget, or start to lose hope, something always came back to remind me of this. The reminders would come in the form of loved ones, other times it came in the form of books. (I am extremely grateful that Spirit never gave up on me—it never gives up on anyone).

It wasn't long before I had a simple but profound realization: I was not having fun. I've never fully grown up: I am 40 today, and the child in me is still alive and well. I am always looking for ways to have fun, to be silly, to laugh until it almost hurts. Those are rampant in my lightest childhood memories. Yet back in the mid-90s, fun had been nearly absent from my life for a while.

I could not be happy unless I found a way to create fun in every aspect of my life. Fortunately, we had a radio at just about every workstation in the lab, which really helped me get through the hours I was there. Music had always been a source of great joy for me. Also, a lot of the people I worked with had a great sense of humor. Finding the bright spots is what helped me remain at that job for the length of time I did.

In the spring of 2002, I was diagnosed with multiple sclerosis. This forced me to literally sit back and re-evaluate my priorities. The job had begun to take a real toll on me, as my physical functions had become quite limited. Fatigue and muscle weakness—particularly in my legs— had caused me to really slow down. This was not the ideal situation in a workplace where I almost *never* got to sit down.

I still had much for which to be grateful. Aside from the MS, I was actually quite healthy. I had a loving family and friends. I had met and married my husband the year before this, thanks to the hospital (we were co-workers). Being with my husband is still something for which I am extremely grateful. We have always found a way to have fun together and we have common interests and values. He remains Spirit's match for me to this day.

The only difficult portion of my decision to leave my job was the fact that I would no longer be working near my husband. We had decided to start a family, since both of us had always wanted children. Somehow we knew everything would be okay with my health—and with the children. I was pregnant with our first child when I left the lab. I had started going to an energy-healing school, and I loved it there. So when the opportunity arose to work there, I was happy to make that change (even though the pay was significantly less). Every positive emotion (including fun) that I have ever had in my life resulted in something great. So this was a leap of faith, but certainly not one of blind faith.

In 2004 I graduated from energy-healing school, and later that year finished a program in massage. Right after that, I started my own business. I truly enjoyed bringing relaxation and wellness to people who often did not have much of either in their lives. The work was amazing—I loved seeing the difference in clients after a session. They looked so much healthier and happier walking out of my office. I also got to work alongside some beautiful, positive, successful healers and therapists. It was the ideal business for a new mom.

So in my job at the hospital, I got to make a pretty good living. In my business, there was not much repeat business but I was able to have fun. Unfortunately, the income was nowhere near what I needed to make ends meet. It was time to look for something I would really enjoy *and* that would provide a steady income.

Since having our second child in 2005, I wanted to spend as much time at home with my boys as possible. I was so grateful I had the chance to be at home with them, so I also needed to find something I could do part-time.

After I closed down my business, it took quite a while for me to find something that fit what I was looking for. In 2009, I found a great health and nutrition business opportunity that was almost entirely online. This could be really helpful with my physical challenges, as I had always believed on good health and nutrition. This business find was ideal, because I found that I could be self-employed yet work with a company where I would never be without a coach for guidance.

At this point I learned about personal development. Anyone that is in business for themselves will face challenges—too many challenges to list in this chapter. I had discovered that with this business, I could not be successful unless I learned how to improve my attitude and skills on a daily basis.

This was huge for me! There were many times when the people I was coaching quit or just wouldn't do the work they needed to make themselves successful. I really did not enjoy this business until I understood that in order for things to change, _I_ had to change. A successful business doesn't just happen because we want it. It comes from hard work and commitment on a daily basis. It also happens if we enjoy what we are doing. So again, I had to find ways to make work fun.

By finding ways to improve my time-management and communication skills, work actually started to become a lot more fun. My business is much more enjoyable now, since I have been playing music at my desk and taking breaks to spend time with my children. Great lessons on fun have come from them! I have also realized that I have needed to do work that I truly love as my main business.

I have had a passion for writing and speaking since I was a child. Because of this, I have become a published author, certified coach and public speaker. I am having so much fun—because I have found a way to be home with my family, and I help people live healthier, happier lives.

After years of searching, success is finally happening as a direct result of learning how to make work fun. I believe that it is due to making that commitment and continuing to work on myself. My husband and I are building a financial wall around our family that will withstand any economy. Knowing that makes what I do even more fun. I am so excited and grateful that even more fun and success us coming our way!

SEVEN STEPS TO SUCCESS

It is the positive stream of emotions we generate that will help us to create and receive all that we desire. The following seven steps outline a direct path to success.

1. **Find a career or business that feeds your passion.** This can often be a lengthy process, but it doesn't have to be. Take a look at what has really created joy in your heart, and find out

how you can turn that into a way to success. A life coach or business coach can help you bring out and focus on what your goals are.

2. **Keep in mind that you also need to either earn a good wage or make a profit.**
As I have learned, just doing what you love isn't always enough. Research fields and businesses that have stood the test of time—even during a weaker economy.

3. *Toiling endlessly and without purpose is <u>not</u> the way to success.*
In other words, you do not have to work yourself sick to be successful. Make sure you get enough rest, exercise, and proper nutrition. Your body and mind will thank you—and you will actually become more productive!

4. **Spend at least 10-15 minutes every day on time-management and organization.**
Keep a schedule and stick to it. You will know what you need to do and when you need to do it. Start cleaning up the clutter in your workspace so you will know where everything is—and a well-organized space will clear up the clutter in your brain too! (This comes from the CEO of Brain Clutter, by the way.)

5. **As mentioned earlier, personal development is how to work the smart way.**
Read, listen to and study the work of wise business philosophers and coaches like Jim Rohn, Anthony Robbins, Brian Tracy, Loral Langemeier and many other successful businesspeople. Learn how to do what people who have gone before you have done. Personal development is the fuel that ignited the flames of lasting success.

6. **Learn to work with the Law of Attraction: what you think about, you bring about.**
Personal development and this law go hand-in-hand. When we change ourselves on the inside, things will change for us on the outside. This is when the magic of success really happens.

7. The Attitude of Gratitude keeps it flowing!

The more positive feelings you have within you, such as feeling grateful for what you already have, will bring you more and more positive results. It works *every time*. Even if the success you want has not come to you yet, practicing this and the previous steps will get you there much more quickly and easily.

If you decide to become successful by having fun, you will!

About Genevieve

Genevieve Kohn, also known as the "Yes I Can Coach", is a best-selling author, success coach and public speaker who writes, coaches and gives workshops with her online, at-home business and all over the United States. She shares her expertise and teaches others how they can create the lives of their dreams.

She has developed a system called Parent-GOALS for parents who are also entrepreneurs. This system helps parents balance their family and work lives so they can take care of themselves, their families and of building their fortunes while helping others.

With the simplicity of the Parent-GOALS system, parents have a clear roadmap to their destinations, while reminding them to also enjoy the journey.

To learn more about Genevieve Kohn, "The Yes I Can Coach" and how you can receive the free Special Report "Finding Your Own Happiness with Mom-GOALS" (can be used by dads too), visit triadsuccesscoaching.com or genevievekohn.com.

CHAPTER 48

911 Fitness:
Leading to Life Transformations

By Jim Sayih

A few years ago, I was named "The Toughest Cop Alive." I could say, "Take that, Dirty Harry," but I won't. I will say that if I have a success secret, it's that I dedicate myself fully to whatever task is at hand —and that kind of dedication is the foundation of any meaningful Life Transformation.

Life Transformations aren't easy. They require hard work, dedication and the will to succeed—and not on a "One Time Only" basis. Consistent follow-through and review are necessary to make any meaningful transformation stick until that transformation is truly a part of your day-to-day life. Only when the extraordinary is ordinary is transformation complete and change accomplished.

I'm proud to say that thousands of people all across the country participate in fitness regimens I invented. I'm especially proud to work extensively with many police and firemen—our 911 "First Responders"– to make sure they're in the best physical condition possible to do their very important work.

However, the biggest Life Transformation I've been through personally had nothing to do with being tough or with getting in shape. It had to do with my son and the heights he propelled me to. In sharing my personal Life Transformation, I hope I can help others make the changes they want to see in their lives and share a few tips on how you can achieve your own.

I call what I do 911 Fitness because it's about becoming everything you can be—so you're ready for anything that life throws at you.

THE JOURNEY OF AN ATHLETE

Fitness has always been very important to me, as I've been an athlete since I was 10 years old. As a boy, I studied judo, played football and competed in track and field and wrestling. After high school, I enlisted in the U.S. Air Force for six years, where I also played football and got into competitive power lifting.

When I was stationed in Japan, I reconnected with my passion for the martial arts. I studied Kempo Karate with an old master who spoke no English, which was interesting. Fortunately, movements transcend language and I was able to learn the discipline well.

My fitness interests continued to evolve when I was next assigned to Italy. I stopped power lifting and again tried something completely new for me—bodybuilding. Again, I was determined to succeed. I entered many European competitions and ended up winning Mr. Italy twice. At my peak, I was rated the number five bodybuilder in Europe for the U.S. military.

After my honorable discharge, I began my career in law enforcement. I was hired by the Miami police department and ended up serving there for two decades, retiring as a Police Lieutenant. About halfway through those twenty years, I competed in the World Police and Fire Games (sort of the Olympics for first responders) and that's when I won medals in The Toughest Competitor Alive title. I also won medals in the Toughest Cop Alive at the International Law Enforcement Games. No, it had nothing to do with me taking down bad guys or executing crazy car chases like in the movies; this was an athletic competition featuring running, climbing, swimming, and other contests.

Because I was involved in so many competitions, this brought me to my first Life Transformation. Met-Rx Sports Nutrition, which sells many acclaimed nutrition products, hired me to be their rep in sport for 911 responders. This was an awesome opportunity and opened the door to what would be my post-policeman career.

I was given my own division by the company to study the effects of the Met-Rx products on the training of police and firemen across the country. I selected the cities and departments to work with. In each department, 20 people would participate in a training regimen. One group would use Met-Rx and the other wouldn't. The objective was to see if the Met-Rx group would get the best results (which they did).

While working on this project, I was shocked to discover that police and firemen in other cities were in much worse shape than I ever imagined. Miami had spoiled me, because most of the guys working in South Florida kept themselves in great shape—that's what living by the beach will do to you! I realized there was an extreme need for education, guidance and leadership when it came to getting 911 first responders into shape.

So, in 1994, I created 911 Fitness, my business which continues to this day.

Yet, this was not my most defining moment as an adult. No, the event that caused my biggest Life Transformation was very personal, not professional.

MICHAEL AND ME

In 1992, I had the honor of having my second son born. Michael was born June 15, two months premature with severe brain damage that was diagnosed as cerebral palsy. His emergency delivery was on the day of his brother Adam's first birthday.

This happened during an incredibly active time for me. 911 Fitness was still a relatively new business that required a lot of time and attention, I was still working on my own personal development, and I was still working full-time with the Miami police department. Now, I was dealt a deck of cards that would turn my priorities upside down.

I spoke to four top neurologists to get their opinion. All four gave me a firm consensus—they all said that Michael's mother and I should institutionalize Michael for the rest of his life. They said he'll never speak, he'll never walk, he'll never be able to feed himself. Well, because of my fitness background, it was impossible for me to accept that my son would not be able to make any kind of physical progress throughout his life.

I dedicated myself to the task at hand with everything I had. I took two courses in child brain development to understand how I could help Michael as he grew up. I also turned my home into a physical therapy center, thanks to Home Depot, by putting up different apparatuses that would help Michael work his body in different ways. I also had volunteers who were gracious enough to come by and help out with his workouts.

Michael's mother and I had different philosophies on raising my boys. We ended up divorced; I fought for and received full legal custody of both of my sons.

Thankfully, I proved the doctors wrong. Today, at the age of 19, Michael speaks with a slurred speech. He can converse with friends on cell phones, and also communicates with them through Facebook and email. He can't walk independently, but he has a walker that he can use to run sprints. He is also able to feed himself.

And the greatest thing about him is that he wants to give back to other special needs kids. He volunteers for a lot of different organizations, including Shriner's Hospitals for Children, which provides free surgery, equipment and therapy for children. The Hospitals are funded by Shriner's, a world organization to which I am proud to have been a member of for over twenty years. Before Michael came into my life, I had volunteered at the Shriner's Hospital for Children in Tampa transporting kids to the Hospital. After Michael was born, I came back to the hospital not as a volunteer, but as a father, and they gave my son great care. Now, Michael serves the hospital that served him as an ambassador

Yes, Michael's growth and development has been amazing and an inspiration. And he created my own biggest Life Transformation. I honestly think I would not be the person I am today if he had not come into my life. I had to carefully manage my time to include time with his brother Adam. Both boys taught me what patience, love and perseverance are all about and that is a wonderful gift to receive from anyone. They both have become a vital part of my fitness endeavors. My sons and I participated in Best Buddies' 100-mile bike rides (I pull Michael in a jogging stroller), ran the Marine Corps Marathon and we also created Michael's Special 5k Run/Walk on Hollywood Beach, to benefit United Cerebral Palsy. Adam has made me very proud in how he has embraced his brother's abilities; he includes him when going out with friends and mentors him to engage with his peers and community. I'm very thankful for Adam.

THE 911 FITNESS CHALLENGE

As Michael was turning three, I had to balance the responsibilities of helping him develop to his full potential with the responsibilities of running my own 911 Fitness business. My company was hired to develop a wellness program for the North Miami Beach Police Department. I created an exercise program for the officers that I knew would do the trick.

Of course, to do the trick, the officers had to actually *do* the exercises—and it was very apparent after the first month, they weren't. How could we motivate them to follow through?

That's when I knew an incentive was needed. I offered an award of $1000 to whoever lost the most fat and gained the most muscle. Suddenly, the gym was filling up and everyone was *very* engaged in the program. Since I've always been very self-motivated in my fitness objectives, this was a new experience for me—and one I knew I would repeat, once I saw how this incentive worked.

The guy who won the challenge was vacationing in Orlando with his family when the official weigh-in was to take place. He actually drove all the way down to go through the weigh-in. When I proclaimed him the winner, he yelled, "I'm going to Disney World!" and drove all the way back to Orlando. *The Miami Herald* was even there to make sure it all got in the paper!

That inspired me to broaden the competition. I created the 911 Fitness Challenge, which takes place from January through April of every year. Police and firefighters in the U.S. and Canada go to fitness centers and work with certified trainers that are aligned with my organization. The team that gains the most muscle wins $5000. The proceeds from registration fees benefit the Shriner's Children's Hospitals and the first responders who participate get valuable free health education from webinars and other informational materials we provide. It's a competition where everybody wins—and we've kept it going and growing for 14 years.

HELPING OTHERS WITH THEIR LIFE TRANSFORMATIONS

From pursuing my own health goals to working with my son to helping to motivate police officers and firefighters, I've learned a lot about what it takes to help someone make dramatic Life Transformations that lead to a happier, healthier life. And I'm dedicated to helping anyone who wants to really make that kind of change. I have all kinds of clients—some have missing limbs or serious afflictions.

I only give new clients one rule to begin with—they are not to use the word "can't." The first thing they need to change is their language in a positive way. When you change the way you think and the way you act, you're on the road to your first significant breakthrough.

And you must lose your fear of change. I have many of my clients work up to walking a plank set up between two buildings, high above the ground. The purpose is to overcome whatever they're scared to do. When you focus on the finish line instead of your fear, you are able to achieve at a higher level.

Every person is unique and every fitness program should be tailored to that person. I truly believe that and apply it to my business. Everyone that starts with my club or one of my programs has to start the same way—by spending two complete days with me, 9 a.m. to 5 p.m. During those two days, usually a Saturday and a Sunday, I get to know who they are and what they're all about, one-on-one, without any distractions for either of us.

Why is that continuous time important? Because when you're with someone for two days, at some point, their true self will emerge. The first few hours, everyone is on their best behavior. In some respects, it's like they're on a job interview, trying not to do anything that might come across as negative. But, eventually, they drop the guard, I get a real reading on who they really are and I am able to identify the right program for them. Sometimes I *do* determine that they can't do certain things. For example, I'm not going to make someone climb trees if I don't feel they're capable of that.

From there we work on their nutrition, mostly on managing their Ph levels in their bodies. Ph helps control the acid levels in our body. We generate that acid through our emotions, both good and bad. Yes, tension and stress can generate acid, but so can working out and the other physical exertions we're going to introduce into their lives. So we direct them to eat foods that will elevate their Ph, foods such as green vegetables, almonds, and citrus fruits, as opposed to foods that are heavy in saturated fat and fried.

Once I am able to understand who our clients are and start them on a proper diet, we then work on challenging them physically, with tasks that take them out of their comfort zones so they can achieve things they've never achieved before. It's not just about doing push-ups in the gym—we get them to canoe across a big lake, we get them to hike up mountains, we get them to push cars, we do everything to get them to experience the potential and fullness of *life*. And that just inspires them to do even more. I've watched clients' self-esteem skyrocket and confidence levels soar. This is very rewarding to me, because my clients end up feeling like family. Watching them achieve greatness is similar to attending a graduation ceremony– priceless.

If you are seeking your own Life Transformation, look for what will spark that transformation and motivate you forward. Ask yourself WHY you want that goal. I've learned it's simply not enough to just lay out a program of diet and exercise. Incentive and inspiration are also necessary to push people forward to where they want to be. I've made it my life's work to put those elements in place so that my clients will successfully complete their own individual Life Transformations. And I'm proud of all of them that achieved these transformations - especially, of course, both my sons.

I wish you luck in your Life Transformation and I invite you to contact me should you wish to receive some advice on how to make yours work for you.

About Jim

Jim Sayih, CrossFit Level 1 Trainer, has a Masters Degree in Sports Science and Exercise Physiology. Jim is a Professor at Broward College, teaching Physical Sciences. Jim has a distinguished career (20 years) in Law Enforcement, currently retired a Police Lieutenant from the Miami Police Department, recognized for numerous commendations, contributions and awards. Jim served six years in the U.S. Air Force, studied Kempo Karate in Misawa, Japan, grew up Wrestling and favored Judo. Stationed In Italy, Jim competed in Bodybuilding, winning the middle weight division for the US Air Force twice and competed in the European Championships. He also participated in Strongman Power-lifting tournaments in Far East Asia. Jim regularly competes in 5Ks, Adventure Races and Duathlon Races, including the Marine Corps Marathon with his two sons, pushing one of his sons, which is a Quadriplegic with cerebral palsy. He and his special needs son created and founded Michael's Special 5K Run/Walk, benefiting United Cerebral Palsy. Jim is an NSCA Certified Strength & Conditioning Specialist, ACSM, Health Fitness Instructor, Certified ISSA in Nutrition, NESTA Certified Nutrition and numerous other fitness certifications.

Jim won the Toughest Cop Alive (TCA), International Law Enforcement Games and competed in numerous World Police and Fire Games in the TCA. Each week, thousands of people around the country enjoy a fitness program created by Jim Sayih. He is the CEO of 911 Fitness and Director of Fitness Commitment Institute. These two professional associations have over 40,000 members nationwide. Jim is also Founder of the 911 Fitness Challenge, benefiting the Shriner's Children's Hospitals, fourteen consecutive years. His fitness programs are implemented in Police & Fire Stations in the US and Canada. Jim has been featured on Good Morning America, Discovery Channel, FOX Sports, NBC, CBS and The Christina Show. His programs are used by the DEA, U.S. Secret Service, and SWAT Teams.

The President's Council on Physical Fitness & Sports Awarded Jim the coveted Community Leadership Award for his outstanding contribution and involvement in helping communities, nationwide, improve their fitness while raising money for Shriner's Children's Hospitals and the American Diabetes Association combined. Learn more at www.JimSayih.com.

CHAPTER 49

Dancing Through The Dark To Come Alive:

Become The Miracle You Are

By Julianne Blake, Ph.D

Every caterpillar goes through massive transformation to become a beautiful butterfly.

If you don't know about the butterfly and you open the cocoon mid-process, you find a creature with strange deformities (ultimately its gorgeous wings). You only see a distorted body, incapable of function.

That's what people experience when new obstacles or symptoms of "disease" manifest in their bodies.

So, how do *you* become a butterfly?

....

The following is this author's story. I am a mentor for healing chronic pain and illness. I have been trained as a Success Coach and as a Gestalt therapist with a doctorate in psychology. But primarily I am trained by my dance with life, and the body I find myself in, honed by dancing through the darkness of it into my own life force, where I can live my passion with purpose.

Even as a girl, I had always loved to dance. Disco, salsa, ethnic–it didn't matter the style. When dancing, I was passionately engaged. The rush

447

of adrenaline and endorphins flowing through me became my favorite "high," favorite way to feel fabulous, and I just couldn't get enough.

That didn't matter now. I kept falling down and could hardly move my knee. I went to the chiropractor, crying, "Usually you get my leg back together, then I'm strong again. But it's not working anymore! What's wrong?"

He curtly replied, "You need to see a neurologist."Distraught, I saw one of UCLA medical school's top neurologists, who diagnosed multiple sclerosis–MS, explaining that the MS would get progressively worse.

To this dancer, those words were death.

The doctor repeated four times, "You know, you can live a long, healthy life with MS."

The first couple times, it rolled by me. Inside I went "Yeah, yeah. That *sounds* good. But I'm a dancer! That's not what I want."

The fourth time, I erupted in anger. Frustrated and defiant, I asked the doctor (just returning from maternity leave), "If you were just diagnosed with MS, would you have a baby?"

After a long pause, the doctor said, "If that's what I wanted, and I had the support system, Yes."

I thought about that…

Did I have a support system? No.

In fact, I went into denial.

Then, I went for a second opinion and more tests. It was frustrating, because I was ill, fatigued, and had trouble walking. So there was no getting around it. The diagnosis was the same.

The doctor recommended finding a support group of people with MS, so I obliged. At the first meeting, it was immediately clear that almost everyone there was focused on drug side effects, depression, complaining, and asking "Why me?" The negativity was overwhelming. I felt sick to my stomach and ran out.

"If that's support," I thought, "I don't want any!"

I yearned to feel uplifted, to make a difference, to do what I loved!

Grief at the loss of dancing caused me deep pain. Dance is what I used to uplift myself and heal. At first I was disturbed. Seeing myself as pathetic and without energy, I withdrew and resigned myself to the worst, as advised.

Then, in the midst of despair, there was an inner pull to invent new ways to dance. Gratefully, I started doing that. It kept me motivated and alive.

But it wasn't enough. I had a burning desire for dynamic movement. I urgently wanted to heal, to stand on my feet and dance joyfully again!

I thought, "That's my movie and I'm going to live it!" Taking yoga, learning to rest, eating differently and nourishing myself wasn't always easy. Sometimes I wanted to succumb to fatigue and despair, and curl up in a ball. But living my depression was intolerable, and I got myself moving outdoors. That infused my mind and soul with new energy.

Finding effective things that doctors would not prescribe, like physical therapy, I became proactive, even inventing devices to help me function. The fatigue resolved and I got stronger. There were things I wanted to do.

As a nature lover, I had a lifelong dream of seeing gorillas in the wild. I wanted to "dance" with the magnificent endangered creatures in their natural jungle habitat. The thought filled me with awe. Feeling strong, I took a trip to Africa. Unfortunately, in Nairobi I tripped, crashing my knees on concrete, injuring one badly.

Then everything changed.The fear came in: "Oh no, now they'll notice I'm the one with the problem, with trouble walking." Others might think being with me could impair their trip to find gorillas.

The expedition director said, "If you recover, fine. But fall again, and you can't go to the gorillas."

That was devastating. I couldn't bear the thought. This was the trip of a lifetime, and my heart ached to get there. I had a week to get into shape.

So I took action. I thought of every possible way to strengthen myself in the short amount of time. I needed every advantage. It was a challenging hike, taking two to five hours to even find gorillas, as they were constantly moving.

Olympic athletes train their body, mind and emotions in the feeling of having already accomplished the goal. Determined, I trained for the competition of a lifetime.

Three times daily, I meditated and visualized, seeing myself walking well, energized, with all my strength. I became creative with my visualizations, using every sense to make them as real as possible, so I would truly feel as if I had already seen the gorillas in their natural habitat. In my imagination, I felt the ground under my feet for strength and balance... I heard soothing rustling leaves in the wind... I smelled dampness in the air, as if I were hiking there now.

In my meditation, I used deep relaxation to relax and center emotionally, giving myself power. The meditation (which research has shown can be more effective than morphine at reducing pain) let me glide as effortlessly as possible through the pain of the injury. It brought resilience and strength back to the weakened knee joint.

Striving to get each part of this body in shape and enlivened, I exercised. I started with a little, gently increasing it, celebrating every bit accomplished.

I was living my movie. I was dancing my dance. Native guides were available to help carry packs and gear in the jungle. Reasoning that no matter what happened, they could help me get back down the mountain, I hired a guide. Now I knew I wouldn't jeopardize anyone's trip.

Finally, the day came, and I was ready.

A Rwandan native led the hikers. He kept me next to him, taking me under his wing. I felt honored. When we came to a stump or large roots that he felt could cause struggle or slow me down, he simply leaned me across his shoulder and lifted me over it.

To me it was like floating and landing perfectly on the ground again. It felt like I was living a miracle.

I was "in the zone."

To our amazement, it didn't take long before we found gorillas munching and napping. Standing ten feet from a 600-pound silverback, I was awed by his impressive force field as he took in our profound respect and appreciation.

He moved in a slow, purposeful, graceful dance, clearly aware of my presence as he foraged. Watching indirectly, he signaled permission to share the food supply. It was magnificent.

What an awesome encounter. A breathtaking moment, full of wonder.

As I sat, energy from the ground filled and enlivened me. It gave me strength to walk back easily! I returned uplifted, overflowing with energy.

What are the primary tools for success here?

Whenever you need to empower yourself, remember two things:

1.) <u>envision the exact conditions you want to enliven</u> and

2.) <u>relax, and know that they are real.</u>

Believe your vision completely, which takes courage and faith. And make it feel real. Know it has already happened.

At the same time, detach, knowing it is not in your hands alone. *Do everything in your power,* with full force and enthusiasm, then *let go,* and give control to your higher power inside, or the Higher Power.

Whether you call it God, Source, Creator or Higher Self, this relationship is critical to creating your new reality.

WHAT METHODS CAN MAKE AN ENORMOUS DIFFERENCE—UPLIFTING AND EMPOWERING YOU?

Step 1. Positive focus.
So how do you stay positive in a negative world (like when your body isn't working)? How can you keep positive focus, and what does it take to find inner strength?

It takes wanting to believe in yourself, and stand up for yourself.

Most of all, it takes <u>caring</u> about yourself. You want to know you matter, you make a difference, and you are loved.

I wanted to make a difference. For me, seeing gorillas wasn't just an adventure; it was doing something that mattered, making a deep connection with phenomenal endangered creatures.

Step 2. Finding and holding your vision.

Honoring people also matters profoundly. I love to help people heal, be strong in the face of illness and pain, and create lives they love to live.

One compelling way to help people heal is to draw out their visions of their greatest life, empowering them to make those visions real. No matter what their physical condition, or their challenge. People with the most severe challenges have lived their vision.

Stephen Hawking is the master physicist who can't move or speak without mechanical assistance to power his lungs and give voice to his brilliant thoughts, which are acknowledged worldwide as an incredible gift.

A six-year-old boy, double amputee below the knees, who wears curved metal prosthetics and runs with a huge glowing smile, showing us all that our rationalizations are invalid.

Kyle Maynard, an inspiring athlete with no hands or feet, has actually become a world champion wrestler. His compelling autobiography is titled, *No Excuses.*

That power is available to anyone who wants it. You can live it. It involves reaching deep inside to discover who you are. People do incredible things regardless of physical circumstances.

Because we're taught to not be overly proud, we can all be blind to our true power and strength. Yet a keen listener can draw out essential qualities that we don't even recognize as our gifts.

For example, Peter doesn't see himself as good at what he wants to do. He's in constant study mode, but says, "I'm not a natural at listening. I'm used to talking a lot."

As his coach, I came fully present to interview, listen to what he yearned for, and uncover his brilliance. At the next session, I presented him a vision of gifts he was ready to share and potential he would develop, so that he could see himself in his full glory.

As I finished, he was speechless. Asked how he was doing, he replied with a beaming smile, "It's so rare for me. I usually can't wait to talk and have too much to say. Now I'm very quiet inside and have nothing to say. I'm just streaming with energy."

To create your vision, contemplate your natural talents. More importantly, think of the things you love to do. What would make you want to jump out of bed in the morning because you couldn't wait to get started?

Then dare to start imagining your life doing that.

If you practice imagining that, it will change your life.

Then continue to visualize, making it real with all your senses, until you experience it as if it has already happened. Hold firmly to that image, as your mind will want to return to its familiar comfort zone. If you hold to that vision with regular dedication and practice, it will empower you beyond belief.

Step 3. Dancing through the dark to come alive. Emerging from the cocoon. The healing power of love overcomes the greatest obstacles.

As you can see, dedicated caring attention, meditative practice, envisioning and guided visualization have been cornerstones in my own healing "dance," as well as in my coaching and training. I know them as primary elements of self-empowerment.

One day I got a faint message from Diane (one of my clients) to please call back.

When I called, she sounded wounded, desperate. She cried, "I'm at the point where I can't go on. I'm suicidal. If I had a way, I'd kill myself. I can't even call 911. I've been crying nonstop for days and I have a huge lump in my throat. I can't even swallow. I can hardly move."

I spoke with her, but mostly listened. I powerfully listened in a very different way, asking questions to draw out what she needed to share and to release. Diane had been through several deaths of the people closest to her.

What took her to the edge, where she didn't want to go on, was her mother dying without reconciliation. Diane knew her whole life that her mother hated her. Yet she always imagined they'd connect before it was too late. When her mother died, that dream died too.

When reconciliation became impossible, she was paralyzed. She had dealt with a degenerative illness for years. Her symptoms would get better, then worse. The final emotional shock, after her mother passed, was the realization that her beloved son–who she had nursed through cancer–couldn't connect with her. He just wasn't available. He didn't understand her feeling completely alone, useless and without purpose.

Diane couldn't lift herself out of that feeling. I listened to her with interest and compassion, to hear her pain and acknowledge it. Sensitive questioning drew out her deep needs and wants. Clearly she needed to heal, to feel connection and purpose.

She began to recognize and accept her pain and grief. She took time to honor her feelings, without judging them. They had been her truth. Yet, now she could release them! She breathed deeply for the first time.

Then, Diane went into a custom guided visualization to bring in appreciation and love. She reconnected with people she knew deeply loved her, and had a spiritual moment with her mother. In the safety of the healing space, she spontaneously heard her mother apologize for not being able to love her. And ask her forgiveness. Diane rocked with pain, and with relief.

Afterwards, Diane had new strength in her legs, walking with more vitality than she had for a long time. She felt new life.

Her words were: "My muscles have been so hard they didn't work. My whole body was like stone. As I shifted out of fear, my muscles became fluid, so I could actually move them. I could walk again. I did not have any physical pain in my body after I hung up. None. I was out of the pain. I've never gone back to that previous level of devastation."

For Diane, the vision was as real as her body. Feeling herself walk strong in the vision translated into her physical reality in her body. Her whole reality shifted when she full experienced the love and let it in.

She was empowered and uplifted.

Then she laughed as she shared what she'd do with the new energy, and how she could contribute to others. It was beautiful to hear. She brought her gift into the world!

Awakening and gifting is a miraculous dance. It is dancing with disease, dancing with healing, and dancing the gift of your heart.

Your gift can be given, no matter what your physical condition.

We all have that ability.

You are not that unrecognizable creature incapable of function in the cocoon. You are the butterfly, miraculously transforming yourself.

You can empower yourself to manifest *your movie* whenever you choose. **So choose the movie you love to live.**

Choose to become the miracle that is who you truly are.

About Julianne

Dr. Julianne Blake, Ph.D., is a Certified Professional Success Coach who offers high-level training in Jack Canfield's outstanding system for attaining ultimate success. As a coach and trainer, she guides you in breaking through obstacles and limitations to create lives you love to live.

The onetime professional dancer earned her doctorate in clinical psychology and was a practicing psychotherapist for eighteen years. As a therapist, she developed exciting, innovative methods in Gestalt art therapy. Her practice focused on teens and adults with self-esteem issues, women in relationship crisis, and she also specialized in effectively counseling people challenged by chronic or life-threatening illness, particularly cancer.

Julianne's quest for a deeper understanding of healing led her to travel the world researching new paths to physical and spiritual health. Her journey took her from milking sheep (for making cheese) on a Sufi farm in England to studying acupuncture and medicinal tonics at a Taiwanese hermitage, to learning ancient meditation techniques at a Buddhist monastery in Nepal.

Then suddenly, Julianne was confronted within her own crisis when she was diagnosed with MS (Multiple Sclerosis) and faced the possibility of never dancing again. Determined to overcome her pain and her own feelings of helplessness, anger—and fear, she journeyed again—this time into the world of medicine, research journals and alternative practitioners, where she experienced acupuncture, osteopathy, chiropractic, and many systems of natural healing.

With newfound knowledge and skills, Julianne parlayed the broad range of her experiences into a new career as a professional success coach. Julianne's exceptional insight allows her to enable you to access your core, your true self. Her program includes personalized guided meditation sessions that empower you to release past trauma and pain, and offers step-by-step guidance in developing the action plan to take you to your ultimate success.

Her own personal challenge gives Julianne a unique ability to work with clients who are challenged with chronic and life-threatening illness and pain, helping them find relief, thrive and live their dreams with passion.

In addition to her designation as a Certified Professional Success Coach, Julianne is a licensed Marriage and Family Therapist in California, as well as a certified member of the Gestalt Therapy Institute of Los Angeles. Today, twenty-six years after her MS diagnosis, Julianne is on the move, and living a courageously creative life, both personally and professionally. She loves to paint, garden, and walk by the ocean, and has found marvelous, inventive ways to continue to do what she loves most–dance!

Julianne Blake is passionate about connecting with people who want to grow exponentially and to heal. Her profound desire, above all, is to inspire those who seek coaching to know who they are, to empower themselves to heal and to succeed in creating a life they love to live.

CHAPTER 50

Write Your Own Story

By Sigrun Lilja Gudjonsdottir

I have always been a positive person with large dreams—but once I allowed myself to turn my dreams into actual goals and tried my best to always use positive perspective in communication with other people, my life took a U-turn and completely changed.

Later in the chapter I will reveal the steps that have worked very well for me. Some of them I created for myself and some I have learned along the way. I encourage you to try it and see how you can start to attract the things in your life that you dream about and desire. I can assure you that if you follow these steps you will start to see opportunities that will bring you closer to the things you really want, meet the right people that can help in bringing your dreams closer and you will begin writing you own story rather than letting others write it for you.

AT LEAST IT WORKED FOR ME!

Today I'm a best-selling author, fashion entrepreneur, designer and perfumista, with both men and women fragrances that are one of the best-selling perfumes in my home country, Iceland. I work in my dream job. I'm living my passion, and that happens to be my job. I run my own lifestyle fashion brand called Gydja Collection. 'Gydja' meaning goddess in Icelandic. I have been given the privilege to build up my "baby," (my company and my brand) from scratch. And believe me, I wasn't born into wealth. For some people it is hard to believe that a young woman is able to build up a company like I have from scratch without a strong financial background. But I did! It hasn't been easy but I loved every minute of it.

In 2010, I had launched several accessory collections, as well as my first signature perfume which I was distributing throughout Iceland with huge success in both sales and marketing. In 2011, my first best-selling book was published in the US.

But I can tell you that for me, this is only the beginning. I have very lofty goals and they keep me from giving up when times are tough, and it also motivates me to be brave and act on the opportunities when they arrive to bring me closer in achieving the life that I desire.

Before I go deeper into explaining how you can attract the things you really want into your life, I've created a few guidelines:

1. **Be brave, and don't let any people say that you can't do something.**
   Remember the story about a Monkey trying to compete to get to the top of the hill and every one was chanting that he wouldn't make it? Well he did, and out of all the contestants, he was the only one who made it to the top! Once he came back down the mountain, the crowd asked him how he did it, when they were all saying he wouldn't. The monkey was deaf. He never heard them. He did what HE wanted on HIS time.

2. **Always follow your heart.**
   This is your passion, your business and you are the true heart in it. Without you it would not be able to grow.

3. **Be a leader, not a follower.**
   There are two different types of people in this world—the Leaders and The Followers. The Leaders make the new trends, the new products, the new techniques and the new unique stuff. The Followers copy the trends and the products. Which group do you want to belong to?

4. **Be persistent.**
   Making and building a company is not easy, don't even dream about it. But it is so much FUN. To see your dream come to life, there is nothing like it. It takes time and you will make many mistakes and there will be many barriers, but it is *yours* to look at it as a project that needs to be fixed rather than a barrier. To be persistent is probably one of the most important features that entrepreneur can have; it determines the successful from the rest.

5. Stay grounded.

There are few things as repellent as arrogant individuals and there are few things as charming as humble people. A person who respects all individuals and treats them as she wants to be treated has much greater chance of success then person who doesn't treat others well. To be able to succeed the people that you surround yourself with is one of the most important thing, no one can build a successful business all by themselves. People want to help people that they respect, that are kind and that gives them their opportunity to shine. Always treat people in a nice way, with respect and I can promise that you will get it thousand times back.

NOW IT'S YOUR TURN.

Since I dedicated myself to positive thinking, my life has really changed.

Eight years ago I wasn't really sure what I wanted to do in my life, I knew I felt passion me inside but I wasn't sure where my passion resided. I was working a full-time job in the family business, a promotional product company in Iceland, and now I can honestly say that it was one of the most important schools in my life so far.

I recently found a memo book of mine from eight years ago, where I had written my goals at the time. The goals were about how I wanted to become a better version of myself. I really wanted to make those changes in myself, and step by step, I did it.

Here are the four steps that can lift your life, your relationships and your career into new and higher levels that you hadn't even dreamt of reaching before.

STEP 1. GRATITUDE

Gratitude is the first step and most important step that will fulfill your life with happiness and help to make your dreams come true. You can't expect anything new to come into your life unless you open yourself up to be grateful for what you already have. To get you started, you should begin by making a list of the things that you are grateful for and short description why. For example: Family, Love, Friends, Work. By doing this your focus will change from focusing on complaining about the things that you don't have into appreciating the things you already have. You should list all the wonderful things you don't take for granted. When the list is ready, you should read it every morning for a few days, to remind you (and your subconscious) on your new way of thinking.

By now you have probably memorized the most important things you are thankful for, then you should find the perfect time every day, to go over the list in your mind and be thankful for what you have. I use the time when I am driving to work in the morning. It doesn't always have to be the same things and it doesn't have to take long. But just by doing this, you will remind yourself of all the wonderful things you have to be thankful for. You will start to feel better, and you will see that complaining about things doesn't really matter. Gratitude will help you stay grounded when your dreams start to come true and you achieve the success that you want.

STEP 2. COMMUNICATION

We communicate every day, whether it's with our partner, our co-workers, family, friends or even customers. Having positive and good communication with other people doesn't only help us feel good, it also brings your dreams closer within reach. We all need the right people in our lives to be successful and to reach our goals. But if you don't treat people like they deserve to be treated, you will not be able attract the right people into your life.

Start by taking the key relationships in your life that you would like to fix.

Ask yourself what are the things that I am grateful for in that person? What are the things that I appreciate about this person? Make a list about all the positive things and read it every day for a few days. Also try to stop the negative complaining with the other person and when you talk about her/him with other people, instead start telling her/him every day what you like about them, give large compliments when deserved. When you start focusing on the strengths, I can promise you will get more of them, and a lot more. That same technique works in all relationships that you have, albeit your co-workers, your family and friends. Let people know what they are doing right, give them as many compliments as you possible can and they will want to continue to do more positive things. The energy starts flowing into that direction and your communications will be fulfilled with good energy and love, which will help you to feel good about yourself and will also help you to reach your success.

Release yourself from being the victim in your relationships and take control of your own destiny.

STEP 3. VISUALIZE

There is a very strong, helpful tool I frequently use to help me focus on my goals.

Below are a few options to do it, and you can choose whichever technique you believe will work best for you.

- **Vision board:** Cut out strong images from magazines, newspapers and print outs of the things you want in your life, also cut out motivational quotes that fit perfectly. Glue the images on a board or a wall in a way that it says everything about what you desire. Put it up were you feel comfortable having it, but make sure you see it every day. I use a large vision board in the Icelandic Gydja office, to motivate myself and the team. We have two large walls in our meeting room that are covered with photos of our next assignments and the future of the brand. It is not only very motivating for us, but also our customers notice the boards and can feel the amazing creativity that lies within our company.

- **Reality book:** I use this for my personal desires that I want to attract into my life. Instead of naming it dream book, I call it reality book because it is the reality of my future. To make a reality book, buy a blank book that you think fits perfectly as your canvas. You start by planning your book and divide it into chapters that cover all of your desires. At first I recommend that you don't try to fill your book, because your dreams will probably change and get bigger on the way, so it is important to leave spaces to change when needed. My book has family, friends, career, health, happiness and wealth. In each chapter, you glue related photos of your dream house, car, body, job and everything else you want in your life. You can write sentences in there for you to read when you look at the photos, but it is very important that the sentences are written out in a way that sounds like you already *have* all of those things. Write: I live in this house, I make this amount of money and I have this kind of car. When you have made your book, you need to have it on your nightstand and read it and look at the images as often as you can. I try to do it at least four times a week.

- **Motivational video:** It is easy to make a short video to watch your future life while a very strong motivational music is played in the background. This is one of the strongest ways to create the important feeling within you. Every time I watch my video I get goose bumps of excitement for my future. You can use any slide show program that gives you the option to create a video, but I like to use Photo Story 3. You start by collecting and saving the images that describe the things you want in your perfect world. In some photos you can take a small photo of yourself and put into the image, to make it more powerful. When you have up-loaded the photos into the program you write text with the photos and you end by choosing a song that touches you and creates excitement. Then you save your video and voila, you have your motivational video ready.

STEP 4. REALITY DAY

The last step but a very important one is the Reality day. To start attracting your desires into your life, you need to begin by figuring out where you want to go. That's often the hard part. If you can't decide on what you want and where you want to go, it's impossible to attract your desires into your life.

What are your hopes and dreams? Now it is time to start figuring out what it is you want in your life to achieve the success that will fulfill your heart. The Reality day is a very good way. I have used it and have encouraged others to use it and it has helped many make life changing decisions. Now let's begin by finding out what you really want. Make sure you do this alone and without interruptions. Do this when you are feeling good and positive. Start by thinking if you had no barriers at all in life, if you could get and have anything you wanted, anything at all, anything you wished to have in your life. If you would have your wildest dreams come true, what would your perfect day look like? Start by writing down where you would wake up, in what country, who would lie by your side, who would live in your home, what your home looks like, what kind of a car would you drive and where would you drive off to go to work? How would your job be? What would your day look like from A-Z if all of your dreams could come true?

Remember this is your reality day, so you write it down like it is true. Do not use "I would wake up in a house," but instead "I wake up in this house" etc.

After you have allowed yourself to write your dream day down, you have figured out what it is that you desire, and that is the first step to achieve the success you want in your life. Now it is important to focus on it, because what you focus on gets bigger. You do that by reading over your Reality day every morning, and I want you to visualize and feel it from the bottom of your heart like it is already your reality.

Now it is your turn to start writing your own story!

About Sigrun

Sigrun Lilja Gudjonsdottir—the best-selling author and fashion entrepreneur, known as Lilja—is the founder, CEO, and head designer of the Icelandic luxury fashion brand Gydja Collection. With her own sense of style and a nose for business, she managed to become a successful entrepreneur, designer and perfumista within a short period of time. Lilja has been fascinated with fashion and business and from a very young age she was linked to four words: entrepreneurship, marketing, business and fashion. She has a keen sense for business thanks to being surrounded by industry leading business entrepreneurs throughout her life. Her family runs a promotional product company, to which Lilja credits to her business acumen through first hand experience. Aged just 24, Lilja started developing her own fashion and accessories brand, called Gydja Collection. Over the years, Lilja's business has gone from strength-to-strength and lately, her name as a business women, marketing expert and creative fashion designer has been rising worldwide.

 She managed to successfully expand and grow the company's products and her lifestyle brand (that is getting to be a well known label) worldwide in a very short period of time. With an eye for marketing and business opportunities and a heart for fashion, Lilja has grown the Gydja Collection into one of the best known designer brands in Iceland – a brand that is quickly working its way to become a worldwide brand.

Collections consisting of feminine accessories and sophisticated designs are a hit with women everywhere; from A-list celebrities in Hollywood to Europeans elite. One of Lilja's greatest achievements was to take on the perfume world by storm when she launched her first signature fragrance called EFJ Eyjafjallajokull by Gydja for women, made from the Icelandic glacier and volcano Eyjafjallajokull, that erupted in 2010. This exotic perfume became one of the best-selling fragrances nationwide right away. The global press became found of the perfumes unique concept and was very interested about this businesswoman and fashion designer from Iceland who gets big ideas and actually implements them.

Thousands of articles and online news were published worldwide about the brand and Lilja was interviewed by many large media outlets, giving the brand an opportunity to grow into foreign markets. In the near future, Lilja is determined to expand the business into new markets with several accessories collections, a range of perfumes and a lot more exciting stuff. She is set to conquer the UK, the US and then... the rest of the world. Find out more about Lilja and Gydja here: www.sigrunlilja.com and www.gydja.is

Awards:

2011 – EUWIIN European Union Women Inventors & Innovators Network; Lilja received a Special Recognition Award.

2011 – The National academy of Best-Selling Authors; Lilja received a Golden Quill Award for her chapter in a book called *The Next Big Thing.*

CHAPTER 51

Rejuvenation: Look Better, Feel Better and Build Your Business!

By Luba Winter

I confess: I am a junkie for inspirational quotes. I love to read, especially books that are uplifting to the spirit. There are times when I come across an expression that stops me in my tracks and sends me reaching for a highlighter. After I mark the quotation in the book for easy reference, I then copy it carefully into my personal journal. I am amazed at how a mere turn of phrase can sometimes oust the noisy gremlins of negativity and allow the songs of angels to fill the mind with positive thought.

One of my favorites is from the late author and motivational speaker, Leo F. Buscaglia:

"Too often we underestimate the power of a touch, a smile, a kind word, a listening ear, an honest compliment, or the smallest act of caring, all of which have the potential to turn a life around."

Such a turning point in my life came when I was 30 years old and living in Portland, Oregon. I was in the process of opening a new beauty salon, and I needed to paint and decorate. Since work always draws a crowd, it wasn't long before I had help from friends and future clients, complete with lively conversation to break up the tedious work of changing the wall color.

"You're only as old as you feel," said one friend, "at least that's what my mother always says."

"You don't agree?" I asked.

"Well, it would be a lot easier to believe in that sentiment if you didn't discover a new wrinkle every time you looked into the mirror," was her reply. She went on to relate the details of her skin-care regime and complain about how painful and expensive it had become.

"You know, if they can put a man on the moon and make computers the size of a finger nail, you would think they could come up with a device to eliminate wrinkles." She said, looking at her face in a mirror.

It was what is called a "germ" of an idea, but one that would not let me sleep that night. I couldn't get the woman's words out of my mind. "A device to eliminate wrinkles…" Where had I heard that before?

In my journal, interspersed with inspirational quotes, are pages of ideas. I call it my "brainstorm gallery." When I have an idea that just won't let go of me, I write it down. It is almost a physical relief to transfer it from my mind onto the page. I carefully wrote down what the woman had said: "device to eliminate wrinkles". Next to that, I added, in bold block letters: **"FIND ONE , MAKE ONE!"**

As I sat on the edge of my bed, holding my journal, I thought about my Ukrainian homeland in eastern Europe, and my grandmother (my "Grannie"), whose home I spent so many summers. As a young girl, my Grannie and I would often take long walks together, surrounded by the luscious green Ukranian hillsides. I remember feeling the silky grass between my toes as I walked barefoot, picking flowers. I can still remember seeing the sparkling droplets of early evening dew that sparkled in a setting sun that seemed to become liquid gold as it nestled into the tops of the hills.

It was on one of these walks that my grandmother, whose voice was always so sweet when she spoke to me, stoked my cheek and told me how soft and pretty my skin was.

"You're pretty too, Grannie," I said, touching her cheek.

"No, child," she said. "See these wrinkles? Maybe someone will invent a machine that will get rid of them, and I too can have soft and beautiful skin like yours."

Were her words prophetic? I would soon find out.

FINDING A WAY

It may have been the influence of inspirational books, or it may have just been the idealism of youth, but I was a supremely confident young woman when I was in possession of a powerful idea.

To borrow the words of Zig Ziglar, another noted author and inspirational speaker, I was the kind of person who would "go after Moby Dick in a rowboat and take the tartar sauce with me." I had no doubt that I could somehow create a device such as the one alluded to by first my grandmother, and then my friend from the conversation in the salon. If I was successful, I could actually change people's lives and make them more beautiful. I was inspired!

The device I envisioned would replace the need for expensive and invasive surgery. While women want to look younger and more beautiful, many tend to balk at the idea of having a cosmetic surgeon. There are too many images of the irreversible damage done by surgery gone wrong. Perhaps those images are the exception rather than the rule, but there had to be a better way, I thought. I began writing down what I needed to do to make the idea blossom into reality. Again, in large block letters, I began compiling a list of characteristics such a device must possess. I wrote down three bullet points:

- Easy to use
- Safe
- Portable

That's all I had so far, but it was a start. Soon, another of my favorite inspirational quotes came to mind:

> *"I not only use all the brains I that I have,*
> *but all the brains I can borrow"*
>
> – Woodrow Wilson.

I began writing down the names of people with whom I needed to talk in order to bring my idea to life. I would soon discover I wasn't the only one intrigued with the idea of skin rejuvenation. I was pleasantly surprised to discover how easy it was to partner with top engineers in the field of skin treatment therapy, and work with leading dermatologists and even cosmetic surgeons from Sweden, Italy and the United States. My passion to find a way elicited from them a willingness to help, and after many years of testing and research, the Rejuvenation G4 was born.

REJUVENATION AT LAST!

The dream of my beautiful grandmother had become a reality. The whimsical wish of my friend in the salon had come to pass. When the team of cosmetology engineers and designers finally released the prototype of the device, and when we finally received the "thumbs up" by the scientists involved who had declared it effective and safe, I felt as happy as I could ever remember feeling. Not even my childhood days in those sun-filled fields in the Ukraine were as joyous. We called the device the "Rejuvenation G4" because of what it was capable of doing. Rejuvenation means "a return to youth." No, the device didn't reverse the aging process, but it did seem to peel away years of aging from the skin, restoring some of its youthful glow without the fine-line wrinkles. The "G4" stands for "Generation 4." The device we finally released to the public was the fourth model we had developed and tested.

As soon as I saw the results of the Rejuvenation G4 on its first users, I knew that it would change many lives by helping people look younger and feel better. As I write this, thousands of men and women who have seen phenomenal results of the device by using it as part of a daily skin-care routine. But what is even more rewarding to me is knowing that so many have reclaimed their self esteem, and are able to lead bolder and happier lives because of it.

TRANSFORMATION

With the proper tools, beauty need not be unduly time consuming or hard work. The Rejuvenation G4, as a skin-care strategy, has been described as transformational, not because "peels away the years," but because it peels away the layers of conventional wisdom when it comes to skin care. One myth that this new strategy debunks is that effective anti-aging has to involve extreme, tedious—even dangerous—measures.

Some think that the more skin-care products, creams, lotions and emulsifiers that line the shelves of our vanity, the better. But do you honestly need all those bottles and tubes? Working with top beauty and skin-care specialists around the world has taught me that the answer is no. Years ago, when the Rejuvenation G4 was still in its development stages, I wrote these three words in my "brainstorm gallery" and they have guided me in my work:

- Cohesion
- Relevance
- Simplicity

Cohesive skin-care products are those that work in harmony with your regime, not at cross purposes with it. If your skin is naturally oily, then applying products that contain oil is not *relevant* to you. If your skin is naturally dry, then products that dry the skin out are not relevant. *Simplicity* speaks for itself. If a regime calls for one hour of this and two hours of that, I'm sorry, but it's just too much.

Youthful beauty can be achieved by simply removing and controlling the effects of the aging process *as they occur*. That means it's never too early to start, and incremental treatment is much more effective than radical treatment. By focusing on these three watchwords of effective skin care strategy, I know that you will neither waste your time nor try your patience. The Rejuvenation G4 plays into those concepts quite nicely, because it is noninvasive, simple to use, compact and requires no more time than taking a shower.

MALE BEAUTY

One of the most pervasive—and I think even dangerous—myths is that men don't need skin care. That's not even close to being true! With the changing standards of aesthetics among males, and more liberal attitudes concerning facial rejuvenation, many men are now seeking anti-aging treatment

In cosmetic surgery, the concept of face lift and neck lift in men is essentially the same as it is in women, but the approach is tailored to highlight and sharpen the angular structures of the jaw, neck and chin, with less emphasis on crow's feet, cheekbones and naso-labial (fold from nose to corners of the mouth) regions. The aim of a face lift and neck lift is to restore the major facial contours, especially the jawline.

I hope that men will develop more confidence in cosmetic anti-aging products and strategies. Doing so will result in the delivery of energy to the level of muscles where the face lift normally would be done. How many men know that they can, in the privacy of their own home, obtain professional results by following a brief skin-care regime that involves treatment only two to three times a week? If they travel, it is something they can take with them.

Feeling good about oneself is not an exclusive emotion, limited strictly to women. Men need the kind of confidence that comes from looking younger and feeling better too. For some, it could open pathways of unexplored potential. There is nothing unmasculine about feeling wonderful and loving the life you're living.

YOUTH HAS NO AGE

In my profession, I cannot literally reverse the aging process, not yours, not mine, not anyone's, anymore than I can make a river run upstream or recapture yesterday and live it again. But I can, to a greater degree now more than ever, help correct the aberration of the cosmetic effects of aging quelling what would otherwise be a youthful spirit. Another of my favorite quotes is by Pablo Picasso, who said: "Youth has no age." That's one you have to read a time or two to get the sense of it. In other words, one can be chronologically older, but have a youthful spirit. Who is to say that individual is not young? Well, most often it is the individual himself or herself. When people do not like what they see in the mirror, it has a negative psychological effect. Change what they see in the mirror, and you turn that emotion from negative to positive. It may sound a bit smarmy to some, but I truly believe the words of Emily Dickenson – *"We turn not older with years, but newer each day."*

About Luba

Luba Winter developed Rejuvenation G4 from Nu Way Beauty and is on mission to guide men and women around the world to love what they see in the mirror. She created three "ABC-Skin Care" steps to help them unlock the secret to healthy skin and start loving their lives as soon as possible.

Her popular Rejuvenation G4 FDA cleared, patent pending device is safe and easy to use, celebrating by hundred men and women who have get amazing results from their daily skin care routine, reclaimed self-esteem, and started bold, happy lives with Luba and her proven Rejuvenation program.

Being inspired by her grandmother 27 years ego, Luba along with top worldwide engineers and cosmetologists, developed a very unique device where she put all the amazing beauty technology of "Galvanic, Ultrasound and Photo Therapy" in one convenient unit to begin a journey to guide others men and women to live more joyous, balanced lives. Luba believes that self love and right skin care is where the transformation begins.

Luba's Rejuvenation G4 device and "ABC-Skin Care" steps are a life-changing program for men and women who struggle with skin care routine and want to prevent themselves from aging process. Learn more about Rejuvenation G4 at www.nuwaybeauty.com.

CHAPTER 52

Cash in on Your Wealth IQ

By Morris Nutt

Do you believe that you have to be smart to be rich? Have you been taught that wealthy people have high IQs and they simply know more than the average person, so they accumulate more wealth? Or perhaps you believe people with much higher levels of education are *destined* to be more successful than those without as much education.

What if I told you that none of those belief systems were true and that there are lots of successful and wealthy people with basic education skills and average IQs? You might be shocked to find out these people are wait for it....wait for it....Tremendously HAPPY!

An interesting survey was published five years ago in *Science Daily* whereby 7,400 Americans were tracked annually for more than 25 years to study their education, intelligence, income, wealth and financial difficulties with credit cards, bankruptcy or paying bills. Adding validity to the study and its results was the fact that the study was funded primarily by the U.S. Bureau of Labor Statistics; the study was a national representative sampling of people who are now in their early 50s. The results were amazing (and surprising) compared to what we have been taught to believe as accepted norms.

For example, the study found that people of below average intelligence were just as wealthy as those in similar circumstances but with higher scores on IQ tests. In fact, Jay Zagorsky, a research scientist and author of the study, stated, "People don't become rich just because they are smart." The study backed up this quote as it found that a number of extremely intelligent people had gotten themselves into severe financial difficulty. Zagorsky also stated, "Your IQ has really no relationship to your wealth. And being very smart does not protect you from getting into financial difficulty."

The one financial indicator that indicated that it paid to be smart was income. Those with higher IQ scores on average were paid more than others. Previous studies have been done and found the IQ to income link but this study was the first to also look at the relationship between intelligence, wealth and financial difficulty, Zagorsky claimed. Participants completed the Armed Forces Qualification Test (AFQT), a general aptitude test used by the Department of Defense. Researchers have long used AFQT scores as a measure of intelligence.

After having read Zagorsky's study it made me think of a quote my father would often recite when I was younger, "A and B students do okay in life but C and D students have buildings named after them." That quote used to really bug me. I mean after all, aren't we supposed to strive to be straight-A students? I certainly don't remember my Father extolling to me the wisdom of this quote when I had brought home a test score lower than a B. He didn't throw a party in my honor for making a 71 on a biology exam and brag to the neighbors, 'Hey did you see my boy's grades this past week? I tell ya, the kid is going to have a building named after him one day!'"

Oh, no. In fact, I remember quite the opposite. I remember the, "Son, you are better than that" speech. Just his disapproving look towards me for underperforming scared me, so much so that I graduated from high school with honors. I did it because that is what society said made you special. I did it because I wanted to please others and myself and to prove I wasn't "average." Did it make a difference? Let's explore a concept I have tinkered with for some time: **Wealth-IQ.** Many of us had our IQs measured at one time or another, perhaps in school. You can even do it online now for free. It is quite the controversial subject, as is any standardized type of test. For one thing, who creates the questions that determine whether or not you are the next Einstein or the next Forrest Gump? Another problem with tests such as these are how they are scored. Does each question have equal weighting to the final outcome or are other questions more heavily weighted and if so, why? You can see why many groups have poked fun at tests such as these over time and why they are heavily contested. Yet we as humans somehow need a measurement of some kind of ourselves even if it is for self-satisfaction or potential application into the local MENSA club.

One author even wrote a book challenging the misplaced importance of IQ tests and alternately suggested that EQ or Emotional Quotient was a far better predictor of life success. I choose to not place all of my eggs in either basket, because it is easy for me to see the virtues of scoring high in either department. IQ/EQ, tomato/tomahto. It doesn't matter to me because I am a money guy. I study wealth and also believe there is an IQ associated with the wealth making abilities of a person. So I created Wealth-IQ. And like the EQ guy, I think there is more than one way to look at an issue and certainly more than one way to solve a complex problem.

The fact is many of us want to be wealthier, but wealth can mean many things. For most, it means money or material possessions. For others, wealth means a well-balanced life containing good health, lots of love and healthy relationships combined with plenty of money, passions, work and community involvement and giving back. I choose to think of simple wealth and being truly wealthy as two very distinct and very different concepts. Simple wealth to me is only about money and material possessions. A truly wealthy person in my opinion really does have a balanced life full of great relationships, good health, lots of respect for others *and from* others, gives just as much as they receive and they have a feeling that they matter. And yes, this person also has plenty of the green stuff.

Becoming wealthy however is a real problem for many. High IQ people can just as easily be broke as low IQ people. The challenge isn't really about raising our IQ or going back to school to get the PHD so we can finally become wealthy. It isn't even a brain issue at all. It is a heart issue. Do you love the life you have? Are you in love with something bigger than yourself? Scientists have recently discovered that the heart, and not the brain, may control more of our decision making than previously thought. So the old saying, "Go with your gut" or "follow your heart" may have been more spot-on than previously considered.

So what is your Wealth-IQ and how does it work? Wealth-IQ is a measurement of life balance and potential success in each of the five key areas of life: Health, Money, Relationships, Spiritual and Pursuits (career/ passions). A perfect score is 500 (100 in each category). The goal is not to achieve a perfect score. You won't be handed a fancy ice sculpture and a cup of magic juice if you do. What the goal should be is to discover more about who you are and what your imbalances are, so you may choose to focus on achieving more balance and producing extreme happiness and satisfaction as a byproduct.

For example, you may be a marathon runner worth millions. That could be a perfect two for two right there (200 score). But you may also be lonely with few close relationships, lack any connection to a higher source and you find you lack any passions or outside interests anymore. These last three areas are big goose eggs for you, because you have scored only 200 out of a possible 500. With low scores in these other three areas, it might not be long before your health and money could be affected as well. It is very hard to hurt only pieces of your body and not hurt the entire body eventually. It doesn't mean you have lost the battle or should feel bad. It simply helps you realize your Wealth-IQ so you can get a handle on areas holding your overall happiness and livelihood back. We must strive for balance and excellence in all of these five key areas so we may truly enjoy our great potential.

Wealth-IQ is deeper than just the five key areas and a simple score. It is a transformational process. I will explain later how you can obtain your score so you can begin living better right away. And if you need help in applying your Wealth-IQ score or improving your Wealth-IQ, you can reach out and receive help. But first, let's examine a bit more from the study about regular IQ and Wealth.

The study established that there was an income to IQ link whereby each point increase in IQ was associated with $202 to $616 more income per year. This meant the average income difference with a normal IQ(100) and someone in the top 2 percent of society(130+) was between $6,000 to $18,500 per year. However, when the likelihood of financial difficulties was considered, people of below average and average intelligence did as well as people who were considered super intelligent.

The golden nugget of the study was this: **The study could find no strong relationship between total wealth and intelligence.**

How could this be? We have been taught you earn more when you have more education; therefore, more degrees should automatically mean more wealth, right? Not exactly. Zagorsky suggests that high IQ people are not saving as much as others. They may earn more but they aren't keeping or building wealth like they should.

"Just because you're smart doesn't mean you don't get into trouble. Among the smartest people, those with IQ scores above 125, 6 percent of them have maxed out their credit cards and 11 percent occasionally miss payments." Zagorsky says even at some of the nation's top universities, intelligence and wealth are not necessarily linked. "Professors tend to be very smart people," he said. "But if you look at university parking lots, you don't see a lot of Rolls Royces, Porsches or other very expensive cars. Instead you see a lot of old, low-value vehicles."

To be fair, perhaps the professors are simply miserly and frugal not wanting huge depreciation on flashy expensive cars. They may prefer "older, low-value vehicles." In their defense, they may enjoy great health, a loving relationship, respect among their peers, a healthy work-out routine at the University gym and perhaps even a healthy 401k and pension balance to boot. They might enjoy the simpler things in life now and have a tremendously high Wealth-IQ score. Or they may be broke and forced to drive the 1990 Civic. The point is not to worry about what the professors are doing and worry about yourself and how you can improve.

One way to do this is through a simple yet effective assessment that can point you in the right direction and help you gain control over your life and your future. Zagorsky says the lesson is simple. "Intelligence is not a factor for explaining wealth. Those with low intelligence should not believe they are handicapped, and those with high intelligence should not believe they have an advantage." Amen, brother. We all need help.

If you would like help and want to take the next step in discovering your Wealth-IQ, one of the great Success Secrets in this book, go to www. morrisnutt.com and take the free assessment. After you finish your assessment you will receive your score along with the opportunity to learn how you can improve your score and as a result achieve a happier life as a result.

About Morris

Morris Nutt was raised on a Family Farm, where he learned important life lessons like team work, business management and family values. He grew his skills to start several businesses in the fields of business, investments, real estate and inspiration. Morris brings a down home sense of practicality and humor mixed with strategic business common sense to the table when speaking to or consulting with corporations, trade groups or individual audiences world wide.

Morris has authored and co-authored several best-selling books including: *Counter-Attack* with Brian Tracy and *The Art and Science of Success* with Matt Morris (Author of *The Unemployed Millionaire*). He is also author of *The Laws of Financial Success and The Laws of Financial Success Weekend* and workbook. Morris leads others in finding their success through his workshops like "The Laws of Leadership Mastery Class."

He was admitted into The National Academy of Best-Selling Authors in 2011 for his work with Brian Tracy. Morris was also bestowed with the Golden Quill Award for his writing skills in 2011. A true people person, Morris enjoys helping others reach for and attain their biggest goals and dreams.

Morris is considered a Wealth Mindset expert. He believes that all worthy success can be traced to a healthy Wealth Mindset. He leads others to discover and develop their own special Wealth Mindset through his speaking, books, webinars, classes and workshops.

When not writing or speaking on Wealth Mindset, Morris enjoys spending time with his spouse, Kelly, and their two children engaged in family activities. They enjoy traveling, family movies, boating and charitable causes.

Morris desires to reach out to as many people as possible with his message of hope, humor, wealth mindset, leadership and happiness. He is currently involved in several new writing and speaking projects for 2012. To book Morris for your upcoming conference, workshop or corporate event, go to morrisnutt.com and click on the Contact tab.

CHAPTER 53

Acquired Immunity to Viral Marketing

By Paul Edgewater

I'm a huge fan of Jay Conrad Livingston and his line of "Guerilla Marketing" books which are some of the most clever and informative series of works in the history our industry. It's not a stretch to say that he was the founding father of modern promotions. "Guerilla" is also a great way to define his message. He used the word as a metaphor for his brand of marketing although it is a term that initially entered the modern vernacular with negative connotations.

I remember when I first heard the word "guerilla." I was watching The CBS Evening News anchored by Walter Cronkite with my mom, dad and big brother. The details escape me because I was so young, but I remember it was about bad guys in Lebanon. My father also had to explain to me that Mr. Cronkite wasn't calling these bad guys "gorillas." It was my first lesson on homonyms, but I digress. It helps to remind ourselves that Mr. Livingston's message succeeded in spite of the negative connotation, not because of it. No one believes his intention was that we'd take his terminology literally and start shooting up Beirut whilst passing out branded tchotchkes. He was just telling us there was another way to get our point across which involved tactics not unlike a guerrilla ambush on an unsuspecting—but ultimately grateful—public. Juxtapose that tactic with what's happening now; he took a negative term and turned it into a positive euphemism. The exact opposite is happening in the marketing world today.

Allow me to set the stage: We've all been exposed to euphemistic re-branding of negative terms in the sterile corridors of the corporate world. Long ago and in more pragmatic times, we may have heard someone say something akin to, "We have a problem and it needs to be fixed." It was clear, concise, to the point and we understood there was a problem and it needed to be fixed. No further explanation was needed. However sometime in the last 20 or 30 years, some mid-level manager raised on Dick & Jane and new math (and who may have just been subjected to sensitivity training), proselytized that people ran for cover when hearing the word "problem," lest their self esteem be irreparably damaged as a result of the exposure. By some decree, the word "problem" was substituted with the word "challenge." After all, everyone likes a challenge, don't they? When "Challenge" lost its luster (after a very short while, incidentally), it was unceremoniously replaced with "issues." That wasn't good enough either and now we actually call problems "opportunities." Good grief. Isn't it sad to think that soon, that wonderfully positive word will be laden with negative connotations?

Euphonies do indeed have their place in the lexicon though. When someone's vital signs cease to be apparent, it blunts the trauma to survivors when we say this person has "passed on" or "passed" versus this person "died." We don't get buried, we get "interred." In fact, life insurance companies go so far as to tell survivors that the policy in question had "matured." We can forgive euphony in businesses that deal with death, but for the rest of us, it borders on ridiculous and it implies that everyone on the payroll is an easily traumatized child. I think it's time to come full circle; indeed we have a 'problem' and it needs to be fixed. You'd never know it, with all the "Johnny-come-lately-me-too" terms in the marketing world we are being subjected to. I believe these new buzz words and phrases try in vain to capture the clever and whimsical spirit and vibe of Mr. Livingston's epiphany. For instance, can we all agree that 'viral marketing' is a vile term? Why must our industry come up with these negative-sounding names to describe what we do? Viruses are bad. No one wants one and if we can help it, we'd never seek one out to bring home to the family.

This chapter will date this book as a work from its era as I'm certain we will stop using this buzz term shortly (wishful thinking?). But I can't help thinking it will be replaced with another, even more negative sounding name. 'Disruptive' is another gem. It's as if the only way to get the attention of our target consumer is to disrupt them (read: Piss them off). If someone disrupts me while I'm busy living my life, I can tell you with complete certainty I will not be investing in their product, company, cause, or service. I would also maintain that I'm not alone in this sentiment. You get the point; I'm illustrating, with absurdity, the absurd. What we do in marketing and promotions is an honorable endeavor but with names like "Viral Marketing" floating around out there defining what we do, at best you'd think that we're up to no good and at worst, trying to infect the public with something that may kill them. If we just call what we're doing "marketing" and "promotions," we're being honest with the consumer. If on the other hand, our product, service or cause needs to be spread by such disgusting sounding names as 'viral marketing,' we shouldn't be surprised when our demographic target moves from our sights and hides where we can't find him or her. It may be for the aforementioned reasons we have to keep on re-inventing, or 'mutating' ways to get our message in front of consumers. No one wants our viruses; hence the name of this chapter, "acquired immunity" and I believe these terms and tactics are creating an ever-resistant strain of consumer. Note that the author is keenly aware that 'viral' is a metaphor, but words have meaning and by continuously using negative words in our communications, it reinforces negativism. Keep in mind the term, "guerrilla marketing" is the exception to inverted euphony; it worked. Most, if not all the others, don't.

Recently, one of our executive Bees, Geoff, had a refreshing and extremely clever idea for a new marketing moniker (everyone at our company, Busy Bee Promotions, is referred to as a "Bee"). He called it "Pollination Marketing." That his idea succinctly complimented the name of our organization, made it all the more appealing to us. Alas, a little research in the availability of the domain was unfortunately an object lesson in the phenomena of universal consciousness; someone had beaten us to the punch. We first checked the availability of the domain. When we saw that it was already taken, we visited the site (www.pollinationmarketing.com) and it was very nice. From what we could tell, they were a stand-up bunch. They are based in the U.K. If it's not too late to make a long story short, had Geoff's brainchild been applied to *our* Business model, the idea was that we would send our Bees out into the marketing world with 'pollen' in the form of samples, talking points, tchotchkes & literature. The Bees pollinate the consumer with this information and create new customers that would then bloom the world over. Cool, huh? It gets better; not only do the worker Bees go out and spread the word about our clients (or Busy Bee for that matter), they return to the hive with new 'pollen' from cross-pollinating/ cross-promoting with contacts they have encountered in their travels in the form of collected literature, photos, business cards, quotes from the public, specific metrics and other anecdotal information that we relay back to our clients and incorporate into our ever-evolving business model. As far as I was concerned, it was a honey of an idea. Which, of course, is why someone else was already implementing many elements of what Geoff was discussing with me. As it is, at Busy Bee Promotions, we create a buzz for our clients. It's a great descriptor of our service, it's brand appropriate and we can live with it for the foreseeable future. Much more importantly though, it's appropriate for our clients and is an activity that their customers won't run for cover from either. Everyone wins.

Perhaps this is a good time to step back from what we are selling for a moment and revisit *why* we are selling it. If we have a product, service or cause that we believe in, we have to ask ourselves; "how did I become aware of this?" Did someone disrupt me? Did someone virally market me? If we ourselves came upon this product or service by more traditional means of data transference, let's give our potential customers the same opportunity to reach the same conclusion—in the same manner that we did. It's the best way to show respect for those who will be parting with their hard-earned money when purchasing our goods and services.

In a world where euphony is the norm, our profession has decided to invert euphony. It's baffling and it's a problem. The 'opportunity' to address this 'issue' is a 'challenge' that we in our industry all need to be up for, or eventually, our clients will avoid us like the plague.

To recap:

- Be honest and frank with your target consumer. Don't try to bamboozle them into opting in to your product or service by cloaking your intentions in euphony. There is nothing wrong with closing a deal and charging a fee for service; it's the free enterprise system and we need make no apologies for engaging in it.

486

- While it's acceptable and encouraged to use euphony (in serious personal matters, for instance), it should be discouraged in business vernacular. It's a waste of time and disperses the focus needed to accomplish goals and resolve problems.

- Come up with a creative way to describe how you're marketing your product, service or cause (i.e. "pollination marketing"/ "creating a buzz"). Make it brand appropriate and it'll be something that'll grow with your organization and not have to be reinvented ad nauseam as consumers won't become resistant to it.

About Paul

Paul Edgewater, is a best-selling and award winning author and CMO & co-founder of Chicago, IL-based, Busy Bee Promotions, Inc. Busy Bee opened its doors in 1998 and conducts an average of 400 events monthly coast-to-coast.

Paul is America's "Promotions Powerhouse" and has been featured in *The Wall Street Journal, USA Today, Promo* Magazine, and on FOX News, CNN, CNBC, MSNBC, FOX, ABC, NBC and CBS news affiliates promoting products and services for clients such as Coca-Cola, Starbucks Coffee, Verizon Wireless, Groupon, Whole Foods Market, Macy's and many, many more. His specialty is in maximizing his clients' exposure in and out of their respective market places by executing very unconventional, attention-getting tactics including an acclaimed, free 20-second spot he garnered for Starbucks Coffee on Fox News by rattling off talking points while doing "360s" on a branded Segway Personal Transporter!

Paul is the author of The Book On Promotions, series, *Counter Attack - Business Strategies For Explosive Growth In The New Economy* co-authored with world renowned business leader, Brian Tracy, *The Only Business Book You'll Ever Need,* co-authored with Robert G. Allen and Ron LeGrand, *In It To Win It,* co-authored with legendary sales trainer, Tom Hopkins and *It's All Up To You - The Top 10 Things You Should Know To Have The Best Life Possible,* co-authored with best-selling author, speaker and coach, Grace Daly (all available at: www.PaulEdgewater.com). He has more than 30 years of sales, marketing and promotions experience, is motivated by his intense love of the private sector and the free market system, and takes great pleasure in creatively connecting his clients with new customers. In addition to his business pursuits, he is a weekend athlete with three marathons under his belt and also an accomplished musician and animal lover.

Paul lives steps off the Magnificent Mile in beautiful downtown Chicago and is available for speaking engagements and consultations.

For booking information or to contact Paul directly, visit: www.BusyBeePromotions.com or call Toll-Free (888) 438-9995.

CHAPTER 54

Tenacity, Fortitude and True Grit

By Phil Cioppa

I was taught that the only way to succeed is to keep trying, if indeed you fail the first time. When I was young, everything seemed to come so easily. I had no idea what it meant to really fail. Yet, as I grew older, it became more and more difficult to always come out on top. In fact, not achieving what I set out to do would send me into an emotional tailspin and deter whatever else was occurring in my life. As I look back, much of this was due to immaturity and false expectations of me and those around me.

I am not so sure that with age comes grace, but what does come, if you are honest with yourself, is the realization of three important things to achieve in life. Set realistic goals without negotiating your dreams; tenacity; fortitude in achieving what you set out to do (knowing that the road is not easy); and grit, to withstand the many obstacles along the way to success.

First, let's define success. The world has many definitions of this concept, most of which are wrong. Success cannot be measured by how much wealth one has accumulated, not what titles(s) one may hold. Success is the inner realization that one has achieved all that has been set out to do in a manner which shows excellence for that person. My success cannot be measured against another's. My success is unique to my personality, abilities and desires. One of the most heartwarming examples I saw of success is when a young man I knew was able to take a few steps four months after an automobile accident. For him the world opened up, and I could genuinely experience the feeling of success that emanated from him. No one could ever say that his success in those first steps was not equal to the U.S. experiencing the first person to walk on the Moon.

To reach his goal, he worked every day for 2-3 hours falling, perspiring, crying and laughing. He never gave up. Although he would be consigned to a wheelchair for life, he was able to prove to himself that he could walk a few steps and it was okay to stumble. He developed his inner strength and truly felt successful in his own right. He went on to be a very prominent businessman in the community. He did not reach that by gliding through life, but by realizing he always had to set up a new goal, once one had already been accomplished. He knew what hard work was and he never gave up. He drew the strength to accomplish from the innermost places of his soul and psyche. He never thought of quitting because he had the raw nerves and thirst for what he wanted to accomplish. His was a journey of tenacity, fortitude and true grit.

Tenacity is a virtue that one develops as a young child and is instilled only from within. Unfortunately, tenacity is seen as something that only very few possess in our culture. We refer to those individuals as the strong ones, the ones who can withstand the pressures of life. Yet, we fail to realize that each one of us has the ability to form tenacity in our being. It is a discipline; it is not easy. It requires hoping against hope and knowing that, at times, failure will be incurred, but strength can resolve that failure. It allows us the strength to truly move beyond the moment into the realization of that which can be. It is as if we transcend ourselves, keeping our eye on the prize. No one is able to stop us when we are tenacious. There may be a need to tweak along the way, but the end goal always remains the same." To be tenacious means that we are not deterred from our ultimate outcome. At times, it may mean that we are not always the popular ones. It may mean that we are seen as 'not in rhythm' with those around us. Yet, tenacity moves us forward against the current to achieve what we seek.

Sister to tenacity is fortitude. Fortitude rises from the depth of our very being, and gives us the strength we need to be tenacious. It fuels tenacity and gives rise to one who is tenacious. It is the sub-virtue that slowly creeps into our soul and propels us with the drive to achieve. Without fortitude, tenacity remains a virtue that lies still without its impetus. Fortitude is likened to a brick wall. No matter how much you batter it, it emerges to rise again. It is stalwart and defiant as a sub-virtue. It withstands both internal and external pressures and constantly drives us to persevere. It heightens our senses and allows us the ability to be creative in our solution-making. It gives us the iron will to keep going. It was often said of the late Prime Minister of the United Kingdom, Margaret Thatcher, that, above else, she had fortitude. She stood for her convictions and never wavered. Whether she was agreed with or not, she kept moving and turning back any obstacle that was placed in her path. She was considered successful in her cause, but it would be more interesting to know if she truly felt that success herself.

Then there is grit—this is when we get "down and dirty." The movie *True Grit* gave rise to a classic Western movie definition of the word. Grit is the characteristic one needs to mix with fortitude and tenacity to make it all run. Grit is so powerful, it eludes a complete definition. We know when we see grit and when we experience it. Grit is found deep in the caverns of our being and is a characteristic that is overpowering, and at times is overwhelming. It is the movement that provides the music to the rhythm of our desires. It allows us the ability to face all challenges and accomplish that to which we place our mind.

With all of this said and done, how do we translate tenacity, fortitude and grit into the everyday marketplace as entrepreneurs and business owners? After all, we are living in a time unlike any other time in history. This is an exciting time; technology is bursting, opportunities lay before us and challenges are being met with new insight and acumen. However, this is also a time of peril and danger for the small business owner and entrepreneur. Thousands of businesses are closing their doors every year, and the majority of them are the small businesses we find on "Main St." In and of itself, this may not be alarming, as this is part of the unfortunate business cycle of our economy, yet what is alarming is that our business owners and entrepreneurs seem to lack the fortitude, tenacity and grit as found in generations before us.

There are those who say that America is not as strong as it once was. I find that hard to believe. In the face of calamities and other events, Americans have risen to the occasion. What is happening is an underlying presence of depression within the entrepreneurial community. I am not speaking about an economic depression, but an emotional and psychological one. The "can do" spirit (albeit a cliché), is lacking. The ability to put "elbow grease" into one's business venture is not apparently present. There is no one person to blame for this, but an overall malaise that permeates the small business community today.

Perhaps we expect things to come easy for us. Or even worse, we believe that financial aid should be provided for our venture, and that our making it on our own is not an expectation. We look to government, banks and other lenders to resolve our difficulties, but forget to look at ourselves and realize that success and failure is, of course, based on the financial bottom line, but just as equally, on our ability to endure. In other words, if we are to succeed, we must look at truly becoming masters of our domain.

In order to do so, we must face the fear of failure. It is my experience that there is truth behind the philosophy of self-fulfilling prophecy. If we plan for disaster in our venture, disaster is almost certainly to follow. What kind of attitude is it when we see entrepreneurs planning for bankruptcy before they even open their doors? I am not proposing that we do not plan for the unexpected, but we should not invite the unexpected in as we begin to pursue our dreams. It is the dream and vision of the entrepreneur that has always been the driving force in our culture. If we lose that or look forward to failure, what do we expect will happen? As the adage goes; "you get what you ask for." We allow ourselves to reach a very dark place in our souls, so much so, that we are unable to function. This is the vicious cycle that I believe is dragging the entrepreneur down.

So now, we look to tenacity, fortitude and grit. It seems very realistic that these qualities, as discussed above, are the qualities lacking in entrepreneurship today. Without these qualities, how would we ever expect to reach success? Beginning a business venture requires more than a 40-hour work week. It requires long hours of planning, executing, monitoring and reworking the plan of action developed. It requires hanging on to the vision and dream that ignited the entrepreneurship inside of you. It means being tenacious in seeking the end goal with the spirit of fortitude and the presence of grit in the pit of your stomach. So often that which seems easy on paper is actually a very difficult task at hand. Many entrepreneurs have an idea and believe that everyone will rush to buy their product and/or service. When that doesn't happen, we wonder what went wrong and the blame game begins. It seems to be everybody else's fault, but never our own. The bank will not give me a loan, the people around me do not understand, the area in which I live doesn't want what I have to offer, and the list goes on and on. Although some of this may very well be true, the blame must rest on ourselves, and we must look for the answers not only externally, but internally as well.

Events and people around us are explainable, but our interior conflict is less so. It is virtually impossible to define how we "feel" or what we are "thinking." All human language falls short of that linguistic ability. Yet, none of that discounts the fact that those feelings are present. They are real, and they impede our progress with any venture we seek. How can we change those emotions and thoughts? How do we turn off the fountain of negativity? The only possible way is to change how we perceive our situation. We must convince ourselves that all is not lost, and opportunity is still present. When we look to other places for answers, we forget to look deep down inside of ourselves. When despair sets in, our psyche is not even aware that defeatism has begun. It is in those moments that the failure, negativity, anger and depression slips in. However, it is at those times that we must dig down deep and transform those inner obstacles to a win-win situation. Easier said than done, but this is able to be accomplished.

I have lived this experience. my business partner and I were in the depths of despair when we thought our venture was on the verge of bankruptcy. Everything we tried seemed to fail, and we found ourselves going down psychologically and emotionally. It finally dawned on us one day that we were falling into the same old trap that we always discussed we would fight against.

I clearly remember the day of that revelation. In one sense, we laughed, and then we picked ourselves up. We realized that the answer was actually deep inside us and we needed to return to the excitement and tenacity we promised each other to have. It went beyond the fact that we had mouths to feed at home. It was more the absolute resolve that no matter the obstacle, we would tackle it with strength and, yes, grit. It would be great to say that everything from that moment was perfect. It was not.

There were a lot of uphill battles to overcome. However, once in the "we will never give up" mode, we never looked back. A tenacious person is always looking ahead. It is too easy to go back and look at the mistakes of yesterday. The real test of one's fortitude is to see if you are able to overcome the feelings of failure and/or discouragement, and move to the next level. If so, then a great deal has been accomplished. I am not saying this will lead you to instant prosperity, but it levels the playing field, and allows you to more resolutely see the possibilities.

Ultimately, the decision to be a person with the qualities I discussed is a decision that rests with each person who decides to embark on an adventure of entrepreneurship. There are those for whom success has come easily. Of course, remember, how do you define success? There are those that struggle, and there are those who are unable to continue on their venture for one reason or the other. That does not mean that they have failed. However, you owe it to yourself to begin with the right attitude and maintain it along the way. Climb the mountain, keep strong, and do not look back!

About Phil

Phil Cioppa is the Managing Principal of a full service financial services firm located in Norwalk, CT and Harrisburg, PA. With over 10 years of financial services experience, he has served as a Certified Trust and Financial Advisor and has distinguished himself among his peers as a top advisor prior to co-founding Arbol Financial Strategies. Phil brings a proprietary and unique client- centered approach and a sense of humor to his work as a financial advisor. He is very passionate about his work with clients and as Chief Investment Officer, he specializes in asset management strategies, insurance planning and taxation issues.

Prior to starting his journey in financial services, Phil pursued his passion for religious studies with a Bachelor of Arts from State University of New York at Albany, Masters of Divinity at St. Bernard's Institute in Rochester and his Doctor of Ministry from Graduate Theological Foundation in Mishawaka, Indiana. Phil served as a Roman Catholic Priest for 18 ½ years, leaving active ministry in excellent standing to pursue his new passage.

Phil has been seen as a guest expert on "*The Brian Tracy Show*" featured on ABC, NBC, CBS and FOX, as well as being named as a "Trendsetter in the New Economy" by *USA Today*. He regularly appears on TV on FOX Business and FOXNews.com TV. He also is featured weekly on two nationally-syndicated radio shows, The Lars Larsen Show and Live with Bill Martinez, as well as numerous regional and local radio programs. He is currently co-author of a book with Brian Tracy, as well as another book with Jack Canfield (author of *Chicken Soup for the Soul*), which will be launched this year at The National Academy of Best-Selling Authors.

The *Phil Cioppa Show* is syndicated via BusinessTalk Radio Network, Radio-Linx and Cable Radio Network to over 145 markets. Phil is married to a wonderful wife, Janie and lives in Danbury, CT.

CHAPTER 55

Turn the Tables on Toxic Workplace

By Dr. Serena Reep

I frequently ask senior project managers and corporate executives: "How many of your direct reports would come to work tomorrow if they won a million dollars in the lottery tonight?" Many of them candidly confess: "not too many." In fact, I had a few go a step further and say: "Heck, I wouldn't come to work if I won a million dollars in the lottery tonight. How can I expect my team to be any different?"

The question, as well as the answers, has profound implications for one of the most challenging issues of our time: the employee engagement. This single question says a lot more than a hundred surveys on worker satisfaction, employee morale and commitment to work. When your job is simply a way to pay your bills and nothing more, any job will do. When the work is not a source of identity and self actualization, it simply becomes a commodity. And, understandably, the highest bidder gets your loyalty for the day. When purpose and passion are lacking from the work we do, it becomes just a job that pays the bills. People are more likely to trade their bodies and time for the paycheck but not their hearts and souls. This is the nature of the toxic workplace.

In fact, according to the PricewaterhouseCoopers' 2010 data, 33% of the US workforce is highly disengaged. So the problem of disenchantment and disconnect from work has become a serious issue for corporations. It has been reported in books, articles and surveys that a great majority of the American workers are only partially engaged and only 12 % are "fully engaged" with their jobs. This is not strictly a U.S. phenomenon either; it has indeed become a worldwide trend. In Germany, for example, surveys have shown that 79 to 90% of the employees report feeling disengaged from their work.

WHAT IS ENGAGEMENT?

Engagement is the commitment to another person, or a purpose, higher than oneself. For our purposes, we can define it as a bond between people working in a team or on a project based on shared sense of belonging, shared identity and empathy. Michael Stallard, in his book *Fired Up or Burned Out*, defines the process of engagement as a move from self-centered identity to group-centered identity.

Generally we can identify people as one of these three types of employees:

Engaged–these are passionate, connected, and actively working on contributing to the group's performance.

Not engaged–these are marginally, if at all, involved with their work (this is what my primary school teacher used to call "body present, mind absent").

Actively disengaged–not only are these alienated from the work they do, but their unhappiness is disruptive of others and is a cancer on the group's morale.

A toxic workplace is one where a great majority of the workers are either not engaged or actively disengaged, to the point of causing morale problems and disenchantment for even the most dedicated of employees. The dominant culture of such an organization has built-in disincentives to become or stay engaged and be passionate about work.

CULTURE OF "ESPRIT DE CORPS"

Recently someone asked me at a conference, "How do we keep engaged employees motivated?" This is like putting the cart before the horse. Motivation is a precursor to engagement, not the other way around. That is, motivation to engage comes first and then the resultant behavior is engagement and identification with the work. A culture of mutuality and cooperation acts as a motivator and a predictor of employee engagement.

Competition is the very backbone of the American enterprise system. "May the best ideas, the best products and best processes win" has been the long-standing American credo. However, there is an important place for *cooperation* in the workplace. The virtues and the importance of cooperation are evident in creating and nurturing employee morale and increased performance. *Collaboration* is the most important cultural ingredient in fostering employee engagement. When a corporate culture emphasizes cooperation within and between teams, there is a greater opportunity for employee engagement and job satisfaction.

But as long as employee engagement remains an "initiative," it is clearly an alien concept trying to fit into the current culture–a proverbial square peg trying to fit in a round hole. On the other hand, when a fully engaged workforce is the pervasive mode of operation in a corporation, and all the systems and processes in the corporation are designed to automatically create and sustain a culture of engagement, no further initiatives are needed. At that point, the engagement principle has become woven into the very fabric of the corporation.

In recent years, team building exercises have become a standard staple in the HR world as a way of humanizing the work environment and creating greater engagement at the workplace. I asked some of my colleagues to recount and evaluate their team-building experiences.

One colleague told me about his recent team building experience.

"We went to a half-day, offsite picnic. There was a weeklong preparation, planning and buying food, collecting recipes, arranging for a place to hold the picnic, keeping track of who would and would not attend the event, number of cars needed for transportation to the picnic site, and of course the logistics of cooking, serving food and cleaning up afterwards. This could have served as a great metaphor for the team to work together and reap the benefits beyond the picnic experience. But somehow this does not translate into a more effective cooperative group at work. Once the picnic is over, we are back to the same "each to their own" modus operandi. We look forward to next year's picnic but don't see the connection of the picnic to our everyday work. We see it simply as a break from the work routine."

Another colleague spoke of his experience:

"We have two team building exercises in a year–one in the spring and one in the fall. We hold it at a hotel. It is a nice catered event, and lots of fun stuff to do. But the highlight of the event is when we all sit in a circle and talk about ourselves. We are supposed to reveal something about ourselves that our teammates don't know. This time the theme was what annoys us the most. One person said she is annoyed with all the burnt popcorn smell from the office kitchen and it distracts her from work. Another person said he gets ticked off when someone cuts him off on the road on his way to work and that ruins his day. I am not sure how these revelations create a sense of camaraderie. But we keep doing these team building exercises anyway. Most of us see this as a way to get out of the office and nothing more."

Most team building efforts are a forced exercise done at some retreat or hotel conference room away from the office and from the everyday work life. After the off-site exercise, we come back to the real world of work and everything is the same as it was the day before.

Ongoing engagement is done every day face-to-face with people you work with on a daily basis–people whose livelihood is intricately tied to your own, and whose success will impact your own success. A new living breathing culture of caring, compassion and camaraderie takes time to implement and nurture. But when it is done right, it is the best antidote to a toxic workplace, one that provides long term dividends on the corporate investment.

As a side note, let me add that there is nothing wrong with giving people a break from work on a regular basis. The only problem is when this is seen as automatically "building a team spirit" or *esprit de corps*. It can't do that. Of course, the only thing worse than assuming it will cure the ills of disengagement is if this is the *only* "initiative" the HR engages in all year and expects the magic of team spirit to envelope the group and drive away the spirit of disengagement. No *one thing* is the cure-all.

BOB'S STORY

Bob is a middle-aged executive in a multi-national corporation. He came to me when he was at the end of his wits, worried sick that he was going to lose his job, his marriage and his life. He was clinically depressed and completely disengaged from his work.

He had seen several waves of layoffs all around him in his company. He witnessed his best friend have a heart attack at work and die before the ambulance arrived. He slowly started to withdraw emotionally from work. And the negative downward spiral continued. His wife served notice that she was going to leave him. The fear of losing his job and his wife actually paralyzed him and marginalized him even further from his work. Ironically his disengagement at work was giving his supervisors every excuse to do what he was most afraid of–fire him.

Bob was feeling powerless to steer his ship in the direction that he knows he needs. He was frozen in place. He was being tossed around by the strong winds of circumstances. His life balance was off kilter. His world was collapsing under its own weight. The macroeconomic turmoil added fuel to the fire and caused him to wonder if giving a lifetime of loyalty and commitment to the corporation was the right thing to do.

MARTHA'S STORY

Contrast Bob's with Martha's story. A clear example of what a "fully engaged employee" looks like.

Martha was the most pleasant, vibrant, and positive woman I've ever met. She was a volunteer at a cancer awareness charity. She didn't make a dime from her work but somehow you knew her sentiment was worth more than a paycheck. She helped, she advised, she rolled up her sleeves, she marched, raised money and answered the phones when needed. Martha was the perfect employee who wasn't hired. I couldn't help but wonder why more people like Martha weren't actually working at a for-profit company. How can we bottle her incredible attitude and infectious optimism? Why is the nine-to-five worker largely unhappy and disengaged from work while this unpaid woman is eager to get to work every morning? Why?

There is clearly a lack of meaning and passion, lack of relevance, in their jobs, compared to Martha's. Everything Martha did as a volunteer had meaning and was fueled by inspiration. She had beaten the breast cancer that took her mother. Her motivation was not only personal but positively vengeful. After seven years of intense chemo, losing all her hair, her confidence and her marriage, she had one chance left. That chance came in the form of a little known alternative cancer treatment used widely in Asia. She traveled there as a last resort, and this became her saving grace. Now back in the U.S., Martha had made it an obsession to have alternative remedies approved by the FDA, so other women can have access to treatment options. She was passionate and unrelenting. She squeezed more productivity out of one day than most people do in a month, because she found meaning for her remaining days here on earth. Using Stallard's continuum of engagement, we can see Bob is a classic example of the "burnt out" end of the engagement spectrum while Martha is on the "fired up" end of the spectrum.

Who is responsible for Employee Engagement?

The answer is: *every one.*

Engagement can be affected at three levels:

1. Individual level
2. Supervisor / manager level
3. Corporate level

Each of the above is, individually and mutually, responsible for the creation of the esprit de corps, and the full engagement of the talents and resources.

THE INDIVIDUAL

One can ask why engagement is important to the individual. After all, it is the corporation's bottom-line that benefits from an engaged workforce.

Engagement and passion for the work has significant implications for the mental health of the individual. The brain holds the key to how the worker's emotional engagement is processed by the body. There are four major areas of the brain: the frontal lobe, the anterior cingulate, the parietal lobe, and the limbic system. Activation of the first two is associated with positive effects on health. Activation of the last two is associated with negative effects on health.

Passion and commitment to ideas and work that is bigger than our selves and our personal interests seems to stimulate the frontal lobe, help keep it healthy, and prevent age-related decline. The anterior cingulate is activated when we feel empathy and compassion for others. The activity in the parietal lobes gives us a sense of self awareness but it can also activate a feeling of alienation from others and loneliness. The time we spend in camaraderie with others, engage in social activities and completing group tasks can disengage the parietal lobes. This helps to forget our problems and instead feel love and compassion for others. The limbic system is where negative emotions such as anger, fear, and resentment are produced. So, being actively engaged in other people and social causes and passion for work can greatly reduce these tendencies and contribute to increased optimism and positive mental attitude.

The more we diminish activity in our parietal lobes and limbic system and at the same time increase the activity in the frontal lobe and anterior cingulate, our chances of happiness and optimism increase and physical health improves. So commitment and engagement with work pays significant dividends to the employee, not just the employer.

MANAGE PEOPLE, NOT PROJECTS

Project managers are trained in the mechanics of project management–how to bring a project or product to successful completion on time and under budget. But not as much emphasis is placed on *people management*. In order to create a culture in which the individual thrives and gets emotionally engaged, the manager is required to be trained in emotional intelligence, not just spreadsheet intelligence. Studies have shown that how the supervisor treats the employees is the most critical factor in employees feeling engaged with the work and with the group. Open and honest communication is critical for creating an environment of trust and commitment.

Learning to deal with the emotional component of people, their unique circumstances, motivations and interpersonal skills helps the supervisors to leverage the human resources to the benefit of the organization and the individual concurrently. Unless it is a win for all, it is a win for none.

CORPORATION

In his book *Good for Business: Rise of a Conscious Corporation,* Andrew Benett shows that a culture of transparency and engagement is critical for the corporation to survive and thrive in the new millennium. He lists the following four cornerstones of the Conscious Corporation:

- Purpose Beyond Profit
- Humanized Leadership
- Corporate Consciousness
- Collaborative Partnerships

It is clear that corporations need to create and nurture the culture of engagement and humanized communication channels within and between groups to reduce toxicity in the workplace and increase employee morale, job satisfaction and increased commitment.

How do we turn the tables on the toxicity in the workplace? As we have seen, the creation of a positive, vibrant environment in the workplace is good for everyone. My proprietary training program pulls together all the threads of evidence and proposes the 5-Rs of employee engagement. This provides the framework for a cultural transformation where the employees will not only give their time and body, but also their heart and soul:

- Respect
- Reward
- Recognition
- Relevance
- Relationship

There are no quick fixes for a long standing, deeply entrenched problem of employee morale and engagement. But it is possible to transform a culture of a corporation to meet the challenges of the new millennium with the 5-Rs program. A fully engaged workforce is good for the organization as well as the individual. A culture built around the 5-Rs is a starting point for this transformation.

About Serena Reep, Ph.D., PMP

Dr. Serena Reep is the President of Transformational Communications. She is an Ex-College Professor, communication and relationship management coach, corporate project management trainer, author and motivational speaker. She considers herself a social-entrepreneur and likes to promote social causes in all her ventures.

Serena Reep received her Ph.D. in Social Psychology. Her specialization is Social Structure and Personality. She also holds an active PMP (Project Management Professional) certification. She frequently speaks on best practices in communication for successful project management as well as successful interpersonal relationship management. She spent eight years as a Professor at Rutgers University, and has been a consultant in the corporate world for almost two decades. She has worked as a contractor/consultant for clients ranging from private corporations such as CA, NCS and IBM to government agencies such as the DOE, CMS and FDIC.

Dr. Serena has been seen on NBC, CBS, ABC and Fox affiliates. She is an Expert Blogger for *Fast Company* and the *Huffington Post.* Her book *Work-Life Balance is DEAD!* is a very thought-provoking and paradigm-shifting manifesto on living an authentic life, unfettered by the weight of outmoded constructs about balancing work and life. She also sounds a wake-up call to the corporations on the effectiveness of the work-life balance perks they provide and offers a fresh perspective on increasing their ROI.

Serena's current mission is to raise "One Million $ in One Year" for charities. To learn more about this project or to contact Dr. Serena Reep for your speaking or training needs, please visit http://www.serenasez.com.

CHAPTER 56

Completely Organize All of Your Stuff in a Half Day – 10 Steps to Less Stress and More Success

By Steve Norton

It was now clear; "Larry" (a soon to be client whose name has been changed) was going to fail high school. February had arrived and with only four months to go, Larry, his parents, and teachers had all come to the same conclusion. With so much work still to be done, so many different things in so many different areas, there was no way Larry was going to finish in time to graduate with his classmates. In fact, just thinking about all the projects, classes, papers, quizzes, tests, and other things that had to be done gave Larry a headache and made his head spin. Too many things to do and many overdue, too many things that all had to be done *now*, everything seemed critical, *nothing* could be ignored. The proverbial elephant was alive and well, standing directly in front of Larry; just daring to be eaten.

And it was then, as in all good stories, that the miracle occurred. Not just a run of the mill, everyday miracle, but a true bona fide, just-in-the-nick-of-time miracle; one that in hindsight doesn't even look like a miracle. What once was completely impossible became, within a matter of hours, not just possible but *probable*!

In less than four hours, Larry and I laid out all the actions that needed to be completed to finish high school and then laid those actions over time. A couple of short iterations later, a specific road map was in place that Larry could follow like a yellow brick road. Sure it would take some effort; I mean you still have to *do* the schoolwork to graduate. But what once appeared impossible and chaotic was now a very clear road map to success.

The beauty of the process we went through is both in the simplicity and in the fact that it can be used for large businesses, small businesses, entrepreneurs, or individuals like you. I've used it with clients from a number of industries and with people from varying experience levels.

The miracle came disguised as a roll end of newsprint, bought for $3.50 from the local newspaper. About four feet wide, the roll becomes waste when it gets down to about a hundred feet long, because they don't want it to run out during printing. One man's waste is another man's miracle as they say (or they *should* say, at least).

Here is how you turn despair, depression, overwhelming challenges, and newsprint into success. You simply turn them into the Triple A's of **Areas**, **Activities**, and **Actions**. The **Areas** are the main areas you want to organize, **Activities** are the next level of detail, and **Actions** are the lowest level of detail–the specific tasks by a date to get you where you want to go.

Tape a big piece of newsprint (6'-8' long) up on the wall and double the thickness so the marking pens don't bleed through. As cool as this will end up, it will get old after a few months, if permanent ink bleeds through the newsprint onto your wall.

Step 1: Decide how much of your world you want to organize. In this case we could have taken Larry's entire world including church activities, scouts, etc. or we could have narrowed it down to one class he was having trouble with. But the part of his world he needed to get his hands around was "all of school." Err on the side of making your scope too big rather than too small if in doubt, because it's better to manage all the factors critical for success (and maybe a few extras) rather than to leave some out and be surprised at the end.

Step 2: Across the top of the newsprint list the 4-7 main **Areas** that make up the world you are addressing (use all the room across the newsprint). In Larry's case, these were the seven classes required to graduate. For others clients I have seen this top level include the person's job, volunteer roles, personal projects underway, house projects, relationship(s), night school, acquiring a professional certification, etc. The **Areas** you identify should fully encompass the world you want to organize. If Larry had only included only 5 of his 7 classes, he'd have set himself up for failure by not planning for and tracking two **Areas** critical for his success (passing 5 of 7 classes does not lead to graduation ceremonies at most schools).

Step 3: Pick one of the 4-7 main **Areas** (e.g. "Senior Project" which was one of the seven classes in this example) and below it list 4-7 main **Activities** that have to be completed to complete that **Area**. Again, these 4-7 **Activities** should encompass all that needs to be done to complete that **Area**. For example, the senior project **Area** might include **Activities** such as: get topic approved, acquire pilot's license, prepare report, create photo collage, and produce Power Point presentation.

Step 4: For each of the **Activities**, develop and list the 4-7 **Actions** that have to be taken to complete that **Activity**. Continuing this example, the **Actions** required to "acquire pilot's license" might include, complete ground school, complete final 8 hours flying time, complete solo touch-and-goes, and pass final exam. **Action** steps should be verb/noun and be specific such as "produce Power Point presentation" so you know exactly what it means a week or month from now. If you just write "presentation" you'll later wonder if this was "start the presentation", "draft the presentation", "send presentation out for comments", etc. Your mind has a way of playing tricks on you when you leave yourself wiggle room. Complete all **Actions** for all **Activities** for all **Areas**.

Step 5: Assign a date to each **Action**. This will be a combination of working forward and backward. Have a calendar handy that you have marked existing commitments on e.g. vacations, holidays, scheduled events, etc., so you have a realistic view of times available to work on your stuff. Give it your best shot. It won't be perfect, but you'll adjust it soon.

Working forward is the typical, "If I start this on the 10th, I can complete it by the 20th and then I'll start the next action which will take me until the 30th..." etc. Working backwards is useful when you have deadlines or hard constraints. For example, "School ends on June 6, so I'll want to hand in all senior project material by May 31. That means I'll want to have completed my pilot's license exam by May 23 (to allow a few days buffer before the Memorial Day holiday), therefore I'll target completing my touch-and-goes by May 9, my final 8 hours of flight time by May 1, and ground school by April 15."

Step 6: After assigning dates to all **Actions**, give it a sanity check and revise the dates. Depending on your time horizon, go through the list of **Actions** and highlight everything that takes place in the first third or quarter of your total time window. For example, our total time window was 4 months, so we highlighted everything due in the first month. Now look at each of those highlighted dates and see if they are reasonably spread out. Sometimes they'll be grouped at the end of a month with little due during the month. Adjust these dates so the **Actions** are more evenly spaced out, yet still serve your needs. Now do this for the next thirds (or quarters) until you've adjusted all **Actions** as needed.

Step 7: Put up a new piece of doubled newsprint, just like the first, and keep the first one where you can still see it. Save about ¼ of the left side of this new one to write **Actions** on and then across the top (the right ¾) make a calendar (usually in weeks but whatever increments you need to encompass your timeline). In the example above, we had a 4-month total window so we made about 16 entries of "week ending ...2/4, 2/11, 2/18, 2/25..." etc.

Step 8: Begin listing the **Action** steps down the left ¼ of the paper (the space that you saved for this purpose) and putting an "X" under the week that each is due. Sometimes it makes sense to reword an **Action** slightly to break it up further and make it easier to track. For example, if the **Action** "complete 8 hours flight time" is due for completion 8 weeks from now, you might want to write the **Action** as "complete 2 hours flight time" and then put an "X" every other week so you're sure to track it more closely. Continue this for the rest of the **Actions**.

Step 9: Marvel at your work! This is a colossal achievement! You have identified everything necessary to succeed and you've laid it out over a time horizon that makes sense. Celebrate this milestone by taking someone out to dinner! Now take a piece of paper and write down the things you have to complete in weeks 1, 2, and 3. These are the things that get put in your day planner (on the days you need to be working on them), onto your to-do list with due dates, into your iPhone task list, or whatever system you use to keep track of what needs to be done. What type of system you use is not nearly as important as the fact that you *use a system*. I've helped people set up systems, but that's another chapter.

Step 10: Each week on the newsprint, check off the completed **Actions**. Pull another week's **Activities** into your planner or onto your to-do list. Adjust as needed. Sometimes you won't complete an **Action** exactly when planned, so establish a new date that works in the overall plan. The best planned schedules are seldom (if ever) executed as originally written. The most important feature is that you have a schedule and a plan to measure your progress against. If you're a week behind on something, you will know it and you can ask yourself, "What do I need to do to hold my end date?" Sometimes the answer is "Finishing this **Action** 5 days late will be okay." Or the answer might be, "Since I'm going to be 5 days late completing this **Action**, I'm going to have to complete my 8 hours flight time 2 days faster than I'd planned and my touch-and-goes 3 days faster than I'd planned."

Extra Credit: After developing it on the newsprint, I actually transfer my clients' work onto an Excel spreadsheet. I find it easier to add new **Actions**, update status, sort by **Area**, by **Activity**, or by date depending on how we want to view it. Not everyone is a spreadsheet wizard so I've created a Triple A's Fast Track Worksheet that you can download for free at my website (see Resources section below).

Summary: Every single one of us faces the challenge of juggling too many things in what seems like a limited amount of time. Without clear organization and a plan to get from where you are to your goal, these things often stack up into that elephant that others tell us to eat one bite at a time. But we have to know where to start biting, how many bites per day or week we need to make, and halfway through the carcass, we need to know we are either on track to have it out of the living room before the anniversary party or that we need to make adjustments to our eating plan.

I've done this for individuals, for non-profit organization boards of directors, and for growing companies; the principles are the same. We scope out the world we want to get a better handle on, break that up into the 4-7 main **Areas** that are involved, break each of those down into the 4-7 main **Activities** required for **Area** success, and then break each **Activity** down into the 4-7 specific **Actions** that will be taken to complete the **Activity**. The importance of "4-7" is that if you have less than four you are probably still up at too high a level and need to be thinking in more detail. If you have more than seven, then you've gotten down into the weeds too quickly and you won't see the forest for the trees. Those aren't absolute numbers but they are a very good rule of thumb that you should think twice about before violating.

Why bother to spend the time (and therefore money) to do this? The benefit is not the organization itself; the benefits are the dramatically reduced stress you will experience by having a clear plan in place to work from and the dramatically improved success you will experience because of the thought process you will have gone through. Any journey will be more successful with a good map; any person or business will be more successful with a well-developed plan of action. Schedule a time to do this right now. In the overall scheme of things, this upfront investment of your time is likely to give you the biggest return on investment that you have experienced to date.

Resources: You can go to my website (http://stevenortonpmp.com/) and get a template to use (8.5" X 11") to draft up the **Areas** and **Activities** for the newsprint. I also have a Triple A's Fast Track Worksheet you can populate if you choose to use that as your tracking method rather than, or in conjunction with, a day planner or to-do list. Feel free to contact me for help too (steve@stevenortonpmp.com). Sometimes a little one-on-one explanation goes a long ways.

About Steve

Steve Norton, PMP, is one of the most highly rated instructors and speakers in his field. Steve Norton has become a regular request for dozens of Fortune 500 companies when it comes to growing their project management skills and developing their staff to become more successful. He's also known as the "go-to guy" for small businesses, entrepreneurs, and professionals who want to turn great ideas into reality.

Well known for his organization, planning, and execution skills, Steve Norton has helped senior managers from global companies, entrepreneurs, and students of all ages. He provides simple tools, techniques, and practices that help organize thoughts and ideas, prepare meaningful goals that lead to the desired destination, plan out the actions necessary to accomplish those goals, and complete and track those actions in a simple fashion. Clients and students alike have commented on Steve's ability to make complex topics understandable and on his ability to use real life stories to make the key points memorable.

As a senior manager for several of the Fortune 500 companies, Steve Norton has had the opportunity to lead a variety of organizations including strategic planning, financial, scheduling, plant operations, and facility startups. He's managed large nuclear waste processing facilities, he's been the project manager for award winning fast track projects, and he's been responsible for portfolios of projects valued in the hundreds of millions of dollars. He's also started up several profitable companies as an entrepreneur.

With a Master of Sciences degree in Project Management from Boston University and a Project Management Professional (PMP) certification from the Project Management Institute (PMI), Steve Norton volunteers on the Board of Directors for the local PMI chapter and teaches project management based courses. Steve has trained with America's #1 Success Coach Jack Canfield, co-creator of the *Chicken Soup for the Soul* book series and author of the best-selling book, *The Success Principles*. Jack also interviewed Steve for an instructional video series including other contributors such as James Malinchak (author and star of ABC television's hit series, *Secret Millionaire, Season One*) and Timothy Ferris (author of *The 4-Hour Work Week*).

Steve Norton has a unique perspective from this diverse background. He's combined a lifetime of experience with his study of success principles and other best practices to help people from all walks of life become more effective. He helps people and companies discern the important "needle movers" from the noise and brings focus to the few critical elements. Steve is one of the best at organizing multiple priorities, developing a plan, and giving others the tools and knowledge required to execute the plan. A resident of Richland, Washington, Steve Norton frequently travels to conferences and events worldwide.

For more information see http://stevenortonpmp.com/.

CHAPTER 57

Leverage Your <u>ASS</u>ets: Win From Behind!

By Dr. Veronica Anderson

If you follow the crowd, you might get lost in it.
— Author Unknown

Yes, the underlining in this chapter title *is* intentional....and yes, this is almost definitely the most unusual title you'll come across in this book!

But there's a very *big branding* idea behind this title, as well as an unexpected Success Secret. And I promise, we won't go beyond a PG-13 rating here.

A few years ago, I realized I was very unhappy and needed to take my life in a totally new direction. I wanted to pursue a high-profile media career, and I wanted to make sure I succeeded in that pursuit.

Luckily I knew, from my training as a physician, the absolute necessity of getting instruction and direction from experts—the kind of people I like to call "Masters," because they're at the top of their game in their specific fields and understand what it takes to succeed.

One of the Masters I was lucky enough to discuss my new life plan with was someone I continue to work with to this day: LeGrande Green, an Emmy-award winning producer who worked with the legendary Oprah. He, as well as others, advised me to do one thing before anything else: *Develop my brand.*

517

That advice was so incredibly right.

Branding myself properly helped me achieve many of my personal and professional goals in an incredibly short time. Many of you might know me from my weekly internet radio show, "Wellness for the Real World." I'm happy to report its growth has been explosive, with an estimated 33 million listeners weekly outside the U.S. and 5 to 7 million inside the U.S. As a matter of fact, it's been rated as the *number one* internet radio health show.

I believe a big reason for that is I deal with issues bluntly and honestly— it's a big part of *my* brand. I don't believe in dancing around controversy. We dish on relationships, diet and fitness, spiritual growth, corporate responsibility, and more—anything that affects our lives and our overall "wellness" in a profound way.

I see that as a very positive aspect of my brand. Unfortunately, I wasn't applying my trademark honesty and bluntness to *another* aspect of my brand that I wanted to just go away. As a matter of fact, I tried very hard *to* make it go away. Then I stopped worrying and learned to love...

...my big butt.

DEALING WITH THE END

I am a black woman. And we black women, quite frankly, are well known for having...well, some extra padding on our posteriors. And we just have to accept that, right?

Wrong. The truth of the matter was...*I was ashamed of it.*

Why should I be ashamed? Well, despite this facet of my physicality being celebrated in such timeless classics as the old Sir Mix-A-Lot song, "Baby's Got Back," our society actually hasn't been all that supportive of women with larger "features." As I write these words, the James Cameron classic, "Titanic" has been re-released in theatres in 3D—and people were actually commenting online about Kate Winslet being "fat" in that movie.

Of course, that's only the tip of the iceberg, pun intended. You need only look at magazine covers, fashion and cosmetic ads, and the vast majority of leading ladies in TV shows and movies to know that the popular ideal of a woman's body image is severely underfed—no hips, no thighs and *no butts*!

I don't mean to be glib about this, because it does seriously affect every woman's consciousness. At worst, it causes some of us to develop eating disorders, and at best, we're confronted with the results of the survey posed on an episode of the "Family Feud" game show, "What do women worry about the most?" Number one answer? Weight!

So I wasn't alone in wanting to lose some curves. The problem was that, no matter how fervently I dedicated myself to the task, I was losing to nature.

And recently, I finally decided it was a battle I *should* lose.

ACCEPTING MY ASSET

It took me way too long to come to grips with something that probably seems very obvious to men; real women tend not to have the shape (or the lack of shape!) of the women on the magazine covers. I've also discovered that most men don't mind this fact - they *like* some curves, as a matter of fact.

Now, after all this, you, the reader, are probably wondering...*what the hell does this have to do with branding???*

Simple. A big reason I came to accept my ample rear end is that I realized my brand should encompass *everything* about me—including that particular part. I'm Dr. Veronica. I'm a radio host, a writer, a coach, and a guest on national talk shows. I have a black belt in tae kwon do and I've run two marathons. And, I am a black woman with a shapely butt.

So, now, I don't mind turning around and showing the back of me - because I've decided to embrace *all* of me as something positive and part of my overall USP (Unique Selling Proposition). Because I believe in using everything you have as part of your brand, even if it's something that at first glance might appear to be a negative.

Why is that important? And aren't you really hurting your brand by including something that might make you look bad in other people's eyes?

Not at all.

Here's why. People buy people. Relationships make things happen. Potential customers will buy your products, will buy your services, will opt for your coaching, will go for whatever you have to offer...*if they like you.*

And they like you if they can *identify* with you. If they can see you're a human being who has things about you that aren't all perfect and polished. Think about it. Who have you bonded with the most closely in the past? Someone who tried to pass themselves off as not having any faults, or someone who might share some of your shortcomings?

For example, I'm talking to a lot of women on my radio show. It goes without saying there are plenty of them out there who have some real shape to their rear ends too. Isn't it going to be more interesting to them if I admit and talk about my own? Aren't they going to bond with me on a deeper level, knowing that I'm no different from them?

The fact is you can use everything about you to advance your brand, to make yourself more memorable and more likable. When people have something in common with you, they are more likely to buy from you. Many of the biggest branding successes proudly fly their freak flags high and turn their negatives into lucrative positives.

Let's talk about a few of them!

TURNING NEGATIVES TO POSITIVES

Would you ever imagine a fat black woman who was the victim of sexual abuse when she was young would become an incredible national rags-to-riches story—as well as a hugely inspirational figure to millions of women of every race, creed and color?

You don't have to imagine it, because Oprah Winfrey is a very genuine reality. We know all these things about her might ordinarily be seen as a negative, but really are symbols of her triumph over her humble beginnings. They're all vital aspects of *her* unique USP—the qualities that allow the world to identify with and admire her.

Of course, she's not famous because of all that—she also happens to be incredibly talented as an entrepreneur, as a business woman, as a TV host and interviewer. But the other things are what make people *love her,* and a huge reason why she's become one of the biggest superstars of all time.

Oprah positively overflows with warmth and empathy, so it's easy to love her in a way we can't love some brash arrogant white man who only brags about how much money he makes. Some guy who's ruthless and doesn't hesitate to fire someone when it needs to be done.

Well, actually, we *can* love a guy like that—if it's Donald Trump.

Think of all the negatives that the Donald carries around him. Seriously. He's always getting into public feuds with other celebrities, his personality is always being mocked and—let's get real,—*he always has that weird hair thing going on.*

And yet, his popular network show, "The Apprentice," has run for 12 seasons. He has a best-selling book out every year or so. Everyone around the world pays him a pretty penny just to put the Trump name on their developments and products, even though he doesn't put a single dime into those projects.

His arrogance, his ruthlessness, his flaunting of his wealth and, yes, even that thing that's on the top of his head, are all things that actually *endear* him to us. People may say they dislike him, but *they can't stop watching him.*

And people can't stop giving him money.

MIXING IT UP AND PUTTING IT ALL TOGETHER

There's something else about branding that I need to stop and address here. People say that in order to build an effective brand, you have to pick *one* thing and stick to it.

Again, totally incorrect.

To create your brand, you need to figure out *all* the things special about you and package it into a compelling combination. The two people we just talked about, Oprah and Donald Trump, can't just be reduced to one-dimensional cartoons; they're both complex people known for their strong and interesting personalities as well as their wide variety of accomplishments.

Another person who's created an amazing brand by putting all his attributes together in a powerful package is Sean Combs, who you may know better by a few of his stage names, such as Puff Daddy, P. Diddy and, yes, just plain Diddy.

He gained his fame for being a music performer and producer—but since then, he's become known for TV shows such as the ABC/MTV reality show, "The Making of the Band," his own vodka label, Circ Vodka, his own award-winning clothing line, Sean John, and his legendary annual White Party, which has an all-white dress code and features a white carpet instead of a red carpet. He talks up (and sings about) such luxury items as Cristal and the super-elite American Express card, the Centurion "black card." He's even raised money for charity by running in the New York City Marathon.

Just focus on one thing for an awesome brand? How about a couple thousand things?

Combs' brand appeals to others' wannabe entrepreneurial aspirations. He's just another form of Trump's success brand—a brand that encompasses a multitude of endeavors all combined to create a great effect.

It's a concept that Dr. Nido Qubein, a business consultant and educator, calls "intentional congruence." He works with a bread company, a furniture company, a bank and many other business ventures, he's the president of High Point University, and is also one of the most well-paid success coaches in the world. And he makes it a priority to make sure that all these different pursuits feed into each other and make the whole bigger than the sum of the parts, just as Sean Combs does.

That's intentional congruence and that's how you build a powerful brand. And the people I'm talking about here are the Masters that can teach you how to make it happen at an incredibly high level.

ADVANCING YOUR BRAND

My advice to anyone who wants to achieve a successful brand is to bring people into your life to help you figure out *what* your brand truly is. Outside experts, skilled at branding, can be objective about your qualities and help you identify what works for your brand.

And remember, even if you don't think you have a brand—you do. Ask anybody who knows you to contribute to your brand conversation as well. They might surprise you with their ideas gained just from spending a lot of time in your company.

There will be four stages to your brand trajectory, if it is successful:

Stage 1: Brand Awareness
People become aware of your brand and what it's all about.

Stage 2: Brand Preference
People begin to choose *you* over the competition because of your brand.

Stage 3: Brand Insistence
People *have* to buy from you because of your successful brand (think of Apple and the peer pressure to own an iPad or iPhone).

Stage 4: Brand Advocacy
This is the ultimate goal—where people tell others that they *must* buy your brand because it's the best (again, when the iPhone first came out, how many people told you that you *have* to get one??).

You only reach Stage 4 when you employ intentional congruence and leverage your assets into a meaningful, potent and attractive brand. This is where the experts really come in handy when it comes to pointing you in the right direction to achieve this lofty level—and can also provide the needed exposure to the right media.

COACHING FOR LIFE

I learned a lot from these experts—including the man whose name is in the title of this book, Jack Canfield.

You might think *Chicken Soup for the Soul* is the lynchpin of his brand, but not to me. I think success through perseverance is his real message. The initial "Chicken Soup" book was rejected *over one hundred and forty times*. Yet, he didn't stop until he did get it published. And now, as of this writing, there are over 200 titles in this series—an incredible branding success story.

In 2010, I joined the Jack Canfield coaching program. A year later, I told my success coach that one day I would write a book with Jack Canfield. Well, out of nowhere, a few months later, that opportunity unexpectedly came my way—and the result is the chapter you're reading now. That's what I like to call the "Law of Attraction *and* Taking Action!"

Today, I work with renowned success coach Mike Collier. I enjoy working with talented coaches who tell me the truth and hold me accountable, even as they inspire and motivate me to greater heights. Also, I enjoy sharing all they've taught me when I coach my clients.

Yes, even people like me who coach professionally continue to have coaches and advisors in their lives. Just as top athletes like Tiger Woods and LeBron James retain many high-paid coaches to reach new levels of excellences, all of us require objective outside help to keep us moving forward. I will always coach, and I will always be coached.

Because we always need someone in our lives willing to kick us in the butt—no matter how big that butt might be!

Talent is hitting a target no one else can hit.
Genius is hitting a target no one else can see.
—Author Unknown

About Veronica

Dr. Veronica Anderson is the new generation of medicine; she transcends all boundaries with her passion for wellness through her unique brand of Social Media Medicine™. Through her artfully blended and controversial perspectives, Dr. Veronica shares her belief that wellness encompasses everything from mind, body and spirit to happiness, personal growth, sex and relationships.

Currently with a listener base of over 30 million worldwide weekly on BlogTalkRadio and Old Grumpy Radio Networks, her popularity continues to tip the scales. Her weekly talk radio show Wellness for the REAL World touches on health, politics and pop culture, with edgy viewpoints that engage her guests and listeners while often exploring uncharted territory.

A graduate of Princeton University, Dr. Veronica is repeatedly requested to appear on news and commentary programs, including Nancy Grace (CNN), *Our World with Neil Cavuto (Fox News Channel)* and *Live with Adam Corolla*. Her fans clamor to get more of Dr. Veronica's straightforward, pull-no-punches philosophy on Facebook, Twitter (@DrVeronicaEyeMD), LinkedIn and Pinterest. Fans can get more of her on her popular, edgy blog on DrVeronica.com. She also hosts popular webinars through AskDrVeronica.com and Facebook. In addition, Dr. Veronica coaches and consults for entrepreneurs through RichDoctorCoaching.com and has been featured at such conferences as "Internet Prophets LIVE".

Having practiced at Robert Wood Johnson Hospital and on staff at Philadelphia's Willis Eye Hospital, this American Board of Ophthalmology diplomat and fellow of the American Academy of Ophthalmology chose to shift gears and realize her dream, emerging as a technology-savvy, smart, outspoken sagacious voice for healthy living in today's world. Dr. Veronica left practice as an Eye Surgeon to bring to the world wellness through Social Media Medicine.